Introductory Phonolo

D0870985

Bruce Hayes

A John Wiley & Sons, Ltd., Publication

This edition first published 2009
© 2009 Bruce Hayes

Blackwell Publishing was acquired by John Wiley & Sons in February 2007. Blackwell's publishing program has been merged with Wiley's global Scientific, Technical, and Medical business to form Wiley-Blackwell.

Registered Office
John Wiley & Sons Ltd, The Atrium, Southern Gate, Chichester, West Sussex, PO19 8SQ, United Kingdom

Editorial Offices
350 Main Street, Malden, MA 02148-5020, USA
9600 Garsington Road, Oxford, OX4 2DQ, UK
The Atrium, Southern Gate, Chichester, West Sussex, PO19 8SQ, UK

For details of our global editorial offices, for customer services, and for information about how to apply for permission to reuse the copyright material in this book please see our website at www.wiley.com/wiley-blackwell.

The right of Bruce Hayes to be identified as the author of this work has been asserted in accordance with the Copyright, Designs and Patents Act 1988.

Wiley also publishes its books in a variety of electronic formats. Some content that appears in print may not be available in electronic books.

Designations used by companies to distinguish their products are often claimed as trademarks. All brand names and product names used in this book are trade names, service marks, trademarks or registered trademarks of their respective owners. The publisher is not associated with any product or vendor mentioned in this book. This publication is designed to provide accurate and authoritative information in regard to the subject matter covered. It is sold on the understanding that the publisher is not engaged in rendering professional services. If professional advice or other expert assistance is required, the services of a competent professional should be sought.

Library of Congress Cataloging-in-Publication Data

Hayes, Bruce, 1955–
   Introductory phonology / Bruce Hayes.
      p. cm. – (Blackwell textbooks in linguistics ; 23)
   Includes bibliographical references and index.
   ISBN 978-1-4051-8411-3 (pbk. : alk. paper) – ISBN 978-1-4051-8412-0 (hardcover : alk. paper)
 1. Grammar, Comparative and general–Phonology.   I. Title.

   P217.H346 2009
   415–dc22

                                                                                    2008009666

A catalogue record for this book is available from the British Library.

Set in 10/13 point Sabon by Graphicraft Limited, Hong Kong
Printed in Singapre by Markono Print Media Pte Ltd

4   2010

For Pat and Peter

Contents

Preface

This text is meant as a first course book in phonology. The book has evolved as the textbook for a course taught to a mostly undergraduate audience over a number of years in the Department of Linguistics at UCLA. The course meets in lecture for four hours per week, with a one-hour problem-solving session, during a ten-week term.

The ideal audience for this book is a student who has studied some linguistics before (and thus has some idea of what linguists are trying to accomplish), and has already taken a course in general phonetics, covering at least the basics of articulatory phonetics and the International Phonetic Alphabet. It is possible to make up this material on the fly through reading and practice,[1] but I consider this strategy second-best. A short chapter on phonetics, intended for review, is included in this text.

As the title implies, this book is meant to be an introductory text. By this I mean not that it is meant to be easier than other texts, but rather that it emphasizes the following two things:

- **Analysis of phonological data,** along with methods that experience has shown can be useful in leading to accurate analyses.
- The **scientific context** of phonological analysis: what are we trying to understand when we carry out formal analyses of the phonological patterns of languages?

I consider the first item to be crucial in an introductory course, because if analysis is not well done at a basic level, all of the more sophisticated theoretical conclusions that might be drawn from it become untrustable. The second item is likewise crucial, to make phonological analysis meaningful.

As a consequence of these general goals, I have left out quite a few topics that currently are of great interest to many phonologists, myself included. This reflects

---

[1] Some recommended material for this purpose: Peter Ladefoged, *A Course in Phonetics* (5th ed., 2005, Heinle), and the accompanying sound materials made available at http://hctv.humnet.ucla.edu/ departments/linguistics/VowelsandConsonants.

my goal of teaching first the material that will provide the most solid foundation for more advanced theoretical study.[2]

I have tried to avoid a common problem of linguistics textbooks, that of presenting data simplified for pedagogical purposes without providing some means for the student to access more information about the language. This is provided in the "Further reading" section at the end of each chapter.

A number of passages in the text offer guidance in eliciting useful and valid data from native speakers. This relates to the phonology course I teach, in which one of the major assignments is a term paper involving analysis of data gathered first hand from a native speaker.

A computer resource for phonology that I have found useful in conjunction with this text is **UCLA FeaturePad**, a computer program created by Kie Zuraw, which helps students to learn and use features by showing the natural classes that correspond to any selection of feature values. It also shows how the sounds are changed when any feature values are changed. The program may be downloaded for free from www.linguistics.ucla.edu/people/hayes/120a/.

Many people provided me with help and feedback on this text, for which I am very grateful. Among them were Marco Baroni, Christine Bartels, Roger Billerey, Abigail Cohn, Maria Gouskova, Jongho Jun, Sun-Ah Jun, Patricia Keating, Charles Kisseberth, the late Peter Ladefoged, Lisa Lavoie, Margaret MacEachern, Donka Minkova, Susan Moskwa, Pamela Munro, Russell Schuh, Shabnam Shademan, Bernard Tranel, Adam Ussishkin, Keli Vaughan, and Kie Zuraw. I'm certain that I've left names out here, and in cases where my memory has failed me I hope the unthanked person will understand.

I welcome comments and error corrections concerning this text, which may be sent to bhayes@humnet.ucla.edu or Department of Linguistics, UCLA, Los Angeles, CA 90095-1543.

For sound files, updated web links, typo corrections, and other material, please visit the website for this text at www.linguistics.ucla.edu/people/hayes/IP.

Portions of chapters 2, 3, 6, and 7 appeared in earlier form as chapter 12 of *Linguistics: An Introduction to Linguistic Theory* by Victoria Fromkin et al. (2000, Blackwell).

---

[2] For students going on to more advanced topics, I have found the following texts to be helpful: John Goldsmith, *Autosegmental and Metrical Phonology* (1990, Basil Blackwell); Michael Kenstowicz, *Phonology in Generative Grammar* (1994, Basil Blackwell); René Kager, *Optimality Theory* (1999, Cambridge University Press); John McCarthy, *A Thematic Guide to Optimality Theory* (2002, Blackwell).

1 Phonetics

1.1 Phonetics and Phonology

There are two branches of linguistic science that deal with speech sounds: **phonetics** and **phonology**.

Phonetics is primarily an experimental science, which studies speech sounds from three viewpoints:

- **Production**: how sounds are made in the human vocal tract
- **Acoustics**: the study of the waveforms by which speech is transmitted through the atmosphere
- **Perception**: how the incoming acoustic signal is processed to detect the sound sequence originally intended by the speaker

Phonology is also, sometimes, an experimental science, though it also involves a fair degree of formal analysis and abstract theorizing. The primary data on which phonological theory rests are phonetic data, that is, observations of the phonetic form of utterances. The goal of phonology is to understand the tacit system of rules that the speaker uses in apprehending and manipulating the sounds of her language (more on this in chapter 2).

Since phonological data are phonetic, and since (as we will see) the very nature of phonological rules depends on phonetics, it is appropriate for beginning students to study phonetics first. In particular, a phonologist who tries to elicit data from native speakers without prior training in the production and perception of speech sounds will be likely to have a hard time. The material that follows can be taken to be a quick review of phonetics, or else a very quick introduction that can be amplified with reading and practical training from materials such as those listed at the end of the chapter.

In principle, a phonologist should understand all three of the areas of phonetics listed above: production, acoustics, and perception. Of these, production probably has the greatest practical importance for the study of phonology. Since it is also the simplest to describe, it is what will be covered here.

1.2   The Vocal Tract

The term "vocal tract" designates all the portions of the human anatomy through which air flows in the course of speech production (see figure 1.1). These include (from bottom to top):

- The lungs and lower respiratory passages
- The **larynx** (colloquially: "voice box"). This is the primary (but not the only) source of sound in speech production
- The passages above the larynx, called the **pharynx, oral cavity** (mouth), and **nasal cavity**

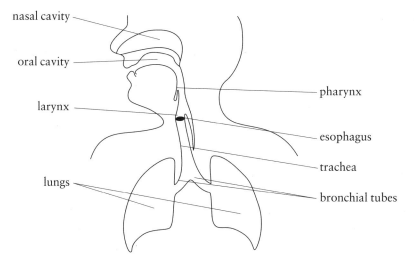

Figure 1.1   The vocal tract

The lungs and respiratory muscles produce a fairly steady level of air pressure, which powers the creation of sound. There are occasional momentary peaks of pressure for certain speech sounds and for emphatically stressed syllables. Air from the lungs ascends through the **bronchial tubes,** which join to form the **trachea** (windpipe). The bronchial tubes and the trachea form an inverted Y-shape.

1.2.1   *The larynx*

The larynx is a complex structure of cartilage and muscle, located in the neck and partly visible in adult males (whose larynxes are the largest) as the "Adam's apple." Figure 1.2 shows two diagrams of the larynx:

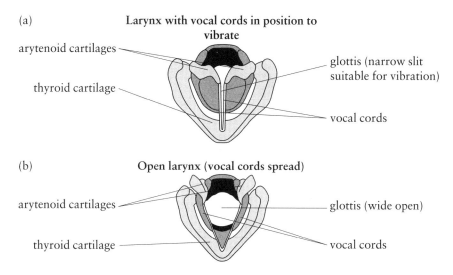

Figure 1.2 The larynx

The larynx contains the **vocal cords** (not "chords"), which are parallel flaps of tissue extending from each side of the interior larynx wall. The vocal cords have a slit between them, called the **glottis**. The vocal cords are held at their rear ends by two small cartilages called the **arytenoid cartilages**. Since these cartilages are mobile, they can be used to adjust the distance between the vocal cords.

When the vocal cords are held tightly together, the sound known as a **glottal stop** is produced; it can be heard in the middle of the expression "uh-oh" and is used as a speech sound in many languages.

If the vocal cords are placed close to each other but not tightly shut, and there is sufficient airflow from the lungs, then the vocal cords will vibrate, creating **voicing**. This is the configuration shown in figure 1.2(a). Voicing is the most important and noticeable sound source in speech.

The vocal cords can also be spread somewhat apart, so that air passing through the glottis creates turbulent noise. This is the way an "h" sound is produced. The vocal cords are spread farther still for normal breathing, in which airflow through the larynx is smooth and silent. This is the configuration shown in figure 1.2(b).

The cartilages of the larynx, especially the **thyroid cartilage** to which the front ends of the vocal cords attach, can stretch and slacken the vocal cords, thus raising and lowering the pitch of the voice. This is somewhat analogous to the changes in pitch that occur when a guitar string is tightened or loosened.

1.2.2 The upper vocal tract

Sound created at the larynx is modified and filtered as it passes through the upper vocal tract. This area is the most complex and needs the most detailed discussion; you should refer to figure 1.3 while reading the text.

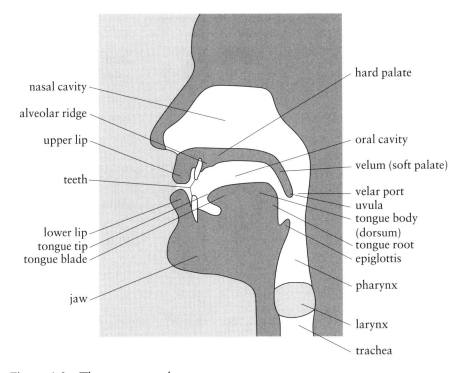

Figure 1.3   The upper vocal tract

The main route through the upper vocal tract is a kind of arch, starting vertically upward from the larynx and bending forward through the mouth. There is an opening about half way from larynx to lips, called the **velar port,** through which air can pass into the nasal passage and outward through the nostrils. In figure 1.3, the velar port is wide open.

We will first cover the upper surface of the upper vocal tract (the roof of the mouth and the back of the pharynx), then the lower surface (floor of mouth, continued as the front wall of the pharynx).

Going in the "upstream" direction, the crucial landmarks of the upper surface are:

- The upper **lip.**
- The upper **teeth** (in particular, the incisors).
- The **alveolar ridge,** a bony ridge just behind the base of the upper incisors. Most people can feel their alveolar ridge by moving the tongue along the roof of the mouth.[1]

---

[1]   Some people do not have a sharply defined alveolar ridge.

- The **hard palate**, which is that part of the roof of the mouth underlain by bone. You can feel the hard palate, and its rear edge, with the tip of your tongue.
- The **velum**, or **soft palate**. This is a flap of soft tissue that separates the mouth from the nasal passages. It is attached at the front (to the hard palate) and at the sides, but hangs loose at its rear edge. Various muscles can raise and lower the velum. When the velum is high, then the velar port is closed, and air is confined to the oral passage.[2]
- The **uvula** (['juːvjələ]). The little thing that dangles from the rear edge of the velum is called the uvula, Latin for 'little grape'. The uvula is vibrated (trilled) as a speech sound in some languages.
- The **pharynx**. Once we are past the velum, we are no longer in the mouth proper but in the rearward part of the upper vocal tract, commonly called the pharynx. The rear pharyngeal wall is continuous and has no significant landmarks all the way down to the larynx.

The crucial parts of the lower surface of the upper vocal tract are as follows:

- The lower lip and the tongue rest on the **jaw**, which raises and lowers the lower lip and tongue when it moves during speech.
- The **lower lip** is more mobile than the **upper** in speaking, though both move considerably. They can touch one another, closing the mouth, or the corners of the lips can be pulled in, creating lip rounding.
- The **tongue** is somewhat deceptive in its size and shape. The parts that are obvious to an external observer are the **tip** (sometimes called the **apex**) and the **blade**. These are merely an appendage to the much larger tongue **body** (also called **dorsum**), a roundish muscular body that can move in all directions. Movements of the dorsum can radically change the shape of the vocal tract, a fact that is crucial in the production of distinct vowel sounds.
- The rear surface of the dorsum is called the **tongue root**. Behind it is a flap called the **epiglottis**.

1.3 Describing Speech Sounds

The human vocal tract can produce thousands of audibly distinct sounds. Of these, only a subset are actually used in human languages. Moreover, of this subset, some

---

[2] If you can produce a distinction between nasal and oral vowels, as in French or Portuguese, then it is possible to watch the velum work, using a flashlight and a mirror. When a speaker alternates between oral and nasal vowels, the velum is seen to billow up and down like a sail (which is what "velum" literally means in Latin).

sounds are much more common than others. For example, almost every language has a *t*-like sound, whereas very few languages have an epiglottal stop or a bilabial trill. Any one language uses only a fairly small inventory of distinct speech sounds, usually no more than a few dozen.

The commonsense distinction of **vowels and consonants** is a generally valid one for phonetics and phonology. Roughly, vowels are highly sonorous sounds, made with a relatively open vocal tract. Consonants involve some kind of constriction (or more than one constriction) in the vocal tract. They are quieter than vowels, and often are detectable by the ear not so much by their own sound as by the transitional acoustic events that occur at the boundaries of consonants and vowels.

For both vowels and consonants, phonetic description involves assigning a **phonetic symbol** to each sound. This book will use the standard, internationally accepted phonetic symbol set called the International Phonetic Alphabet (IPA), promulgated by the International Phonetic Association.

It should be clear why the use of standard symbols, rather than spelling, is crucial. The spelling systems of most languages are ambiguous (consider *read*, *bow*) and inconsistent in the depiction of identical sounds (consider *whole/hole*, *real/reel*). Cross-linguistically, the situation is even worse, as different languages employ the same letters to depict different sounds: the letter *j* spells four quite different sounds in English, French, Spanish, and German (in IPA these are [d͡ʒ], [ʒ], [x], and [j]). Since this book will be presenting data from many languages, I will standardize all data using IPA transcription.

Phonetic transcription is traditionally given surrounded by square brackets. Thus, one possible rendition of the previous sentence in IPA (as pronounced in my own dialect of English) is:

[fə'nɛɾɪk t͡ʂɹæn'skɹɪpʃən ɨz t͡ʂɹɑ'dɪʃɪnəli 'gɪvən sə'ɹæʊndɨd baɪ 'skwɛɹ 'bɹækɨts]

1.4   Consonants

Consonants are classified along three dimensions: **voicing, place of articulation, and manner of articulation**.

1.4.1   *Voicing*

In a voiced consonant, the vocal cords vibrate. For example, the "s" sound, for which the IPA symbol is simply [s], is voiceless, whereas the "z" sound (IPA [z]) is voiced. If you say "sa, za" while planting the palm of your hand firmly on the top of your head, you should feel the vibrations for [z] but not for [s].

petaka

bodega

The sounds [p t k] are voiceless. The sounds [b d g] as they occur in (for example) French or Japanese are voiced; in English they are often voiced for only part of their duration or even not at all; nevertheless the symbols [b d g] are traditionally used for them.

1.4.2 Manner

There are various manners of articulation.

In a **stop,** the airflow through the mouth is momentarily closed off. This can be done by the two lips, forming [p] or [b]; by the tongue tip touching the alveolar ridge, forming [t] or [d]; by the tongue body touching the palate, forming [k] or [g]; and in other ways.

In a **fricative,** a tight constriction is made, so that air passing through the constriction flows turbulently, making a hissing noise. Some of the fricatives of English are [f], [v], [θ] (the first sound of *thin*), and [ð] (the first sound of *the*). In **sibilant** fricatives, the mechanism of production is more complex: a stream of air is directed at the upper teeth, creating noisy turbulent flow. The four sibilant fricatives of English are [s], [z], [ʃ] (the first sound of *shin*), and [ʒ] (the consonant spelled *s* in *pleasure*).

An **affricate** is a stop followed by a fricative, made at the same location in the mouth in rapid succession so that the result has the typical duration of a single speech sound. English has two affricates: voiceless [tʃ] (as in *church*) and voiced [dʒ] (as in *judge*). As can be seen, the IPA symbol for an affricate is made with the symbols for the appropriate stop and fricative, optionally joined with a ligature.

Affricates are often considered to be a species of stop; that is, "affricated stops."

In a **nasal consonant,** the velum is lowered, allowing air to escape through the nose. Most nasal consonants have a complete blockage within the mouth at the same time. The places of articulation for nasals are mostly the same as those for stops. The nasal consonants of English are [m] (*mime*), [n] (*none*), and [ŋ] (*young*).

Nasals like [m, n, ŋ] in a certain sense are also stops, since they involve complete closure in the mouth; hence the term "stop" is ambiguous. I will use this term here in its strict sense, which includes oral stops only.

In **taps** and **flaps,** an articulator makes a rapid brush against some articulatory surface. The motion of the articulator is forward in a flap, backward in a tap. North American varieties of English have alveolar taps (IPA [ɾ]) in words like *lighter* and *rider*.

In a **trill,** an articulator is made to vibrate by placing it near an articulatory surface and letting air flow through the gap. Many dialects of Spanish have an alveolar trill (IPA [r]) in words like *perro* 'dog'. The uvula ([ʀ]) and lips ([ʙ]) can also be trilled.

Approximants are consonants in which the constriction is fairly wide, so that air passes through without creating turbulence or trilling. In **lateral approximants,**

the air passes around the sides of the tongue, as in English [l]. In **central approximants**, the flow is through a gap in the center. English dialects have (at least) three central approximants, namely [j],[3] as in *youth*, [w], as in *win*, and [ɹ], as in *ray*.

The last three categories just given are sometimes presented with a different classification. The **liquids** are the sounds that have the characteristic acoustic quality of *l*-like and *r*-like sounds.[4] This term groups [l] and similar sounds together with tap [ɾ], trilled [r], approximant [ɹ], and various similar "r" sounds. Under this same scheme, the **glides** (also called **semivowels**) are the central approximants; that is, [j], [w], and similar sounds covered below.

1.4.3   *Place of articulation*

I will cover most of the possible places of articulation, proceeding from front to back. Each place is shown in figure 1.4: dotted lines indicate the approximate path taken by an articulator in making contact with the opposite wall of the vocal tract.

- **Bilabial** sounds are made by touching the upper and lower lips together. English has a voiceless bilabial stop [p], a voiced bilabial stop [b], and a (voiced) bilabial nasal [m].

  Note that the description just given follows the standard form for describing a consonant: **voicing**, then **place**, then **manner**. In the case of nasals and approximants, which are normally voiced, it is common to specify only place and manner.
- **Labiodental** sounds are made by touching the lower lip to the upper teeth. English has a voiceless labiodental fricative [f] and a voiced one, [v].
- **Dental** sounds are made by touching the tongue to the upper teeth. This can be done in a number of ways. If the tongue is stuck out beyond the teeth, the sound is called an **interdental**, though we will not be concerned with so fine a distinction. English has a voiceless dental fricative [θ] (*thin*) and a voiced one [ð] (*the*).
- **Alveolar** sounds are made by touching the tip or blade of the tongue to a location just forward of the alveolar ridge. English has a voiceless alveolar stop [t], a voiced alveolar stop [d], voiceless and voiced alveolar fricatives [s] and

---

[3]   The IPA symbol is modeled after the spelling of German, Dutch, Polish, Swedish, and various other languages. The letter *y*, used in English, has a different meaning in IPA, given below.

[4]   In terms of speech acoustics, *l*-like sounds have an exceptionally high third **formant** (band of acoustic energy), and *r*-like sounds have an exceptionally low third formant. Non-liquid approximants have third formants that would be expected, given their first and second formants.

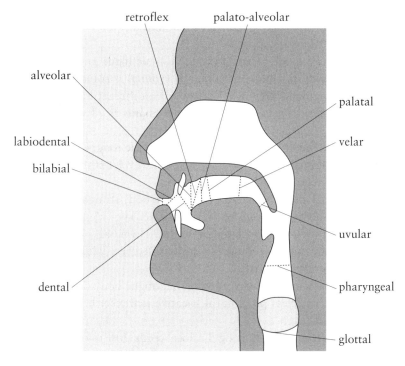

Figure 1.4 Place of articulation

[z] (both of them sibilants), a voiced alveolar nasal [n], a voiced alveolar lateral approximant [l],[5] and a voiced alveolar central approximant [ɹ].

- **Palato-alveolar** sounds (sometimes called **post-alveolar**) are made by touching the blade of the tongue to a location just behind the alveolar ridge. English has a voiceless palato-alveolar fricative [ʃ] (*shoe*), a voiced palato-alveolar fricative [ʒ] (*vision*), a voiceless palato-alveolar affricate [tʃ], (*church*), and a voiced palato-alveolar affricate [dʒ] (*judge*).
- **Retroflex** sounds are made by curling the tongue tip backward, and touching the area just behind the alveolar ridge. Some English speakers lack the alveolar approximant [ɹ] and instead have a retroflex one, transcribed [ɻ]; retroflex stops and affricates are common in languages of India and Australia.

In the strict sense of the term, palato-alveolars and retroflexes have the same place of articulation: the same place on the roof of the mouth is contacted.

---

[5] For many speakers of English, the "l" sound is actually dental [l̪].

They differ in the part of the tongue (blade or tip) that makes the contact. Conventionally, however, palato-alveolar and retroflex are referred to as separate places of articulation.

- **Palatal** sounds are made by touching the tongue blade and the forward part of the tongue body to the hard palate. [j] (*young*) is sometimes described as a palatal approximant (see §1.5.5 below for a different kind of description); various languages have a variety of other manners of articulation at the palatal place.
- **Velar** sounds are made by touching the body of the tongue to the hard or soft palate. English has three velar sounds: a voiceless velar stop [k], a voiced velar stop [g], and a velar nasal [ŋ] (*sing*).
- **Uvular** sounds are made by moving the tongue body straight back to touch the uvula and neighboring portions of the soft palate. The "r" sound of French and German is usually a voiced uvular fricative, [ʁ]. The nasal consonant that occurs at the end of many words in Japanese, transcribed here with [ŋ], is pronounced by many speakers as uvular [N].
- **Pharyngeal** sounds are made by moving the tongue body down and back into the pharynx. A voiceless pharyngeal fricative is transcribed [ħ]; it occurs for example in Arabic.
- **Glottal** sounds are made by moving the vocal cords close to one another. English has a voiceless glottal fricative [h].

1.4.4   Consonant chart

Table 1.1 reproduces the part of the official IPA chart covering consonants.

It can be seen that any consonant in the chart is describable with the terminology given in table 1.1, and that a fair number of sounds are listed that do not occur in English. Quite a few of these will come up in the chapters to follow.

The symbols for dentals, alveolars, and palato-alveolars are systematically ambiguous. Where it is important to make a distinction, it is possible to do so with diacritics:

[t̪] = voiceless dental stop
[t] = voiceless alveolar stop
[t̠] = voiceless palato-alveolar (= post-alveolar) stop

Affricates are formed by joining a stop and fricative symbol together, as in for instance [tʃ] the first and last sound of *church*. The same ligature may be used for so-called "complex segments" such as labial-velar [k͡p], which are formed at two places of articulation simultaneously.

A subsidiary part of the IPA chart (table 1.2) covers consonants in which the airflow comes not from the lungs, but from motions of the larynx (**implosives**, with inward airflow, and **ejectives**, with outward), or of the tongue body (**clicks**).

Table 1.3 shows consonants that don't fit into the main IPA chart.

Table 1.1 The main portion of the IPA consonant chart.
www.arts.gla.ac.uk/IPA/IPA_chart_(c)2005.pdf

	Bilabial	Labiodental	Dental	Alveolar	Post-alveolar [= palatoalveolar]	Retroflex	Palatal	Velar	Uvular	Pharyngeal	Glottal
Plosive [= stop]	p b			t d		ʈ ɖ	c ɟ	k ɡ	q ɢ		ʔ
Nasal	m	ɱ		n		ɳ	ɲ	ŋ	ɴ		
Trill	ʙ			r					ʀ		
Tap or Flap		ⱱ		ɾ		ɽ					
Fricative	ɸ β	f v	θ ð	s z	ʃ ʒ	ʂ ʐ	ç ʝ	x ɣ	χ ʁ	ħ ʕ	h ɦ
Lateral fricative				ɬ ɮ							
[Central] approximant		ʋ		ɹ		ɻ	j	ɰ			
Lateral approximant				l		ɭ	ʎ	ʟ			

Where symbols appear in pairs, the one to the right represents a voiced consonant. Shaded areas denote articulations judged impossible.

Table 1.2   The IPA chart: non-pulmonic consonants.
www.arts.gla.ac.uk/IPA/IPA_chart_(c)2005.pdf

Clicks		Voiced implosives		Ejectives	
ʘ	Bilabial	ɓ	Bilabial	'	as in
ǀ	Dental	ɗ	Dental/alveolar	p'	Bilabial
!	(Post)alveolar	ʄ	Palatal	t'	Dental/alveolar
ǂ	Palatoalveolar	ɠ	Velar	k'	Velar
‖	Alveolar lateral	ʛ	Uvular	s'	Alveolar fricative

Table 1.3   The IPA chart: other consonants.
www.arts.gla.ac.uk/IPA/IPA_chart_(c)2005.pdf

ʍ	Voiceless labial-velar fricative
w	Voiced labial-velar approximant
ɥ	Voiced labial-palatal approximant
ʜ	Voiceless epiglottal fricative[a]
ʕ	Voiced epiglottal fricative
ʡ	Epiglottal plosive
ɕ ʑ	Alveolo-palatal fricatives
ɺ	Alveolar lateral flap
ɧ	Simultaneous ʃ and x

Note: [a] Epiglottals are made by touching the upper edge of the epiglottis (see figure 1.3) to the rear wall of the pharynx.

1.5   Vowels

Vowels differ from consonants in that they do not have "places of articulation," that is, points of major constriction in the vocal tract. Rather, the vocal tract as a whole acts as a resonating chamber. Modifying the shape of this chamber using movements of the tongue, jaw, and lips causes different timbres to be imparted to the basic sound produced at the vocal cords.

There are three basic modifications that one can make to the shape of the vocal tract. Vowels are described by specifying each modification used.

1.5.1   *Rounding*

An obvious modification one can make to the shape of the vocal tract is to round the lips, thus narrowing the passage at the exit. This happens, for example, in the vowels that many English dialects have for *boot* [u], *book* [ʊ], and *boat* [o]. These are called **rounded** or simply **round** vowels. Other vowels, such as the [i] of *beet* or the [ʌ] of *cut*, are called **unrounded**.

1.5.2 Height

Another modification one can make to the shape of the vocal tract is to make the passage through the mouth wider or narrower. Widening is accomplished by opening the jaw and/or lowering the body of the tongue towards the bottom of the mouth. Narrowing is accomplished by raising the jaw and/or raising the body of the tongue.

The terminology for describing these changes is based on the height of the tongue body, without regard to whether this is due to jaw movement or tongue movement. Vowels are classified as **high, mid, or low.** In effect, high vowels have a narrow passage for the air to pass through, and low vowels have a wide passage. Another terminology, which appears on the IPA chart, is to call the high vowels **close** and the low vowels **open**.

high – close
low – open

Examples of high vowels in English are [i], the vowel of *beat*, and [u], the vowel of *boot* (for some English speakers; see below). Examples of low vowels are [ɑ], the vowel of *spa*, and [æ], the vowel of *bat*. You can feel the oral passage widening and narrowing if you pronounce a sequence of vowels that alternates between high and low, such as [i æ i æ i æ].

1.5.3 Backness

The third primary way of changing the vocal tract shape is to place the body of the tongue towards the front part of the mouth or towards the back. Vowels so made are called **front and back vowels**, respectively; and vowels that are neither front nor back are called **central**. For example, [i] (*beat*) is a high front unrounded vowel, and the [u] vowel that appears in many languages (e.g. Spanish, French, and Persian) is a high back rounded vowel: French [ʁuʒ] 'red'.

[u] is often described as being the vowel of English words like *boot*. This is true, but only for certain dialects of English; other dialects have a vowel that is closer to central than back: [bʉt].

A way to feel backness, particularly if you know how to say a true [u] instead of [ʉ], is to say the sequence [i u i u i u i u . . .] and feel your tongue body sliding forward and backward along the roof of your mouth.

1.5.4 Describing vowels systematically

We now have three dimensions for classifying vowels, each based on a particular modification of the vocal tract shape: rounding, height, and backness. The three dimensions allow us to describe vowels clearly and to organize them in a chart.

The IPA chart for vowels is shown in figure 1.5:

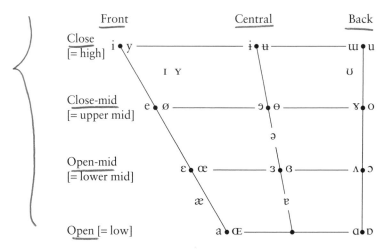

Where symbols appear in pairs, the one to the right represents a rounded vowel.

Figure 1.5 The IPA chart for vowels.
www.arts.gla.ac.uk/IPA/IPA_chart_(c)2005.pdf

For the use of these symbols in depicting the vowels of English, see p. 21.

An awkward problem with the IPA is that there is no symbol for the low central unrounded vowel, which appears to be the most common of all vowels in the world's languages. Below, I will follow the practice of many other linguists in adapting the symbol [a], which strictly speaking designates a front vowel in IPA, to denote the central vowel; where it is crucial, I will state which vowel is being described.

The IPA chart is also a bit puzzling for offering vowel symbols that have no description in terms of categories; for instance [ɪ] floats in the upper left part of the chart without any row or column label. We will remedy this below when we set up a system of **features** (chapter 4) to classify vowels; see p. 82.

1.5.5   Glide–vowel correspondences

Glides can be described in two ways, because they are essentially the non-syllabic equivalents of vowels (semivowels). Thus, [j] is in IPA terms a palatal central approximant, but it is also describable as a high front unrounded glide, and is thus the consonant counterpart of [i]. Likewise, [w] is a labial-velar central approximant, but it is also treatable as a high back rounded glide, the counterpart of [u].

1.5.6   Diphthongs

A **diphthong** (note the spelling) is a sequence of two vowels that functions as a single sound. Further, a diphthong always forms just one syllable, whereas a two-vowel sequence forms two. You can transcribe a diphthong by stringing together two vowel symbols denoting its beginning and end, and optionally connecting them with a ligature.

English has numerous diphthongs, the number depending on dialect. The three most noticeable ones are [aɪ], which appears in *ride*; [ɔɪ], which appears in *boy*; and [aʊ], which appears in *how*. (The diphthong [aʊ] is pronounced [æʊ] by many speakers.) In addition, most dialects have diphthongs in which the difference between the two component vowels is more subtle, and a rough transcription can use a monophthong symbol. Thus, the sound of *bay*, which some sources transcribe as [e], is [eɪ] for most English speakers, and [o] (*go*) is most often [oʊ]. Other vowels of English can be more or less subtly diphthongal; for example, [ɛə] for what is normally transcribed [ɛ] (as in *bed*).

1.5.7 Syllabic consonants

It is possible for sounds that are normally consonants to be prolonged slightly and serve as the nucleus of a syllable. Such sounds are called **syllabic consonants**; they are transcribed by placing the IPA syllabic marker under them, as in [n̩] (*button*, IPA [ˈbʌtn̩]). Generally, only the more sonorous consonants, such as liquids or nasals, can occur as syllabic.[6] Syllabic glides are simply vowels, as noted above in §1.5.5.

1.6 Stress and Tone

Many languages make distinctions of stress; roughly, the degree of loudness or effort with which a syllable is pronounced. IPA provides the symbol [ˈ] to indicate a strong stress, and [ˌ] to indicate a relatively weak (secondary) stress. These marks are placed just before the *syllable*, not the vowel, thus [ˈɹæbɪt] *rabbit*, [əˈbaʊt] *about*.

A great many of the world's languages are tone languages, using differences of pitch to distinguish words from one another. The IPA offers two distinct systems of tonal transcription. In table 1.4, the symbols given first in each category are ordinarily used for languages with mostly level tones; the ones given second are for languages in which the tones often glide up or down within a syllable.

Intonation is use of the voice for linguistic purposes other than distinguishing words; for instance, for distinguish questions from statements. The IPA intonation marks will not suffice for our purposes (see chapter 15), and are omitted from table 1.4.

---

[6] Various Berber languages have syllabic fricatives and stops.

Table 1.4 The IPA chart: suprasegmentals.
www.arts.gla.ac.uk/IPA/IPA_chart_(c)2005.pdf

The two example words in this chart are *phonetician* and *react*.

		TONES AND WORDS ACCENTS			
ˈ Primary stress	ˌfoʊnəˈtɪʃən	LEVEL		CONTOUR	
ˌ Secondary stress		e̋ or ˥ extra high	ě or ˄	rising	
ː Long	eː	é ˦ high	ê	˅ falling	
ˑ Half-long	eˑ	ē ˧ mid	ế	˧˥ high rising	
˘ Extra-short	ĕ	è ˨ low	ề	˩˧ low rising	
. Syllable break	ri.ækt	ȅ ˩ extra low	e᷈	˧˩˧ rising-falling etc.	

1.7 Diacritics

The IPA provides a number of diacritics that may be attached to symbols to modify their meaning. Of these, the most important ones used here are as follows:

- [ʰ], for **aspiration**. In [pʰ, tʰ, kʰ], aspiration is a puff of breath (which in English can be felt with the fingers, placed in front of the mouth), with a delay in the onset of voicing in a following vowel.
- [˳], used to denote **voicelessness** in a symbol that is otherwise interpreted as voiced. For example, [i̥] is a voiceless vowel, found for instance in Japanese.
- [˞], the **rhoticity** diacritic, meaning that the tongue tip or blade is curled backward. Rhoticized schwa, [ɚ], is a common way of transcribing the syllabic consonant [ɻ]. (Note that this is essentially parallel to the vowel–glide correspondences described in §1.5.7 above. [ɚ] and [ɹ], are essentially the same sound, described from the viewpoint of vowels and consonants.)
- [ː] is placed after vowels (and occasionally consonants[7]) to show they are **long**; likewise [˘] is placed over a speech sound to show that it is extra **short**.
- [˜], a tilde placed over a symbol, indicates that it is **nasalized**; that is, pronounced with the velum lowered as in French [mɛ̃] 'hand'.
- Tiny **adjustments for vowel quality**: [˔] a bit higher, [˕] a bit lower, [̠] a bit backer, [̟] a bit fronter. The backer/fronter diacritics may also be used for place of articulation in consonants.

---

[7] For consonants, probably the more common practice is to indicate length by doubling.

1.8 Phonetic Transcription

The accurate rendering of pronunciation using phonetic symbols is a skill learned through practice; see Exercises below. Here I will note only that different transcriptions are appropriate for different purposes.

- On occasion, issues of phonological importance will hinge on matters of tiny phonetic detail. Here, the wide range of diacritics offered by the IPA can be very useful. Transcription that attempts to use symbols to represent speech as accurately as possible is called **narrow** transcription.
- Otherwise, a so-called **broad** transcription, abstracting away from non-crucial detail, usually suffices. Often, transcription is narrow in one part of a word (the part containing the matter of interest), but broad elsewhere.
- In selecting a broad transcription, sometimes it is useful to idealize across speakers somewhat. Thus, the various English dialects have a remarkable range of phonetic qualities for the vowel of the word *out* ([aʊ], [æʊ], [ɑʊ], [ɑo], [ɛʊ], [ʌʊ], etc.), but if one's focus is on other matters, it is harmless to use [aʊ], which is fairly standard in reference sources. The advantage is that the experienced reader can read a standardized transcription more quickly.

Exercises

1   Web exercises

Phonetic exercises usually involve production or perception, so they are best done on line where sound files can be provided. The exercises for Peter Ladefoged's textbook (see Further reading, below) are posted at www.phonetics.ucla.edu. Some exercises used in the author's own phonetics teaching are available at:

www.linguistics.ucla.edu/people/hayes/103/EnglishTranscriptionPractice/
www.linguistics.ucla.edu/people/hayes/103/Allophones/
www.linguistics.ucla.edu/people/hayes/103/CTranscriptionPractice/

2   Study guide questions for this chapter

a. The IPA consonant chart (p. 11) includes a shaded cell for pharyngeal nasals, claiming that such a sound is "judged impossible." Why is this so? Explain your answer.

b. Same question as (a), but for the voiced counterpart of the glottal stop.
c. Find a pair of contrasting examples showing that we need to be able to transcribe [t͡ʃ] distinct from [tʃ]. Give IPA transcriptions for your examples. (Hint: try stringing words together.)
d. Construct an unambiguous IPA symbol to depict a voiceless dental sibilant affricate, explaining each diacritic that you use.
e. Would it be sensible to use [o̥] in an IPA transcription? Explain your answer.
f. In articulating a velar nasal, the tongue body need not move as far to achieve closure as in a velar stop. Explain why, referring to figure 1.3.
g. Give three ways to use the IPA diacritics to transcribe a low central unrounded vowel.
h. Find the errors in the following IPA transcriptions and correct them: *sing* [sɪŋ], *threat* [thɹɛt], *table* [ˈteɪ̄ble], *exit* [ˈɛxɪt], *ballad* [bˈæləd], *heraldry* [ˈhɛɹəldri], *easy* [ízi], *music* [ˈmusɪk].

Further reading

Some important resources for the International Phonetic Alphabet are:

*   The *Handbook of the International Phonetic Association: A Guide to the Use of the International Phonetic Alphabet* (1999, Cambridge University Press).
*   A website containing sound files for all the examples given in the Handbook: http://web.uvic.ca/ling/resources/ipa/handbook.htm.
*   The official IPA website (http://www2.arts.gla.ac.uk/IPA/ipa.html).
*   The widely used free IPA fonts distributed by the Summer Institute of Linguistics (http://scripts.sil.org/cms/scripts/page.php?site_id=nrsi&id=IPAhome).

An introductory phonetics textbook that I rely on in my own phonetics teaching is *A Course in Phonetics*, by Peter Ladefoged (5th ed., 2005, Heinle). This text is accompanied by downloadable sound files: see www.phonetics.ucla.edu. A wide-ranging study of speech sounds is in Peter Ladefoged and Ian Maddieson, *The Sounds of the World's Languages* (1996, Blackwell).

The student who examines journal articles and other reference sources in phonology will encounter, in addition to IPA, a bewildering variety of other phonetic symbols. One also often finds the same symbol used in radically different ways. A useful resource for navigating this thicket is the *Phonetic Symbol Guide*, by Geoffrey Pullum and William Ladusaw (2nd ed., 1996, University of Chicago Press).

A useful webpage on vocal tract anatomy is www.phon.ox.ac.uk/~jcoleman/phonation.htm.

2 Phonemic Analysis

2.1 Phonology and Phonetics

As noted in the previous chapter, there are two branches of linguistics that deal with speech sounds. Phonetics studies speech sounds in ways that are close to the speech stream, focusing on production, acoustics, and perception. Phonology tends to be more abstract, dealing not directly with the physical nature of speech sounds (though that is of course quite relevant), but rather with the largely unconscious **rules** for sound patterning that are found in the mind/brain of a person who speaks a particular language. It could be said that a phonologist is a kind of grammarian, and the area of grammar that she studies is the sound pattern of a language.

The rules studied by phonologists come in various kinds. First, phonetic study shows that sounds *vary with their context*, often in complex ways; and phonologists hypothesize rules to characterize this variation. Second, the *sequencing and distribution* of speech sounds is not arbitrary, but follows patterns also describable with rules. Third, phonology is *interfaced* with other components of the grammar, particularly morphology and syntax, and there are rules that characterize the way in which sound patterning reflects information that arises within these components.

The phonologies of many languages often show a level of complexity that make them a worthwhile intellectual challenge for the phonologist trying to understand them. It can take many years of careful research to fully explicate the sound pattern of a language. What is remarkable is that the same pattern is learned quite rapidly, at the intuitive level, by humans when they are exposed to it in childhood.

2.2 Distinctiveness and Contrast

The sounds of a language are intrinsically meaningless: their only purpose is to form the building blocks of which words are made. For example, because English has the sounds [t] and [d], the possibility exists of English having the word *time* [taɪm], distinct from the word *dime* [daɪm]. One could put it this way: the only real purpose of a speech sound is to sound different from the other sounds of the language; this is what makes a spoken vocabulary possible.

To begin the analysis of a language's phonology, we therefore seek to locate all of its basic sounds, the minimal units that serve to distinguish words from each other. These basic speech sounds are the **phonemes** of the language. The phonemes of one commonly spoken dialect of American English are arranged phonetically in tables 2.1 and 2.2; that is, more or less in the manner of the IPA chart, though not necessarily the exact same rows, columns, or order that the IPA uses. The sound symbols are in slant brackets, which is the standard way of indicating phonemes. An example word is given beneath each phoneme to illustrate it.

Other English dialects differ from the above, having additional phonemes such as /ʍ/, /ʌɪ/, /ɛə/, /ɒ/; or fewer phonemes.

Languages vary in their number of phonemes. The record low is believed to be held by Rotokas (East Papuan, New Guinea), with 11, and the record high by !Xóõ (Khoisan, Botswana/Namibia), with 160. English has roughly 37–41, depending on the dialect and the analysis. The average across languages is about 30.

Below, we will discuss detailed methods for establishing the phoneme inventory of a language or dialect. But the most important point can be stated right away: *if any two words of a language are pronounced differently, they must differ in at least one phoneme.* This follows from the basic idea of the phoneme; that is, that the phoneme inventory is the set of "building blocks" out of which all the words of the language are constructed.

The example given above, *time* [taɪm] vs. *dime* [daɪm], was strategically arranged to make this point. These words are identical, except for their initial sounds; that is, they are both of the form [Xaɪm]. Since they are different words, it follows that [t] and [d] are distinct sounds; that is, they are separate phonemes. A pair like ([taɪm], [daɪm]), differing in just one single location, is called a **minimal pair**. A minimal pair is the most effective way to show that two sounds are distinct phonemes.

There are quite a few ways in phonology of saying that two sounds are separate phonemes. Equivalently, we say that the English sounds /t/ and /d/ **contrast** with each other, that they are **in contrast**, or that they are **phonemically distinct**, or that the difference between them is **distinctive**. All of these terms are essentially equivalent.

The concept of minimal pair can be extended to cover larger sets. A set like *time* [taɪm] – *dime* [daɪm] – *lime* [laɪm] is a **minimal triplet**, showing that /t/, /d/, and /l/ are distinct phonemes; and the concept clearly generalizes to as many members as one can find. Tables 2.1 and 2.2 include examples forming a minimal 13-tuplet for consonants and a minimal 12-tuplet for vowels. Such sets are useful for demonstrating a large fraction of the phonemic system of a language all at once.

Table 2.1 English phonemes: consonants

	Bilabial	Labiodental	Dental	Alveolar	Palatoalveolar	Palatal	Velar	Glottal
Stops *voiceless*	/p/ pin			/t/ tin			/k/ kin	
voiced	/b/ bin			/d/ din			/g/ gill	
Affricates *voiceless*					/tʃ/ chin			
voiced					/dʒ/ gin			
Fricatives *voiceless*		/f/ fin	/θ/ thin	/s/ sin	/ʃ/ shin			/h/ hymn
voiced		/v/ vim	/ð/ this	/z/ zip	/ʒ/ vision			
Nasals	/m/ mitt			/n/ nip			/ŋ/ sing	
Approximants *lateral*				/l/ Lynn				
central	/w/ win			/ɹ/ rim		/j/ ying		

Table 2.2   English phonemes: vowels and diphthongs

	Front Unrounded	Central Unrounded	Back Unrounded	Back Rounded	Diphthongs
Upper high	/i/ beat			/u/ boot	/aɪ/, /aʊ/, /ɔɪ/ bite, bout, Coit
Lower high	/ɪ/ bit			/ʊ/ foot	
Upper mid	/eɪ/ bait	/ə/ abbot		/oʊ/ boat	*Rhotacized upper mid central unrounded*
Lower mid	/ɛ/ bet		/ʌ/ but	/ɔ/ bought	
Low	/æ/ bat		/ɑ/ father		/ɚ/ Bert

2.3   Sounds that Do Not Contrast

For a reason to be given, there are also many pairs of sounds (in any language) that do *not* contrast. Here is a simple case from English, involving the length of vowels. If you listen to a native speaker say the following pairs of words (or better, measure with acoustic equipment), you will find that the vowel phoneme /eɪ/ is quite a bit **shorter** in the second member of each pair. I've indicated this in the transcription with the IPA shortness marker on the [e] part of the [eɪ] diphthong:

save	[seɪv]	*safe*	[sĕɪf]
Abe	[eɪb]	*ape*	[ĕɪp]
made	[meɪd]	*mate*	[mĕɪt]
maze	[meɪz]	*mace*	[mĕɪs]
age	[eɪdʒ]	*H*	[ĕɪtʃ]
Haig	[heɪg]	*ache*	[ĕɪk]

Although [eɪ] and [ĕɪ] are audibly different, they are not separate phonemes – one could not use them to form a distinction between words. The reason is that their distribution is predictable. In the data given, which are representative, there is a straightforward fact that determines which of the two will appear. (You should take a look at the data now if you have not yet seen what this factor is.)

The relevant factor is the voicing of the immediately following sound. [eɪ] occurs when this sound in the word is voiced (here: [v, b, d, z, dʒ, g]), and [ĕɪ] occurs when the next sound in the word in voiceless (here: [f, p, t, s, tʃ, k]). The fact that the appearance of [eɪ] vs. [ĕɪ] is predictable is important, because it shows that the difference between the two could never be the (sole) distinction between words; there will always be a difference in the voicing of the following consonant as well. It follows that there can be no minimal pair for [eɪ] and [ĕɪ].

A term that is commonly used to describe this is **complementary distribution**: two sounds are said to be in complementary distribution if one sound never occurs in the environments in which the other occurs.

Thus, in phonological analysis, for any pair of sounds it is necessary to establish their phonological status: either they are separate phonemes, capable of distinguishing words, or mere variants, whose distribution in the language is determined by context, in a way that can be expressed by a rule (here, the rule relating length to voicing). We will see refinements on this point later on, but it will suffice for now.

To complete the description of [eɪ] and [ĕɪ], we must dispose of an alternative possibility: that [eɪ] and [ĕɪ] really are distinct phonemes, and it is the voicing of the following consonant that is predictable. This possibility is eliminated by the fact that minimal pairs occur for consonant voicing in other contexts (for example, *few* vs. *view*); thus it has to be the voicing that is phonemic and the length that is predictable.

2.4 Phonemes as Categories

Another important aspect of the [eɪ]–[ĕɪ] data under discussion is that virtually every English speaker is unaware of the difference until it has been pointed out. That is to say, speakers are willing, intuitively, to accept [eɪ] and [ĕɪ] as being the "same vowel."[1] Phonologists hypothesize that sounds [eɪ] and [ĕɪ] in the present case (and similarly in parallel cases) form an abstract phonological *category*, namely, the phoneme /eɪ/. The concrete, observable sounds [eɪ] and [ĕɪ] are called the **allophones** of /eɪ/. This is illustrated as follows:

Abstract level:	/eɪ/	⟵ phoneme
Concrete level:	[eɪ] [ĕɪ]	⟵ allophones
	used before used before ⟵ environments for allophones	
	voiced voiceless	
	consonants consonants	

---

[1] This is true even when the sounds are spelled differently, as in *Haig* vs. *ache*. The intuitive judgments are of sound, not spelling.

The idea is that the fundamental phonological categories (the phonemes) can be used to distinguish words from each other, but the variants of a particular phoneme (the allophones), cannot. As a metaphor, you could imagine that the phoneme inventory of a language is the fundamental "alphabet" (an alphabet of sound) out of which all the words of a language are composed; but each letter is subject to contextual variation. At the level of conscious awareness, people are characteristically attuned only to the distinctions between phonemes; to make people aware of allophones requires that their attention be carefully directed to the distinction.

2.5   More Instances of Allophonic Variation

Before moving on, let us consider some other cases of allophonic variation in English. The following pair illustrates words containing alveolar [n] and dental [n̪]. Check the environments for each sound, establishing the complementary distribution, before you read further.

Words with [n]		Words with [n̪]	
know	[ˈnoʊ]	*tenth*	[ˈtɛn̪θ]
annoy	[əˈnɔɪ]	*month*	[ˈmʌn̪θ]
onion	[ˈʌnjən]	*panther*	[ˈpæn̪θɚ]
nun	[ˈnʌn]	*chrysanthemum*	[kɹəˈsæn̪θəməm]

It is not hard to see that the dental [n̪] occurs in a specific context: before [θ]. There is no particular context for alveolar [n]; it occurs pretty much everywhere else. Thus, the phonemic pattern is as follows:

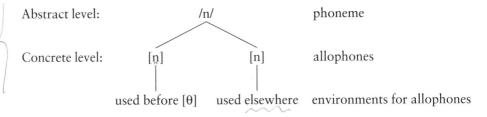

The "elsewhere" environment seen here is quite common in phonology, and cases like the [n] in this example are often called elsewhere allophones. The allophone [eɪ], seen in the previous example, is actually an elsewhere allophone; it occurs not just before voiced consonants, but at the end of a word, as in *bay* [beɪ] or *day* [deɪ].

The next data set illustrates four allophones of the /l/ phoneme as they occur in a number of dialects of English. [ɫ] is a velarized l, articulated with high back tongue body position. [ɫ̪] is the same as [ɫ], only with a dental instead of alveolar place of articulation. [l̥l] is an l which starts out voiceless and ends voiced. Before you read further, inspect the following data and determine the environment characterizing each sound.

Words with [ɬ]	Words with [l̥̃]		Words with [ɫ̪]	Words with [l]	
file ['faɪɬ]	*slight* ['sl̥aɪt]		*wealth* ['wɛɫ̪θ]	*listen* ['lɪsən]	
fool ['fuɬ]	*flight* ['fl̥aɪt]		*health* ['hɛɫ̪θ]	*lose* ['luz]	
all ['ɔɬ]	*plow* ['pl̥aʊ]		*filthy* ['fɪɫ̪θi]	*allow* [ə'laʊ]	
ball ['bɔɬ]	*cling* ['kl̥ɪŋ]		*tilth* ['tɪɫ̪θ]	*aglow* [ə'gloʊ]	
fell ['fɛɬ]	*discipline* ['dɪsəpl̥ən]		*stealth* ['stɛɫ̪θ]	*blend* ['blɛnd]	
feel ['fiɬ]					

The pattern can be described as follows:

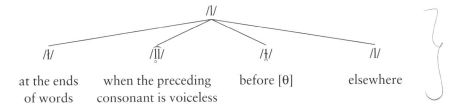

As before, this description appears to hold for the entire language, not just the sample data given here. Since none of these environments overlap,[2] the description establishes complementary distribution, and we can claim that all four of these sounds are allophones of the same phoneme.

The three examples just given are only the tip of the iceberg; in fact, virtually all the phonemes in English show variation based on their context. If we looked at English in full phonetic detail, taking all the allophonic variation into account, we would find that it has not several dozen speech sounds, but thousands.

All this gives rise to an overview of how a phonological system is "designed." In every language, the number of sounds that can be uttered is very large. But the phonological system organizes these sounds in a particular way, such that only a small subset of phonetic differences (for example, in English [t] vs. [d], or [ɪ] vs. [ɛ]) can serve to distinguish words. The remaining phonetic differences are allophonic, and determined by rule.

2.6 Phonemic Transcription

When a linguist records words as sequences of phonemes (under a particular phonemic analysis), the result is termed a **phonemic transcription**. This is to be

---

[2] The environments "after a voiceless consonant" and "at the end of a word" cannot overlap, because English has no words ending in a voiceless consonant followed by /l/.

distinguished from a **phonetic transcription**, which includes allophonic detail – the degree of detail recorded being up to the transcriber. The term **orthographic transcription** simply means that the words are written down using the customary spelling system (orthography) of the language. Below I give the same sentence in orthographic, phonemic, and phonetic transcription.

This is an orthographic transcription.

/ðɪs ɪz ə fou'nimɪk træn'skɹɪpʃən/   (This is a phonemic transcription.)

['d̥ðɪs ɪz ə fə̃'nɛɾɨʔk t͡sʰɹɛ̃ə̃n'skɹɪpʃɨ̃n]   (This is a phonetic transcription.)

The attractiveness of a phonemic transcription for practical purposes is that it is far simpler than a phonetic transcription, yet (provided one knows the rules) it conveys the same information. One need only apply the rules to derive the correct allophones.

Reference grammars (books addressed to linguists that offer a description of a language) often begin by setting out the phonemes and allophones. The first few transcriptions in a grammar are usually phonetic; then, once the allophonic rules have been duly set out, all the remaining transcriptions can safely be phonemic, without any loss of information.[3]

2.7   Phonological Rules

Generalizations about the patterning of allophones can be stated as phonological rules. For instance, to describe the patterning of [eɪ] and [ĕɪ] given above, one might write a rule like this:

/eɪ/ Shortening
The phoneme /eɪ/ is realized as extra short when a voiceless consonant follows.

We will refine our rules in many ways below, but this should get across the basic idea. The concept of rule is central to phonology; here are some elaborations.

First, rules are language-specific: the shortening of /eɪ/ (and, as it turns out, of other vowels) must be considered as a rule *of English*; it is not a universal rule, nor some kind of general principle of speech articulation. We know this because we have data from other languages that apparently lack any rule of this kind. For instance, neither Polish nor Saudi Arabic shortens vowels before voiceless consonants. The shortening rule of English is part of the phonological pattern of the English language, and must be learned in some form by children acquiring English.

---

[3] For convenience, authors of reference grammars usually take the further step of setting up a **practical orthography**, in which each phoneme is spelled using an ordinary letter or letter combination.

Second, rules are usually productive in the sense that they extend to novel cases. "*Vake*" and "*praig*" are not words of English, but if they become words, we can be confident that they will obey the rules and be pronounced [vĕɪk] and [pɹeɪg]. For more on productivity, see chapter 9.

Third, rules give rise to well-formedness intuitions. If a phonetician, or a speech synthesizer, were to create exceptions to the rule, English speakers sense the awkwardness of the result; thus [sĕɪv] and [seɪf] are inappropriate as natural renditions of *save* and *safe*. In other words, rule violations are sensed intuitively.

Fourth, phonological rules are untaught. Instead, they are learned intuitively by children from the ambient language data, using mechanisms that are as yet unknown. In this respect, phonological rules are very different from rules that are imparted by direct instruction, like (for example) the rules for traffic lights, or rules of **normative grammar** like "don't end a sentence with a preposition."

Lastly, phonological rules are evidently a form of unconscious knowledge. No matter how hard we try, we cannot access our phonological rules through introspection.

One shouldn't be surprised that this is so, because most of the computations that our brains carry out are similarly inaccessible to consciousness. For example, we can detect color constancy under variable conditions of light and shadow, or the direction of sound sources by the time delay between our ears. These processes involve rapid, automatic mental computations that cannot be intuited by the conscious mind as they occur. We consciously notice the *result* of such computations ("this object is uniformly red"; "a car is approaching from my left"), but not the way it is done. To understand such processes, cognitive scientists *infer* their mechanisms on the basis of observation, experimentation, and theorizing. No one bothers to ask people how they do these things, because people don't know.

Phonology is similar. When we speak, we automatically obey hundreds, perhaps thousands of phonological rules, but we can neither observe nor articulate what these rules are. Thus, when this book discusses "rules," what is meant is rules of the unconscious kind. We cannot learn about these processes through introspection, but must proceed indirectly, through data gathering, experiment, and construction of theories.

2.8   Formalizing Phonological Rules

We turn now to the problem of expressing the phonological rules precisely. In principle, we could just write all of the rules in prose – and indeed, this is usually done as backup, to help the reader understand the rules more easily. But in general, phonologists have found that use of a formal notation permits greater precision and clarity. Throughout this book, we will gradually accumulate more notational apparatus with this purpose in mind. The notations used here are drawn from the research literature in phonology; I have tried to limit myself to notations that would be widely recognized among phonologists.

2.8.1 *Expressing environments*

Let us start with some formalism for describing the environments where allophones occur. The symbol slash, "/", as used in phonology, means "in the environment." A long underline stands for where the allophone occurs relative to its neighbors. Thus the following expression:

is to be read "in the environment 'before theta'", or, for short, just "before theta." If instead we had written "/ θ ___", it would be read "after theta."

In expressing the environment of an allophone, we often must specify not just a single sound like [θ], but a whole class of sounds. For example, the environment for [l̥] (p. 25) includes the class of voiceless consonants. To describe such classes, we use **square brackets**, containing the particular phonetic properties – which, in the context of phonology, are called **features** – that designate the relevant class of sounds. (Features are covered in detail in chapter 4.) Thus, the following notation can be read "after a voiceless consonant":

$$/\begin{bmatrix} \text{consonant} \\ \text{voiceless} \end{bmatrix} \underline{\qquad}$$

As can be seen, square brackets in phonology essentially mean "*and*"; hence $\begin{bmatrix} \text{consonant} \\ \text{voiceless} \end{bmatrix}$ means "a segment[4] which is a consonant *and* is voiceless."

The symbols "+" and "−" are used before feature names to mean that a segment either has, or does not have, the phonetic property that a feature designates. Thus, in more standard notation the environment just given would appear as:

$$/\begin{bmatrix} +\text{consonant} \\ -\text{voice} \end{bmatrix} \underline{\qquad}$$

Where we want to refer to the beginnings and ends of grammatical constituents like words, we can use brackets, much as is done in the study of syntax and morphology. For example, the notation given below can be read "at the end of a word."

$$/ \underline{\qquad}]_{\text{word}}$$

"At the beginning of a word" would be "/ [$_{\text{word}}$ ___."

---

4   As phonologists generally do, I will use the term "segment" to refer to a single speech sound.

2.8.2 *Underlying representations and derivations*

We turn next to the task of characterizing allophones as the variants of a single abstract phoneme. A widely adopted theoretical approach in phonology is to characterize the phoneme by setting up an abstract level of representation called the **underlying representation**, also called the **phonemic representation, underlying form, or base form**. The idea is that phonemes have an essential, characteristic form, which is altered in particular contexts by the rules of the phonology, applying in a derivation.

In a system of this kind, it is rational to adopt as the underlying representation of the phoneme its "elsewhere" allophone. Recall (p. 24) that the elsewhere allophone is the allophone that is not affiliated with any particular context, but rather is the sound that appears when no other special context is met. The phonological derivation starts out with the underlying form, and rules apply to derive from it the various allophones in their appropriate contexts. If no rule is applicable, the underlying form emerges unaltered as the output of the phonology.[5]

Using this approach, we can develop an explicit description of the system of allophones for the English phoneme /l/. We select /l/ as the underlying representation, and posit three rules, stated below in both formalism and prose.

/l/ Devoicing

$$/l/ \rightarrow [\widehat{\overset{\circ}{l}}] \quad / \begin{bmatrix} +\text{consonant} \\ -\text{voice} \end{bmatrix} \underline{\quad}$$

Partially devoice /l/ after a voiceless consonant.

/l/ Dentalization

$$/l/ \rightarrow [\overset{\smallfrown}{ɫ}] \quad / \underline{\quad} θ$$

/l/ is rendered as velarized and dental before [θ].

/l/ Velarization

$$/l/ \rightarrow [ɫ] \quad / \underline{\quad}]_{\text{word}}$$

/l/ is velarized word-finally.

Along with the posited underlying forms and rules, an analysis of this type is usually illustrated by providing sample derivations. A derivation consists of a series of lines. The first contains the underlying representations of a set of forms, and the last contains the actual phonetic forms, which in this context are often

---

[5] A caution: I find that students sometimes spontaneously adopt a terminology in which the elsewhere allophone is termed "the phoneme" and the contextual allophones derived by rule are called the "allophones." This is perfectly coherent, but is not standard usage. Among phonologists, the elsewhere allophone counts as an allophone just like all the others, and the phoneme is a separate, abstract entity – it occurs at a deeper level of representation.

called surface representations. The intermediate lines show the application of the rules in order. Where a rule is inapplicable, the notation "—" is used to designate this.

Here is a derivation for four words containing /l/, specifically chosen to illustrate all of the rules above.

file	*slight*	*wealth*	*listen*	
/faɪl/	/slaɪt/	/wɛlθ/	/ˈlɪsən/	underlying forms
—	sl̥aɪt	—	—	/l/ Devoicing
—	—	wɛl̪θ	—	/l/ Dentalization
faɪɫ	—	—	—	/l/ Velarization
[ˈfaɪɫ]	[sl̥aɪt]	[ˈwɛl̪θ]	[ˈlɪsən]	surface forms

In this approach, we need not specify that the elsewhere allophone is [l]; that is simply the base form whenever none of the phonological rules happen to alter it. In other words, a phonological rule like "/l/ → [l] / elsewhere" is unnecessary.

The idea of a phonological derivation has over time proven fruitful. Often, the rules apply in an intricate, cross-cutting pattern, creating large numbers of allophones.[6] It also turns out (chapter 7) that, in many cases, the order in which the rules apply is crucial.

The derivations form the heart of a phonological discussion, and the reader of a phonological analysis is well advised to inspect rather than skim them.[7] In particular, in each case it is important to understand, by comparing the rule to the form, why the rule applied or did not apply. Thus, in reading the first line of the derivation above, you would want to reassure yourself that /l/ Devoicing did indeed apply correctly to *slight*, because /s/ is a member of the class of voiceless consonants; and similarly in all other cases.

2.9   Phonemes in Other Languages

A great number of languages have been subjected to phonemic analysis. This typological study has found great diversity, but also a certain degree of unity. As an example of the latter, there is a certain "core" set of speech sounds that tend to be employed as phonemes in a great number of languages. The following set, for example, constitutes all the sounds that occurred in at least 40 percent of the

---

[6]   For instance, we can note that /l/ Dentalization probably doesn't need to carry out the full change /l/ → [l̪]; rather, it should only make the change /l/ → [l̪], and a suitably generalized version of /l/ Velarization can handle that part of the change that velarizes the /l/.

[7]   I find that in hard cases it is helpful to copy them down.

languages in Maddieson's (1984) survey of phonemic systems. It might be thought of as a "maximally ordinary" phonemic system.

p	t	tʃ	k		i		u
b	d	dʒ[8]	g		e		o
f	s	ʃ				a	
m	n		ŋ				
	l						
	ɾ						
w	j						

On the other hand, most phonemic inventories are not restricted to just these "core" sounds; more normally, an inventory will contain additional, more unusual sounds. For example, the typologically unusual aspects of English include /θ/, /ð/, the syllabic consonants, and the heavy representation of diphthongs in the vowel inventory. Unusual sounds often occur in multiple languages in the same geographic area; e.g., retroflexes in India and Australia, diphthongs in Northern Europe, and gliding tones in East Asia.

However, phonemic diversity extends beyond just phoneme inventories. A more subtle cross-linguistic difference concerns how the phonetic inventory of a language (that is, the complete collection of allophones) is organized into phonemes. In particular, a distinction that is phonemic (serves to distinguish words) in one language might be allophonic (predictably distributed) in another.

An example is found in the phonemic systems of English and Spanish. Spanish has many sounds that resemble sounds of English (we will consider only North American dialects of English here). In particular, English has a [t] and a tap [ɾ]. The [d] of Spanish is dental rather than alveolar, and there are also slight differences in the tap, but these are small enough to ignore for our purposes.

In North American English [ɾ] is (to a rough approximation) an allophone of the /t/ phoneme. The environment for [ɾ] is between two vowels of which the second is stressless. Words having /t/ that fit this environment, and which therefore show a tap, are given in the first column below.

	Phonemic	Phonetic			Phonemic	Phonetic
data	/ˈdeɪtə/	[ˈdeɪɾə]		*tan*	/ˈtæn/	[ˈtæn]
latter	/ˈlætɚ/	[ˈlæɾɚ]		*attend*	/əˈtɛnd/	[əˈtɛnd]
eating	/ˈitɪŋ/	[ˈiɾɪŋ]		*guilty*	/ˈgɪlti/	[ˈgɪlti]
Ottoman	/ˈatəmən/	[ˈaɾəmən]		*cat*	/ˈkæt/	[ˈkæt]
rhetoric	/ˈɹɛtəɹɪk/	[ˈɹɛɾəɹɪk]		*active*	/ˈæktɪv/	[ˈæktɪv]
automatic	/ˌɔtəˈmætɪk/	[ˌɔɾəˈmæɾɪk]		*Atkins*	/ˈætkɪnz/	[ˈætkɪnz]

---

[8] [dʒ] actually falls somewhat short of 40%; it is included in the list above because of another strong cross-linguistic tendency, i.e. for the sounds to occur in complete, symmetrical series (e.g., voiced matching up with voiceless).

The second column combines other allophones of /t/, without narrowly transcribing their specific properties. In this column, we see where /t/ does **not** appear as the [ɾ] allophone: either because it fails to follow a syllabic sound (*tan, guilty, active*) or because it fails to precede a syllabic sound (*cat, Atkins*), or because the following syllabic sound is stressed (*attend*). But if all the right conditions are met simultaneously, as in the first column, we get [ɾ].

It can be seen that the difference between [t] and [ɾ] is not distinctive in English: the tap is a conditioned variant of the /t/ phoneme that shows up in a particular environment. The Tapping rule can be stated, as a first approximation, as follows:

Tapping

$$/t/ \quad \rightarrow \quad [ɾ] \; / \; [+\text{vowel}] \; \underline{\hspace{1cm}} \; \begin{bmatrix} +\text{vowel} \\ -\text{stress} \end{bmatrix}$$

The phoneme /t/ is realized as [ɾ] when it is preceded by a vowel and followed by a stressless vowel.

Here are derivations:

data	tan	attend	cat	guilty	
/ˈdeɪtə/	/ˈtæn/	/əˈtɛnd/	/ˈkæt/	/ˈɡɪlti/	underlying forms
ɾ	—	—	—	—	Tapping
[ˈdeɪɾə]	[ˈtæn]	[əˈtɛnd]	[ˈkæt]	[ˈɡɪlti]	surface forms

In Spanish, /t/ and /ɾ/ are separate phonemes, as is demonstrated by minimal pairs such as the following:

[ˈpita]   'century plant'
[ˈpiɾa]   'funeral pyre'

As with the minimal pairs given for English above, this one demonstrates that for Spanish, the difference between [t] and [ɾ] signals a difference in meaning. That is to say, [t] and [ɾ] are in contrast, and are separate phonemes, /t/ vs. /ɾ/.

Comparing English and Spanish, we see that the [t] vs. [ɾ] difference is allophonic (non-distinctive) for English, but phonemic (distinctive) for Spanish. Thus, in this area, the two languages are *phonetically similar but phonologically different.*

Here is a similar case. Both English and Spanish have a [d] and a [ð] (the voiced dental fricative). In English, we know that the two sounds are separate phonemes, because minimal pairs exist:

die	[daɪ]	vs.	thy	[ðaɪ]
bayed	[beɪd]	vs.	bathe	[beɪð]
den	[dɛn]	vs.	then	[ðɛn]

But in Spanish, there are no such pairs. Furthermore, by looking at Spanish data one can determine that [d] and [ð] are allophonic variants:

[daðo]   'given'
[deðo]   'finger'
[usteð]   'you (polite)'
[donde]   'where'
[de ðonde]   'from where'

These and other data indicate that [ð] occurs only after a vowel, while [d] is the elsewhere allophone, occurring after consonants and initially. Thus [ð] and [d] are allophones of the same phoneme.

We can set up the following phonological analysis for the sounds of Spanish discussed so far.

Phonemes: /t/, /d/, /ɾ/

Phonological rule: **/d/ Spirantization**
                   /d/ → [ð] / [+vowel] ___
                   The phoneme /d/ is realized as [ð] when it follows a vowel.

Derivations: 'given'   'you'   'where'
                 /dado/   /usted/   /donde/   underlying forms
                   ð   ð   —   /d/ Spirantization
                 [daðo]   [usteð]   [donde]   surface forms

Regarding the name of the rule, spirantization is the conventional term in phonology for rules that convert stops to fricatives; such rules are common. "Spirant" is a mostly obsolete synonym for "fricative."

The differences in phonological organization between English and Spanish reflect a different division of phonetic space. Suppose we construe phonetic space as made up of multiple dimensions. We place [d] at the center of this space, and in different directions show [ð] as differing from [d] minimally in its fricative character ("continuancy"); [ɾ] differing from [d] in having short, weak closure; and [t] differing minimally from [d] in voicing:

The phones of this phonetic space are grouped into phonemes differently by Spanish and English, as shown below:

Spanish   English

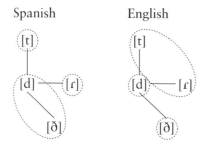

The dotted lines surround groups of sounds that fail to contrast, and thus form single phonemes in the language in question. English has /d/, /ð/, and /t/, with the latter having two allophones [t] and [ɾ]. Spanish has /t/, /ɾ/, and /d/, with the latter having two allophones [d] and [ð]. The chart shows that the sound systems of languages can differ in their phonological organization, as well as in the sounds that they contain. In principle, we could imagine two languages that had exactly the same sounds, but a radically different phonological organization. This would happen if the two languages selected different phonetic distinctions to be contrastive vs. non-contrastive. Using the phonemic method, we would analyze such languages as having the same set of sounds, grouped into phonemes in two different ways.

2.10   Phonemicization

Phonemicization is the body of knowledge and techniques that can be used to work out the phonemic system of a language. The method described below has been in existence for several decades and has been used on many languages. Of course, no recipe in linguistics provides certain results, and later on in this text we will see cases where the method falls short. But it is usually the starting point for working out the phonology of a language.

A really solid phonemicization is often the result of years of hard work, carried out by linguists with good ears and extensive experience with the target language. The reason that phonemicization takes so long is that the first linguist or team of linguists to encounter a language will quite often fail to notice a difficult-to-hear contrast. Another factor is that certain phonemes might be rare, and will be encountered only after the linguist has collected a large vocabulary.

2.10.1   *Minimal pairs*

By far the most effective method in phonemicization is to look for **minimal pairs**, which (to review) are defined as two different words that differ in exactly one sound in the same location. Some examples: *sip* [sɪp] and *zip* [zɪp] in English form a minimal pair for the phonemes /s/ and /z/; *sill* [sɪl] and *zeal* [zil] are not

a minimal pair, because they differ in two locations; *seal* [sil] and *eels* [ilz] are
not a minimal pair because the /s/ and /z/ occur in different places. Two sounds
that appear in a minimal pair are almost always distinct phonemes.[9]

The **absence** of a minimal pair does not prove much. Often, a language will
lack minimal pairs for a pair of relatively rare phonemes simply by accident.
A method for dealing with such cases is given in the next section.

As noted earlier, minimal pairs generalize to minimal triplets, quadruplets,
and so on. Often, selecting a good "frame" or phonological context will make it
possible to justify quite a bit of the phonemic inventory of a language. A notation
that is commonly used for such frames is to place the environment sounds on
either side of an underlined blank, which represents the sound being manipulated
in the pair, quadruplet, etc. Thus for American English vowels, the frame /h __ d/
gets all but /ɔɪ/, though admittedly some of the words are a bit forced:[10]

heed	[hid]			*who'd*	[hud]
hid	[hɪd]			*hood*	[hʊd]
hayed	[heɪd]			*hoed*	[hoʊd]
head	[hɛd]	*HUD*	[hʌd]		
had	[hæd]	*hod*	[hɑd]	*hawed*	[hɔd]
hide	[haɪd]	*how'd*	[haʊd]		
heard	[hɚd]				

For the missing /ɔɪ/, it is easy to imagine that "*hoid*" *could* be a word; its absence
from English is essentially an accident.

2.10.2 Near-minimal pairs

There are cases in which it is impossible to find minimal pairs for a phoneme.
This probably occurs more frequently in languages with long words and large
phoneme inventories. In English there appear to be cases where, at least for some
idiolects, a minimal pair cannot be found.[11] Conducting a search in an electronic
dictionary for minimal pairs for English /ð/ and /ʒ/, I found that it included only
three plausible candidates:

bathe	['beɪð]	vs.	*beige*	['beɪʒ]
leather	['lɛðɚ]	vs.	*leisure*	['lɛʒɚ]
seethe	['sið]	vs.	*siege*	['siʒ]

---

[9] The exceptions are discussed below in §7.1.1 and §10.3.
[10] *hayed* 'made hay', *HUD* 'colloquial abbreviation for United States Department of Housing and
Urban Development.'
[11] An **idiolect** is a language as it is learned and internalized by a single individual. A dialect is a
collection of closely similar idiolects, characterizable by region or social class. I refer to idiolects here
because I doubt that there is any English dialect whose speakers uniformly lack minimal pairs of the
kind under discussion.

However, for all three [ʒ] words, the pronunciation varies by dialect: there are many speakers who have [ˈbeɪd͡ʒ] for *beige*, [ˈliʒɚ] or [ˈlɛʒʊɹ] for *leisure*, and [ˈsid͡ʒ] for *siege*. For such a speaker, there are presumably no minimal pairs for [ð] vs. [ʒ].

Despite this, it is impossible that [ð] and [ʒ] could be allophones of the same phoneme, even in such a dialect. If they were allophones, we would expect that we could locate the **rules** that determine which allophone occurs where. But a moment's reflection will show that there could be no such rules.

This is shown by the existence of **near-minimal pairs,** which can be defined as pairs which would be minimal except for some evidently irrelevant difference. Here are some near-minimal pairs for /ð/ vs. /ʒ/:

tether	[ˈtɛðɚ]	vs.	*pleasure*	[ˈplɛʒɚ]
		or	*measure*	[ˈmɛʒɚ]
neither	[ˈniðɚ]	vs.	*seizure*	[ˈsiʒɚ]
lather	[ˈlæðɚ]	vs.	*azure*	[ˈæʒɚ]
heathen	[ˈhiðən]	vs.	*adhesion*	[ədˈhiʒən]
smoothen	[ˈsmuðən]	vs.	*illusion*	[ɪˈluʒən]
		or	*intrusion*	[ɪnˈtɹuʒən]
		or	*fusion*	[ˈfjuʒən]

Key

This list shows that the phonetic environment has nothing to do with whether [ð] or [ʒ] occurs – there is no *consistent* factor that could determine which segment appears. Any effort to find the rules that determine the appearance of [ð] vs. [ʒ] would have to make use of a completely arbitrary collection of "environments" for these phones. If the rules cannot be found, then an analysis that claims that [ð] and [ʒ] are allophones cannot be justified.

It is also easy to imagine that if a new word came into English that created a true minimal pair (say, '*hesion*' to go with *heathen*), such a word would readily be accepted. It is logical, then, to assume that /ð/ and /ʒ/ are separate phonemes, and that (for some speakers) no minimal pairs happen to be available. The near-minimal pairs suffice to show this.

Plainly, the near-minimal pair method of establishing phonemes requires more work than minimal pairs do: it is the accumulation of forms, and the ruling out of all reasonable hypotheses concerning allophone environments, that ultimately permits near-minimal pairs to be used as evidence.

2.10.3   *Using local environments to establish complementary distribution*

The methods of minimal and near-minimal pairs are used to establish that two sounds belong to separate phonemes. For establishing that two sounds are in the same phoneme, we need to establish that they are in complementary distribution, and therefore we need to find the environments in which they occur. For this purpose, it is often useful to follow the method of compiling local environments, illustrated below.

The language we will examine is Maasai (Nilotic, spoken in Kenya and Tanzania), and our focus is solely on the following set of sounds: [p, t, k, b, d, g, β, ð, ɣ]. The last three of these are voiced fricatives: [β] is bilabial, [ð] dental, and [ɣ] velar. Below are 63 words containing these sounds.

Maasai data

1	[ailap]	'to hate'	35	[imbok]	'you clean ceremonially'
2	[aret]	'to help'			
3	[arup]	'to heap up'	36	[indai]	'you-plural'
4	[asip]	'to speak truly'	37	[ijːoːk]	'we'
5	[ɓarːiɣoi]	'reddish brown'	38	[kaɣe]	'but'
6	[ɓaða]	'dangerous'	39	[keɗianje]	'left side'
7	[ɗalut]	'mischievous'	40	[keβer]	'heaven'
8	[diɣai]	'elsewhere'	41	[kiɓiroðo]	'stunted'
9	[ɗorːop]	'short'	42	[koɣoː]	'grandmother'
10	[emɓiðir]	'female wart hog'	43	[olɗiret]	'pack saddle'
11	[emaɲaða]	'warriors' village'	44	[olɗuɣa]	'shop'
12	[embiʃan]	'bravery'	45	[olɟilaða]	'room'
13	[emburuo]	'smoke'	46	[olʃiβet]	'stake'
14	[enɗaraða]	'thunder'	47	[olkila]	'garment'
15	[enɗuβai]	'sisal'	48	[olkiɣuei]	'thorn'
16	[eŋgirut]	'silent-feminine'	49	[olporːor]	'age set'
17	[eŋɟoː]	'small chest'	50	[olpul]	'slaughtering place'
18	[enaiβoʃa]	'Naivasha Lake'	51	[olpurɗa]	'meat preserved in fat'
19	[endaːraða]	'fight each other'			
20	[endorop]	'bribe him'	52	[olpurkel]	'dry steppes'
21	[endulelei]	'sodom apple'	53	[oltaː]	'lamp'
22	[enduβeiðai]	'Taveta woman'	54	[oltulet]	'gourd in natural state'
23	[eŋgamaniɣi]	'name of age-set'			
24	[eŋgila]	'garment-diminutive'	55	[oltuli]	'buttock'
25	[eŋgiruðoðo]	'fright'	56	[paɗan]	'skilled in shooting'
26	[eŋgoː]	'advise him'			
27	[eŋoɣi]	'sin'	57	[poɣira]	'all'
28	[ilarak]	'murderers'	58	[pus]	'light colored'
29	[ilkeːk]	'trees'	59	[sarkin]	'intermarriage taboo'
30	[ilpaβit]	'hairs'			
31	[iltoːi]	'barrel'	60	[taruɓini]	'binoculars'
32	[imɓok]	'you detain'	61	[tasat]	'disabled'
33	[imbala]	'papers'	62	[tisila]	'sift it'
34	[imbaɣiβak]	'you are restless'	63	[tiʃila]	'scrutinize it'

The first thing to notice about the data is that they include an additional series of stops: /ɓ ɗ ʄ ɠ/. These are voiced implosives, made by lowering the larynx to form a slight vacuum in the mouth during closure. The implosives form a separate series of phonemes in Maasai, as can be shown by minimal and near-minimal pairs such as the following:

35.	[imbok]	'you clean ceremonially'
vs. 32.	[imɓok]	'you detain'
7.	[ɗalut]	'mischievous'
vs. 61.	[tasat]	'disabled'
26.	[eŋgoː]	'advise him'
vs. 17.	[eŋɠoː]	'small chest'
41.	[kiɓiroðo]	'stunted'
vs. 40.	[keβer]	'heaven'

Having established this, we will ignore the implosives henceforth.

The method of compiling local environments works as follows: for each sound, we construct a list of all its appearances, each time including the preceding segment, if any, and the following segment, if any. For example, word #5, [ɓarːiɣoi] 'reddish brown' contains the target sound [ɣ]. This sound is preceded by [i] and followed by [o]. Thus, we add to our chart the following entry, in a column headed [ɣ]:

$$[\gamma]$$
$$/\,i \,\_\_\_\, o \quad (5)$$

This chart entry may be read "[ɣ] occurs where preceded by [i] and followed by [o], in example (5)."

Where the target sound is the initial or final segment in the word, one includes in the environment a bracket of the type]ₐₒᵣd to designate this environment:

$$[k]$$
$$/\,oː \,\_\_\_\,]_{word} \quad (37)$$

This expression may be read "[k] occurs where preceded by [oː] and word-final."

One then continues through the whole set of data in this way. If this is done for the **velar** sounds only, one gets the following:

[k]			[g]			[ɣ]		
/ [word ___ a	(38)		/ ŋ ___ a	(23)		/ a ___ e	(38)	
/ [word ___ e	(39, 40)		/ ŋ ___ i	(24, 25)		/ a ___ i	(34)	
/ [word ___ i	(41)		/ ŋ ___ o	(26)		/ i ___ a	(8)	
/ [word ___ o	(42)					/ i ___ i	(23)	
/ l ___ e	(29)					/ i ___ o	(5)	
/ l ___ i	(47, 48)					/ i ___ u	(48)	
/ r ___ e	(52)					/ o ___ i	(27, 57)	
/ r ___ i	(59)					/ o ___ oː	(42)	
/ a ___]word	(28, 34)					/ u ___ a	(44)	
/ eː ___]word	(29)							
/ o ___]word	(32, 35)							
/ oː ___]word	(37)							

At this point, one inspects the data in hopes of locating general patterns. For these data, notice that [g] may occur only when the sound [ŋ] immediately precedes it. Further, and crucially, the sounds [k] and [ɣ] are **never** preceded by [ŋ] – which makes the distribution complementary. It thus looks likely that [g] is just one allophone of a phoneme, because it has such a highly restricted distribution. The preceding [ŋ] is likely to be the context that requires this allophone.

Inspecting the third column, we see another particular property: all cases of [ɣ] are surrounded by vowels. As before, this is not the case with the other candidate phones. The pattern suggests that [ɣ] is another allophone of the phoneme that includes [g].

Inspection of the [k] column shows no particularly interesting property: [k] may occur initially, after [r] or [l], and in final position. The only really important property here is that these various environments do *not* include the environments for [ɣ] or [g]. This makes [k] a good candidate for being an "elsewhere" allophone, in the sense described on p. 24 above.

We have established, then, that [k], [ɣ], and [g] are in complementary distribution: none occurs when any of the others may occur. The environments are shown below.

[g] / ŋ ___
[ɣ] / V ___ V   where V stands for any vowel
[k] / elsewhere

It is reasonable to suppose that [k], as the elsewhere allophone, is the normal, unperturbed member of the phoneme, which we set up as the underlying representation. [g] and [ɣ] are particular allophones resulting from phonological rules applying in particular environments. Note finally that, once we write the rules, the changes that they will carry out are not drastic: [k] and [g] differ only in voicing, while [k] and [ɣ] differ only in voicing and manner. This gives some additional plausibility to the idea that these sounds are related by rule.

Pursuing this, we can state the phonological analysis of these sounds as follows. First, /k/ is assumed to be a phoneme of Maasai, which undergoes the following two phonological rules.

/k/ Spirantization

k → ɣ / [+vowel] ___ [+vowel]
/k/ is realized as [ɣ] between vowels.

Postnasal Voicing

k → g / ŋ ___
/k/ is realized as [g] after [ŋ].

Sample phonological derivations for three representative words of Maasai are as follows:

'grandmother'	'garment-dim.'	'trees'	
/koko:/	/eŋkila/	/ilke:k/	underlying forms
ɣ	—	—	/k/ Spirantization
—	g	—	Postnasal Voicing
[koɣo:]	[eŋgila]	[ilke:k]	surface forms

It should be clear why the method of collecting local environments was useful here: as it turned out, the environments for the rules were in fact local, involving adjacent segments. While this is not true of all phonological rules,[12] it is common enough to make the strategy worthwhile.

Plainly, the procedure is tedious. It is possible, for many people and in many cases, to skip steps. If you have a knack for this, phoneme problems can be solved by inspection, without the tedious charting of all environments.

Another asset in solving such problems is experience. The same rules often show up in many different languages, so someone who has examined extensive phonological data before has a leg up in solving new problems. In the present case, we can note some languages that realize /k/ as [ɣ] between vowels: Taiwanese, Ewe (Ghana), and Tümpisa Shoshone (Death Valley, California). Languages that realize [k] as [g] after a nasal include Modern Greek, Leurbost Gaelic (Scotland), and Waorani (Amazon basin, Peru). The questions of *why* the same rules recur in many different languages is one of the outstanding issues in phonological theory.

---

[12] The primary exceptions are vowel-to-vowel rules (example on p. 154), stress rules (treated in ch. 14), and the occasional long-distance consonant-to-consonant rule (see p. 84).

2.10.4 More Maasai: natural classes

We have not yet considered six of the nine Maasai sounds we set out to analyze, namely [p, b, β] and [t, ð, d]. Before proceeding, it is useful to arrange the relevant sounds into phonetic charts. Ideally, we would do this for all of the sounds of Maasai, but for present purposes the following will suffice:

	Bilabial	*Dental*	*Velar*
voiceless stops	p	t	k
plain voiced stops	b	d	g
voiced implosive stops	ɓ	ɗ	ɠ
voiced fricatives	β	ð	ɣ
voiced nasals	m	n	ŋ

If we sort out the target sounds in the way we did before, we will get the following:

[p]
/ [word ___ a   (56)
/ [word ___ o   (57)
/ [word ___ u   (58)
/ l ___ a   (30)
/ l ___ o   (49)
/ l ___ u   (50, 51, 52)
/ a ___]word (1)
/ i ___]word (4)
/ o ___]word (9, 20)
/ u ___]word (3)

[b]
/ m ___ a (33, 34)
/ m ___ i (12)
/ m ___ o (35)
/ m ___ u (13)

[β]
/ a ___ i (30)
/ e ___ e (40)
/ i ___ a (34)
/ i ___ e (46)
/ i ___ o (18)
/ u ___ a (15)
/ u ___ e (22)

[t]
/ [word ___ a   (60, 61)
/ [word ___ i   (62, 63)
/ l ___ aː   (53)
/ l ___ oː   (31)
/ l ___ u   (54, 55)
/ a ___]word (61)
/ e ___]word (2, 43, 46, 54)
/ i ___]word (30)
/ u ___]word (7, 16)

[d]
/ n ___ aː (19)
/ n ___ a   (36)
/ n ___ o   (20)
/ n ___ u   (21, 22)

[ð]
/ a ___ a (6, 11, 14, 19, 45)
/ i ___ a (22)
/ i ___ i (10)
/ o ___ o (25, 41)
/ u ___ o (25)

If you consider both the phonetic chart and the list of environments, you can see that the distribution of the bilabial and dental sounds is in complete parallel with the velars: voiced stops appear after nasal consonants, voiced fricatives occur between vowels, and voiceless stops occur elsewhere.

Thus, although we are dealing with three phonemes and nine allophones, we do not need a large number of rules to cover the data. Rather, we can use features to write general rules that cover all three phonemes at once. The specific analysis sets up the three phonemes /p/, /t/, and /k/ and posits two generalized phonological rules.

Spirantization

$$\begin{bmatrix} +\text{stop} \\ -\text{voice} \end{bmatrix} \rightarrow \begin{bmatrix} +\text{voice} \\ -\text{stop} \\ +\text{fricative} \end{bmatrix} / [+\text{vowel}] \_\_\_ [+\text{vowel}]$$

A voiceless stop is realized as the corresponding voiced fricative when surrounded by vowels.

Postnasal Voicing

$[+\text{stop}] \rightarrow [+\text{voice}] / [+\text{nasal}] \_\_\_$
A voiceless stop is realized as the corresponding voiced stop when it follows a nasal consonant.

For this approach to work, we need to be explicit about how features are used in rules. If a feature occurs on the right side of the arrow, that feature is changed, whenever the rule applies. But *all other features are assumed to remain unaltered.* Thus, if we are considering a sequence like /mp/ and apply Postnasal Voicing (as in #33, /impala/ → [imbala]), the [−voice] of the /p/ is changed to [+voice], so that /p/ is altered to [b]. But the features [+bilabial] and [+stop] remain unaltered. In this way, we can express rules that alter whole classes of segments (such as all the voiceless stops) in parallel. The features therefore permit a simpler and more general analysis than would be available if all the allophones of each phoneme were derived separately.

The fact that the stop phonemes of Maasai vary in parallel fashion is not an accident. The same phenomenon shows up in a great number of languages. Here are two examples we've already covered of how rules apply to classes of sounds.

Vowel Shortening in English: The shortening of /eɪ/ to [ĕɪ] before voiceless consonants in English (p. 26) is not unique to /eɪ/: all vowels of English are shortened in this environment. Examples: *coat* [kŏʊt] vs. *code* [koʊd], *lap* [lǽp] vs. *lab* [læb], etc.

Spirantization in Spanish: Spanish not only has [ð] as a post-vowel allophone of /d/ (p. 33), but also [β] as a post-vowel allophone of /b/ and [ɣ] as a post-vowel allophone of /g/. In other words, all voiced stops are converted to the corresponding fricatives in the post-vowel environment. Examples: /'lobo/ ['loβo] 'wolf', /'lago/ ['laɣo] 'lake'.

The general lesson that we learn from these examples (and countless others) is this: *phonological rules are based on phonetic features*. This general principle has three specific subcases.

First, the *set of sounds a rule applies to* is normally a set of sounds that share a particular phonetic feature or set of features. For example, the Spirantization rule of Spanish applies to all and only the voiced stops, characterized as [+stop, +voice].

Second, rules often change only *one or two features* of a sound, rather than making massive alterations. For example, the rules for Maasai alter only voicing and the stop/fricative distinction.

Lastly, the *sounds appearing in the environment of a rule* are almost always a set of sounds that share a particular phonetic feature or features. For example, the rule of English that shortens vowels applies before the complete set of consonants in English that are [−voice].

A **natural class** of sounds is defined as any complete set of sounds in a given language that share the same value for a feature or set of features. For example, /m/, /n/, and /ŋ/ in Maasai and in English form a natural class because they constitute the complete set of sounds that share the feature [+nasal]. Likewise, /p/, /t/, and /k/ form a natural class in Maasai and in English because they constitute all the [+stop, −voiced] sounds of the language.

It can be noted that the natural class defined by a particular feature combination will vary from language to language, simply because different languages have different inventories of sounds. Thus, in English [p t k] form the natural class of voiceless stops ([+stop, −voice]). Yet [p t k] are not a natural class in Persian (Farsi), since Persian contains a fourth voiceless stop, uvular [q]. For Persian, [+stop, −voice] is a natural class, but consists instead of the sounds [p t k q].

To reiterate the point made above with the novel terminology: in most instances, the segments that undergo a rule or appear in the environment of a rule form a natural class in the language in question.

Exercises

1 /ɹ/ in American English

This is a simple allophone problem, to be solved like the Maasai allophone problem in §2.10.3 above. The focus sounds are the voiced alveolar central approximant [ɹ], and the (slightly) rounded voiced alveolar central approximant [ɹʷ].

migrants	[ˈmaɪɡɹʷənts]	*Homeric*	[hoʊˈmɛɹʷɪk]
or	[ˈɔɹ]	*trek*	[ˈtɹʷɛk]
from	[ˈfɹʷʌm]	*debriefed*	[diˈbɹʷift]
shire	[ˈʃaɪɹ]	*reply*	[ɹʷiˈplaɪ]
tripling	[ˈtɹʷɪplɪŋ]	*Iraqi*	[ɪˈɹɹʷɑki]
metaphor	[ˈmɛtəˌfɔɹ]	*preys*	[ˈpɹʷeɪz]
iridium	[ɪˈɹʷɪdiəm]	*ranted*	[ˈɹʷæntəd]
proclivities	[pɹʷoʊˈklɪvəɾiz]	*crucible*	[ˈkɹʷusəbəl]
romancing	[ɹʷoʊˈmænsɪŋ]	*indiscriminately*	[ˌɪndəsˈkɹʷɪmənətli]
February	[ˈfɛbjuɛɹʷi]	*fear*	[ˈfɪɹ]
dwarfing	[ˈdwɔɹfɪŋ]	*dreadful*	[ˈdɹʷɛdfəl]
assure	[əˈʃuɹ]	*feldspar*	[ˈfɛldspɑɹ]

2   Lango phonemes

Lango is a Nilotic language spoken in Uganda.

a.   Make a phonetic chart of all the consonants in the data below (columns: place of articulation; rows: manner of articulation, voicing, and length).

b.   This problem deals just with the sounds [p, pp, ɸ, t, tt, ɾ̥, t͡ɕ, t͡tɕ, ç, k, kk, x]. Collect local environments for these sounds only, following the method given in this chapter.

c.   The sounds [p, pp, ɸ, t, tt, ɾ̥, t͡ɕ, t͡tɕ, ç, k, kk, x] may be grouped into eight phonemes. List the eight phonemes and their allophones. State the environments where the allophones occur. You may use "elsewhere" to simplify your presentation.

d.   State in words the phonological rules that determine the allophones. There is a major ambiguity in determining what is an allophone of what. Figure out this ambiguity, and state analyses for both possibilities.

e.   The word for 'lazy' is [ɲàp], with a [p]. The word for 'laziness' is [ɲáɸô], with a [ɸ]. Explain how this bears on the ambiguity noted in the previous question.

Phonetic symbols:

- [á] marks High tone, [à] marks Low, [â] marks Falling.
- [t͡ɕ] and [d͡ʑ] are alveolopalatal affricates, [ç] is an alveolopalatal fricative.
- [ɾ̥] is a voiceless tap.
- Consonants transcribed as double are simply held longer; they are not "rearticulated." Think of them as single long consonants.

1	[pì]	'because of'	33	[dáxô]	'woman'
2	[kètɕ]	'hunger'	34	[tɕùtɕ]	'pitch black'
3	[tɔ́ŋ]	'spear'	35	[tóddʑó]	'to beat up'
4	[búttɕó]	'to yell at'	36	[wókkí]	'a few minutes ago'
5	[tɕɔ̀ː]	'men'	37	[dìəxə̀]	'wet'
6	[ʔɔ̀t]	'house'	38	[máxâtɕ]	'scissors'
7	[dɔ̀ttɔ̀]	'to suck'	39	[pé]	'snow, hail'
8	[pə̀ppì]	'fathers'	40	[kɔ́ppɔ̀]	'cup'
9	[pójó]	'to remember'	41	[pàttɕó]	'to peel'
10	[ljèt]	'hot'	42	[pámmà]	'cotton'
11	[bókkó]	'to make red'	43	[mɔ̀ɾɔ̀xà]	'car'
12	[júttɕú]	'to throw'	44	[bə̀p]	'to deflate'
13	[èŋə̀ɾó]	'lion'	45	[lwìttê]	'to sneak'
14	[ókkɔ́]	'completely'	46	[ɲàp]	'lazy'
15	[déɸô]	'to collect'	47	[bwɔ̀ttɔ̀]	'to retort insultingly'
16	[dèk]	'stew'	48	[tèttó]	'to forge'
17	[tɕùɸâ]	'bottle'	49	[tɕàmmó]	'to eat'
18	[gwèk]	'gazelle'	50	[tɔ̀p]	'to spoil'
19	[kókkó]	'to cry'	51	[tɕɔ́k]	'near'
20	[ɲáɸô]	'laziness'	52	[pàɸó]	'father'
21	[ɾétɕ]	'fish'	53	[ŋwèttɕó]	'to run from'
22	[bóɾə̀]	'to me'	54	[bót]	'to'
23	[dìppó]	'to smash'	55	[dèppó]	'to collect'
24	[dwéɾê]	'months'	56	[gɔ̀t]	'mountain'
25	[kóddó]	'to blow'	57	[jìtɕ]	'belly'
26	[tɕín]	'intestines'	58	[bìttó]	'to unshell'
27	[gíɾé]	'really'	59	[dɔ̀k]	'to go back'
28	[lòɕə̀]	'man'	60	[kòp]	'matter'
29	[kwə̀ɕê]	'leopards'	61	[tîn]	'today'
30	[kál]	'millet'	62	[kít]	'kind'
31	[màɕê]	'fires'	63	[àkká]	'purposely'
32	[àbíɕèl]	'six'	64	[tɕàk]	'milk'

Further reading

The opening of this chapter states that the central subject matter of phonology
is *sound patterns* in language. This invokes two important early phonological works.
Edward Sapir's "Sound patterns in language" (1925; *Language* 1: 37–51) was
the first work to point out that two languages could have phonetically identical
inventories but quite different phonologies (see §2.9 above). *The Sound Pattern
of English*, by Noam Chomsky and Morris Halle (1968, Harper and Row) is by

consensus the most important single work in phonological theory. Many of the ideas given in this text first appeared there.

The systematization of a procedure for finding the phonemes of a language was one of the major accomplishments of the so-called "American structuralist" school of linguistics, which flourished from approximately the 1920s to the 1950s. A fine presentation of the method of phonemicization by a member of this school may be found in H. A. Gleason's *An Introduction to Descriptive Linguistics* (1961, Holt, Rinehart and Winston). Two works that are widely considered to be gems of American structuralism are *Language* by Leonard Bloomfield (1933, reprinted 1984, University of Chicago Press) and *Language: An Introduction to the Study of Speech* by Edward Sapir (1921, Harcourt Brace; now on line at www.bartleby.com/186/).

The maximum and minimum phoneme counts in §2.2 are taken from Ian Maddieson's *Patterns of Sounds* (1984, Cambridge University Press), a very useful survey of several hundred phoneme inventories.

The point that shortening of vowels before voiceless consonants is a rule specific to particular languages is argued for in Patricia Keating, "Universal phonetics and the organization of grammars," in Victoria Fromkin, ed., *Phonetic Linguistics* (1985, Academic Press).

Maasai phonemes: Archibald N. Tucker and J. Tompo Ole Mpaayei, *A Maasai Grammar with Vocabulary* (1955, Longman, Green).

3   More on Phonemes

3.1   Phonemic Analysis and Writing

The question of phonemicization is in principle independent from the question of writing; that is, there is no necessary connection between letters and phonemes. For example, the English phoneme /eɪ/ can be spelled in quite a few ways: *say* /seɪ/, *Abe* /eɪb/, *main* /meɪn/, *beige* /beɪʒ/, *reggae* /ˈrɛɡeɪ/, *H* /eɪtʃ/. Indeed, there are languages (for example, Mandarin Chinese) that are written with symbols that do not correspond to phonemes at all.

Obviously, there is at least a loose connection between alphabetic letters and phonemes: the designers of an alphabet tend to match up the written symbols with the phonemes of a language. Moreover, the conscious intuitions of speakers about sounds tend to be heavily influenced by their knowledge of spelling – after all, most literate speakers receive extensive training in how to spell during childhood, but no training at all in phonology.

Writing is prestigious, and our spoken pronunciations are sometimes felt to be imperfect realizations of what is written. This is reflected in the common occurrence of **spelling pronunciations**, which are pronunciations that have no historical basis, but which arise as attempts to mimic the spelling, as in *often* [ˈɔftən] or *palm* [pɑlm].

In contrast, most linguists feel that spoken language is primary, and that written language is a derived system, which is mostly parasitic off the spoken language and is often rather artificial in character. Some reasons that support this view are that spoken language is far older than writing, it is acquired first and with greater ease by children, and it is the common property of our species, rather than of just an educated subset of it.

One of the practical applications of phonology (especially, phonemic analysis) is the design of alphabets for languages heretofore unwritten. It is widely agreed that an alphabet will be most useful and easy to use if the letters and sounds are in one-to-one correspondence. What is not commonly realized is that at the level of phonetic detail – with all the allophones considered – every language contains thousands of sounds. What is really needed in a good alphabet is a system in which it is letters and *phonemes* that correspond one-to-one; this will permit all meaning-bearing distinctions to be reflected in the spelling, and it avoids the

needless effort (and perhaps confusion) that arises in spelling allophonic variation. Advocates of "phonetic spelling" are thus really advocates of "phonemic
spelling." Most of the many alphabets designed for hitherto unwritten languages
in the last few decades have been phonemic.

3.2   The Psychological Reality of the Phoneme

Chapter 2 covered a fairly mechanical procedure for extracting a phonemic
analysis from the data of a language. However, the goal of phonology is not really
to contrive useful procedures for arranging linguistic data; rather, we wish to arrive
at a scientific account of the knowledge of language internalized by speakers. We
can ask: is it legitimate to suppose that speakers actually produce and perceive
language (at an unconscious level) in terms of phonemes? A fair amount of
experimentation has been conducted on this issue, and the practical experience
of linguists over many years likewise seems relevant.

We will discuss this question in three parts. Recall that the most fundamental
phenomenon concerns phonetic differences that are contrastive vs. noncon-
trastive. Evidence that this distinction is part of speakers' knowledge is discussed
in §3.2.1 Beyond this, there is the idea that the principle of contrast is expressed
in the grammar by grouping together the non-contrasting sounds into phonemes;
this is covered in 2.2. Lastly, there is the system of phonological rules which derives
the allophones in their proper contexts; this is discussed in 2.3.

3.2.1   Audibility of fine distinctions

There is little doubt that contrastiveness plays a major role in the perceptions of
language users. The auditory processing apparatus is "tuned" through experience
to be able to extract precisely those phonetic distinctions that are phonemic in
the perceiver's own language.

The practical experience of linguists and other language users attests to this. Suppose we are dealing with two sounds that are phonetically rather close. Suppose
further that the two sounds are heard by two different listeners. For listener A,
the two sounds are contrastive, serving to distinguish words in her language. The
two sounds also occur in listener B's language, but are allophones, and are not
contrastive. What usually happens in such a situation is this: A can hear the
difference between the two sounds with perfect ease, but B has great difficulty.

On various occasions I have played the role of both A and B. Here are some
examples.

On one occasion when I was listener B, A was a speaker of a dialect of Bengali
in which dental stops (tongue tip touches upper teeth) contrast with alveolar

stops (tongue tip touches alveolar ridge), as in the following minimal and near-minimal pairs:

[t̪an]	'(vocal) tune'	[tan]	'pull!'
[sat̪]	'seven'	[sat]	'sixty'
[d̪an]	'donation'	[dan]	'right (hand)'
[d̪in]	'day'	[dim]	'egg'

Attempting to transcribe A's speech, I found that, despite extensive practice, I was unable to learn to hear the Bengali dental/alveolar distinction. This amused A, who as a native speaker found the distinction to be utterly obvious. (In desperation I tried guessing alveolar on every occasion, a strategy which does better than chance, but my colleague quickly detected this.)

An important additional fact here is that my own native language, a variety of American English, does include both dental and alveolar consonants. The dentals occur as allophones of the alveolars, and are derived by a rule that replaces alveolars by dentals before dental fricatives (this is a generalized version of the rules seen for /n/ and /l/ dentalization in chapter 2).

/eɪtθ/	[eɪt̪θ]	*eighth*	/eɪt ðə/	[eɪt̪ ðə]	*ate the . . .*
/wʊd θɪŋk/	[wʊd̪ θɪŋk]	*would think*	/sɛd ðə/	[sɛd̪ ðɪs]	*said this*
/tɛnθ/	[tɛn̪θ]	*tenth*	/ɪn ðə/	[ɪn̪ ðə]	*in the . . .*

The point is that my inability to hear the dental/alveolar distinction is not due to a lack of experience with dentals. Rather, it is because my native language does not have a phonemic contrast between alveolars and dentals.

I have also played the role of A, as a native speaker of a dialect of English that contrasts /ɑ/ with the lower mid back rounded vowel /ɔ/. In this dialect, there are minimal pairs such as the following:

caught	['kɔt]	*cot*	['kɑt]
Kaun	['kɔn]	*con*	['kɑn]
paw	['pɔ]	*Pa*	['pɑ]
auto	['ɔɾoʊ]	*Otto*	['ɑɾoʊ]

This dialect is spoken by perhaps half of the American population, and coexists with a historically innovating dialect in which all occurrences of the old phoneme /ɔ/ have been replaced by /ɑ/.[1] Thus in the new dialect, *caught* is [kɑt], *Kaun* is [kɑn], *paw* is [pɑ], and *auto* is ['ɑɾoʊ], all homophonous with their counterparts that had [ɑ] from earlier on.

Speakers of this newer dialect often claim that hearing the [ɑ]/[ɔ] distinction is quite difficult for them. In contrast, speakers of the older dialect, which makes a distinction, feel that it would be very strange *not* to be able to hear it.

---

[1] A map showing where the two dialects are spoken may be examined at www.ling.upenn.edu/phono_atlas/maps/Map1.html (Telsur Project, University of Pennsylvania).

Such stories are easily multiplied. They have also been backed up by extensive experimental work, which can now actually trace the time course whereby humans change from unbiased perceivers to phonological perceivers, who fluently detect the contrasts of their own language, but not that of others. Strikingly, much of the process appears to take place in infancy: ten-month-olds already show a strong tendency to hear only those phonetic distinctions that are present in the ambient language.

To summarize: the contrastiveness of two phonetically similar sounds leads speakers of a language or dialect that has the contrast to focus their perceptual attention on the contrasting sounds, and fail to hear other distinctions. In a phoneme-based approach to phonology, we would interpret this as indicating that native speakers hear the differences between phonemes, but not between allophones.

There is a practical consequence of all this: if you are trying to elicit new data from a native speaker, and are not a native speaker yourself, it is likely that you will have trouble in hearing the finer phonemic distinctions that do not occur in your own language. In such cases, you can often improve the quality of your data by having your consultant *help you listen*, using the method of **keywords**. If, for instance, you speak a dialect of English that has no contrast between /ɑ/ and /ɔ/, and you were eliciting from me a series of words that contained either /ɑ/ or /ɔ/, I could help you out in identifying the correct vowels – my phonemic distinction (and lifelong experience in hearing it) makes it highly detectable for me. This can be achieved by setting up keywords which unambiguously identify the target vowel. For example, for English /ɑ/ vs. /ɔ/, one could establish *shah* [ʃɑ] as the keyword for /ɑ/ and *saw* [sɔ] as the keyword for /ɔ/. Then, whenever the identity of a vowel is not clear, it can be determined by asking the consultant "vowel of *shah* or vowel of *saw*?"

3.2.2   The notion of "same sound"

The evidence above focuses on the most fundamental claim of phonemic theory – that distinctive differences have a different linguistic status from non-distinctive ones. But phonemic theory goes beyond this primary claim: it posits that groups of mutually non-distinctive sounds are grouped together into categories, that is, the phonemes.

On the whole, linguists have found that speakers usually believe that two allophones of the same phoneme are the "same sound," despite the phonetic difference between them. Here are some examples.

The words *ten* and *Ted* have phonetically different vowels. In *ten*, the phoneme /ɛ/ occurs before a nasal sound, and is therefore eligible for a phonological rule which we can state as follows.

Vowel Nasalization
[+vowel] → [+nasal] / ___ [+nasal]
A vowel is realized as nasalized when it precedes a nasal consonant.

The application of the rule is shown below:

ten	Ted	
/tɛn/	/tɛd/	underlying forms
ɛ̃	—	Vowel Nasalization
[tɛ̃n]	[tɛd]	surface forms

In my experience, English speakers are quite willing to say that *ten* and *Ted* have "the same vowel." Indeed, the difference between the two sounds is felt to be subtle, and observable only with careful attention, for example, by greatly prolonging them.

For this phonetic difference, it is useful to compare the behavior of (for example) French speakers. Minimal pairs show that in French, nasal vowels are phonemically distinct from oral vowels:

[mɛ]	'but'	vs.	[mɛ̃]	'hand'
[tʁɛ]	'very'	vs.	[tʁɛ̃]	'train'

For French speakers, it is plain that [ɛ] and [ɛ̃] are different sounds. The crucial difference between a French speaker and an English speaker in this respect is the phonemic structure of the two languages: corresponding nasal and oral vowels in French count as different sounds because they are different phonemes; they count as the same sound in English because they are allophones of the same phoneme.

The same would hold true for the case of dental [t̪] and alveolar [t] in English and Bengali, mentioned above. Very few if any English speakers would sense that the [t̪] in *eighth* is not the "same sound" as the [t] in *eight*. Bengali speakers, however, have a strong sense that [t̪] and [t] are different.

We can conclude that, to a rough approximation, if two phones are allophones of the same phoneme, a speaker of the language in question will feel that they are the same sound.

However, we must supplement this conclusion with certain reservations about conscious awareness of sounds in general. It would appear that the natural state of humans is to be unaware that languages have speech sounds at all. What leads speakers to become consciously aware of their phonemes is typically the process of learning to read and write in an alphabetic system, since this focuses the learner's attention on the sounds that correspond to the letters.[2]

---

[2] A stronger position sometimes taken is that phonemic awareness is based *exclusively* on orthography. I'm skeptical of this position, in part because of my experience as a teacher: it is really quite easy to teach people to hear phonemic distinctions, such as /θ/ vs. /ð/, that are spelled inconsistently. Moreover, there are English dialects that have phonemes that have no distinctive spelling (for example, /ʌɪ/, in contrast with /aɪ/; or /ɛə/, in contrast with /æ/). In my elicitation experience, native speakers of these dialects have proven highly aware of these phonemes.

To state the original claim more accurately, then: *once speakers have been made aware* of the existence of speech sounds in their language, they will naturally tend to consider allophones of the same phoneme as counting as the same sound.

3.2.3 Foreign accents and transfer

The third fundamental claim made by phonemic theory is that speakers internalize rules that derive the various allophones in their appropriate environments. One of the best sources of evidence for the existence of such rules comes from second language acquisition, in particular, the behavior of speakers who are attempting to pronounce the sounds of a language new to them. The usual result, at least at first, is a rather poor imitation of the second language. Indeed, a foreign accent often persists even after years of practice with a second language.

Foreign accents are not the result of just "missing the mark" in random ways. To the contrary, careful inspection shows that the deviations between the goal and what is achieved are systematic; and can usually be attributed to the phonology, including the phonological rules, of one's native language. The phenomenon of mispronunciations in a second language in ways attributable to the phonology of the first language is called **transfer**.

To understand transfer, it helps to consider a phonology as specifying the set of *things that are pronounceable* in a given language. This set consists of the legal sequences of phonemes, realized as the appropriate allophones for their context. In other words, anything outside this (very large) set will necessarily involve one of three properties:

- It can be phonologically illegal (in a given language) because it contains an **illegal phoneme**. For example, in English any utterance containing the voiced uvular fricative [ʁ], a voiced aspirated stop, or a front rounded vowel is illegal.
- It can be phonologically illegal because it corresponds to an **illegal sequence** of phonemes (even where the phonemes themselves are legal). Thus, [bnɪk] consists of four English phonemes, arranged in an order which English phonology does not permit. (This point is treated in more detail below in §3.6 below.)
- It can be phonologically illegal because it corresponds to an **impossible distribution of allophones**. For example, [fil], with a non-velarized [l], is illegal in English, because English has an allophonic rule requiring the use of velarized [ɫ] in word-final position, as in the correct pronunciation [fiɫ] 'feel'.

If a word of a foreign language is phonologically illegal in English, for any of the above three reasons, it will typically not be pronounced correctly by English speakers, at least without practice.

Here are some examples. The German proper name *Gödel* is phonetically ['gøːdəl], with a long upper mid front rounded vowel. Many English dialects have no /øː/ phoneme, but do have the acoustically similar phoneme /ɚ/. Speakers of these dialects tend to pronounce *Gödel* as *girdle*. French *thé* 'tea' is phonetically [t̪e]. Most English speakers speak a dialect in which the monophthong [e] does not occur; the diphthong [eɪ] occurs instead. These speakers must fight the tendency to substitute their own [eɪ] for French [e]; less conspicuously, they need to suppress their own native alveolar [t] and use dental [t̪] instead.

These are cases in which foreign accents arise from substituting native phonemes for phonetically similar foreign ones. We also get cases of substitution of native allophones for phonetically similar foreign sounds, through application of the phonological rules. For example, a typical English mispronunciation of French *thé* is [tʰeɪ], with an aspirated [tʰ], since that is the allophone of /t/ that occurs word-initially in English. Likewise, *Gödel* as pronounced by English speakers tends to receive the velarized [ɫ] allophone of /l/ (p. 25), which further mutilates it to [ˈgɚdəɫ].

The path from foreign source word to native rendition is sometimes a bit more crooked. French *tante* 'aunt' [t̪ɑ̃t] has a nasalized vowel alien to the English phoneme inventory. In an English accent, this usually comes out [tɑ̃n̆t], where [n̆] is a particularly short [n]. The derivation (that is, in English) here seems to be something like:

/tɑnt/ underlying form: choice of native phonemes

ɑ̃   **Nasalization** (p. 50):   [+vowel] → [+nasal] / ___ [+nasal]

n̆   **Nasal Consonant** $\begin{bmatrix} +\text{consonant} \\ +\text{nasal} \end{bmatrix}$ → [+short] / ___ $\begin{bmatrix} +\text{consonant} \\ -\text{voice} \end{bmatrix}$
     Shortening:

[tɑ̃n̆t] surface form

You can see that the derivation is rather "strategic": the insertion of /n/ disagrees sharply with the original French, yet this /n/ gives rise to an allophone, [ɑ̃], which considerably improves the matchup to the French vowel phoneme /ɑ̃/. Moreover, since nasal consonants are allophonically shortened before voiceless consonants in English, the offending /n/ ends up reduced in its perceptual salience. It seems to be the resemblance of the end result to the foreign word, and not some kind of step-by-step procedure, that guides the choice of phonemic accommodation.

To sum up, to a greater or lesser extent, learners of foreign languages are prisoners of their own phonologies. Lifelong experience leads them strongly to favor the legal phonological sequences of their native language, which may be defined as the sequences of allophones that are derived from legal sequences of native phonemes. The psychological reality of the constraints of the native phonology becomes blatant when one sees them determine the outcome of the native speaker's attempts to pronounce a second language.

Naturally, individuals differ greatly in their ability to overcome the transfer effect; in other words, to assimilate a novel phonology. In principle, explicit knowledge of the phonology of both native and learned language could be of help to foreign language learners in achieving a correct accent, and some foreign language textbooks do provide systematic training of this kind.

3.3   The Criterion of Phonetic Similarity

With the introduction of a criterion of psychological reality into phonological analysis, we find that in a number of cases, phonemicization cannot be done in purely mechanical fashion, as was done in the Maasai example of chapter 2. Here, we will consider some cases in which merely collecting and arranging the non-contrasting phonetic segments is insufficient.

A simple case arises in English, involving the sounds [h] and [ŋ]. [h] occurs at the beginnings of words and before stressed vowels, as in the examples below:

hill	[ˈhɪl]	*ahead*	[əˈhɛd]
high	[ˈhaɪ]	*prohibit*	[proʊˈhɪbɪt]
how	[ˈhaʊ]	*behold*	[bɪˈhold]
Horatio	[həˈɹeɪʃoʊ]	*rehearse*	[ɹiˈhɚs]

The sound [ŋ] occurs at the ends of words, before consonants, and (at least in the dialects we will consider) between vowels of which the second is stressless:

sing	[ˈsɪŋ]	*sink*	[ˈsɪŋk]	*singer*	[ˈsɪŋɚ]
pang	[ˈpæŋ]	*anger*	[ˈæŋgɚ]	*Singapore*	[ˈsɪŋəˌpɔɹ]
running	[ˈɹʌnɪŋ]	*hangs*	[ˈhæŋz]	*dinghy*	[ˈdɪŋi]
		Langley	[ˈlæŋli]	*hangar*	[ˈhæŋɚ]

There are no cases of [h] occurring at ends of words, or before consonants, or between vowels of which the second is stressless. Likewise, there are no cases of [ŋ] occurring at the beginning of a word, or before a stressed vowel. Therefore, [h] and [ŋ] *do not contrast*. Given the phonological patterning of English, there is no way that they could distinguish words from each other, because they occur in entirely different contexts.

Since [h] and [ŋ] do not contrast, should we regard them as allophones of a single phoneme? The traditional answer of phonologists is no, for the following reason. When two sounds are allophones of the same phoneme, they will be felt by native speakers to be the same sound. This is plainly not the case for [ŋ] and [h]. It seems appropriate here to say that /h/ and /ŋ/ are separate phonemes of English, and that for accidental reasons (having to do with where it is legal for them to occur), they are unable to form contrasts. In other words, we reject the idea that phonemes can be established purely on distributional grounds; rather, if we are to posit that two sounds are allophones of a single phoneme, they must be related to each other phonetically in some way.

A similar example makes the same point. By reexamining the distributions of Maasai [p b t d k g] given on pp. 39 and 41, you should convince yourself of the following facts:

- [p] and [d] are in complementary distribution.
- [t] and [g] are in complementary distribution.
- [k] and [b] are in complementary distribution.

This is true because the voiced stops in Maasai always come after nasals, and the voiceless ones never do. We could imagine, then, a phonemic analysis of Maasai that grouped [p] and [d] together into the same phoneme, and similarly with [t]–[g] and [k]–[b]. Such an analysis indeed works on distributional grounds, but would almost certainly fail as a means of capturing the intuitions of the native speaker, who sensibly regards the phonetically similar [t] and [d] as being the same sound, and similarly with [p]/[b], [k]/[g].

At the level of phonological theory, it seems that we must impose some criterion of **phonetic similarity** on analyses: the allophones of a single phoneme should resemble one another to a particular degree. The case of Maasai is rather straightforward, since all we are trying to do is compare a sensible analysis, in which [b] is an allophone of /p/, [d] of /t/, and [g] of /k/, with a bizarre alternative that mixes up the places of articulation. By any criterion, the sensible analysis makes the allophones more mutually similar than the bizarre analysis does, and thus is to be preferred.

The case of /h/–/ŋ/, where we choose not to group two sounds into one phoneme despite their complementary distribution, is harder, because it raises the question of where to draw the line: what is the degree of dissimilarity beyond which the association of sounds into a single phoneme becomes impossible? [h] and [ŋ] are certainly far enough apart, but there are many other cases where the outcome is not so clear. It is possible that during language change, new phonemes might be created when two allophones drift apart too far to count any more as variants of the same basic linguistic unit.

3.4   Other Problems in Phonemicization

Defining the phonetic similarity criterion rigorously is by no means the only conundrum in traditional phonemicization; here are some others.

3.4.1   *Contour segments and the segment/sequence problem*

Sounds like diphthongs ([a͡ɪ]), affricates ([t͡ʃ]), and prenasalized stops ([m͡b]) are often called **contour segments**: they have two phonetic qualities in sequence, but are often treated phonologically as a single sound. The recognition of the contour segments is often an analytic difficulty faced in phonemicization. For example, given a sequence like [ai] in the data, we need to decide whether it should be treated

as a diphthong (that is, as a single phonemic unit), or as a sequence of /a/ + /i/.
The same issue arises for [tʃ] (is it the affricate [t͡ʃ], or is it /t/ + /ʃ/?) and for
[mb, nd, ŋg] (prenasalized stops or *nasal + stop* sequences)? This analytical issue
might be called the **segment/sequence problem**.

The problem is easy to solve if there is an actual contrast between segment and
sequence. For instance, the analysis of [t͡ʃ] as an affricate in Polish is uncontroversial, because this sound contrasts with the stop + fricative sequence [tʃ].
The following minimal pair illustrate this:

[tʃɨ]   *trzy*   'three'
[t͡ʃɨ]   *czy*   'if, whether'

[tʃ] and [t͡ʃ] are phonetically different; in particular, [tʃ] is noticeably longer
than [t͡ʃ]. The affricate [t͡ʃ] must be analyzed as a single segmental unit in Polish,
since otherwise we could not express the contrast between monosegmental /t͡ʃ/
and bisegmental /tʃ/. Similarly, in other languages diphthongs contrast with two-
vowel sequences (English *boing* [bɔ͡ɪŋ] vs. *sawing* [sɔɪŋ]), and prenasalized stops
contrast (for example in Sinhala) with nasal + stop sequences. In Turkish, long
vowels contrast with identical vowel sequences, as in [daː] 'mountain-nom. sg.'
vs. [da.a] 'mountain-dat. sg.', which leads to the clear conclusion that the long
vowels must be single phonemic units in Turkish.

Sometimes phonologists choose between segments and sequence on the basis
of the overall pattern of the language. Suppose that a language has five monoph-
thongs /i, e, a, o, u/, and that moreover any one of the 25 logical possibilities for
putting any two of these vowels together occurs in the language; that is, we observe:

[iː]	[ie]	[ia]	[io]	[iu]
[ei]	[eː]	[ea]	[eo]	[eu]
[ai]	[ae]	[aː]	[ao]	[au]
[oi]	[oe]	[oa]	[oː]	[ou]
[ui]	[ue]	[ua]	[uo]	[uː]

In this case, we would be sensible to opt for a sequence analysis, in which these
putative "diphthongs" are not phonemes, but merely sequences of the independently existing vowel phonemes /i, e, a, o, u/, as follows:

/ii/	/ie/	/ia/	/io/	/iu/
/ei/	/ee/	/ea/	/eo/	/eu/
/ai/	/ae/	/aa/	/ao/	/au/
/oi/	/oe/	/oa/	/oo/	/ou/
/ui/	/ue/	/ua/	/uo/	/uu/

The two criteria just given do not always suffice to determine an analysis. The
apparent diphthongs of Mandarin Chinese are a classical example; they have been

treated by some analysts as monophonematic diphthongs and by others as sequences. To consider just a subset of the Mandarin problem, observe that Mandarin has the following sounds: [ə], [i], [u], [ei], and [ou]. [e] and [o] never occur alone, but only as part of the diphthongs [ei] and [ou]. One possible phonemicization is the following:

/ə/	/əi/	/əu/	/i/	/u/	underlying forms
—	ei	—	—	—	Vowel Assimilation I: ə → e / ___ i
—	—	ou	—	—	Vowel Assimilation II: ə → o / ___ u
[ə]	[ei]	[ou]	[i]	[u]	surface forms

The appeal of this analysis is that we can get by with just three phonemes (/ə/, /i/, /u/) to derive five sounds. Moreover, the rules make sense as **assimilation** rules; the vowel /ə/ is assimilated to [i] or [u], become phonetically more similar to its neighbor; and assimilation is a very common process in phonology. However, not all phonologists would necessarily agree that this is an iron-clad argument – in principle, we want to know not just a convenient and elegant way to symbolize Mandarin sounds, but the way that actually is found in the internalized grammars of native speakers. In general, the issue of how to segment the speech stream into its phonemes is an unsettled one in phonology.

3.4.2 Borrowed sounds

We live in a time in which the phonology of a great number of the world's languages is in flux, as a result of new borrowed sounds. When a borrowed sound is used for the very first time by a single speaker, it cannot count as a phoneme of the language. But with time, borrowed words come to be used by larger numbers of speakers. Eventually, they are felt by native speakers to be an integral part of the language. One example is English /v/, which centuries ago was a borrowed phoneme (see §11.7) but is now fully integrated into the English phoneme inventory.

The difficulty for phonological analysis is that the process is gradual. Contemporary Japanese provides an example. In Japanese as it was spoken not long ago, the sound [ɸ] (voiceless bilabial fricative) was plainly an allophone of /h/. It occurred only in the environment / ___ u, and was in complementary distribution with [h], which occurred in most other environments and thus was the elsewhere allophone.

As Japanese has evolved under the influence of English and other foreign languages, [ɸ] has extended its usage: it is the usual way to approximate a foreign [f] sound. If we are willing to include recently borrowed words in our data set for phonemicization, then we can now find many near-minimal pairs for [ɸ] vs. [h], as follows:

before /a/: [ɸaito] 'fight', [ɸaŋ] 'fan'   (vs. [haiku] 'type of poetry')
before /e/: [ɸesutibaɾu] 'festival', [ɸeɾuto] 'felt'   (vs. [hema] 'blunder')
before /i/: [suɸiŋkusu] 'sphinx', [ɸiɾumu] 'film'   (see footnote[3])
before /o/: [ʃiɸoŋ] 'chiffon', [ɸoːku] 'fork'   (vs. [hoŋ] 'book')

To the extent that we can consider the words in the left column to be authentic words in the vocabularies of innovating speakers, we must say that the dialect spoken by these speakers has acquired a new phoneme, having promoted [ɸ] from allophone to phoneme status.

But the crucial question is whether such words really *can* be considered authentic words of contemporary Japanese. Different speakers feel differently about whether the words above are normal, everyday words. Speakers of the more conservative variety of Japanese consider them to be exotic imports. This may be compared with the way English speakers regard words and phrases like [ˌfæ də siˈɛklə] 'end of the century', [ˈbɑx] 'Bach', and [t͡suˈnɑmi] 'wave caused by an earthquake',[4] taken from French, German, and Japanese respectively.

That there really is a continuum is suggested by the fact that there are some sounds that are less far along in the process of becoming Japanese phonemes. According to my reference source (see below), younger, cosmopolitan speakers of Japanese have an emergent phonemic distinction between /d/ and /d͡z/; for all other speakers [d͡z] is merely the allophone of /d/ that occurs before /u/. For these younger speakers, in certain speaking styles, it is possible to say words like [**du**ː itto juaseɾuɸu] 'do-it-yourself' and [**du**ː-wappu] 'doo-wop (music)'.

In the end, we must recognize that a phonemic analysis is a phonemic analysis of a **particular stratum** of the vocabulary. Such strata can include the core vocabulary, the vocabulary as it includes mildly non-native words, or even the vocabulary as amplified by words still recognized as quite foreign. The blurriness of the phonemic analysis arises from the blurriness of the concept "member of the language's vocabulary." Careful presentation of a phonemic analysis must therefore specify the vocabulary strata on which the analysis rests.

3.5 Free Variation

Languages are permeated with variation: we frequently say the same thing in different ways. In phonology, free variation takes two forms. One is the phenomenon of **phonological doublets**, in which one word happens to have two different phonemic forms. For instance, in many people's speech, the word *envelope* can be pronounced as either [ˈɛnvəˌloʊp] or [ˈɑnvəˌloʊp]; *economics* as either

---

[3]   Before /i/, /h/ has the allophone [ç] (voiceless palatal fricative), as in /himo/ [çimo] 'string'.
[4]   These are how I usually pronounce these words when using them in English. These pronunciations are not the same as those used in the source languages.

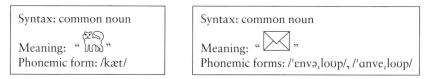

Syntax: common noun	Syntax: common noun
Meaning: " 🐈 "	Meaning: " ✉ "
Phonemic form: /kæt/	Phonemic forms: /'ɛnvə,loʊp/, /'ɑnve,loʊp/

Figure 3.1 Lexical entries for "cat" and "envelope"

[ˌikə'namɪks] or [ˌɛkə'namɪks], *deity* as either ['diəɾi] or ['deɪəɾi]. This does *not* refer to instances in which different people say certain words differently; rather, a doublet is a case where one and the same person uses both variants.

The usual treatment of phonological doublets posits that in the **lexicon** (the mental store of words in the mind/brain), they have just one listing for their syntactic properties and meaning, but more than one phonemic representation, as shown in figure 3.1.

The other kind of variation in phonology is when a single phonemic representation gives rise to more than one phonetic form; this is called **free variation**. Here is one example found in the speech of many Americans. In the dialect in question, the vowel phoneme /æ/ has a diphthongal allophone I will transcribe as [ɛ̃ə̃]. Some data on the distribution of [ɛ̃ə̃] vs. [æ] are given below:

	[æ]			[ɛ̃ə̃]	
lap	/læp/	[læp]	*man*	/mæn/	[mɛ̃ə̃n], [mæ̃n]
pal	/pæl/	[pæl]	*Spanish*	/spænɪʃ/	[spɛ̃ə̃nɪʃ], [spæ̃nɪʃ]
pack	/pæk/	[pæk]	*dance*	/dæns/	[dɛ̃ə̃ns], [dæ̃ns]
lab	/læb/	[læb]	*flannel*	/'flænəl/	['flɛ̃ə̃nəl], ['flæ̃nəl]

To summarize the pattern: if an /n/ follows /æ/, then there are two outputs, one with [ɛ̃ə̃] and one with [æ̃]. Otherwise, the observed allophone is [æ]. This [ɛ̃ə̃]–[æ̃] pattern is systematic; it holds not just for these four words, but for any word in this dialect in which /æ/ precedes /n/. Indeed, even if we make up a completely new word ("Hello, my name is *Thran*"), it too would behave this way: [θɹɛ̃ə̃n], [θɹæ̃n].

In analyzing the data, we should first dispose of the distribution of nasality. The nasalization seen on both [ɛ̃ə̃] and [æ̃] is plainly the consequence of Vowel Nasalization (p. 50). More crucial is the free variation between the monophthongal and diphthongal allophones. These cannot be phonological doublets, in the sense given above, because they are part of a systematic pattern rather than being idiosyncratic. We need to express the variation with a rule.

An appropriate analysis, then, would be as follows. We set up /æ/ as the basic form of the phoneme, and include the following rule.

/æ/ Diphthongization (preliminary)
æ → ɛə / ___ n
The phoneme /æ/ is realized as [ɛə] when it precedes /n/.

Together with Vowel Nasalization, /æ/ Diphthongization suffices to derive the [ɛ̃ə̃] variants, as illustrated below.

ban: /bæn/   underlying form
       bɛən   /æ/ Diphthongization
       bɛ̃ə̃n   Vowel Nasalization
       [bɛ̃ə̃n]   surface form

We can derive the non-diphthongized variants as well, provided that we indicate that /æ/ Diphthongization **applies optionally**; that is, on any given speaking occasion, the speaker may apply the rule or not. I will designate optional rules simply by including the word "optional" in parentheses after the statement of the rule:

/æ/ Diphthongization (revised)
æ → ɛə / ___ n   (optional)
The phoneme /æ/ may be realized as [ɛə] when it precedes /n/.

We can explicitly show the effects of optional rules with **branching derivations**, which include arrows to indicate what happens when an optional rule does or does not apply. The derivation for *ban* below is a branching derivation.

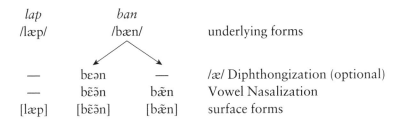

lap   *ban*
/læp/   /bæn/   underlying forms

—   bɛən   —   /æ/ Diphthongization (optional)
—   bɛ̃ə̃n   bæ̃n   Vowel Nasalization
[læp]   [bɛ̃ə̃n]   [bæ̃n]   surface forms

Another optional rule of English, at least for some speakers, is the Tapping rule discussed on p. 32. For such speakers, the derivation of *data*, given earlier, should actually be a branching derivation:

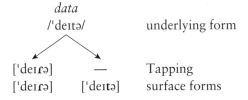

       data
       /'deɪtə/   underlying form

['deɪɾə]   —   Tapping
['deɪɾə]   ['deɪtə]   surface forms

As with /æ/ Diphthongization, the phenomenon occurs across the board, and is not specific to the word *data*; similar variation is found for *outer* ['aʊɾɚ]/['aʊtɚ], *attic* ['æɾɪk]/['ætɪk], *catapult* ['kæɾəpʊlt]/['kætəpʊlt], and so on.

Not all phonological rules are optional. Vowel Nasalization, for instance, is obligatory: while [bɛ̃ə̃n] and [bæ̃n] are both options for *ban* (in the relevant dialect), *[bɛən] and *[bæn], with oral vowels, are impossible. (I follow normal practice in linguistics in using asterisks to designate impossible forms.) Similarly, the rule that assimilates alveolar /n/ to dental [n̪] before /θ/ (p. 49) is obligatory: to say the word *tenth* as [tɛnθ], with a true alveolar [n], is difficult and artificial.

The same rule can be optional in one dialect of a language and obligatory in a closely related dialect; this is true, for instance, of both Tapping and /æ/ Diphthongization.

3.5.1   Optional rules and speech style

When a language has an optional rule, it is often the case that the choice of whether to apply the rule or not is determined by the style of speech. A typical pattern is that in solemn or careful speech, application of an optional rule is suppressed, whereas in casual or rapid speech, it will apply. This can be seen clearly if you pick a sequence of words that allows for the application of more than one optional rule. For example, the phrase *tan attic* is phonemically /ˈtæn ˈætɪk/. It can undergo Tapping and [æ] Diphthongization (along with obligatory Vowel Nasalization) to become [ˈtẽə̃n ˈæɾɪk], a casual pronunciation. Alternatively, Tapping and [æ] Diphthongization could be suppressed, yielding [ˈtæ̃n ˈætɪk], a solemn and careful pronunciation. There could also be intermediate variants, in which only one of the optional rules is suppressed.

In most languages and dialects, speakers command a broad range of speaking styles, of which they may be only dimly aware. This variation is amenable to phonological analysis: typically, there are particular optional phonological rules that apply with greater frequency (or derive more dramatically deviating outputs) when the speaker is in a more casual social context. Speakers unconsciously tune their phonological style so as to produce appropriate speech behavior for each context.

The word "appropriate" in the previous paragraph deserves clarification. In literate societies, people are often told how they *should* speak; that is, there are many **normative** beliefs about language, which include beliefs about pronunciation. The sense of "appropriate" here is descriptive, not normative. While there exist contexts where informal speaking styles are felt to be inappropriate, there are also contexts where formal styles are likewise perceived as inappropriate – that is, as pretentious or pedantic.

3.5.2   Variation and elicitation

Free variation can pose problems for the linguist who is eliciting new data from a native speaker consultant. For one thing, the linguist is seldom in a good position to get the speaker to say each variant – usually the speaker will say the one that is appropriate for the social context (namely, elicitation), and the other variant(s) will go undetected.

The missing variant will normally be the one characteristic of informal speech. The reason is that most consultants construe elicitation, where attention is focused on their speech, to be a rather formal speaking context. Simply requesting the consultant to speak casually may not help much, since speakers often have little conscious control over their speaking style.

The problem of "missing free variants" often arises when a student attempts to hear from a native speaker the application of a rule that she has read about in a reference source. If the rule applies only in more casual speech, and the consultant adopts a formal speaking style, then the researcher may wrongly draw the conclusion that the rule simply doesn't exist in the consultant's speech.

Here is some practical advice on how to elicit informal variants from a consultant. First, one can at least make clear to your consultant that you are interested in casual as well as formal speech. Second, it often pays to turn off any recording equipment and rely (at least temporarily) on one's ability to transcribe on the spot, since recording equipment often can intimidate the consultant. Third, it usually helps to elicit words in **connected speech** rather than in isolation (say "Could you use that word in a sentence?"); connected speech almost always produces more rule application than citation forms. Lastly, in a pinch it sometimes helps to ask a consultant to say the same thing many times; often boredom will set in and the consultant will speak more casually.

The ultimate method for investigating casual speech is to abandon elicitation entirely, and let the consultant speak spontaneously. This is the central research method of **sociolinguistics**, a field which has developed methods for studying casual speech systematically (see Further reading, at the end of this chapter). Recorded conversations among family members or friends[5] will often reveal optional phonological rules that could never have been detected in elicitation. Of course, the disadvantage of sociolinguistic methods is that they require a great deal of work to get the data, since one must wait until the data of the type one is looking for turn up by accident.

When one's goal is to elicit *formal* speech, the task is of course much easier. Elicitation tactics that are likely to evoke formal speech include: (a) asking the consultant to speak "correctly"; (b) use of recording equipment; (c) asking the speaker to pronounce individual words, especially minimal pairs; and (d) asking the consultant to make a recording in a soundproof booth, if one is available.

3.6 Contextually Limited Contrasts and Phonotactics

Phonemic contrast is often not an across-the-board matter, but is confined to particular contexts. For instance, in Toba Batak (Austronesian, Sumatra), there

---

[5] It helps to let the recording equipment run for quite a while before transcribing; this permits the consultants to become more used to its presence.

is a general contrast between voiced and voiceless stops and affricates, as the following near-minimal pairs attest:

[**p**inoppar]   'descendant'
[**b**iaŋ]   'dog'
[**d**ukkar]   'let out'
[**t**uak]   'palm wine'
[**k**orea]   'Korea'[6]
[**g**arut]   (name of town in Indonesia)

Many words of Toba Batak also end in voiceless stops:

[sukku**p**]   'adequate'
[hoto**p**]   'fast'
[doho**t**]   'with'
[sura**t**]   'letter'
[rappo**k**]   'steal'
[hala**k**]   'man'

However, no word in the language ever ends in a voiced stop: hypothetical words like *[sukku**b**], *[doho**d**], or *[rappo**g**] sound "un-Batak" to native speakers.

Thus, we have a phonological contrast of voicing, but it is a **contextually limited contrast**. A full description of Toba Batak must include a characterization not just of the contrasting phonemes, but also a characterization of where the contrast is allowed.

3.6.1   *Analyzing phonotactics and contextually limited contrast*

Two formal approaches have been taken to contextually restricted contrast. In one, we write rules that would have the effect of eliminating the contrast. For the Toba Batak case given above, a suitable rule would be the following:

Final Devoicing (Toba Batak)
[+stop] → [−voice] / ___]$_{word}$
Stops are devoiced at the end of a word.

This approach may seem slightly counterintuitive, since one wonders: what are the forms to which the rule applies? There is no reason to set up any underlying forms in Toba Batak that would qualify. The idea behind positing such a rule is

---

[6]   A caution: /k/ is a borrowed phoneme in Toba Batak, so that this (unlike /p/–/b/ and /t/–/d/) is a marginal contrast.

to say, "even if Toba Batak *did* have final voiced stops in its underlying forms, they would be pronounced as voiceless in surface forms." The result is in fact a correct prediction, as no Toba Batak word can end with a voiced stop.

A different approach to contextually limited contrast posits that phonological theory involves not just rules but also **constraints**. A constraint is a formal characterization of a structure that is illegal in a particular language. In the constraint below, the asterisk may be read "is illegal" or "is ill-formed."

Constraint against Final Voiced Stops (Toba Batak)

$$*\begin{bmatrix} +\text{stop} \\ +\text{voice} \end{bmatrix} / \underline{\quad}]_{\text{word}}$$

It is illegal to have a voiced stop in word-final position.

Such constraints are sometimes called **phonotactic constraints**, "phonotactics" being a general term for the principles (however stated) of phonological well-formedness in a particular language. Phonologists debate what are the roles and relative importance of rules and constraints in phonology. Some theories make use only of rules, some use both, and some theories use only constraints.

3.6.2   Contrast with zero

The notion of phonological contrast can be broadened to include **contrast with zero**. For instance, English allows contrasts like *tax* [tæks] vs. *tack* [tæk], where the [s] of *tax* is said to be in contrast with zero. The following diagram illustrates this; ∅ is the symbol representing the null string.

```
t   æ   k   s
t   æ   k   ∅
```

Contrast with zero can also be contextually limited. Thus, for instance, Toba Batak has no contrasts like the one just given, because it never permits two consonants to occur at the end of a word. Consonants do contrast with zero in other environments of Toba Batak, for example in the context / V ___]_{word}. One of many examples would be [laŋa] 'empty' vs. [laŋan] 'pale'. In fact, Toba Batak falls into a very widespread phonological pattern whereby consonants may contrast with zero only when they are adjacent to a vowel.

To ban the CC vs. C contrast in final position, we formulate either a rule or a constraint, as shown below. Note that "X → ∅" is the usual notation in phonology for deletion.

Rule: Cluster Simplification
C → ∅ / C ___]_{word}
Delete a word-final consonant if a consonant precedes.

Constraint: Ban on final clusters

*CC]~word~

In comparing these two approaches, we see one possible objection to the rule-based theory: it often forces us to make arbitrary analytic decisions. In particular, given the data we have, there seems to be no reason to delete the second consonant rather than the first (C → ∅ / C ___]~word~); both rules would suffice to enforce the one-consonant limit.[7] Often, there is further evidence from the language that tells us which rule is correct; see chapter 6. In addition, one should bear in mind that it is perhaps not so bad to have two possible analyses available, when both of them happen to work.

Concluding up to this point, we have now considered most, though not all, of the basic goals of phonological analysis. In analyzing a language, we seek first to isolate its inventory of phonemes. The allophonic variation of phonemes, both contextual (chapter 2) and free (§3.5), must be characterized with appropriate phonological rules. Lastly, the limitations on contrast, both between phonemes and between phonemes and zero, must be characterized with rules or constraints. There remains one further (large) area, phonological alternation, to which we will turn in chapter 6. Since alternation is dependent on morphology, chapter 5 gives an overview of this topic.

Exercises

1 Psychological reality of the phoneme in Ilokano

In the following (partly true, partly fictional) dialogues, BH is me. MA is a UCLA undergraduate. MA had studied some linguistics, including phonetics, and was collaborating with me on a research project on Ilokano (Austronesian, Northern Philippines), which is her native language.

Ilokano has no minimal pairs for [ʔ] vs. [t]. [ʔ] is derived from /t/, by an optional rule of **/t/ Glottalization**: t → ʔ / ___ C. The dialogue is from an elicitation session that focused in part on /t/ Glottalization.

BH₁:	"egg"

BH₁: "egg"
MA₁: "[itˈlog]"
BH₂: "Say it three times, please."
MA₂: "[itˈlog], [iʔˈlog], [iʔˈlog]"
BH₃: "men"

---

[7]   More precisely, they suffice if applied iteratively (see §14.4) to make sure that clusters of any length are reduced to just one.

MA₃: "[tat'tao] . . . [taʔ'tao]"
BH₄: "to fall"
MA₄: "[mat'twaŋ]"
BH₅: "Would [maʔ'twaŋ] also be ok?"
MA₅: "Sure, [maʔ'twaŋ] is fine."
BH₆: "the egg of the chicken"
MA₆: "[ti it'log ti ma'nok]"
BH₇: "Would [ti iʔ'log ti ma'nok] be ok?"
MA₇: "Yes."
BH₈: "What about [ʔi 'iʔlog ʔi ma'nok]?"
MA₈: "No, completely impossible."

Questions:

a.   Why did BH request repetition at BH₂?
b.   What explains MA's reply in MA₈?

Here is another dialogue, this time MA eliciting from her mother, JA:[8]

MA₁: "to smell like candy"
JA₁: "[agat'dulse] . . . [agaʔ'dulse]"
MA₂: "egg"
JA₂: "[it'log]"
MA₃: "Could you also say [iʔ'log]?"
JA₃: "Of course; I just *did*: [it'log]".

c.   What do we learn about JA's idiolect[9] from JA₁?
d.   Explain why JA said what she did at JA₃, making use of the material in this
     chapter about conscious awareness of speech sounds. You should assume that
     listening conditions were excellent and that JA's hearing is fine.
e.   Compare JA₃ with MA₅ in the previous dialogue. Why are they different?

2   *Final stop clusters in English*

English words can end in two stops, but only if the second is alveolar:

concept	['kansɛpt]	contact	['kɑntækt]
jumped	[dʒʌmpt]	milked	[mɪlkt]
rubbed	[ɹʌbd]	bagged	[bægd]

Thus, there are no words in English like *['kansɛtp], *['kɑntætk], *[mɪlkp], *[bædg],
or *[ɹʌdb]. Speakers of English immediately recognize such hypothetical words as

---

[8]   MA and JA are fluent bilinguals. They tend to use English in discussions of schoolwork and Ilokano
for domestic topics.
[9]   For "idiolect" see fn. 11, p. 35.

ill-formed, and often regard them as hard to pronounce. Following the discussion in §3.6 above, give two analyses, one based on rules, the other on constraints.

3 Contextually limited contrast in Japanese

In most dialects of Japanese, there are several nasal consonants: [m, n, ŋ, w̃, j̃] (the latter two are nasalized glides). However, not all of these are phonemic, and the phonemic distinctions are limited to certain contexts.
    Examine the Japanese data given below.

a.   There is a phonemic contrast for place of articulation in Japanese nasals. Find this contrast and give three minimal pairs to justify it.
b.   Collect local environments (§2.10.3) for the sounds [m, n, ŋ, j̃, w̃].
c.   The phonemic contrast you located in (a) occurs in a certain position. State in words what this position is.
d.   In all other contexts, there is no contrast for place of articulation in nasals, and the place of articulation of nasals is predictable. State phonological rules that determine the place of articulation for these other contexts. If you cannot think of a formalism for a particular rule, either invent one or state the rule as clearly as possible in words.

1	[mi]	'body'	24	[sʉpeiŋ]	'Spain'
2	[me]	'eye'	25	[deŋ]	'palace'
3	[ma]	'interval'	26	[nihomppoi]	'Japanesey'
4	[muʃi]	'neglect'	27	[zambuɾi]	'with a splash'
5	[matte]	'wait'	28	[ʃimmiɾi]	'quiet sympathy'
6	[mo]	'also'	29	[hommo]	'book-too'
7	[ni]	'two'	30	[aɾimasentte]	'that there isn't'
8	[na]	'name'	31	[kentoː]	'examination'
9	[no]	'field'	32	[honda]	'brand of automobile'
10	[nuʃi]	'owner'	33	[jonda]	'read-past'
11	[hema]	'blunder'	34	[onna]	'woman'
12	[ʃima]	'island'	35	[kaɾendaː]	'calendar'
13	[çimo]	'string'	36	[hoj̃ja]	'bookstore'
14	[zama]	'state'	37	[boj̃jaɾi]	'vacantly'
15	[jomu]	'read-nonpast'	38	[zaŋki]	'remaining time'
16	[oːkami]	'wolf'	39	[ɾondoŋkko]	'Londoner'
17	[samui]	'cold'	40	[nippoŋgiŋkoː]	'Bank of Japan'
18	[oneːsaŋ]	'older sister'	41	[oŋgaku]	'music'
19	[katana]	'sword'	42	[geŋgogaku]	'linguistics'
20	[tanuki]	'raccoon dog'	43	[jaw̃waɾi]	'softly'
21	[hoŋ]	'book'	44	[how̃wa]	'book-topic'
22	[paŋ]	'bread'	45	[ikebana]	'flower arranging'
23	[ʃizuŋ]	'season'	46	[ɸudʒijama]	'Mount Fuji'

Further reading

Phonemic principle in alphabet design: Joseph E. Grimes and Raymond G. Gordon, Jr., "Design of new orthographies," in James F. Kavanagh and Richard L. Venezky, eds., *Orthography, Reading, and Dyslexia* (1980, University Park Press).

Effect of native phonology on the audibility of phonetic distinctions: a literature summary with references is given on pp. 105–6 of Sharon Peperkamp (2004) "Lexical exceptions in stress systems: arguments from early language acquisition and adult speech perception," *Language* 80: 98–126 [www.ehess.fr/centres/lscp/persons/peperkamp/Language.pdf]. The native-phonology effect is found even in infants under one year of age, as was originally shown by Janet Werker and Richard Tees (1984) "Cross-language speech perception: evidence for perceptual reorganization during the first year of life," *Infant Behavior and Development* 7: 49–63. For further references on phonemic perception in infants, see pp. 99–100 of the Peperkamp article.

Experimental evidence bearing on whether speakers hear two allophones of the same phoneme as "the same sound": Jeri J. Jaeger (1980) "Testing the psychological reality of phonemes," *Language and Speech* 23: 233–53; Bruce Derwing, Terrance M. Nearey, and Maureen L. Dow (1986) "On the phoneme as the unit of the 'second articulation,'" *Phonology Yearbook* 3: 45–70.

I know of little psycholinguistic work that has been done on how native speakers tacitly decide whether to treat phonetic sequences as contour segments or as phoneme sequences (§3.4.1). A paper that at least presents a method that could be useful in future work is Linnea C. Ehri and Lee S. Wilce (1980) "The effect of orthography on readers' conceptualizations of the phonemic structure of words," *Applied Psycholinguistics* 1: 371–85.

Sociolinguistics and casual speech data: work of William Labov, particularly *Sociolinguistic Patterns* (1972, University of Pennsylvania Press), *Language in the Inner City* (1972, University of Pennsylvania Press), *Principles of Linguistic Change*, Vols. 1 and 2. (1994, 2001, Blackwell). Peter Trudgill's *Sociolinguistics: An Introduction to Language and Society* (4th ed., 2001, Penguin) is a good short introduction.

Rules and constraints in phonology: two current textbooks cover Optimality Theory, a constraints-only approach. See René Kager (1999) *Optimality Theory* (Cambridge University Press) and John McCarthy (2001) *A Thematic Guide to Optimality Theory* (Cambridge University Press).

Polish affricates: Maria Zagorska Brooks (1965) "On Polish affricates," *Word* 20: 207–10. Borrowed phonemes in Japanese: Timothy Vance, *An Introduction to Japanese Phonology* (1987, State University of New York Press); Junko Ito and Armin Mester "Japanese Phonology," in *Handbook of Phonology*, John Goldsmith, ed. (1995, Blackwell). Turkish [daː] vs. [da.a]: G. N. Clements and S. J. Keyser, *CV Phonology* (1983, MIT Press). Mandarin diphthongs: the analysis given is modeled on Lawton Hartman III (1944) "The segmental phonemes of the Peiping dialect," *Language* 20: 28–42. Final Devoicing in Toba Batak: P. W. J. Nababan, *A Grammar of Toba-Batak* and W. Keith Percival, *A Grammar of the Urbanised Toba Batak of Medan* (both 1981, Australian National University).

4 Features

4.1 Introduction to Features: Representations

Feature theory is part of a general approach in cognitive science which hypothesizes formal **representations of mental phenomena**. A representation is an abstract formal object that characterizes the essential properties of a mental entity.

To begin with an example, most readers of this book are familiar with the words and music of the song "Happy Birthday to You." The question is: what is it that they know? Or, to put it very literally, what information is embodied in their neurons that distinguishes a knower of "Happy Birthday" from a hypothetical person who is identical in every other respect but does not know the song?

Much of this knowledge must be abstract. People can recognize "Happy Birthday" when it is sung in a novel key, or by an unfamiliar voice, or using a different tempo or form of musical expression. Somehow, they can ignore (or cope in some other way with) inessential traits and attend to the essential ones. The latter include the linguistic text, the (relative) pitch sequences of the notes, the relative note durations, and the musical harmonies that (often tacitly) accompany the tune.

Cognitive science posits that humans possess *mental representations*, that is, formal mental objects depicting the structure of things we know or do. A typical claim is that we are capable of singing "Happy Birthday" because we have (during childhood) internalized a mental representation, fairly abstract in character, that embodies the structure of this song. The process of singing accesses this representation, and uses it to guide behavior: in this case, our own rendition.

Linguistic theory seeks to develop appropriate representations for the mental objects of language. One such representation is the tree diagram, used to represent the structure of phrases:

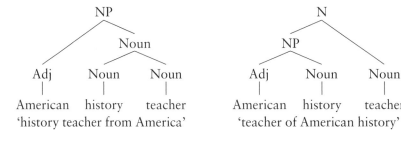

The utterances above are (at least at faster speaking rates) homophonous; the fact that people can perceive two different meanings when they hear [ə'meɹikin'hɪstəɹi,titʃɚ] is attributed to the possibility of their assigning two distinct representations to the same phonetic string.

Representations are generally stated in a formal notation; this permits us to be more precise about the predictions they make and how rules apply to them.

4.2   Representations in Phonology

Phonology faces the issue of what are the appropriate representations for its mental objects. How are the sounds of speech, and the morphemes and words assembled from them, represented in the mind? This is a difficult issue to settle, and a reliable answer is unlikely to emerge for some time.

However, we do have an important clue, namely the pervasive tendency of phonological rules to apply to **natural classes** (§2.10.4). If phonological rules group segments in particular ways according to the phonetic properties of the segments, it may be a clue that it is precisely the phonetic properties of the segments that constitute their substance.

4.2.1   *Feature matrices*

Let us suppose, then, that each segment is represented simply as a bundle of features, which collectively define it. The usual formal notation for this is the **feature matrix**. The features are placed in vertical columns enclosed by square brackets, as in the following example:

map ([mæp]):
$$
\begin{bmatrix} -\text{syllabic} \\ +\text{sonorant} \\ +\text{stop} \\ +\text{nasal} \\ +\text{labial} \\ +\text{voice} \end{bmatrix}
\begin{bmatrix} +\text{syllabic} \\ +\text{sonorant} \\ -\text{stop} \\ -\text{nasal} \\ +\text{low} \\ -\text{back} \\ +\text{front} \\ -\text{round} \end{bmatrix}
\begin{bmatrix} -\text{syllabic} \\ -\text{sonorant} \\ +\text{stop} \\ -\text{nasal} \\ +\text{labial} \\ -\text{voice} \end{bmatrix}
$$

The columns of the representation are sets of features that define /m/, /æ/, and /p/. Indeed, we may now consider (within the theory we are developing), that symbols such as /m/ and /æ/ are merely convenient abbreviations for the real representations, which, though fully explicit, are an annoyance to write whenever we simply want to identify a segment.

4.2.2 *Applying rules to featural representations*

Given an explicit featural representation for sounds, we can state more precisely what it means for a rule to apply to a form. Here is a simple example. As already noted, it is a rule of English that all vowels are realized as nasalized when they precede nasals; they appear as oral in all other contexts; thus *cam* [kæ̃m] vs. *cab* [kæb]. The Vowel Nasalization rule given on p. 50 is restated below using the features to be covered in this chapter; the feature [+syllabic] in this context abbreviates essentially the class of vowels.

Vowel Nasalization

[+syllabic] → [+nasal] / ___ [+nasal]

The goal here is to apply the rule carefully to the proper name *Pom* (= /pɑm/), deriving [pɑ̃m]. The formal representation for /pɑm/ is as follows.

$$
Pom: \quad = \quad
\begin{bmatrix}
-\text{syllabic} \\
-\text{sonorant} \\
+\text{stop} \\
-\text{nasal} \\
+\text{labial} \\
-\text{voice}
\end{bmatrix}
\begin{bmatrix}
+\text{syllabic} \\
+\text{sonorant} \\
-\text{stop} \\
-\text{nasal} \\
+\text{low} \\
+\text{back} \\
-\text{round}
\end{bmatrix}
\begin{bmatrix}
-\text{syllabic} \\
+\text{sonorant} \\
+\text{stop} \\
+\text{nasal} \\
+\text{labial} \\
+\text{voice}
\end{bmatrix}
$$

In matching up a rule to a form, it is useful to restate the rule in equivalent form so that it maps complete strings to complete strings, without distinguishing target segments from context segments:

Vowel Nasalization (restated)

$$
[+\text{syllabic}][+\text{nasal}] \rightarrow
\begin{bmatrix}
+\text{syllabic} \\
+\text{nasal}
\end{bmatrix}
[+\text{nasal}]
$$

This rule can be interpreted as "Seek out a feature matrix that includes [+syllabic] directly followed by a feature matrix that includes [+nasal]. Modify the output so that the first of these two matrices will have the value [+nasal]."

The matchup of rule and form goes like this:

$$
Pom: \quad = \quad
\begin{bmatrix}
-\text{syllabic} \\
-\text{sonorant} \\
+\text{stop} \\
-\text{nasal} \\
+\text{labial} \\
-\text{voice}
\end{bmatrix}
\begin{bmatrix}
\mathbf{+syllabic} \\
+\text{sonorant} \\
-\text{stop} \\
-\text{nasal} \\
+\text{low} \\
+\text{back} \\
-\text{round}
\end{bmatrix}
\begin{bmatrix}
-\text{syllabic} \\
+\text{sonorant} \\
+\text{stop} \\
\mathbf{+nasal} \\
+\text{labial} \\
+\text{voice}
\end{bmatrix}
$$

$$
[\mathbf{+syllabic}]\ [\mathbf{+nasal}] \rightarrow
\begin{bmatrix}
+\text{syllabic} \\
+\text{nasal}
\end{bmatrix}
[+\text{nasal}]
$$

and the application of the rule yields this:

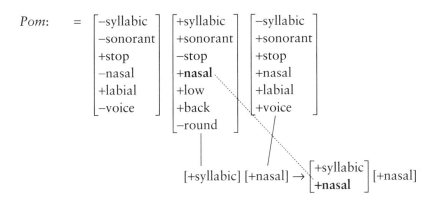

The above derivation is explicit regarding the representations and how they are changed. But we also need to state precisely our assumptions about how rules are matched up to forms. First, all features or segments not changed by a rule are assumed to remain the same. Second, when two feature matrices in a rule are adjacent, they can only be matched to two segments which are adjacent. For example, Vowel Nasalization does not apply to *Whitney* /wɪtni/, because the vowel /ɪ/ does not directly precede the nasal consonant /n/; /t/ intervenes. Third, while it is necessary to match everything in the rule, it is not necessary to match everything in the form. Thus, Vowel Nasalization applies to *plump* /plʌmp/ *plump*, because it matches the contiguous string /ʌm/. The additional material /p . . . mp/ is not analyzed by the rule and remains unchanged. Lastly if a rule matches up to more than one location in a form, it applies to all such locations; thus /fændæŋgoʊ/ *fandango* becomes [fæ̃ndæ̃ŋgoʊ], with two applications of Vowel Nasalization.

One reason for formalizing with this degree of care is that it makes it possible for phonologists to reach full agreement about what an analysis predicts. Theory and analysis in phonology can get rather controversial, and the scholarly debates can't get very far if it is not agreed what the prediction of an analysis is. Such disagreement usually results when the analysis is so casually presented that the derivations need human intuition and insight to be carried out.

A fully worked-out theory of rules and representations in phonology involves more than just segments. The later chapters of this book outline a number of other things that must be included: the grouping of segments into morphemes, words, and phrases (chapter 10), syllabification (chapter 13), and suprasegmental information involving stress (chapter 14) and intonation (chapter 15). For now, however, we will assume that a phonological representation consists simply of a sequence of bundles of features.

4.3   A Feature Set: Preliminaries

Many different proposals for phonological feature systems have been made in the research literature. This book presents a fairly "mainstream" feature set, most of whose features were first proposed in Chomsky and Halle's book *The Sound Pattern of English* (1968). Tonal features are not included here but postponed to chapter 15.

4.3.1   The goal of characterizing natural classes

A question that arises at the outset is why not simply use as our features the standard labels of phonetic terminology given by the IPA (chapter 1)? This is what we have been doing so far, with features like [+stop], [+vowel], and so on. The reason for not doing this is that we want our feature system to be able to characterize natural classes, the groupings of sounds that appear in phonological rules (§2.10.4). There are natural classes that are broader than the IPA categories, and we want our feature system to characterize them.

Perhaps the clearest example of such broader categories are those defined by the feature [**sonorant**], which are as follows: stops, fricatives, and affricates are [–sonorant] and all other sounds are [+sonorant]. The following paragraphs give some of the evidence that the feature values [+sonorant] and [–sonorant] define natural classes.

- In Spanish, Japanese, Swahili, and a great number of other languages, it is the class of stops, fricatives, and affricates (that is, the [–sonorant] sounds) that can bear a phonemic contrast for voicing. In [+sonorant] sounds, the value of [voice] is usually predictably [+voice].
- Many languages (e.g. French, Catalan, Russian, Polish, Maltese Arabic) have a rule of Voicing Assimilation, in which a consonant is assigned the same voicing as an immediately following consonant; see p. 133 for an example. Typically, both the set of triggering consonants and those which undergo the rule are restricted to the class of [–sonorant] segments; that is, stops, affricates, and fricatives.
- In many languages (for example German, Dutch, Russian, Polish, and Catalan) there is a rule of Final Devoicing which is similar to the Toba Batak rule on p. 63 but which targets the full class of stops, affricates, and fricatives. It can be stated [–sonorant] → [–voice] / ___]_word.[1]

---

[1]   In fact, the Toba Batak rule could just as easily be written [–sonorant] → [–voice] / ___]_word as well. Toba Batak has no final affricates (even voiceless ones), and has no voiced fricatives, so the formulation with [–sonorant] would work.

- In certain tonal languages (Lithuanian, some ancient Greek dialects), syllables ending in consonants can bear contrastive rising and falling tones (chapter 15) just in case the consonant is *not* a stop, affricate, or fricative; that is, it must be [+sonorant].
- The sound [ŋ] is deleted from the Indonesian prefix [məŋ-] just in case the following sound is a consonant other than a stop, affricate or fricative; that is, [–syllabic, +sonorant].

The conclusion drawn is that the class consisting of stops, affricates, and fricatives, and its complement class, should be considered natural classes in phonology, and the feature set should include a feature, [sonorant], that permits them to be characterized as such. The IPA terminology is inadequate as a feature system because it offers no such feature.

Another name for sounds that are [–sonorant] is **obstruent**. *–Sonorant*

4.3.2 Defining features

In a complete feature theory, the features will be defined not as lists (like {stop, fricative, affricate}) but with phonetic properties, which can be articulatory, acoustic, or both.

For instance, [+sonorant] segments characteristically have greater acoustic energy than [–sonorant] segments, though the cutoff point is difficult to define. At the articulatory level, [–sonorant] segments have a constriction sufficiently narrow to cause a buildup of air pressure in the vocal tract. You can feel this buildup when you articulate sounds slowly and forcefully: [pa], [t͡ʃa], [sa] etc. have it; [ma], [la], [wa] etc. do not.

Below, the features are identified both by their phonological purpose (that is, the way they classify segments), and more concretely by their phonetic correlates.

4.4   Manner Features

4.4.1   The sonority hierarchy

Since the work of Eduard Sievers in the nineteenth century, phonologists have found it useful to arrange the manners of articulation in a hierarchy based loosely on the acoustic sonority (loudness) of sounds; this is called the **Sonority Hierarchy**. The hierarchy is stated in different versions, of which a fairly simple one is the following:

greater sonority   less sonority
←――――――――――――――――――――――――――――――――――――→   } Key
vowels   glides   liquids   nasals   obstruents

The natural classes found in phonological rules often consist of some **contiguous set** of manner types drawn from the hierarchy, such as {vowels, glides, liquids} or {liquids, nasals}. On the other hand, noncontiguous sets, like {glides, nasals}, seldom pattern as natural classes.

A simple scheme to capture this pattern is to adopt four features, each of which defines a particular cutoff point along the sonority hierarchy. The feature [sonorant], just defined, forms one such cutoff point; [+sonorant] segments are more sonorous than [−sonorant]. To cover the complete hierarchy, we add three further features: **[syllabic]**, **[consonantal]**, and **[approximant]**. Along with [sonorant], they divide up the sonority hierarchy as in table 4.1:

Table 4.1   The sonority hierarchy

Vowels	Glides	Liquids	Nasals	Obstruents
[+syllabic]	[−syllabic]			
[−consonantal]		[+consonantal]		
[+approximant]			[−approximant]	
[+sonorant]				[−sonorant]

The features [consonantal] and [approximant] can be phonetically defined, in principle, with cutoff points along the hierarchy of acoustic sonority, just like [sonorant]; unlike [sonorant] they appear to lack a clear articulatory definition. The case of [syllabic] is slightly different and is discussed below.

In this system, all of the contiguous sets along the hierarchy are expressible as natural classes. For example, we can describe the set of glides, liquids, and nasals with the formula [−syllabic, +sonorant] (the sonorant consonants). A claimed advantage of this system is that noncontiguous groups of manner types, such as {stops, liquids} *cannot* be expressed as natural classes. To the extent that such groups do not occur in phonological rules, the theory is making the right predictions.

4.4.2   Reconstructing the traditional manner categories

With such a system of manner features, it is unnecessary to employ our earlier features [glide] and [liquid], and we will henceforth dispense with them. The reason is that they can be restated by combining more general features; thus "glide," for instance, is [−syllabic, −consonantal]. More generally, the following definitions hold:

vowel	=	[+syllabic] (but see next section for a complication)
glide	=	[−syllabic, −consonantal]
liquid	=	[+consonantal, +approximant]
nasal	=	[−approximant, +sonorant]
obstruent	=	[−sonorant]

4.4.3   Syllabic consonants

The feature [syllabic] must be defined rather differently from the other sonority features. We will assume a definition based on syllabification, discussed in more detail in chapter 13. Every syllable may be said to have a nucleus, which is its most sonorous segment. Segments forming the nucleus of a syllable will be classified as [+syllabic], while the remaining segments in the syllables are classified as [−syllabic].

This definition of [syllabic] is necessary because of the occurrence in many languages of **syllabic liquids and nasals**, as in Serbo-Croatian [tr̩g] 'square' or the last sound of English (casual speech) *button* [ˈbʌtn̩]. These sounds lack the sonority of vowels, but nevertheless serve as syllable nuclei and are counted as [+syllabic], as shown below.

$$
\text{syllabic liquid} = \begin{bmatrix} +\text{syllabic} \\ +\text{consonantal} \\ +\text{approximant} \end{bmatrix} \quad \text{syllabic nasal} = \begin{bmatrix} +\text{syllabic} \\ -\text{approximant} \\ +\text{sonorant} \end{bmatrix}
$$

Syllabic fricatives and stops are quite rare (they occur in Berber languages), but can be defined analogously. As for syllabic glides, they are assumed under this system to be the same thing as vowels; thus "syllabic [j]" is simply a rather strange way of describing the vowel [i], and similarly for other glide–vowel pairs made at the same place of articulation. The IPA symbol [ɚ], "rhotacized schwa," is often used as an equivalent of "syllabic r," which in IPA is [ɹ̩].

In general, the higher the sonority of a speech sound, the more likely it is that languages will use it as a [+syllabic] segment. For instance, it would be inconceivable that a language could use only syllabic liquids as its syllable nuclei and have no vowels. Thus, although the feature [syllabic] is logically independent of sonority, it is very closely related.

4.4.4   Sonority sequencing

The Sonority Hierarchy, expressed here with the manner features, has another important role in phonology, that of governing the phonotactics; that is, the legal sequencing of speech sounds (§3.6). It often governs the sequencing of segments within the syllable. In a language which permits clusters of consonants to occur at the margins of syllables, typically the situation will be this: as one proceeds outward from the nucleus towards the edges of the syllable, one encounters segments of progressively decreasing sonority. Here is an example from English:

trance:	[t	ɹ	æ	n	s]
	obstruent	liquid	vowel	nasal	obstruent

This holds true, I suspect, for well over 99 percent of the world's syllables. But there are notable exceptions. Slavic languages and Persian are notable for having some syllables whose segments occur in orders going strongly against the Sonority Hierarchy; for example Russian [rta] 'mouth, gen. sg.', Persian [qæbl] 'before'; both of these words are monosyllabic.

The individual features for sonority defined above play a role in phonological systems. For instance, only [+approximant] consonants may occur after initial stops in English (/l/ [pleɪ] *play*, /ɹ/ [kɹoʊ] *crow*, /w/ [twɪn] *twin*, /j/ [kjut] *cute*). For an example of [syllabic], see §4.2.2 above; for [sonorant], §4.3.1; and for [consonantal], p. 122.

4.4.5 Classifying the stops, affricates, and fricatives

The manner features defined thus far provide no way of distinguishing the stops, fricative, and affricates from each other. We will use two features for this purposes, [continuant] and [delayed release].[2]

4.4.5.1 [continuant]

A sound is said to be [−continuant] if it involves a full closure in the oral portion of the vocal tract. Thus, stops like [p t k] are [−continuant], as is the glottal stop [ʔ] and affricates like [tʃ] and [ts]. Moreover, nasals like [m n ŋ] also involve a complete oral closure and are thus [−continuant]. Fricatives, liquids, glides, and vowels do not have a complete oral closure and are classified as [+continuant].[2]

It can be seen that [continuant] is not a sonority feature: nasals are more sonorous than fricatives, but they are [−continuant] and fricatives are [+continuant].

The feature [continuant] predicts an affinity between true stops and nasals. This is illustrated by an optional rule found in many dialects of English. Consider the following data, which occur in my own casual speech and seem to be fairly common in the language as a whole:

---

[2] In some feature systems, the partial closure (midline of vocal tract) of laterals justifies their being classified as [−continuant]; occasionally the very brief closure of taps, flaps, and trills is taken as justification for their being [−continuant]. The data are problematic, and for simplicity we will classify all laterals, taps, flaps, and trills as [+continuant].

Word	Phonemic	Phonetic
business	/ˈbɪznəs/	[ˈbɪznəs] or [ˈbɪdnəs]
isn't	/ˈɪznt̩ /	[ˈɪznt̩] or [ˈɪdnt̩]
doesn't	/ˈdʌznt̩/	[ˈdʌznt̩] or [ˈdʌdnt̩]

Apparently in these cases the underlying /z/, which is articulated as a fricative, is adjusted so as to take on the stop articulation of the following /n/. That is, articulatorily, /n/ is a kind of stop, even though acoustically it is more sonorous than a true stop. The /z/ assimilates to it in continuancy.

4.4.5.2 [delayed release]

We also need a feature that distinguishes affricates from stops. In the system used here, stops are [−delayed release], and affricates are [+delayed release]. A sound which is [−delayed release] is a stop in the purest sense, being neither affricated nor nasal.

The word "delay" appearing in the name of this feature refers to the period of semi-closure during which frication noise is produced; and the feature can be phonetically defined with the criterion "includes frication noise." Assuming this definition, it would follow that fricatives are [+delayed release] as well. A phonological reason to consider fricatives as [+delayed release] is given below.

4.4.5.3 The natural classes defined by [continuant] and [delayed release]

Under this system, the three-way distinction between fricatives, affricates, and stops is taken to be a three-valued scale, defined in the usual way with two features (table 4.2):

Table 4.2 The features for stops, affricates, and fricatives

Stops	Affricates	Fricatives
[−continuant]		[+continuant]
[−delayed release]	[+delayed release]	

Below are some examples of the natural classes implied by these features.

In Mandarin Chinese, the class of aspirated phonemes (vocal cords abducted; see §4.7.2 for features) is /pʰ/, /tʰ/, /kʰ/, /t͡sʰ/, /t͡ʂʰ/, and /t͡ɕʰ/; that is to say, all and only the stops and affricates. No other sounds (including fricatives) may be [+spread glottis] in this language. The stops and affricates together form the natural class [−sonorant, −continuant]. Limitation of aspiration to this class of sounds is common among languages, including English.

Affricates and fricatives: in Kongo, there is an allophonic rule that takes /t/, /d/, and /s/ to [t͡ʃ], [d͡ʒ], and [ʃ] respectively when /i/ follows. The change involves both place features (alveolar becomes palato-alveolar) and manner features. For the manner features, it suffices to assign the value + to the feature [delayed release]. This will turn the stops /t/ and /d/ into affricates as desired. /s/, in the system given here, is already [+delayed release], and a rule that makes it [+delayed release] will "apply" to it harmlessly, imposing the same feature it already had (this is known as **vacuous application**). The rule for Kongo may be formalized as follows:

Kongo Palatalization

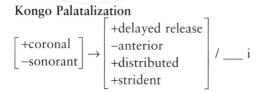

For the place features [coronal], [anterior], [distributed], and [strident], see §4.6 below.

Note that a primitive feature like [+affricate] would be of little help in expressing this rule: a rule that assigned the feature [+affricate] would wrongly convert /s/ into *[tʃ]. As before, it appears that a feature system will work better if it includes higher-level abstract categories, in this case the natural class of affricates and fricatives defined by [+delayed release].

4.4.6   *Trills and taps*

Nothing in the manner features given so far distinguishes the various types of "r"; plausibly trills and taps have their own features, specifically [**+trill**] and [**+tap**]. Flaps (see p. 7) are distinct from taps in IPA terminology; but it appears unnecessary to include a feature [flap] since flaps also differ from taps in place of articulation. Taps are generally [+anterior] (alveolar) and flaps are [−anterior] (retroflex).

4.5   Vowel Features

4.5.1   *Basic vowel features*

The fundamental phonetic basis for classifying vowels (§1.5) is to specify their *height*, *backness*, and *rounding*. As a first step, we can ask how many phonemic vowel distinctions occur along each of these three dimensions.

4.5.1.1   Backness

Norwegian has a three-way distinction for backness in its high rounded vowels: /y/ (front), /ʉ/ (central), and /u/ (back), as shown by the following minimal triplet: [byː] 'town' has a front vowel, [bʉː] 'shack' has a central vowel, and [buː] 'live' has a back vowel; all three are high and rounded. In order to capture such a three-way distinction, we need the features [**back**] and [**front**], defined in table 4.3.

Table 4.3 Backness in vowels

Front	Central	Back
[−back]		[+back]
[+front]	[−front]	

Phonologists sometimes try to make do with a simpler system, using the single feature [back] to render a two-way backness distinction. In such an approach, the central vowels are treated as a subspecies of back vowels. The advantage of a three-way system is that it provides a category for central vowels, allowing systems like Norwegian to be described. Moreover, central vowels such as [ɨ] or the (very common) [a] seem to behave phonologically neither like back vowels nor like front;[3] classifying them as [−front, −back] captures this patterning.

4.5.1.2 Height and tenseness

An unusually rich system of height is found in the front vowels of English, where there is a five-way distinction, going from top to bottom: /i/ (*bead*), /ɪ/ (*bid*), /e/ (more precisely, [eɪ]; *bayed*), /ɛ/ *bed*, /æ/ *bad*. The phonology of English suggests a system with three basic heights (high, mid, low), on which is superimposed an additional, finer distinction commonly called [tense]. (A synonym for [−tense] is "lax.")

Height	IPA symbol	[high]	[low]	[tense]
upper high	[i]	[+high]	[−low]	[+tense]
lower high	[ɪ]	[+high]	[−low]	[−tense]
upper mid	[e]	[−high]	[−low]	[+tense]
lower mid	[ɛ]	[−high]	[−low]	[−tense]
low	[æ]	[−high]	[+low]	

This system deviates from the way we have treated other phonetic continua, with a feature defining each "cutoff point." Yet there is phonological justification for [tense], at least in English and related languages, because it defines a natural class. Among other things, the vowels of English which are [−tense] ([ɪ], [ɛ], [æ], [ʊ], [ʌ], and in British English [ɒ]) cannot end a word or precede another vowel.

---

[3] For example, [a] doesn't trigger palatalization rules, as front vowels do; true back vowels are most often rounded, but low central vowels only seldom.

The tense and lax vowels also differ phonetically. The lax vowels tend to be shorter and more centralized, and under slow or emphatic speech there are differences of diphthongization: [+tense] vowels diphthongize toward a higher vowel (*bayed* [beɪd]), [−tense] vowels tend to diphthongize with an inserted schwa: *bid* [bɪəd].

It would be easy to extend the system above to six heights by making [tense] relevant to low vowels as well. However, since tenseness distinctions among low vowels are hard to find, and it will be easier to deal with English (the language of many of our examples) with a five-height system, I will use this system for height in this book.

4.5.1.3   Rounding

Rounding is generally believed to be a binary distinction. Although the phonetic degree of rounding on vowels can vary greatly, there is at most a two-way phonological distinction of rounding, expressed as [+round] vs. [−round].

4.5.2   *A feature chart for vowels*

It is awkward to reduce the IPA vowel chart (p. 14) to a feature system. The chart offers as many as seven contrasting heights (in the central unrounded vowels), whereas the system used here, intended for use in phonology, uses only five.

Table 4.4 represents an attempt to use the IPA vowel symbols to fill the 30 slots defined by the feature system just given. As can be seen, not every slot has a symbol (one would have to use the IPA diacritics to fill these slots), and not every IPA symbol can be fitted into a slot.

Here are the main divergences between this chart and IPA.

- The chart has no place for [ɐ], a symbol standing for a vowel that is central, unrounded, and a bit higher than low. [ɐ] could fit in the chart as [+low, +tense], were we making tenseness distinctions among low vowels.

Table 4.4   Features used for classifying the dorsals

	[+front, −back]		[−front, −back]		[−front, +back]	
	−round	+round	−round	+round	−round	+round
[+high, −low, +tense]	i	y	ɨ	ʉ	ɯ	u
[+high, −low, −tense]	ɪ	ʏ	–	–	–	ʊ
[−high, −low, +tense]	e	ø	ɘ	ɵ	ɤ	o
[−high, −low, −tense]	ɛ	œ	ə	ɞ	ʌ	ɔ
[−high, +low]	æ	Œ	a	–	ɑ	ɒ

- IPA provides three mid central unrounded vowels: in order of height, [ɘ, ə, ɜ]. Since the feature system here permits only two (and allowing for three seems rather extravagant in any case), we will use [ɘ] for the [+tense] mid central vowel, and [ə] (a more familiar symbol than [ɜ]) for the [−tense] one.
- In IPA, [a] designates the lowest possible front vowel, lower than [æ]. In the five-height system used here, this symbol is deemed unnecessary for purposes of phonology, and [æ] will be used for the lowest front unrounded vowel, following common descriptive practice.
- Following the practice of many linguists, the symbol [a] is used to denote a low central unrounded vowel, filling the gap in the IPA discussed on p. 14.

4.5.3 Other vowel features

Many languages, particularly in sub-Saharan Africa, distinguish vowels with a feature called [Advanced Tongue Root], abbreviated [ATR]. This feature is often involved in **vowel harmony** systems – roughly, all the vowels in a particular word must be either [+ATR] or [−ATR]. It is not yet clear whether [Advanced Tongue Root] is to be considered the same feature as [tense]. Occasionally phonologists use [ATR] instead of [tense] in describing English and other European languages.

There are three more features that are often relevant to vowel inventories:

- [long]: For instance, Classical Latin had five contrasting long and five contrasting short vowels: /i iː e eː a aː o oː u uː/. This feature applies as well to consonants; long consonants are often also called **geminates**.
- [nasal]: This feature is also a feature of consonants, but serves here to distinguish nasalized from non-nasalized vowels.
- [stress]: This turns out to be dubious as a vowel feature; we will later (chapter 14) consider the alternative that it is a feature of syllables, and add other features relevant to stress.

4.6 Place Features for Consonants

4.6.1 Major articulator features

A useful starting point for treating consonant place of articulation is to distinguish the consonants according to the **active articulator** that is used in producing them.

[+labial]   =   articulated with the lips
[+coronal]   =   articulated with the tongue blade and/or tip
[+dorsal]   =   articulated with the tongue body

Often a consonant is made with just one articulator, so it would get the value + for one of the features above and – for the others. In so-called **complex segments**, however, two articulators are involved. Thus, a labial-velar like [k͡p] or [w] involves both lips and tongue body, and thus would be [+labial, +dorsal]. Most clicks, such as [!], involve the tongue tip/blade as well as the tongue body, and are classified as [+coronal, +dorsal]. For more complex segments, see §4.6.5 below.

It is also possible for a consonant to involve none of the articulators just mentioned. This is true for glottal consonants, which in this view are [–labial, –coronal, –dorsal]. For the features that distinguish glottal consonants, see §4.7 below.

The view that place of articulation should be classified by the choice of active articulator receives some confirmation from the phonological pattern of languages. For instance, the following example has been taken as evidence that [+coronal] defines a phonologically relevant class of consonants. Consider the ways in which the definite article of Classical Arabic appears before various stems. It shows up as [ʔal] in the context / ___ [b, f, m, k, x, ɣ, q, ħ, ʕ, ʔ, h, w, j]; that is to say, all but dentals, alveolars and palato-alveolars. Before a consonant of the latter three places of articulation, it is pronounced as a copy of the immediately following consonant, hence producing a geminate ([ˠ] is the IPA diacritic for velarization):

[ʔaθ]	/	___ θ	[ʔas]	/	___ s	
[ʔað]	/	___ ð	[ʔasˠ]	/	___ sˠ	
[ʔaðˠ]	/	___ ðˠ	[ʔaz]	/	___ z	
[ʔat]	/	___ t	[ʔazˠ]	/	___ zˠ	
[ʔatˠ]	/	___ tˠ	[ʔan]	/	___ n	
[ʔad]	/	___ d	[ʔar]	/	___ r	
[ʔadˠ]	/	___ dˠ	[ʔaʃ]	/	___ ʃ	

The feature [coronal] is needed here to generalize over both alveolar/dental and palato-alveolar places of articulation.

4.6.2   *Features for classifying the coronals*

Coronal consonants are commonly classified using four features: [**anterior**], [**distributed**], [**strident**], and [**lateral**].

4.6.2.1   [anterior]

The word "anterior" means "towards the front." [+anterior] coronals are articulated at the alveolar ridge or further forward. The IPA places of articulation that are [+anterior] are the (inter-)dentals and alveolars. [–anterior] coronals are articulated behind the alveolar ridge; the IPA places of articulation that are [–anterior] are the palato-alveolars and retroflexes.

[anterior] defines natural classes in the process of **sibilant harmony**, found in many languages including Navajo, Chumash, and Kinyarwanda. In sibilant harmony, all stridents in a word are required to agree in anteriority. Sibilant harmony is also a common substitution process in children's speech; when my son was little I observed him saying [ʃuʃi] for *sushi* and [ʃʌnʃaɪn] for *sunshine*.

4.6.2.2 [distributed]

Both [+anterior] and [−anterior] coronals can be made with either the tongue blade (called **laminal** coronals) or tongue tip (**apical** coronals). In this book, the feature [distributed] will designate this distinction, with laminals counted as [+distributed] and apicals counted as [−distributed].

[+distributed] = blade = contact is long, measured front to back   *key*
[−distributed] = tip = contact is short, measured front to back

The basis of the term "distributed" is evidently as follows: when the tongue blade is used, there is more contact between tongue and roof of mouth; thus, the tongue is "well distributed" over the roof of the mouth.

Dentals and palato-alveolars are normally laminal and alveolars and retroflexes are normally apical. Thus as a rule of thumb the IPA places of articulation can ordinarily be described as follows:

Lamino-dentals   [t̪, d̪, θ, ð, n̪]   [+coronal, +anterior, +distributed]
Apico-alveolars   [t, d, s, z, n]   [+coronal, +anterior, −distributed]   *key*
Palato-alveolars   [t͡ʃ, d͡ʒ, ʃ, ʒ]   [+coronal, −anterior, +distributed]
Retroflexes   [ʈ, ɖ, ʂ, ʐ, ɳ]   [+coronal, −anterior, −distributed]

For an example in which [distributed] defines natural classes, see p. 179.

4.6.2.3 [strident]

In this book, the [+strident] sounds are the sibilants, such as [s, z, t͡s, d͡z, ʃ, ʒ, t͡ʃ, d͡ʒ]. Only coronal fricatives and affricates can be [+strident]. [+strident] sounds may be defined articulatorily as follows: the airstream is channeled through a groove in the tongue blade and blown at the teeth. Acoustically, [+strident] sounds are louder than nonstrident fricatives or affricates.

The allomorphs of the English plural suffix plainly identify the class of stridents: [əz] appears after /s z ʃ ʒ t͡ʃ d͡ʒ/ (*glasses, mazes, bushes, garages, batches, judges*), while [z] or [s] appear after all other sounds. If one takes the analytic approach that the underlying form of the plural is /-z/, one can say that English employs schwa insertion to break up clusters of [+strident] sounds. The avoidance of strident clusters is common in languages.

English Schwa Epenthesis
∅ → ə / [+strident] ___ [+strident]]_word_
Insert schwa between two word-final stridents.

In the name of the rule, **epenthesis** denotes rules of insertion. $\varnothing \rightarrow X$ ("zero becomes X") is the usual formalism for insertion rules.

The feature [strident] is used by some phonologists in a broader sense that includes certain non-coronal consonants; for discussion see footnote 5 below.

4.6.2.4   [lateral]

[lateral] distinguishes /l/ from other coronal liquids and [ɬ, ɮ] from other coronal fricatives. In a lateral sound, the tongue is compressed laterally, so that contact at the edges is incomplete. In this state, air can pass laterally around the tongue.[4]

4.6.3   *Features used for classifying the labials*

In the system used in this book, the features that subdivide the labials are the following:

[**round**]   = articulated by rounding the lips
[**labiodental**]   = articulated by touching the lower lip to the upper teeth

[round] has already been discussed as a vowel feature. [labiodental] is much more marginal, as only a few languages, such as Ewe and California Spanish, have phonemic contrasts (/ɸ/ vs. /f/, /β/ vs. /v/) based on this feature.[5]

The IPA category of **labialization** (secondary rounding on consonants, as in [k] vs. [kʷ]) can be treated by adding the features [+labial, +round] to whatever values the unlabialized version of the consonant has.

Here are some examples of segments that are [+labial] along with their feature values.

Plain bilabials	[p, b, m, ɸ, β]	[+labial, −round, −labiodental]
Plain labiodentals	[f, v]	[+labial, −round, +labiodental]
Rounded bilabials	[pʷ, bʷ, mʷ, ɸʷ, βʷ]	[+labial, +round, −labiodental]
Rounded labiodentals	[fʷ, vʷ]	[+labial, +round, +labiodental]

---

[4]   [lateral] is, cross-linguistically, overwhelmingly a feature of coronals, and thus is listed in this section. A few languages have velar laterals.

[5]   Distinctive feature theorists have often tried to handle the bilabial-labiodental contrast without adding a new feature. In one view, labiodentals are [−distributed], since they have short front-to-back closure. But this groups them together with the coronal apicals as a natural class, and to my knowledge there is no support for such a class from language data. Another approach is to say that labiodentals are [+strident], based on the fact that they are slightly louder than bilabial [ɸ] and [β]. This groups [f] and [v] with the sibilants, and once again there appears to be no support for such a grouping. For example, if [f] and [v] were [+strident], we would expect the plurals of *cuff* and *dove* to be *['kʌfəz] and *['dʌvəz]. I use [labiodental] instead of trying to shoehorn the labiodentals into a slot they don't fit.

Rounded velars	[w, kʷ, gʷ, xʷ, gʷ]	[+labial, +dorsal, +round, −labiodental]
Labial-velars	[k͡p, g͡b]	[+labial, +dorsal, −round, −labiodental]
Rounded coronals	[tʷ, dʷ, sʷ, zʷ, rʷ]	[+labial, +coronal, +round, −labiodental]

4.6.4 Features used for classifying the dorsals

The [dorsal] articulator (tongue body) is special because it is also the primary articulator for vowels. One appealing strategy for describing the various consonants that can be made with the tongue body is to treat consonants as analogous to the closest similar vowel.

- Fronted velars (the kind in English *keen* [k̟in]) are treated as [+high, −low, +front, −back], like [i] and [y].
- Central velars (the kind in English *collect* [kəˈlɛkt]) are treated as [+high, −low, −front, −back], like [ɨ] and [ʉ].
- Back velars (the kind in English *coo* [k̠u][6] are treated as [+high, −low, −front, +back], like [ɯ] and [u].
- Uvulars (e.g. [q, ɢ, χ, ʁ]), are treated as [−high, −low, −front, +back], like [ɤ] and [o].
- Pharyngeals (e.g. [ħ, ʕ]), are treated as [−high, +low, −front, +back] like [ɑ] and [ɒ].

Table 4.5 shows the equivalences.

There is a certain sensibleness to this proposal, since these features are needed to describe tongue body position in vowels in any event. Moreover, there is a phonetic affinity between the consonants and vowels that are paired this way. English fronts its velars in the environment of front vowels and backs them in the neighborhood of back vowels, Eskimo languages lower their high vowels to mid when they precede uvulars, and Maltese Arabic lowers /i/ to [a] before pharyngeals. Under this feature system, all of these can be construed as assimilations (p. 57).

True palatals (IPA [c, ɟ, ç, ʝ, ɲ] are usually judged to involve the simultaneous participation of both tongue blade and tongue body. They are treated here as [+coronal, −anterior, +distributed, +dorsal, +high, −low, +front, −back].

---

[6] Caution: this example works only for dialects of English that have a true back vowel in *coo*. If you speak a dialect that has central /ʉ/ for this phoneme, then of course the allophone of /k/ that will appear before it will be central [k̟].

Table 4.5   Features used for classifying the dorsals

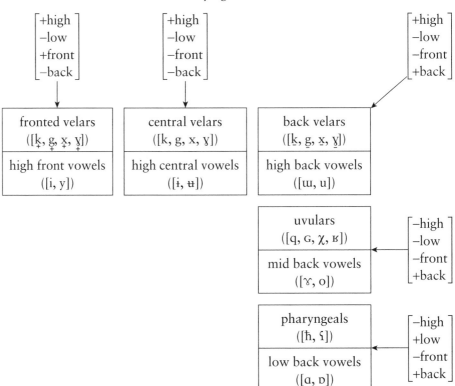

4.6.5   Secondary articulations

The tongue body also participates in secondary articulations, which can be described by adding the appropriate feature values to the base segment:

palatalization (IPA [ʲ]):   add [+dorsal, +high, −low, +front, −back]
velarization (IPA [ˠ]):   add [+dorsal, +high, −low, −front, +back]
pharyngealization (IPA [ˤ]):   add [+dorsal, −high, +low, −front, +back]
labialization (IPA [ʷ]):   add [+labial, +round]

4.6.6   *"Place" as a group concept*

It is commonly noted that the system of features should not be treated as some homogeneous collection, but instead is internally structured: one speaks of place features, manner features, laryngeal features, and a few other categories. Suppose that the following features are specified in the theory as the place features:

[labial]	[coronal]	[dorsal]
[round]	[anterior]	[high]
[labiodental]	[distributed]	[low]
	[strident]	[front]
	[lateral]	[back]

An interesting aspect of many phonological rules is that they manipulate all the place features at once. Thus, in Spanish and many other languages, when underlying /n/ is placed before another consonant, it assimilates in place to that consonant, no matter what place it bears.

in isolation:	[un]	(masculine indefinite article)
before a vowel:	[un oso]	'a bear'
before bilabials:	[um peso]	'a peso'
	[um beso]	'a kiss'
before labiodentals:	[uɱ foko]	'a focus'
before dentals:	[un̪ t̪io]	'an uncle'
	[un̪ d̪ia]	'a day'
before alveolars:	[un sako]	'a sack'
before palatoalveolars:	[un̠ t͡ʃaɾko]	'a pool'
before velars:	[uŋ kakto]	'a cactus'
	[uŋ gato]	'a cat'
	[uŋ xweɣo]	'a game'

Various proposals have been made for treating the place features as a unit. Here we will use the following notation:

/n/ Assimilation

$$n \rightarrow [place_i] / \underline{\quad} \begin{bmatrix} -syllabic \\ place_i \end{bmatrix}$$

The notation "$place_i$" in the environment of the rule should be taken as meaning "all of the values for the place features." Thus, the rule above assigns to /n/ all of the place feature values of the immediately following consonant. (For more on the notation of assimilation rules, see p. 133.)

4.7 Laryngeal Features

4.7.1 [voice]

[voice] can be defined articulatorily as involving vocal cord vibration, and acoustically as involving the characteristic periodic waveform that results from

this vibration. [voice] defines a phonemic distinction among obstruents in the majority of languages, but is seldom phonemic among sonorant consonants, and virtually never phonemic among vowels. Voiceless vowels and sonorant consonants are quite common, however, as allophones.

4.7.2   *[+spread glottis]*

[**+spread glottis**] means that the vocal cords, riding on the arytenoid cartilages (see figure 1.2, p. 3) have been placed relatively far apart, producing a wide glottis. Phonologically, [+spread glottis] is present for [h], for breathy vowels, and for aspirated consonants. [+spread glottis] sounds are normally voiceless, but do occur voiced, notably in the voiced allophone of /h/ in English, [ɦ] (found between two vowels, as in *ahead* [əˈɦɛd]), in breathy vowels, and in the voiced aspirated stops [bʰ dʰ gʰ] found in many languages of India.

The phonetic affinity of [h] and aspirated stops appears to be phonologically relevant. For instance, Ancient Greek and other languages that forbid the appearance of two aspirated stops in the same root also tend to forbid the cooccurrence of aspirated stops and [h]. In English, the aspirated allophones of the voiceless stops occur in the same set of environments that /h/ does (see p. 54): word-initially (*perhaps* [pʰɚˈhæps], *Horatio* [həˈɹeɪʃoʊ]), and medially before a stressed vowel (*competition* [ˌkʰɑmpəˈtʰɪʃən], *prohibit* [proʊˈhɪbɪt]).

4.7.3   *[+constricted glottis]*

[**+constricted glottis**] is the opposite of [spread glottis], involving adduction of the vocal cords to make a narrow or closed glottis. The [+constricted glottis] sounds include the following:

- Glottal stop ([ʔ])
- Ejectives ([p', t', k'])
- Preglottalized sounds like the allophone of /t/ at the end of English *cat* [kæˀt]
- The so-called "tense" stops of Korean, which have glottal closure but are not ejective. (conventional transcription: [p', t', k'])

The features [spread glottis] and [constricted glottis] divide a single phonetic continuum – glottal width – into three categories, [+spread glottis, –constricted glottis], [–spread glottis, –constricted glottis], and [–spread glottis, +constricted glottis]. The majority of speech sounds probably use "normal" phonation and thus are [–spread glottis, –constricted glottis].

4.7.4 [+implosive]

[+implosive] sounds involve a special articulatory gesture in which the larynx is lowered, creating a temporary partial vacuum.

4.8 Zero as a Feature Value

Consider a labial consonant like /p/. What is its value for dorsal features like [high], [low], [front], [back], or [tense]?

If the /p/ is a palatalized ([pʲ]) or velarized ([pˠ]) sound, then the answer is clear (§4.6.5): the palatalization or velarization requires us to invoke dorsal features ([+high, −low, +front, −back] for palatalization, [+high, −low, −front, +back] for velarization). However, where this is not the case, we have to look more closely at the phonetics.

It appears that in most languages with plain /p/, the position of the tongue body during the production of this sound is simply *whatever is most articulatorily convenient*, given the neighboring sounds. Thus, for instance, in [ipa], the tongue body does not adopt any particular position during the /p/; rather, it makes a smooth, continuous gesture moving from the high front position of /i/ to the low central position of /a/. In this sense, the /p/ could be said truly "not to care" about values for dorsal features.

In the system used here, this kind of situation is described by assigning the value **zero** to features for which a segment can be said "not to care." We can assume that in the phonetic realization of phonological form, such "don't care" segments normally are given a smooth contour for the relevant phonetic parameter, achieving a convenient transition among the sounds that do care. The notation used here is simply the digit 0, as in [0back, 0front, 0high, 0low] as the tongue body features for a "don't care" [p].

Velar consonants can often be argued, on the same grounds, to be [0back] and [0front]. In phonetic studies, the tongue body during a velar can sometimes be seen to be sliding along the palate, in smooth transition from the preceding to the following vowel. However, some velars have a specified frontness value; for instance the allophone of /k/ at the end of a word in Persian is [+front, −back], irrespective of the preceding vowel, as for example in [pɑk̟] 'pure'.

Zero values are also set up simply because the feature doesn't seem relevant to the sound in question; in this text sonorants are assumed to be [0delayed release] (this feature only classified obstruents), and low vowels are assumed to be [0tense].

For details on the particular features and segments assumed to have the zero value, see the feature charts at the end of this chapter.

4.9 When and How to Use Features in Writing Rules

4.9.1 *Features vs. phonetic symbols*

A fully explicit phonological analysis of a language would use no phonetic symbols. Only the feature matrices have theoretical status, and the phonetic symbols are meant only as convenient abbreviations for particular feature matrices.

On the other hand, one also wants to be able to describe phonologies in a way that is accessible to human inspection. My own feeling is that in semi-formal presentation, it is appropriate to use a mixed notation, using phonetic symbols where they lead to no harm, and features where they contribute insight. Here are ways in which rules benefit by writing them with features.

To capture a natural class. For example, as noted above (p. 75), Indonesian has a rule that deletes /ŋ/ before nasals, liquids, and glides, the set of sonorant consonants:

Indonesian /ŋ/ Deletion

$$\eta \rightarrow \emptyset \; / \; \underline{\qquad} \begin{bmatrix} -\text{syllabic} \\ +\text{sonorant} \end{bmatrix} \textit{resonante}$$

To capture an assimilation. We do this by showing that the assimilating segment adopts a feature value already possessed by one of its neighbors. For example, in English, /k, g, ŋ/ become fronted [k̟, g̟, ŋ̟] before front vowels, as in *keel* [ˈk̟il], *gale* [ˈg̟eɪl], or *dinghy* [ˈdɪŋ̟i]. This is an assimilation, which can be expressed by:

Velar Fronting

$$\begin{bmatrix} +\text{dorsal} \\ +\text{consonantal} \end{bmatrix} \rightarrow \begin{bmatrix} +\text{front} \\ -\text{back} \end{bmatrix} \; / \; \underline{\qquad} \begin{bmatrix} +\text{syllabic} \\ +\text{front} \end{bmatrix}$$

To show that a change is minor; that is, of only one or two feature values. For example, if a rule changes (only) /p/ to [b], one would write p → [+voice] rather than p → b, to show that nothing other than [voice] is changing.

Otherwise use of plain symbols is a sensible way to make a rule easier to read, provided that it is understood that the "real" rule employs only feature matrices.

4.9.2 *Finding the features needed in a rule*

To find the particular features needed to define a natural class, it helps to start with the complete set of sounds in a language, then use just enough features to take away the sounds not wanted, leaving the target natural class in place. For

Table 4.6 Analysis with a separate devoicing rule for each fricative

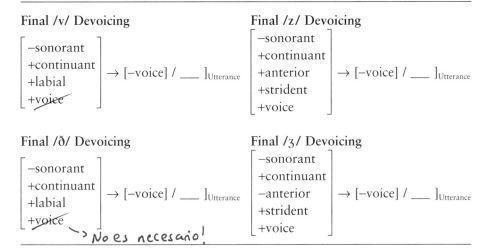

Final /v/ Devoicing

$$\begin{bmatrix} -\text{sonorant} \\ +\text{continuant} \\ +\text{labial} \\ +\text{voice} \end{bmatrix} \rightarrow [-\text{voice}] \text{ / } \underline{\hspace{1em}}]_{\text{Utterance}}$$

Final /z/ Devoicing

$$\begin{bmatrix} -\text{sonorant} \\ +\text{continuant} \\ +\text{anterior} \\ +\text{strident} \\ +\text{voice} \end{bmatrix} \rightarrow [-\text{voice}] \text{ / } \underline{\hspace{1em}}]_{\text{Utterance}}$$

Final /ð/ Devoicing

$$\begin{bmatrix} -\text{sonorant} \\ +\text{continuant} \\ +\text{labial} \\ +\text{voice} \end{bmatrix} \rightarrow [-\text{voice}] \text{ / } \underline{\hspace{1em}}]_{\text{Utterance}}$$

No es necesario!

Final /ʒ/ Devoicing

$$\begin{bmatrix} -\text{sonorant} \\ +\text{continuant} \\ -\text{anterior} \\ +\text{strident} \\ +\text{voice} \end{bmatrix} \rightarrow [-\text{voice}] \text{ / } \underline{\hspace{1em}}]_{\text{Utterance}}$$

instance, if you are seeking to describe the class of glides, you can use [–syllabic] to take away all of the vowels of the language, then [–consonantal] to get rid of the non-glide consonants. At this point, just the glides remain.

There are good reasons to include only just as many features in a rule as are needed. Here is an example. In English, all voiced fricatives can be realized as voiceless when they precede a pause; that is to say, they are at the end of an utterance.[7]

save	/seɪv/	[seɪf], [seɪv]
bathe	/beɪð/	[beɪθ], [beɪð]
maze	/meɪz/	[meɪs], [meɪz]
rouge	/ɹuʒ/	[ɹuʃ], [ɹuʒ]

Since there are four voiced fricatives in English, we could, in principle, write four rules, which in features could be expressed as in table 4.6.

But this flies in the face of our earlier principle that phonological rules make reference to natural classes; certainly a more elegant approach would be to adopt a single rule:

Final Fricative Devoicing

$$\begin{bmatrix} -\text{sonorant} \\ +\text{continuant} \\ +\text{voice} \end{bmatrix} \rightarrow [-\text{voice}] \text{ / } \underline{\hspace{1em}}]_{\text{Utterance}} \quad \text{(optional)}$$

---

[7] You might imagine that this would create considerable confusion, but in fact a basic voiceless fricative can be distinguished in this context because it has shortened the preceding vowel: *safe* is [sĕɪf] while *save* is [seɪf] (or [seɪv]); and similarly with *mace* [mĕɪs] vs. *maze* [meɪs, meɪz]. For more on this, see §7.1.

In fact, there is more than just elegance at stake: unlike the four-rule approach, the single-rule approach makes predictions about new voiced fricatives that could, in principle, enter the language. For example, when I teach phonetics, I find that I am liable to devoice other final voiced fricatives if I am not careful; syllables like [az̜] (retroflex) or [að̼] (linguo-labial) can come out by mistake as [as̜] and [aθ̼]. I interpret this as a transfer effect (§3.2.3), with my native phonology applying to fricatives that are new to me, because they belong to the same natural class. The four-rule approach fails to predict this behavior.

Even where we can't test the generality of a rule in this way, it is widely felt that it is better science to adopt (tentatively) the more general hypothesis in the absence of evidence to the contrary, since it opens our eyes to the cases that ought to be tested.

4.9.3   *Simplifying rules through vacuous application*

Notice that Fricative Devoicing can be made even simpler, as follows:

Final Fricative Devoicing (shortened)
$$\begin{bmatrix} -\text{sonorant} \\ +\text{continuant} \end{bmatrix} \rightarrow [-\text{voice}] \, / \, \underline{} \,]_{\text{Utterance}}$$

This rule would apply *also to voiceless fricatives* and "devoice" them – making no change at all, a form of vacuous application (p. 80). Although it is hard to imagine circumstances in which it would matter, phonologists usually do write their rules in this way, if only to keep them simpler and easier to read.

4.9.4   *Features in the change of a rule*

A common error in writing rules is to neglect some of the features needed in a change. For instance, rules of Tapping (t → ɾ), which occur in a variety of languages, cannot in general be stated as simply adding the feature [+tap], since various other features (such as [sonorant] and [voice]) must change at the same time. It helps to examine the complete list of feature values of both input and output segments, comparing them carefully.

4.10   Feature Charts

In tables 4.7–10 I have aimed at a compromise between maintaining reasonable size and broad coverage. Many sounds absent from the charts can have their

resonante

Table 4.7 Consonants I: single place of articulation

Header groups — **Manner features**: consonantal, sonorant, continuant, delayed release, approximant, tap, trill, nasal · **Laryngeal features**: voice, spread gl, constr gl · **Place features**: labial, round, labiodental, coronal, anterior, distributed, strident, lateral, dorsal, high, low, front, back, tense

		consonantal	sonorant	continuant	delayed release	approximant	tap	trill	nasal	voice	spread gl	constr gl	labial	round	labiodental	coronal	anterior	distributed	strident	lateral	dorsal	high	low	front	back	tense
bilabial	p	+	−	−	−	−	−	−	−	−	−	−	+	−	−	−	0	0	0	−	−	0	0	0	0	0
	b	+	−	−	−	−	−	−	−	+	−	−	+	−	−	−	0	0	0	−	−	0	0	0	0	0
	ɸ	+	−	+	+	−	−	−	−	−	−	−	+	−	−	−	0	0	0	−	−	0	0	0	0	0
	β	+	−	+	+	−	−	−	−	+	−	−	+	−	−	−	0	0	0	−	−	0	0	0	0	0
	m	+	+	−	0	−	−	−	+	+	−	−	+	−	−	−	0	0	0	−	−	0	0	0	0	0
	ʙ	+	+	+	0	+	−	+	−	+	−	−	+	−	−	−	0	0	0	−	−	0	0	0	0	0
labiodental	pf	+	−	−	+	−	−	−	−	−	−	−	+	−	+	−	0	0	0	−	−	0	0	0	0	0
	f	+	−	+	+	−	−	−	−	−	−	−	+	−	+	−	0	0	0	−	−	0	0	0	0	0
	v	+	−	+	+	−	−	−	−	+	−	−	+	−	+	−	0	0	0	−	−	0	0	0	0	0
	ɱ	+	+	−	0	−	−	−	+	+	−	−	+	−	+	−	0	0	0	−	−	0	0	0	0	0
	ʋ	−	+	+	0	+	−	−	−	+	−	−	+	−	+	−	0	0	0	−	−	0	0	0	0	0
dental	t̪	+	−	−	−	−	−	−	−	−	−	−	−	−	−	+	+	+	−	−	−	0	0	0	0	0
	d̪	+	−	−	−	−	−	−	−	+	−	−	−	−	−	+	+	+	−	−	−	0	0	0	0	0
	θ	+	−	+	+	−	−	−	−	−	−	−	−	−	−	+	+	+	−	−	−	0	0	0	0	0
	ð	+	−	+	+	−	−	−	−	+	−	−	−	−	−	+	+	+	−	−	−	0	0	0	0	0
alveolar	t	+	−	−	−	−	−	−	−	−	−	−	−	−	−	+	+	−	−	−	−	0	0	0	0	0
	d	+	−	−	−	−	−	−	−	+	−	−	−	−	−	+	+	−	−	−	−	0	0	0	0	0
	t͡s	+	−	−	+	−	−	−	−	−	−	−	−	−	−	+	+	−	+	−	−	0	0	0	0	0
	d͡z	+	−	−	+	−	−	−	−	+	−	−	−	−	−	+	+	−	+	−	−	0	0	0	0	0
	t͡ɬ	+	−	−	+	−	−	−	−	−	−	−	−	−	−	+	+	−	−	+	−	0	0	0	0	0
	s	+	−	+	+	−	−	−	−	−	−	−	−	−	−	+	+	−	+	−	−	0	0	0	0	0
	z	+	−	+	+	−	−	−	−	+	−	−	−	−	−	+	+	−	+	−	−	0	0	0	0	0
	n	+	+	−	0	−	−	−	+	+	−	−	−	−	−	+	+	−	−	−	−	0	0	0	0	0
	l	+	+	+	0	+	−	−	−	+	−	−	−	−	−	+	+	−	−	+	−	0	0	0	0	0
	ɬ	+	−	+	+	−	−	−	−	−	−	−	−	−	−	+	+	−	−	+	−	0	0	0	0	0
	ɮ	+	−	+	+	−	−	−	−	+	−	−	−	−	−	+	+	−	−	+	−	0	0	0	0	0
	ɾ	+	+	+	0	+	+	−	−	+	−	−	−	−	−	+	+	−	−	−	−	0	0	0	0	0
	ɺ	+	+	+	0	+	+	−	−	+	−	−	−	−	−	+	+	−	−	+	−	0	0	0	0	0
	r	+	+	+	0	+	−	+	−	+	−	−	−	−	−	+	+	−	−	−	−	0	0	0	0	0
palato-alveolar	t͡ʃ	+	−	−	+	−	−	−	−	−	−	−	−	−	−	+	−	+	+	−	−	0	0	0	0	0
	d͡ʒ	+	−	−	+	−	−	−	−	+	−	−	−	−	−	+	−	+	+	−	−	0	0	0	0	0
	ʃ	+	−	+	+	−	−	−	−	−	−	−	−	−	−	+	−	+	+	−	−	0	0	0	0	0
	ʒ	+	−	+	+	−	−	−	−	+	−	−	−	−	−	+	−	+	+	−	−	0	0	0	0	0
	ɹ	−	+	+	0	+	−	−	−	+	−	−	−	−	−	+	−	+	−	−	−	0	0	0	0	0

Table 4.7 (*cont'd*)

		Manner features								Laryngeal features			Place features													
		consonantal	sonorant	continuant	delayed release	approximant	tap	trill	nasal	voice	spread gl	constr gl	labial	round	labiodental	coronal	anterior	distributed	strident	lateral	dorsal	high	low	front	back	tense
retroflex	ʈ	+	−	−	−	−	−	−	−	−	−	−	−	−	−	+	−	−	−	−	−	0	0	0	0	0
	ɖ	+	−	−	−	−	−	−	−	+	−	−	−	−	−	+	−	−	−	−	−	0	0	0	0	0
	ʂ	+	−	+	+	−	−	−	−	−	−	−	−	−	−	+	−	−	+	−	−	0	0	0	0	0
	ʐ	+	−	+	+	−	−	−	−	+	−	−	−	−	−	+	−	−	+	−	−	0	0	0	0	0
	ɳ	+	+	−	0	−	−	−	+	+	−	−	−	−	−	+	−	−	−	−	−	0	0	0	0	0
	ɭ	+	+	+	0	+	−	−	−	+	−	−	−	−	−	+	−	−	−	+	−	0	0	0	0	0
	ɽ	+	+	+	0	+	+	−	−	+	−	−	−	−	−	+	−	−	−	−	−	0	0	0	0	0
	ɻ	+	+	+	0	+	−	−	−	+	−	−	−	−	−	+	−	−	−	−	−	0	0	0	0	0
fronted velar	k̟	+	−	−	−	−	−	−	−	−	−	−	−	0	0	0	0	0	0	−	+	+	−	+	−	0
	g̟	+	−	−	−	−	−	−	−	+	−	−	−	0	0	0	0	0	0	−	+	+	−	+	−	0
	x̟	+	−	+	+	−	−	−	−	−	−	−	−	0	0	0	0	0	0	−	+	+	−	+	−	0
	j	−	+	+	0	+	−	−	−	+	−	−	−	0	0	0	0	0	0	−	+	+	−	+	−	+
velar	k	+	−	−	−	−	−	−	−	−	−	−	−	0	0	0	0	0	0	−	+	+	−	0	0	0
	g	+	−	−	−	−	−	−	−	+	−	−	−	0	0	0	0	0	0	−	+	+	−	0	0	0
	ŋ	+	+	−	0	−	−	−	+	+	−	−	−	0	0	0	0	0	0	−	+	+	−	0	0	0
	k͡x	+	−	−	+	−	−	−	−	−	−	−	−	0	0	0	0	0	0	−	+	+	−	0	0	0
	x	+	−	+	+	−	−	−	−	−	−	−	−	0	0	0	0	0	0	−	+	+	−	0	0	0
	ɣ	+	−	+	+	−	−	−	−	+	−	−	−	0	0	0	0	0	0	−	+	+	−	0	0	0
	ʟ	+	+	+	0	+	−	−	−	+	−	−	−	0	0	0	0	0	0	+	+	+	−	0	0	0
back velar	k̠	+	−	−	−	−	−	−	−	−	−	−	−	0	0	0	0	0	0	−	+	+	−	−	+	0
	g̠	+	−	−	−	−	−	−	−	+	−	−	−	0	0	0	0	0	0	−	+	+	−	−	+	0
	x̠	+	−	+	+	−	−	−	−	−	−	−	−	0	0	0	0	0	0	−	+	+	−	−	+	0
	ɣ̠	+	−	+	+	−	−	−	−	+	−	−	−	0	0	0	0	0	0	−	+	+	−	−	+	0
uvular	q	+	−	−	−	−	−	−	−	−	−	−	−	0	0	0	0	0	0	−	+	−	−	−	+	0
	ɢ	+	−	−	−	−	−	−	−	+	−	−	−	0	0	0	0	0	0	−	+	−	−	−	+	0
	χ	+	−	+	+	−	−	−	−	−	−	−	−	0	0	0	0	0	0	−	+	−	−	−	+	0
	ʁ	+	−	+	+	−	−	−	−	+	−	−	−	0	0	0	0	0	0	−	+	−	−	−	+	0
	ɴ	+	+	−	0	−	−	−	+	+	−	−	−	0	0	0	0	0	0	−	+	−	−	−	+	0
	ʀ	+	+	+	0	+	−	+	−	+	−	−	−	0	0	0	0	0	0	−	+	−	−	−	+	0
pharyn	ħ	+	−	+	+	−	−	−	−	−	−	−	−	0	0	0	0	0	0	−	+	−	+	−	+	0
	ʕ	+	−	+	−	−	−	−	−	+	−	−	−	0	0	0	0	0	0	−	+	−	+	−	+	0
glottal	ʔ	+	−	−	−	−	−	−	−	−	−	+	−	0	0	0	0	0	0	−	−	0	0	0	0	0
	h	−	−	+	+	−	−	−	−	−	+	−	−	0	0	0	0	0	0	−	−	0	0	0	0	0
	ɦ	−	−	+	+	−	−	−	−	+	+	−	−	0	0	0	0	0	0	−	−	0	0	0	0	0

Table 4.8   Consonants II: complex segments

		consonantal	sonorant	continuant	delayed release	approximant	tap	trill	nasal	voice	spread gl	constr gl	labial	round	labiodental	coronal	anterior	distributed	strident	lateral	dorsal	high	low	front	back	tense
		Manner features								Laryngeal features			Place features													
labial-back velar	w	−	+	+	0	+	−	−	−	+	−	−	+	+	−	−	0	0	0	−	+	+	−	−	+	+
labial-back velar	ʍ	−	−	+	+	−	−	−	−	−	+	−	+	+	−	−	0	0	0	−	+	+	−	−	+	+
labial-labial velar	k͡p	+	−	−	−	−	−	−	−	−	−	−	+	−	−	−	0	0	0	−	+	+	−	0	0	0
labial-labial velar	g͡b	+	−	−	−	−	−	−	−	+	−	−	+	−	−	−	0	0	0	−	+	+	−	0	0	0
labial-front velar	ɥ	−	+	+	0	+	−	−	−	+	−	−	+	+	−	−	0	0	0	−	+	+	−	+	−	+
alveolopalatal	t͡ɕ	+	−	−	+	−	−	−	−	−	−	−	−	−	−	+	+	+	+	−	+	+	−	+	−	0
alveolopalatal	d͡ʑ	+	−	−	+	−	−	−	−	+	−	−	−	−	−	+	+	+	+	−	+	+	−	+	−	0
alveolopalatal	ɕ	+	−	+	+	−	−	−	−	−	−	−	−	−	−	+	+	+	+	−	+	+	−	+	−	0
alveolopalatal	ʑ	+	−	+	+	−	−	−	−	+	−	−	−	−	−	+	+	+	+	−	+	+	−	+	−	0
palatal	c	+	−	−	−	−	−	−	−	−	−	−	−	−	−	+	−	+	−	−	+	+	−	+	−	0
palatal	ɟ	+	−	−	−	−	−	−	−	+	−	−	−	−	−	+	−	+	−	−	+	+	−	+	−	0
palatal	ç	+	−	+	+	−	−	−	−	−	−	−	−	−	−	+	−	+	−	−	+	+	−	+	−	0
palatal	ʝ	+	−	+	+	−	−	−	−	+	−	−	−	−	−	+	−	+	−	−	+	+	−	+	−	0
palatal	ɲ	+	+	−	0	−	−	−	+	+	−	−	−	−	−	+	−	+	−	−	+	+	−	+	−	0
palatal	ʎ	+	+	+	0	+	−	−	−	+	−	−	−	−	−	+	−	+	−	+	+	+	−	+	−	0

features deduced by looking up a similar sound and changing the most obvious features; or you can try using the FeaturePad software listed in the Preface to this book. A more complete feature chart can be downloaded as a spreadsheet from www.linguistics.ucla.edu/people/hayes/120a/index.htm#features.

4.10.1   Consonants I: single place of articulation

For consonants that have two places of articulation (complex segments), see the next section. All consonants are [−syllabic], and this feature is not included in the chart.

4.10.2   Consonants II: complex segments

These segments have two places of articulation. They are all [−syllabic], so this feature is not included in the chart.

4.10.3   Vowels

The basic features for vowels (shown in table 4.9 by the basic IPA symbols rather than the diacritics) are [round], [high], [low], [front], and [back]. [labial] is predictable, occurring only in [+round] vowels. All other features are invariant; unless overridden by a diacritic, all vowels are [+syllabic, −consonantal, +sonorant, +continuant, 0delayed release, +approximant, −tap, −trill, −nasal, +voice, −spread glottis, −constricted glottis, −labiodental, −coronal, 0anterior, 0distributed, 0strident].

Table 4.9   Vowels

	high tense						high lax			mid tense					
	i	y	ɨ	ʉ	ɯ	u	ɪ	ʏ	ʊ	e	ø	ɘ	ɵ	ɤ	o
[high]	+	+	+	+	+	+	+	+	+	−	−	−	−	−	−
[low]	−	−	−	−	−	−	−	−	−	−	−	−	−	−	−
[tense]	+	+	+	+	+	+	−	−	−	+	+	+	+	+	+
[front]	+	+	−	−	−	−	+	+	−	+	+	−	−	−	−
[back]	−	−	−	−	+	+	−	−	+	−	−	−	−	+	+
[round]	−	+	−	+	−	+	−	+	+	−	+	−	+	−	+

	mid lax						low				
	ɛ	œ	ə	ɞ	ʌ	ɔ	æ	Œ	a	ɑ	ɒ
[high]	−	−	−	−	−	−	−	−	−	−	−
[low]	−	−	−	−	−	−	+	+	+	+	+
[tense]	−	−	−	−	−	−	0	0	0	0	0
[front]	+	+	−	−	−	−	+	+	−	−	−
[back]	−	−	−	−	+	+	−	−	−	+	+
[round]	−	+	−	+	−	+	−	+	−	−	+

4.10.4 Diacritics

Table 4.10 Diacritics

Diacritic	As applied to	Phonetic definition	Designates these features
̩	a consonant	syllabic	[+syllabic]
̰	voiced sounds	creaky voice	[−spread glottis, +constricted glottis]
̈	voiced sounds	breathy voice	[+spread glottis, −constricted glottis]
̥	voiced sounds	voiceless	[−voice]
̠	alveolar	palato-alveolar	[−anterior, +distributed]
̪	alveolar	dental	[+anterior, +distributed]
̟	velar	fronted velar	[+front, −back]
̠	velar	backed velar	[−front, +back]
ˈ	before a syllable	stressed	[+stress]
ː	any segment	long	[+long]
ʰ	a consonant	aspirated	[+spread glottis, −constricted glottis]
ʲ	a consonant	palatalized	[+dorsal, +high, −low, +front, −back]
ʷ	a consonant	labialized	[+labial, +round]
ˠ	a consonant	velarized	[+dorsal, +high, −low, −front, +back]
ˤ	a consonant	pharyngealized	[+dorsal, −high, +low, −front, +back]
̃	a sonorant	nasalized	[+nasal]
˞	a vowel	rhotic	[+coronal, +anterior, +distributed, −strident]
ʼ	an obstruent	ejective	[−spread glottis, +constr glottis]

Exercises

Note: for software that may help in doing feature exercises, see discussion of "FeaturePad" in the Preface to this book.

1 Natural classes

Assume the vowel inventory shown in table 4.11 and the features [high], [low], [back], and [round] as defined in §4.10.3. For the sake of simplicity, ignore [front] and [tense].

Table 4.11 Vowel chart for exercise 1

Vowels:	Front		Back	
	Unrounded	Rounded	Unrounded	Rounded
high	i	y	ɯ	u
mid	e	ø	ɤ	o
low	æ	Œ	ɑ	ɒ

a. Find as many natural classes as you can that have four members. List them, and define the natural class using features.
b. Find as many natural classes as you can that have six members. List them, and define the natural class using features.
c. Find as many natural classes as you can that have eight members. List them, and define the natural class using features.
d. Find as many natural classes as you can that have five members.
e. Explain why [y, e] is not a natural class.

2 *Hypothetical language*

A hypothetical language has the phonemes shown in table 4.12.

Table 4.12 Consonant chart for exercise 2

Consonants	Labial	Alveolar	Palatoalveolar	Fronted Velar	Velar	Uvular	Pharyngeal	Glottal
Stops	p	t		k̟	k	q		ʔ
Affricates		t͡s						
Fricatives	f	s	ʃ	x̟	x	χ	ħ	h
Nasals	m	n	ɲ	ŋ̟	ŋ	N		
Liquids: Tap Lateral		ɾ l						
Glides	w			j				

Vowels: as in previous problem.

Write the following phonological rules of this language using the features presented in this chapter. In each case I have indicated the real-life rule on which I have modeled the imaginary rule. Some problems will arise in notation; read the footnotes for help with these.

1 [i, y, ɯ, u] become [e, ø, ɤ, o] before [q, ɴ].
(modeled on Eskimo languages)
2 [t] becomes [t͡s] before [i, y, ɯ, u]. (modeled on Japanese)
3 [i, e, æ] become [j] before a vowel. (modeled on Ilokano)
4 When a member of the group [s, t͡s, ʃ] is followed by a member of the group [s, ʃ], the resulting cluster is broken up by the insertion of [i]. Use features, not a phonetic symbol, for [i]. (modeled on English)
5 [n] assimilates in place to a following stop or affricate.
(modeled on Ilokano)
6 All consonants except /t, t͡s, s, n, ɾ, l, ʃ, n̪/ delete word-finally.
(modeled on Lardil (Australia))
7 [l] becomes [ɾ] if another [l] precedes it anywhere in the word.[8]
(modeled on Latin)
8 [ʔ] changes places with an immediately following glide.[9]
(modeled on Ilokano)
9 All unrounded vowels become [ɑ], and all rounded vowels become [ɒ], before [ħ]. (modeled on Maltese Arabic)
10 [e] and [ɤ] become [ø] and [o] if a [ø] or [o] occurs in the preceding syllable.[10] (modeled on Khalkha Mongolian)
11 [k, x, ŋ] become [k̟, x̟, ŋ̟] after [i, j]. (modeled on German)

Further reading

Representations in other areas of cognitive science: Fred Lerdahl and Ray Jackendoff, *A Generative Theory of Tonal Music* (1983, MIT Press); David Marr, *Vision*: *A Computational Investigation into the Human Representation and Processing of Visual Information* (1982, W. H. Freeman).

[8]   The notation to use here is a "variable," like X. X means "any number of segments of any type." So, for instance, the Sibilant Harmony rule from child speech mentioned above (p. 85) was something like:

s → ʃ / ___ X ʃ

[9]   Here is how to do the concept "changes places with." Put a number underneath each segment in the rule. Then, on the right side of the arrow, list everything in the input, using the numbers to show what has changed places. So, for instance, this rule:

V	t	p	V	→	V	p	t	V
1	2	3	4		1	3	2	4

means "reverse the order of /tp/ when surrounded by vowels."

[10]   You need a way to describe the notion "vowel of the preceding/next syllable." For the notation that is needed, look at the rule on p. 154.

Most of the features here are taken from Chomsky and Halle's *The Sound Pattern of English* (1968, Harper and Row). An earlier important work that developed the idea of acoustic features is Roman Jakobson, Gunnar Fant, and Morris Halle, *Preliminaries to Speech Analysis* (1963, MIT Press).

Eduard Sievers on sonority: *Grundzüge der Phonetik*, chapter 3, §2 (5th ed., 1901, Breitkopf und Härtel). The feature [approximant]: G. N. Clements, "The role of the sonority cycle in core syllabification," in John Kingston and Mary E. Beckman, eds., *Papers in Laboratory Phonology I: Between the Grammar and Physics of Speech* (1990, Cambridge University Press). See the same reference (including references cited therein) for the idea of analyzing the sonority hierarchy with a set of features, each defining a cutoff point. Palatals as [+coronal, +dorsal]: Patricia Keating (1988) "Palatals as complex segments: X-ray evidence," *UCLA Working Papers in Phonetics* 69: 77–91.

Phonetic evidence for zero feature values (with smooth transition between the values for neighboring segments): Patricia A. Keating (1988) "Underspecification in phonetics," *Phonology* 5: 275–92.

Syllabic stops and fricatives in Berber: François Dell and Mohamed Elmedlaoui, *Syllables in Tashlhiyt Berber and in Moroccan Arabic* (2002, Springer). Tonal restrictions as an argument for the feature [sonorant]: Matthew Gordon (2001) "A typology of contour tone restrictions," *Studies in Language* 25: 405–44. Kongo affrication: George N. Clements and Morris Halle, *A Problem Book in Phonology* (1983, MIT Press). Arabic assimilation of /l/ to coronals: Alan S. Kaye, "Arabic," in Bernard Comrie, ed., *The World's Major Languages* (1987, Oxford University Press). Vowel lowering and voicing assimilation in Maltese Arabic: Michael K. Brame, "On the abstractness of phonology: Maltese ʕ," in Michael K. Brame, ed., *Contributions to Generative Phonology*, pp. 22–61 (1972, University of Texas Press). Indonesian ŋ deletion: Hans Lapoliwa, *A Generative Approach to the Phonology of Bahasa Indonesia* (1981, Australian National University). Spanish nasal assimilation: James Harris, *Spanish Phonology* (1969, MIT Press).

5 Morphology

5.1 Basics of Morphology

Morphology is the branch of linguistics that studies the structure of words. There are many interactions, often complex, between phonological form and morphological structure, covered in chapters 6–8. The purpose of this chapter is to cover enough morphology to provide the groundwork for later material.

In studying the structure of words there are two basic goals: to isolate the component parts of words, and to determine the rules by which words are formed. For the first task, it is useful to make use of the term **morpheme**, defined as the smallest linguistic unit that bears a meaning. One can often break up a word into its component morphemes by peeling off one morpheme at a time, like this:

unidentifiability	= unidentifiable + ity	'the quality of being unidentifiable'
unidentifiable	= un + identifiable	'not identifiable'
identifiable	= identify + able	'able to be identified'
identify	= ident + ify	'to associate with an identity' (?)

Result: un + ident + ify + able + ity

The stages of decomposition seen above can all be justified by appealing to other words that have the same pattern, for example the division of *unidentifiability* into *unidentifiable + ity* is supported by parallel examples like *obscur-ity*, *pur-ity*, and *obes-ity*, and similarly for the other stages (*un-clear*, *un-willing*; *sell-able*, *visit-able*; *class-ify*, *person-ify*).

Morphemes are not the same as phonemes. A phoneme is the smallest linguistic unit that can *distinguish* meaning, whereas a morpheme is the smallest linguistic unit that *has* a meaning. This is illustrated in the following example:

	tacking	*tagging*
Allophones:	[tʰækĩŋ]	[tʰægĩŋ]
Phonemes:	/tækɪŋ/	/tægɪŋ/
Morphemes:	/tæk/ + /ɪŋ/	/tæg/ + /ɪŋ/

5.2   Formal Types of Morphemes

Most words can be analyzed as having a central morpheme, to which the remaining morphemes are attached. This central morpheme is called the **root**. For example, the root of the word *unidentifiability* is *ident-* and the root of *jumping* is *jump*. The root of the word *jump* is *jump* itself.

Roots can be classified as **bound** vs. **free**. A free root, like *jump*, can stand alone; bound roots, like *ident-*, are those which occur only in the presence of another morpheme. **Prefixes** and **suffixes** are also bound morphemes. When linguists refer to prefixes and suffixes as a class, they use the term **affix**. This term also covers a few additional morpheme types to be mentioned below.

When an affix is attached to something, that thing is called the **base** of attachment.[1] Thus, in *unidentifiable*, the base of attachment for the prefix *un-* is *identifiable*. In *jumping*, the base of attachment for the suffix *-ing* is *jump*. As can be seen, the base sometimes is a root, but sometimes it is a root to which affixes have already been attached. Using this term, we can define a prefix as an affix that precedes its base and a suffix as an affix that follows its base.

An **infix** is an affix that is inserted within its base. Consider the following data from Bontoc (Austronesian, Philippines):

[fikas]	'strong'	[f<u>um</u>ikas]	'he is becoming strong'
[kilad]	'red'	[k<u>um</u>ilad]	'it is becoming red'
[bato]	'stone'	[b<u>um</u>ato]	'it is becoming a stone'
[fusul]	'enemy'	[f<u>um</u>usul]	'he is becoming an enemy'

The affix that means "is becoming" is an infix, *-um-*, which is inserted immediately after the first consonant of the base.

Zero affixation or **conversion** is the use of a word in a different part of speech from its base form, without any affix or other change. Conversion of nouns to verbs in English is common (left column below); and conversion from verbs to nouns (right column) is also found.

to **telephone** one's mother	a close **look**
to **fan** oneself	a three-mile **run**
to **Kleenex** the floor	an expensive **co-pay**

For the first set of examples, most speakers would feel that the noun is somehow "basic" and that the verb is a derived form: we more often speak of *a telephone*,

---

[1]   Another term that is often used to mean "base" is **stem**. However, this term has a number of different usages, and one must be careful to check what an author means by it when it is used.

a fan, a Kleenex. In the right-side examples, the verb is felt to be the base form: *to look, to run, to co-pay*.

Reduplication is a morphological process in which all or part of the base is copied. For example, in Warlpiri, an aboriginal language of Australia, various plurals and semantically similar noun forms are created by making two copies of the base form:

[kuɻu]	'child'	[kuɻukuɻu]	'children'
[wuɭkumanu]	'old woman'	[wuɭkumanuwuɭkumanu]	'old women'
[jatuɭu]	'rock, boulder'	[jatuɭujatuɭu]	'rocky country'
[ʈupulpaɻi]	'prominent hillock'	[ʈupulpaɻiʈupulpaɻi]	'hilly country'

In Ilokano, noun plurals are formed by reduplicating the first *consonant + vowel + consonant* sequence of the base:

[kalˈdiŋ]	'goat'	[kalkalˈdiŋ]	'goats'
[ˈpusa]	'cat'	[pusˈpusa]	'cats'
[ˈjojo]	'yoyo'	[jojˈjojo]	'yoyos'

Reduplication phenomena are often classified into **total reduplication**, with full copy (Warlpiri), and **partial reduplication**, as in Ilokano. Partial reduplication is often considered as a kind of affix whose content varies depending on the segments that it is copied from.

Languages often use reduplication to express plural number or repetitive action. Such meanings are sometimes considered as iconic (meaning reflected in form); multiple things or events in the world are evoked by the multiple copies of phonological material.

5.3 Notation

It is useful, where the morphological structure of words is relevant to the discussion, to separate the morphemes with hyphens, thus:

un-ident-ify-abil-ity Warlpiri: [kuɻu-kuɻu]
tack-ing = [tʰæk-ɪŋ] Ilokano: [kal-kalˈdiŋ]
Bontoc: [f-um-ikas]

As shown in the forms on the right, this is done even when the "morpheme" is a reduplication process. For how to notate morphological conversion, see p. 110.

Hyphens can also be used to indicate the status of a morpheme when it is presented alone, as follows:

prefixes *un-*   bound roots *ident-*
suffixes [-ɪŋ]   free roots   *turnip* (no hyphen)
infixes   [-um-]

The hyphens indicate, as it were, the "gluing point" of the morpheme in question
– the place where another morpheme is required to occur.

5.4 Compounding

This is the formation of a word by combining two (or more) words. A compound
word thus will have more than one root, whereas ordinary words have just one.
Here are some compounds of English:

blackbird	*tongue-lashing*	*coal scuttle*
pancake	*fine-grained*	*pie plate*
intake	*secretary-treasurer*	*lap dog*
bedroom	*front-runner*	*bird bath*

The spelling system of English is inconsistent with regard to compounds; some
are spelled without a space between the component words, some with a hyphen,
and some with a space. It is important to realize that even if there is a space, the
result can still be a compound – syntactically it is treated as a single word.

It is possible to form a compound from two words one of which is itself a
compound. For example, we can combine the compound *law degree* with the
word *requirement* to get the complex compound *law degree requirement*. This
compound can in turn be combined with *changes* to get *law degree requirement
changes*, and so on. The following example suggests that the process is essentially
unlimited:

eggplant	'plant shaped like an egg'
eggplant plant	'factory for manufacturing eggplants'
eggplant plant plant	'factory for manufacturing factories for manufacturing eggplants'

. . .

5.5 Morphological Structure

Morphology creates structure, which can be depicted using the tree notation commonly used in syntax. For example, in compounding, two nouns can be combined
to form a larger noun:

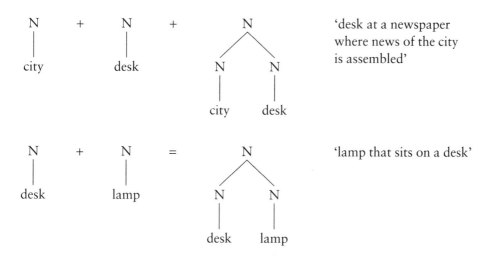

'desk at a newspaper where news of the city is assembled'

'lamp that sits on a desk'

When we repeat the process to create compounds inside compounds, we get more elaborate trees:

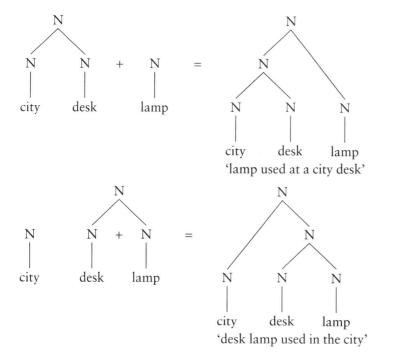

'lamp used at a city desk'

'desk lamp used in the city'

The different groupings of the same words can produce differences in meaning, which the tree structure makes clear. The same can be true with affixes, as we will see shortly.

5.6   The Functions of Morphology

Morphology can be said to perform two functions in language.

Derivation: Derivation expands the stock of words in the language by forming new words from old; thus it is often also called **word formation**. Here is an example of derivation. Given that *identify* is an existing word of English, a derivational process that is part of English morphology can generate a new word, namely *identifiable*. From this, a further derivational process can generate *unidentifiable*, and from this yet another process creates *unidentifiability*.

Compounding is sometimes considered as a form of derivation, though it is not always described in this way.[2]

Inflection: Inflectional morphology is grammatical morphology; the morphology that renders words *syntactically appropriate to their context*. Inflection can often be detected because the choice of inflectional category can be shown to be dependent on other words in the same sentence: thus, *She sings*, with the third person singular inflectional suffix, but *They sing*, without.

Here follows a brief list of some of the kinds of inflectional morphology. In English, we find:

- **Tense** on verbs (present *jump<u>s</u>*, past *jump<u>ed</u>*)
- **Aspect** on verbs (*sings* vs. *is sing<u>ing</u>*)
- **Number** on nouns (singular *cow*, plural *cow<u>s</u>*)
- a small amount of **person and number agreement** in verbs (*She sing<u>s</u>.* vs. *They sing.*)
- **Case** in pronouns (subjective *I* vs. objective *me*)

Many languages have much richer inflectional systems than English. The richness consists sometimes of having more inflectional categories, such as **gender** (masculine, feminine, neuter, others), **evidential status** (events known directly vs. by hearsay), and **degree of respect** (formal vs. informal, often applied to verbs). Another source of richness is having a greater number of possibilities within a category, for example **dual or trial number** in addition to singular and plural number; **remote vs. recent past** in a tense system; **inclusive vs. exclusive** forms of the first person plural, distinguishing whether or not the hearer is included; and **multiple cases** in nouns, each indicating the syntactic role of the noun in the sentence (nominative, accusative, dative, genitive, etc.).

---

[2]   The main rival theory is to suppose that compounding is part of the syntax; such approaches develop alternative explanations for the fact that compounds cannot be interrupted by modifiers, as in **desk bright lamp*. In the traditional view adopted here, this is because words are the units from which sentences are formed.

5.6.1 *Inflectional morphology as obligatory choice*

An important aspect of inflectional morphology is that it can involve **obligatory choices**. When in English one says "I bought the book," it specifically means "one book," not "any number of books." Likewise, "books" necessarily implies the plural. To avoid this obligatory choice, one must resort to awkward circum-locutions like "book or books." There are other languages (for example, Mandarin) that work quite differently. Thus, the following sentence:

wɔ³   mai³   ṣu¹
I   buy   book

is noncommittal about how many books are bought. (It is also noncommittal about when the buying takes place.) Thus an important aspect of the grammar of languages is the set of choices they force speakers to make when speaking; this is determined by their systems of inflectional morphology.

5.7   Writing Morphological Rules

5.7.1   *Rules for derivation*

Consider some words formed with the English suffix *-able*:

-able: *washable, lovable, thinkable, growable, doable*

We wish to write the rule (a **word formation rule**) that attaches *-able* to an existing word to form a new one. There are three kinds of information that must be included in such a rule. First, there is a change of form; the existing word is augmented by the suffix. This could be expressed with the formalism:

$X \rightarrow X + \text{əbəl}$

Second, there is a change of meaning: *Xable* means "able to be Xed." We will not formalize this, since we do not have an explicit way of representing meaning. Finally, there is often a change in **part of speech**: *-able* attaches to Verbs (e.g. *wash, love, think*, etc.) and forms Adjectives.

All three aspects of the rule can be expressed more compactly in the following abbreviated form:

-able **Affixation**
Verb + əbəl → Adjective
Verb + əbəl means "able to be Verbed"

The arrow should be read as follows: "form a new constituent, whose category is given on the right side of the arrow, and whose members are given on the left." We can express the newly formed constituent with a tree diagram, as shown in the following morphological derivation for *washable*:[3]

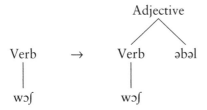

The structure created by the rule can be expressed on just a single line with brackets: [[wɔʃ]_{Verb} əbəl]_{Adj}. Less informatively, linguists sometimes write [[wɔʃ] əbəl], or if the structural information is obvious, even just wɔʃ-əbəl.

Here are some further word formation rules of English. To express the derivation of words in *-ity* (for example, *divinity, obscurity, obesity, insanity, sensitivity*), we could write the rule given below:

-ity Affixation
Adjective + ɪti → Noun
Adjective + ɪti means "the quality of being Adjective"

This creates structures like [[oʊ'bis]_{Adj} ɪti]_N, for *obesity*.

To handle words formed with the prefix *un-* (*unfair, unkind, unjust, unspoken, unattested, unidentifiable*), we could write this rule:

un- Affixation
ʌn + Adjective → Adjective
ʌn + Adjective means "not Adjective"

The rule creates structures like [ʌn [kaɪnd]_{Adj}]_{Adj}, for *unkind*.

Zero affixation (conversion) can be expressed like this:

Noun to Verb Conversion
Noun → Verb
"to do an action involving Noun"

Here, the only change is to create the higher-level constituent labeled as a Verb. An example of the structure created is [['tɛlə,foʊn]_N]_V, 'to telephone'.

---

[3] In some approaches to word structure, affixes are given their own node labels, so [-əbəl] would be dominated by the node Suffix. It's not clear to me that there are any linguistic rules that refer specifically to these nodes, so I will leave them out.

Infixation rules need a slightly more elaborate formalism. Recall that in Bontoc, verbs of becoming are formed by placing the infix *-um-* after the first consonant of an adjective or noun. We can formalize the rule as follows:

Bontoc Infixation
[C X]$_{A,N}$ → [[C um X]$_{A,N}$]$_{Verb}$
Meaning: "is becoming Adjective" or "is becoming a Noun"

X here is a variable; it means "any string of phonemes." Here is an example of an application of the rule. /fikas/ 'strong' is an adjective. We take /f/ to match up with C in the rule; and /ikas/ matches up with X. Placing /um/ between the two, we get *fumikas* 'he is becoming strong'. The line-up is shown explicitly below:

Rule: [C   X   ]$_{A,N}$ →   [[C   um   X   ]$_{A,N}$]$_{Verb}$

Form: [f   ikas   ]$_A$ →   [[f   um   ikas   ]$_A$]$_{Verb}$

Words with multiple morphemes can be derived by applying multiple word formation rules, one after the other. For example, we can derive the long word *unmindfulness* by applying the following rules in succession:

mind + ful → mindful   (Noun + fəl → Adjective)
un + mindful → unmindful   (ʌn + Adjective → Adjective)
unmindful + ness → unmindfulness   (Adjective + nəs → Noun)

The resulting complex word is shown in tree notation below:

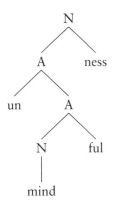

In bracket notation, this would be: [un [[[mind]$_N$ ful]$_A$]$_A$ ness]$_N$, or in phonetic notation [ʌn [[[maɪnd]$_N$ fəl]$_A$]$_A$ nəs]$_N$.

An important point that arises in connection with longer derivations like this is that they clarify the concept of "infix": just because a morpheme is placed in the middle of a word does not mean it is necessarily an infix. For example, linguists would say that in *unmindfulness*, *-ful* is not an infix, but a suffix. The reasoning is based on how the word is put together. At the stage where *-ful* is added, it is attached as a suffix to *mind*, and it shows up in the middle of the word because later on, *-ness* gets added to the result. In contrast, in Bontoc *f-um-ikas*, we do have an infix, because at the stage where *-um-* is added, it really is placed in the middle of the word.

Here is a word formation rule for noun compounding:

Noun Compounding
X + Noun → Noun (where X is a word)
Meaning: "a Noun that has something to do with X"

For example, if we took X to be *tiger* and Noun to be *bird*, we would derive *tigerbird*. Tigerbirds don't exist, but nevertheless, speakers of English who hear the word *tigerbird* already know two things: that a tigerbird is a kind of bird (and not a kind of tiger), and that it has something to do with tigers (perhaps it is striped like a tiger, or it likes to roost on top of sleeping tigers, or it fights like a tiger, etc.).

5.7.2   *Rules for inflection*

For inflection, we assume that the grammar of the language provides words with **morphological features**, things like [+plural], [+3rd person], [−past], and so on. The rules of inflectional morphology then refer to these features to determine what material to add; thus these rules "realize" the features in audible form. For example, we can write (as an approximation) the inflectional rule for forming English past tenses as follows:

Past Tense Formation

$$X \rightarrow Xd \quad \text{when} \quad \begin{bmatrix} \text{Verb} \\ \text{+past} \end{bmatrix}$$

This rule derives, among many other forms, *warned* [wɔɹnd] and *rowed* [ɹoʊd].

The following is an inflectional rule for plurals:

Plural Formation

$$X \rightarrow Xz \quad \text{when} \quad \begin{bmatrix} \text{Noun} \\ \text{+plural} \end{bmatrix}$$

This is not the whole story for these endings, which take on other forms as well ([t] in *jumped*, [əd] in *voted*; and [s] in *cats*, [əz] in *faces*) – more on this in the next chapter.

5.7.3   *The ordering of inflection and derivation*

It is at least a strong cross-linguistic tendency – perhaps a universal – that derivational rules of morphology apply before inflectional rules. Thus, for instance, in English it is possible to have words like *nullifies*, which are derived as follows:

$[n\Lambda l]_A$ root: 'null'

-ify **Attachment** (derivation):
$[[n\Lambda l]_A ɪfaɪ]_V$ Adjective + ɪfaɪ → Verb

3rd Singular Attachment (inflection):

$[[n\Lambda l]_A ɪfaɪ+z]_V$ $X \rightarrow Xz$ when $\begin{bmatrix} \text{Verb} \\ +\text{3rd person} \\ +\text{singular} \\ +\text{present} \end{bmatrix}$

The opposite rule ordering would have derived *$[n\Lambda lzɪfaɪ]$, so that the inflectional suffix would appear "inside" the derivational suffix. Cases of this sort are unusual, though there are cases (e.g. *systems analyst*) whose analysis is controversial.

5.8   Productivity

Rules of derivational morphology commonly differ in their **productivity**, which may be defined as their capacity to apply in novel circumstances. Consider, as an example, the pair of English word formation rules below. Both form adjectives from nouns.

-ical **Affixation**
N + ɪkəl → Adj
N + ɪkəl means "having to do with a N"

-like **Affixation**
N + laɪk → Adj
N + laɪk means "resembling a N"

alphabet	*alphabetical*	*mollusk*	*mollusklike*
farce	*farcical*	*appendage*	*appendagelike*
quiz	*quizzical*	*alphabet*	*alphabetlike*
paradox	*paradoxical*	*koala*	*koalalike*

The suffix *-ical* is not productive in English. We see this when we attempt to attach it to nouns to form new words, and the results sound peculiar: ??*attitudical*, ??*porchical*, ??*breezical*, ??*Rolodexical*, ??*violinical*. Evidently, words like *alphabetical*, given above, are memorized entities. We accept them as words because we have heard them before and are familiar with them; the rule of *-ical* Affixation does not by itself license the existence of a word.

In contrast, the rule for -*like* applies open-endedly; we accept a novel form in -*like* even if we have never heard it before. The following examples were gathered with a search engine:[4]

- *Walking through the retrospective exhibition of Lee Bontecou . . . we encounter some **mollusklike** shapes on pedestals . . .*
- *. . . bluntly triangular, up to 0.4 mm, alternating with well-defined, **appendagelike** plicae . . .*
- *Martin-Gilly makes interesting use of graphic, **alphabetlike** markings on 24 small canvases . . .*
- *. . . small, **koalalike** toys billed as the "always-with-You Otaru" . . .*

None of these forms with -*like* are listed in the comprehensive *Oxford English Dictionary*; nor, in a sense, should they be. They are nonce formations, created on the spot by the authors of these passages using a productive word formation rule.

This constitutes the kind of evidence used to show that -*like* involves a productive rule of word formation, and -*ical* does not. Similar tests can be used to demonstrate the productivity – or perhaps better, the *degree* of productivity – of other word formation rules.

In the description of a language's morphological system, there is good reason to include even the non-productive rules. Even though they cannot be used to derive novel words, they do characterize a systematic relationship among existing words, one which is apprehended by speakers of the language. Thus, even though -*ical* is not productive, speakers of English plainly recognize *alphabetical* as an adjective based on *alphabet*. In cases where there is no systematic pattern in the language, no relationship is perceived: for example, no English speaker feels that *hear* is a prefixed form of *ear*, because there is no justification anywhere else in English for the morphological rule that would be needed to derive it (something like *h*- + Noun → Verb, meaning 'use bodily organ for its purpose').

Productivity is an important phenomenon to keep in mind when eliciting data from native speakers: typically consultants will be reluctant to give a linguist novel forms based on a non-productive morphological process. To the extent that they are able to provide such forms, the result may well be a form of linguistic play and thus unreliable.

Productivity is also an important research topic in morphology. A particularly challenging research question is what *causes* differences in productivity. No one tells young children which of the morphological processes they encounter are productive and which are not; rather, there must be something in the data pattern of the language from which the child is able to determine productivity.

---

[4] To be fair, my search also turned up *attitudical* and *breezical*, from the previous list. Both occurred in contexts indicating that the user was engaged in a form of word play.

5.9   Morphological Analysis

When encountering an unfamiliar language, one of the first tasks a linguist will carry out is to develop an analysis of the morphology. This involves gathering data (usually in a phonemic notation), determining what morphemes are present, and writing the rules that form the words from the morphemes.

In all cases, the basic process of analysis consists of examining morphologically related words and determining which phoneme sequences remain the same whenever an element of meaning remains the same. Two kinds of data are particularly useful:

- A collection of words that are all morphologically derived (or appear to be derived) from the same root. Such a collection is often called a **paradigm**, especially when the morphological processes involved are inflectional rather than derivational.
- A collection of words that are all derived by the same morphological process, for example, a whole sequence of past tense verbs, or a whole sequence of adjectives in *-able*.

The example we will do here involves an inflectional paradigm from Swahili, the most widely spoken language of East Africa.

Swahili verbs involve a much richer morphological system than English. In Swahili, it is possible to indicate the number and person of both the subject and the object of a verb by attaching the appropriate affix in the right place. Here are the data we will use:

Swahili Verbs

1	atanipenda	'he will like me'	10	atanipiga	'he will beat me'
2	atakupenda	'he will like you'	11	atakupiga	'he will beat you'
3	atampenda	'he will like him'	12	atampiga	'he will beat him'
4	atatupenda	'he will like us'	13	ananipiga	'he is beating me'
5	atawapenda	'he will like them'	14	anakupiga	'he is beating you'
6	nitakupenda	'I will like you'	15	anampiga	'he is beating him'
7	nitampenda	'I will like him'	16	amenipiga	'he has beaten me'
8	utanipenda	'you will like me'	17	amekupiga	'he has beaten you'
9	utampenda	'you will like him'	18	amempiga	'he has beaten him'

Forms 1–9 are all forms of the verb 'like'. They all end in the sequence *penda*, and there is no *longer* sequence with which they all end. If seems safe to conclude that the root meaning 'like' is in fact *penda*. The same considerations suggest that the root meaning 'beat' is *piga*.

Rapid progress can be made by isolating minimal pairs, which exist for morphology as well as phonology. For morphology, minimal pairs are words that differ in just one morpheme, rather than in just one phoneme. For example, #1 and #2 in the data (*atanipenda* 'he will like me' and *atakupenda* 'he will like you') form a minimal pair for the morphemes *ni-* 'me-object' and *ku-* 'you-object', as shown below.

```
a    t    a    n    i    p    e    n    d    a
a    t    a    k    u    p    e    n    d    a
```

#2 (*atakupenda* 'he will like you') and #6 (*nitakupenda* 'I will like you') are a morphological minimal pair for *a-* 'he-subject' and *ni-* 'I-subject'. #11 (*atakupiga* 'he will beat you') and #14 (*anakupiga* 'he is beating you') are a morphological minimal pair for the tense morphemes *ta-* 'future' and *na-* 'present'. Lastly, #1 (*atanipenda* 'he will like me') and #10 (*atanipiga* 'he will beat me') are a minimal pair for the stems *penda* 'like' and *piga* 'beat'.

With patience, one can gradually unravel the whole morphology. One will ultimately find that the Swahili verbs in the data are constructed according to the following formula:

SUBJECT PREFIX	–	TENSE PREFIX	–	OBJECT PREFIX	–	ROOT
(a-, ni-, u-)		(ta-, na-, me-)		(ni-, ku-, m-, tu-, wa-)		(penda, piga)

The last step is to express the analysis with a fully explicit set of rules. The positioning of the various morphemes can be accounted for if we require that the rules apply *in a particular order*. Since all the affixes here are prefixes, the ordering of the rules will be the opposite of the left-to-right order in which the morphemes appear in a verb. Here are the rules given in the correct order.

Object Marking

X → OP + X   in [+Verb]

where OP (Object Prefix) is selected on the basis of the object features:

ni-   [+me-object]
ku-   [+you-object]
m-   [+him-object]
tu-   [+us-object]
wa-   [+them-object]

Tense Marking

X → Tense + X in [+Verb]

where Tense is selected on the basis of the tense features:

ta-   [+future]
na-   [+present]
me-   [+past]

Subject Marking

X → SP + X   in [+Verb]

where SP (Subject Prefix) is selected on the basis of the subject features:

a-   [+he-subject]
ni-   [+I-subject]
u-   [+you-subject]

Notice that the subject prefixes sometimes, but not always, take the same form as the corresponding object prefixes.

Here is a morphological derivation for the first form of the data, *atanipenda* 'he will like me', showing the rules applying in order.

penda   root
nipenda   Object Marking
tanipenda   Tense Marking
atanipenda   Subject Marking
atanipenda   output of morphology

5.9.1   *Morphological analysis in elicitation*

The discussion above makes an assumption: that the English glosses[5] accurately reflect the structure of the target language. This is usually true in problem sets. However, when the data are gathered from a bilingual native speaker consultant, the glosses volunteered by the speaker may well be only the roughest guide to the truth. The problem is that inflectional morphemes often have highly abstract meanings, meanings that can be gotten at only through extended examination of data and analysis. Often it is more helpful to ask a consultant for instances in which it is appropriate to use a particular morpheme, rather than asking the consultant to give the meaning herself.

Exercises

---

1   *Derivation*

Consulting the rules in §5.7.1, explain why the following is not a possible tree for the word *unmindfulness*.

---

[5] A *gloss* is a linguist's translation of a smallish linguistic unit, usually a word or a morpheme. Often, a linguist will present a sentence from a language including both glosses (one for each morpheme) and an idiomatic translation of the whole sentence.

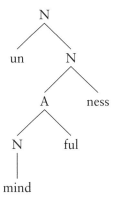

2   Inflection in Japanese verbs

a.   List all eight stems in the data in table 5.1.
b.   Write inflectional rules, following the rule format given in §5.7, that can derive all of the forms of each stem. You may assume the following inflectional features:

Formality: [+/–formal]
Affirmative/negative: [+/–affirmative]
Voice: [+/–passive]
Valence: [+/–causative]

Give your rules descriptive names so you can refer to them in the derivation.
c.   Specify the order in which your inflectional rules must apply.
d.   Provide derivations for the following forms: *ageru*, *agemasen*, *agesaserareru*, *agesaseraremasen*. For each, list the stem with its associated inflectional features and show your rules applying in order.

Table 5.1

	Affirmative informal	Affirmative formal	Negative informal	Negative formal
'*rise*'	ageru	agemasu	agenai	agemasen
'*exit*'	deru	demasu	denai	demasen
'*insert*'	ireru	iremasu	irenai	iremasen
'*exist*'	iru	imasu	inai	imasen
'*change*'	kaeru	kaemasu	kaenai	kaemasen
'*borrow*'	kariru	karimasu	karinai	karimasen
'*see*'	miru	mimasu	minai	mimasen
'*get up*'	okiru	okimasu	okinai	okimasen
	Passive affirmative informal	Passive affirmative formal	Passive negative informal	Passive negative formal
'*rise*'	agerareru	ageraremasu	agerarenai	ageraremasen
'*exit*'	derareru	deraremasu	derarenai	deraremasen
'*insert*'	irerareru	ireraremasu	irerarenai	ireraremasen
'*exist*'	irareru	iraremasu	irarenai	iraremasen
'*change*'	kaerareru	kaeraremasu	kaerarenai	kaeraremasen
'*borrow*'	karirareru	kariraremasu	karirarenai	kariraremasen
'*see*'	mirareru	miraremasu	mirarenai	miraremasen
'*get up*'	okirareru	okiraremasu	okirarenai	okiraremasen
	Causative affirmative informal	Causative affirmative formal	Causative negative informal	Causative negative formal
'*rise*'	agesaseru	agesasemasu	agesasenai	agesasemasen
'*exit*'	desaseru	desasemasu	desasenai	desasemasen
'*insert*'	iresaseru	iresasemasu	iresasenai	iresasemasen
'*exist*'	isaseru	isasemasu	isasenai	isasemasen
'*change*'	kaesaseru	kaesasemasu	kaesasenai	kaesasemasen
'*borrow*'	karisaseru	karisasemasu	karisasenai	karisasemasen
'*see*'	misaseru	misasemasu	misasenai	misasemasen
'*get up*'	okisaseru	okisasemasu	okisasenai	okisasemasen
	Causative passive affirmative informal	Causative passive affirmative formal	Causative passive negative informal	Causative passive negative formal
'*rise*'	agesaserareru	agesaseraremasu	agesaserarenai	agesaseraremasen
'*exit*'	desaserareru	desaseraremasu	desaserarenai	desaseraremasen
'*insert*'	iresaserareru	iresaseraremasu	iresaserarenai	iresaseraremasen
'*exist*'	isaserareru	isaseraremasu	isaserarenai	isaseraremasen
'*change*'	kaesaserareru	kaesaseraremasu	kaesaserarenai	kaesaseraremasen
'*borrow*'	karisaserareru	karisaseraremasu	karisaserarenai	karisaseraremasen
'*see*'	misaserareru	misaseraremasu	misaserarenai	misaseraremasen
'*get up*'	okisaserareru	okisaseraremasu	okisaserarenai	okisaseraremasen

Further reading

For more on morphology in general, I have found Andrew Spencer's text *Morphological Theory* (1991, Blackwell) a useful source. A very old – but still very usable – book of problem sets for morphology is Eugene Nida, *Morphology: The Descriptive Analysis of Words* (1949, University of Michigan).

The formal mechanisms used here for the expression of inflectional rules are taken from work by Stephen R. Anderson: his "Where's Morphology?" (1981), *Linguistic Inquiry*, 13: 571–612; and his 1992 book *A-Morphous Morphology* (Cambridge University Press). Anderson has also produced cross-linguistic surveys of the inflectional and derivational phenomena of the world's languages; see his chapter contributions to Tim Shopen, ed. *Language Typology and Syntactic Fieldwork* (1985, Cambridge University Press).

An influential theoretical approach to derivational morphology is laid out in Paul Kiparsky "Lexical morphology and phonology," in I.-S. Yang, ed., *Linguistics in the Morning Calm* (1982, Hanshin), pp. 3–91. The *tigerbird* example in §5.7.1 is taken from this work.[6]

The example of morphological non-relatedness of *ear* and *hear* is taken from Paul Kiparsky "Remarks on analogical change," in John M. Anderson and Charles Jones, eds., *Historical Linguistics II* (1976, North-Holland), pp. 257–76.

One approach to the problem of explaining morphological productivity is presented in Jen Hay and Harald Baayen (2003) "Phonotactics, parsing and productivity," *Italian Journal of Linguistics* 1: 99–130 (www.ling.canterbury.ac. nz/jen/documents/hayandbaayen.pdf).

Bontoc infixation: Carl Wilhelm Seidenadel, *The First Grammar of the Language Spoken by the Bontoc Igorot* (1909, Open Court Publishing). The data are cited in a form lightly polished by Henry A. Gleason in his *Workbook in Descriptive Linguistics* (1955, Holt, Rinehart and Winston); he removed some inflectional endings and retranscribed Seidenadel's data phonemically. Warlpiri reduplication: David Nash (1980), *Topics in Warlpiri Grammar*, MIT dissertation, available from https://dspace.mit.edu. Ilokano reduplication: Bruce Hayes and May Abad (1989) "Reduplication and syllabification in Ilokano," *Lingua* 77: 331–74; www.linguistics.ucla.edu/people/hayes/Papers/HayesAndAbad1989.pdf. Swahili paradigms: I reprint data from a famous problem set from the book by Gleason cited above, now used in linguistics classrooms around the world. Gleason obtained his data from an earlier edition of Edward Steere's *Swahili Exercises* (1943).

---

[6] Kiparsky made up his example before there were search engines. By using one, I have since learned that in Guyana there is a (striped) bird species that the locals refer to as the tigerbird, and that various national air forces maintain fighter jets that they call tigerbirds. These new observations are quite consistent with the rule on p. 112, adapted from Kiparsky's work.

6 Phonological Alternation I

6.1 Alternation as a Consequence of Phonology–Morphology Interaction

A morpheme is said to **alternate** when it appears in different forms in different contexts. The analysis of alternations is one of the central areas of phonology.

Alternation often arises because of the way that phonology interacts with morphology. To show how this happens, it will be useful first to present some background material on the morphology and phonology of English.

6.1.1 Alternations in English /t/-final stems

Here are some phonological rules of English, some repeated from earlier, all of which apply to the phoneme /t/ and give rise to alternation.

The rule of Preglottalization derives the preglottalized allophones of /p, t, k/ when they occur in word-final position:

Preglottalization

$$\begin{bmatrix} -\text{continuant} \\ -\text{voice} \end{bmatrix} \rightarrow [\text{+constricted glottis}] / \underline{\quad}]_{\text{word}}$$

A voiceless stop is realized as preglottalized when in final position.

By "preglottalized," I mean that the vocal cords slam shut just before the stop is made. This is represented in the feature system with the feature [+constricted glottis], and transcribed here with a preceding superscript glottal stop. Here are representative data:

cap	/kæp/	[kæˀp]
hat	/hæt/	[hæˀt]
hack	/hæk/	[hæˀk]

Preglottalization is optional, but we will ignore this fact here, with no harm to the point being made.

The rule of Tapping (p. 32) realizes the /t/ phoneme as a tap [ɾ] just in case it occurs between two syllabic sounds of which the second is stressless. Using the features of chapter 4, it appears as follows:

Tapping[1]

$$\text{/t/} \rightarrow [\text{ɾ}] \text{ / [−consonantal]} \underline{\quad} \begin{bmatrix} \text{+syllabic} \\ \text{−stress} \end{bmatrix}$$

Tapping is also optional, at least for some speakers.

English also has an allophonic rule of Aspiration, which applies obligatorily to the voiceless stops /p, t, tʃ, k/, rendering them [+spread glottis]. A rough statement of the rule is given below.

Aspiration

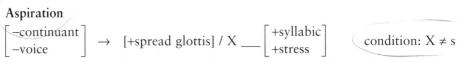

$$\begin{bmatrix} \text{−continuant} \\ \text{−voice} \end{bmatrix} \rightarrow [\text{+spread glottis}] \text{ / X} \underline{\quad} \begin{bmatrix} \text{+syllabic} \\ \text{+stress} \end{bmatrix} \qquad \text{condition: X} \neq \text{s}$$

Voiceless stops are aspirated when they precede a stressed vowel and are not preceded by /s/.

Data showing the effects of this rule for the phoneme /t/ are given below.

Tom	/tɑm/	[ˈtʰɑm]	vs.	*Atlas*	/ætləs/	[ˈætləs]
tell	/tɛl/	[ˈtʰɛl]		*get*	/gɛt/	[ˈgɛt]
obtain	/əbteɪn/	[əbˈtʰeɪn]		*actor*	/ˈæktɚ/	[ˈæktɚ]
attest	/ətɛst/	[əˈtʰɛst]		*terrific*	/tərɪfɪk/	[təˈɹɪfɪk]
retain	/riteɪn/	[ɹiˈtʰeɪn]		*stun*	/stʌn/	[ˈstʌn]

The examples in the left column above illustrate a /t/ that precedes a stressed vowel and thus is aspirated. No aspiration occurs in *Atlas*, *get*, *actor*, and *terrific*[2] because the /t/ does not precede a stressed vowel. *Stun* shows the inhibiting effect of /s/ on aspiration.

We will be observing the relationship of these three phonological rules with two rules of derivational morphology, given below.

---

[1] The left-side environment is given as [−consonantal], rather than [+syllabic], since Tapping may occur following the [−consonantal] sound /ɹ/ in words like *barter* [ˈbɑɹɾɚ]. The assumption that /ɹ/ is [−consonantal] (p. 95) is phonetically plausible, given that this sound is made with a weak glide-like constriction in the vocal tract.

[2] Words like *terrific* actually have an intermediate degree of aspiration, more than *stop* but less than *Tom*. This complication will be ignored here.

-able **Affixation** (from p. 109)
Verb + əbəl → Adjective
Meaning: "able to be Verbed"

-ation **Affixation**
Verb + 'eɪʃən → Noun
Meaning: "the process or product of Verbing"

The reason morphological rules are of phonological interest is that they can rearrange the phonological environments of the phonemes. The segments of prefixes and suffixes can themselves be part of the environment of a phonological process. Consider the following data:

note	*notable*	*notation*
/noʊt/	/noʊtəbəl/	/noʊteɪʃən/
['noʊʔt]	['noʊɾəbəl]	[noʊ'tʰeɪʃən]

quote	*quotable*	*quotation*
/kwoʊt/	/kwoʊtəbəl/	/kwoʊteɪʃən/
['kwoʊʔt]	['kwoʊɾəbəl]	[kwoʊ'tʰeɪʃən]

Let us consider the particular allophone of /t/ that emerges in these forms. In *note* and *quote* occurring by themselves, the /t/ phoneme is at the end of a word. It is thus eligible for Preglottalization, and emerges as the allophone [ʔt]. In *notable* and *quotable*, the suffix /-əbəl/ has added the stressless vowel that is crucial for Tapping, so the /t/ shows up as [ɾ]. Finally, in *notation* and *quotation*, the suffix we've added begins with a stressed syllable (which, in English phonology, has the effect of weakening or eliminating the stress of the base, an effect we will not formalize here). This puts the /t/ phoneme in pre-stress position so that Aspiration can apply, and we get [tʰ].

In other words, once the morphology has arranged the appropriate suffixes, the phonological form of words is accommodated to the new environments that are created. The selection of the proper allophone of /t/ is not established for the stems /noʊt/ and /kwoʊt/ once and for all, but rather is determined on the basis of the environment in which the stem-final /t/ appears.

To illustrate the concept of alternation, we take the forms just given, and "strip away" the suffixes, giving:

note:
without affix: ['noʊʔt]
['noʊɾəbəl], removing [-əbəl], yields: ['noʊɾ]
[noʊ'tʰeɪʃən], removing [-'eɪʃən], yields: [noʊtʰ]

quote:
without affix: ['kwoʊʔt]
['kwoʊɾəbəl], removing [-əbəl], yields: ['kwoʊɾ]
[kwoʊ'tʰeɪʃən], removing [-'eɪʃən], yields: [kwoʊtʰ]

Referring back to the definition of alternation given at the start of this chapter, we see that the morphemes *note* and *quote* do indeed alternate: depending on the context (which the morphology creates for them), they take on different forms.

When a morpheme alternates, the different forms it takes on are called **allomorphs**. Thus ['nouʔt], ['nouɾ], and [noutʰ] are described as allomorphs of the morpheme /noʊt/. Alternating allomorphs are often connected with a tilde: "['nouʔt] ~ ['nouɾ] ~ [noutʰ]" can be read "['nouʔt] alternating with ['nouɾ] alternating with [noutʰ]."

This is a common pattern in languages: alternation results because the phonological rules enforce their demands on the *output* of the morphology. The norm, in fact, is that a morpheme will not have a constant pronunciation. The morphology of a language frequently places morphemes in different phonological contexts, and when this happens, the outcome that is demanded by the phonological rules is often different. The differences that result are sometimes subtle, sometimes drastic.

6.1.2 Components and multi-component derivations

It is commonly proposed in linguistic theory that the rules of the grammar are arranged into **components**; that is to say, into separate systems of rules, each with its own function and rule types. In the present case, we assume (a) a **lexicon**, in which morphemes are stored; (b) a **morphological component**, which assembles words by processes of derivation and inflection; and (c) a **phonological** component, which assigns a phonetic interpretation to the sequences of phonemes emerging from the morphology. In a complete derivation, we show the effects of the two rule components: first the morphology assembles words starting from the lexical entries of their morphemes, then the phonology makes changes in the sounds of the resulting words.

Table 6.1 shows multi-component derivations for *quote*, *quotable*, and *quotation*, discussed in the previous section. It can be seen that the "underlying form" of the phonology is not the deepest representation of a linguistic form. Rather, it represents the deepest level of representation within the phonological component.

The derivation just given, while reasonably explicit, leaves aside some potentially important issues; particularly whether morphological brackets (as in [['kwoʊ't]ᵥeɪʃən]ₙ) are erased prior to the phonology (see chapter 10); and what is the mechanism for the loss of stress on the stem in *quotation*. We will not address these questions here; the crucial point of the derivation is that it illustrates in fairly explicit terms how alternation emerges from the interaction of components.

6.1.3 Alternation and analysis

For linguists working on the phonology of a language, the existence of alternations can be very helpful, because it gives them better control over their material. Should a phonologist wonder, "What would happen to a /p/ if it occurred before a stressless vowel?", then an easy answer is at hand, provided that there are stems

Table 6.1 Derivations for *quote*, *quotable*, and *quotation*

quote	quotable	quotation	
		Lexicon	
[ˈkwoʊt]ᵥ	[ˈkwoʊt]ᵥ	[ˈkwoʊt]ᵥ	Lexical entry for *quote*
		Morphological component	
—	[[ˈkwoʊt]ᵥəbəl]ₐ	—	*-able* Affixation
—	—	[[ˈkwoʊˈt]ᵥeɪʃən]ɴ	*-ation* Affixation
[ˈkwoʊt]ᵥ	[[ˈkwoʊt]ᵥəbəl]ₐ	[[ˈkwoʊˈt]ᵥeɪʃən]ɴ	output of morphological component
		Phonological component	
/ˈkwout/	/ˈkwoʊtəbəl/	/kwoʊˈteɪʃən/	underlying forms
ˀt	—	—	Preglottalization
—	ɾ	—	Tapping
—	—	tʰ	Aspiration
[ˈkwoʊˀt]	[ˈkwoʊɾəbəl]	[ˈkwoʊˈtʰeɪʃən]	surface forms

ending in /p/ and suffixes (particularly productive ones) that begin with stressless vowels. One need only find a relevant stem, attach the suffix to it, and query a native speaker about the result – in effect, performing a miniature experiment.

This kind of experimentation can be done quite systematically. A phonologist doing fieldwork may keep at hand a representative collection of stems including at least one stem ending in each of the phonemes of the language. Then, as new suffixes are discovered, the phonologist can try attaching each suffix to each stem in the list, as a method of systematically searching for alternations. Alternatively, as each new stem is discovered, its paradigm can be collected, adding (where feasible) all possible affixes to learn the allomorphs of the stem and their distribution.

6.1.4 *Rhythmic Lengthening in Choctaw*

Alternation usually affects segments at the edges of morphemes, since these are most likely to be placed in novel phonologically-relevant environments by affixation. But sometimes alternation can affect segments throughout the stem. An example is the phenomenon of Rhythmic Lengthening in Choctaw, a Native American language spoken mostly in Oklahoma.

The stem for "see" in Choctaw is /pisa/, and by itself it is pronounced as such. However, if a suffix consisting of a single syllable is added to /pisa/, the stem is pronounced differently, with a lengthened vowel:

[pisaː-li]   'see-1st person' = 'I see'
[pisaː-tʃi]   'see-causative' = 'cause to see'

In other words, the morpheme *pisa* shows the alternation [pisa] ~ [pisaː]. Given this much information, we could imagine quite a few hypotheses about what is going on: for example, maybe Choctaw always lengthens vowels before suffixes, or perhaps it lengthens the second-to-last vowel of all words, so long as it isn't the first vowel. You can probably think of more possibilities, but to make further progress, we need further data.

Here is an example of what happens when you put a *prefix* before *pisa*:

[tʃi-piːsa]   'you (object)-see'   '(someone) sees you'

The data we've now seen suggest there may be a fairly general phonological principle at work: when a word has two syllables, both are short, but when there are three syllables, then the vowel of the middle syllable is long: [pisaːli], [pisaːtʃi], [tʃipiːsa]. It doesn't seem to matter how the word is divided into prefixes and suffixes.

The pattern begins to make further sense if we look at forms built from *pisa* with four or five syllables (that is, having two or three affixes):

[tʃi-piːsa-li]   'you (object)-see-I (subject)' = 'I see you'
[tʃi-piːsa-tʃi]   'you (object)-see-causative' = '(someone) causes to see you'
[pisaː-tʃi-li]   'see-causative-I (subject)' = 'I cause to see'
[tʃi-piːsa-tʃiː-li]   'you (object)-see-causative-I (subject)' = 'I cause you to see'

The pattern emerges clearly if we take all the forms we have, and align them vowel for vowel, in a left-justified way:

```
[ p   i   s   a ]
[ p   i   s   aː   l    i ]
[ p   i   s   aː   tʃ   i ]
[ tʃ  i   p   iː   s    a ]
[ tʃ  i   p   iː   s    a    l    i ]
[ tʃ  i   p   iː   s    a    tʃ   i ]
[ p   i   s   aː   tʃ   i    l    i ]
[ tʃ  i   p   iː   s    a    tʃ   iː   l   i ]
```

Namely: a vowel must be long if it is in an *even-numbered syllable*, counting from the beginning of the word, and moreover is *not in the last syllable*. Choctaw seems to have a kind of alternating durational rhythm. For this reason the phenomenon has been called Rhythmic Lengthening by Choctaw scholars.

Let us test out Rhythmic Lengthening with another stem, which in this case means 'to receive a present'. The basic data, parallel to what we saw for *pisa*, are as follows:

[habiːna]	'receive a present'
[habiːna-li]	'receive a present-1st person' = 'I receive a present'
[habiːna-tʃi]	'receive a present-causative' = 'cause to receive a present'
[tʃi-haːbina]	'you (object)-receive a present' = '(someone) receives a present for you'
[tʃi-haːbinaː-li]	'you (object)-receive a present-I (subject)' = 'I receive a present for you'
[tʃi-haːbinaː-tʃi]	'you (object)-receive a present-causative' = '(someone) causes to you to receive a present'
[habiːna-tʃiː-li]	'receive a present-causative-I (subject)' = 'I cause to receive a present'
[tʃi-haːbinaː-tʃi-li]	'you (object)-receive a present-causative-I (subject)' = 'I cause you to receive a present'

Examining each form, you can see the alternating pattern of Rhythmic Lengthening affecting all and only the non-final even-numbered vowels.

To set up the analysis more explicitly, we suppose that the phonemic forms for the stems for 'see' and 'receive a present' are /pisa/ and /habina/. The morphological rules of Choctaw may attach to them a variety of prefixes and suffixes. The form that results must comply with the phonological rule of Rhythmic Lengthening, which we state in prose as follows:

Rhythmic Lengthening
Lengthen the vowels of non-final, even-numbered syllables, counting from the beginning of the word.[3]

Thus for the form [tʃipiːsatʃiːli], the derivation is as follows:

	Lexicon:
/pisa/	entry for 'see'
	Morphological component:
tʃi-pisa-tʃi-li	rules (unstated) attaching /tʃi-/, /-tʃi/, and /-li/
	Phonological component:
/tʃi-pisa-tʃi-li/	underlying form
iː iː	Rhythmic Lengthening
[tʃipiːsatʃiːli]	surface form

---

[3]   This isn't formalizable with the notation we have so far; with iterative application (see p. 277), we can write V → [+long] / V C ___ C V, applied iteratively left to right.

In this view, the phonemic form /pisa/ has no long vowels at all: whenever this stem is pronounced with a long vowel, the rule of Rhythmic Lengthening has created it. The stem *habina*, 'to give a present', is more subtle. When this stem is pronounced by itself, it comes out as [habiːna], with a long vowel. But there is good reason to think that this is not a *phonemic* long vowel, because it appears only when the conditions of Rhythmic Lengthening are met for /i/. When they are not, /i/ appears as short, and other vowels which *do* meet the conditions for Rhythmic Lengthening appear as long, as in for example [tʃi-haːbina].

This reasoning can be stated more explicitly if we show precisely what is happening when the two forms are constructed by the grammar:

/habina/	/habina/	phonemic form for 'receive a present'
—	/tʃi-habina/	Morphology: addition of prefix (second column only)
[habiːna]	[tʃihaːbina]	Phonology: Rhythmic Lengthening

We can now summarize the Choctaw example, emphasizing its similarity to the English case. The Choctaw stems that we have phonemicized as /pisa/ and /habina/ each alternate, having the allomorphs [pisa] ~ [pisaː] ~ [piːsa] and [habiːna] ~ [haːbinaː]. As with English, the allomorphs are the consequences of letting the complete word, as it is assembled in the morphology, be accommodated to the requirements of the phonological rules, in this case the rule of Rhythmic Lengthening.

6.2 Neutralization

The examples of alternation we've seen so far involve allophones: a particular morpheme varies because its phonemes show up with different allophones, according to what the morphological component attaches. However, there are examples of alternation which go beyond allophonic alternation. Instead, one phoneme is turned into a sound that exists independently as a phoneme of the language.

6.2.1 Stop Nasalization in Korean

In final position of morphemes, Korean contrasts a series of voiceless stop phonemes /p, t, k/ with the nasals in the same places of articulation /m, n, ŋ/. This is shown by the following minimal pairs.

[otʃiŋə-tʃət]	'squid pickle'
[otʃiŋə-tʃən]	'squid pancake'

[nuɾin-pap]   'scorched rice'
[nuɾin-pam]   'scorched chestnut'

[tʃakin-pak]   'small gourd'
[tʃakin-paŋ]   'small room'

However, this contrast is not always manifested in speech. The reason is that Korean has a phonological rule which forbids voiceless stops from preceding a nasal, requiring that the corresponding nasal appear instead. We will write the rule as follows:

Korean Stop Nasalization

$$[-\text{delayed release}] \quad \rightarrow \quad \begin{bmatrix} +\text{nasal} \\ +\text{voiced} \\ +\text{sonorant} \end{bmatrix} / \underline{\quad} [+\text{nasal}]$$

A stop that immediately precedes a nasal sound must be replaced by the corresponding nasal.

The rule applies to the entire class of stops, which consists in Korean of /p/, /t/, and /k/. Since the rule is formulated to change only voicing and nasality, it leaves place of articulation unaltered. Therefore, it changes /p/ to [m], /t/ to [n], and /k/ to [ŋ].

The significance of this rule can be seen when we take pairs like the ones given above, and so arrange them in a phrase or sentence that the next word begins with a nasal sound. Under such circumstances, the word pairs are pronounced *exactly the same*, as shown in table 6.2. This follows from the statement of Stop Nasalization. Below are given underlying forms and derivations for the third pair of examples:

Table 6.2   Neutralization in Korean

[otʃiɲə-tʃət]	'squid pickle'	[otʃiɲə-tʃən nɛmsɛ-ka]	'squid-pickle smell-nom.' = 'the smell of the squid pickle'
[otʃiɲə-tʃən]	'squid pancake'	[otʃiɲə-tʃən nɛmsɛ-ka]	'squid-pancake smell-nom.' = 'the smell of the squid pancake'
[nuɾin-pap]	'scorched rice'	[nə nuɾin-pam məkəpwan-ni]	'you scorched-rice tried-question' = 'Have you tried scorched rice?'
[nuɾin-pam]	'scorched chestnut'	[nə nuɾin-pam məkəpwan-ni]	'you scorched-chestnut tried-question' = 'Have you tried scorched chestnut?'
[tʃakin-pak]	'small gourd'	[tʃakin-paŋ nɛmsɛ-ka]	'small-gourd smell-nom.' = 'the smell of a small gourd'
[tʃakin-paŋ]	'small room'	[tʃakin-paŋ nɛmsɛ-ka]	'small-room smell-nom.' = 'the smell of a small room'

'smell of small gourd'	'smell of small room'	
/tʃakɨn-pak nɛmsɛ-ka/	/tʃakɨn-paŋ nɛmsɛ-ka/	underlying forms
ŋ	—	Stop Nasalization
[tʃakɨn-paŋ nɛmsɛ-ka]	[tʃakɨn-paŋ nɛmsɛ-ka]	surface forms

There is a practical implication of this rule: when a Korean speaker hears [tʃakɨnpaŋ nɛmsɛka], she cannot determine purely from the phonetic input whether her interlocutor is talking about a gourd or a room. One must either make use of the context of the utterance to figure out what is meant, or request clarification.

The Korean example illustrates the concept of **neutralization**. The phonemic distinction of /p t k/ vs. /m n ŋ/ in Korean is *neutralized* in the context of a following nasal, meaning that the distinction is indeed "there" in the underlying forms of the relevant words, but due to a phonological rule is not actually manifested in pronunciation.

In general, neutralization can be defined as the *identical phonetic realization of distinct phonemic forms*. In Korean, the distinct phonemic forms /tʃakɨn-pak/ 'small gourd' and /tʃakɨn-paŋ/ 'small room' are realized identically as [tʃakɨnpaŋ] in the context of a following nasal. In this case, we are speaking of the neutralization of complete utterances.

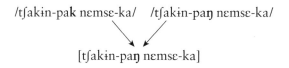

Phonologists also commonly speak of the neutralization of the particular phoneme, or classes of phonemes, that are involved. Here, the entire stop and nasal series are neutralized as nasals:

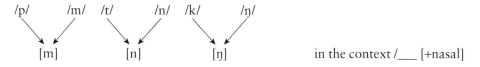

A second lesson of the Korean example concerns the arrangement of grammatical components. The examples given above are syntactic phrases in Korean. Under the assumption that there is a **syntactic component**, responsible for constructing phrases and sentences out of their component words, it would follow that syntax, like morphology, "feeds into" phonology, causing alternation when the right phonological rules are present.

6.2.2 *Postnasal /t/ Deletion in English*

English likewise has rules of phonological neutralization. The one to be discussed here takes the form of a deletion: the contrast that is wiped out is that of /t/ with zero (§3.6.2). Consider first some minimal pairs demonstrating this contrast. We are particularly interested in cases where the /t/ follows an /n/:

plant	[plænt]	vs.	*plan*	[plæn]
stunt	[stʌnt]	vs.	*stun*	[stʌn]
bent	[bɛnt]	vs.	*Ben*	[bɛn]

There are also a fair number of near-minimal pairs:

Bentley	['bɛntli]	vs.	*Henley*	['hɛnli]
until	[ən'tɪl]	vs.	*anneal*	[ə'nil]

Since all of the examples on the left-hand side are selected to have /t/ preceded by /n/, we can also describe the contrast by saying that /nt/ contrasts with /n/.

Now, let us consider a number of groups of words that share the same morphological stem. The pronunciations given are not common to all dialects of English, but are common in North America.

plant	['plænt]	*planter*	['plænɚ]
plan	['plæn]	*planner*	['plænɚ]
stunt	['stʌnt]	*stunting*	['stʌnɪŋ]
stun	['stʌn]	*stunning*	['stʌnɪŋ]
punt	['pʌnt]	*punting*	['pʌnɪŋ]
pun	['pʌn]	*punning*	['pʌnɪŋ]

Our assertion is that, at least for some speakers and in some speech styles, *planter* is pronounced identically to *planner*, and similarly for the other pairs. The rule involved, to which we will now turn, is evidently a neutralizing one.

From the data, we know that the /t/ is maintained after /n/ when the /t/ is at the end of a word (['stʌnt]); moreover, in the relatively few cases where an /nt/ sequence is followed by a consonant (others include *entry* ['ɛntɹi], *antler* ['æntlɚ] and *Antwerp* ['æntwɚp]), the /t/ survives. Additional data given below indicate that stress also plays a role:

plant	[plænt]	*planting*	['plænɪŋ]	*plantation*	[plæn'teɪʃən]
		mental	['mɛnəl]	*mentality*	[mɛn'tælɪɾi]
		scientist	['saɪənəst]	*scientific*	[ˌsaɪən'tɪfɪk]

Apparently, /t/ is vulnerable to deletion when it is followed by a stressless vowel. Thus we can state the rule as follows:

Postnasal /t/ Deletion

$$t \rightarrow \emptyset \; / \; n \; \underline{\hspace{1.5em}} \begin{bmatrix} +\text{syllabic} \\ -\text{stress} \end{bmatrix}$$

/t/ is deleted when it occurs between /n/ and a stressless vowel.

Here are derivations for some crucial cases. We will assume, uncontroversially, that *plant* is phonemically /plænt/ and *plan* is phonemically /plæn/. For the morphology, we assume the rule of *-ation* Affixation, from p. 123, along with an inflectional rule of Present Participle Formation, stated as follows:

Present Participle Formation
X → Xɪŋ   when [+Verb, +present participle]

The relevant derivations are thus as follows:

/ˈplæn/	/ˈplæn/	/ˈplænt/	/ˈplænt/	/ˈplænt/	**Lexical entries:** *plan, plant*
					Morphological component:
—	ˈplænɪŋ	—	ˈplæntɪŋ	—	Pres. Participle Formation
—	—	—	—	plænˈteɪʃən	*-ation* Affixation
					Phonological component:
/ˈplæn/	/ˈplænɪŋ/	/ˈplænt/	/ˈplæntɪŋ/	/plænˈteɪʃən/	underlying forms
—	—	—	ˈplænɪŋ	—	Postnasal /t/ Deletion
[ˈplæn]	[ˈplænɪŋ]	[ˈplænt]	[ˈplænɪŋ]	[plænˈteɪʃən]	surface forms

The relevant neutralization is diagrammed below on the left as a neutraliztion between utterances, and on the right as a neutralization of a particular phoneme sequences:

As in the Korean example, neutralization creates ambiguous utterances; thus on hearing [ðeɪɑɹˈplænɪŋəˈgɑɹdən] from a native speaker of this dialect, one cannot know whether the speaker's intent was to say *They are planting a garden* or *They are planning a garden*; only context or further queries can determine this.

6.2.3 *Russian voicing assimilation*

In Russian, most obstruents occur in pairs, phonemically voiced and voiceless. However, when an obstruent immediately precedes another obstruent, it takes on the voicing of the following obstruent, as in cases like the following.

Underlying form	Before sonorant: underlying form is unaltered	Assimilation before obstruent
/ot/	[ot mami]	/ot babuʃki/ → [od babuʃki]
'from'	'from mama'	'from grandma'
/pod/	[pod mamoj]	/pod papoj/ → [pot papoj]
'locative preposition'	'under mama'	'under papa'

This neutralization is shown in the diagram below: /t/ and /d/ get neutralized either to [t] or to [d] depending on the context.

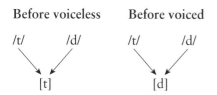

Before voiceless   Before voiced

Similar alternations can be found for the other obstruent consonants of Russian.
  The rule in question can be expressed as follows:

Voicing Assimilation

$$[\text{--sonorant}] \rightarrow [\alpha\text{voice}] \ / \ \underline{\quad} \begin{bmatrix} -\text{sonorant} \\ \alpha\text{voice} \end{bmatrix}$$

An obstruent takes on the voicing of a following obstruent.

The notation of the rule incorporates a Greek letter variable α. The idea is that α can take on either of the two values + or −, but it must take on the same value in both of its appearances when the rule is applied. Thus the rule in effect embodies two rules:

$$[\text{--sonorant}] \rightarrow [+\text{voice}] \ / \ \underline{\quad} \begin{bmatrix} -\text{sonorant} \\ +\text{voice} \end{bmatrix} \qquad (\text{derives [od babuʃki]})$$

$$[\text{--sonorant}] \rightarrow [-\text{voice}] \ / \ \underline{\quad} \begin{bmatrix} -\text{sonorant} \\ -\text{voice} \end{bmatrix} \qquad (\text{derives [pot papoj]}).$$

The [place$_i$] scheme for place assimilation, given above on p. 89, is an extended version of the same idea.

6.3   Dynamic vs. Static Neutralization

Neutralization is closely related to the concept of contextually limited contrast, given in §3.6. We can distinguish here between **dynamic** and **static** patterns of neutralization; I will give an example of each.

In a dynamic neutralization, there is alternation: morphemes are actively changed in order to respect the pattern of contextually limited contrast. Here is an example.

In English words, it is impossible for two final obstruents to disagree in their value for voicing. Thus, we recognize immediately that *[mipz], *[lʌbs], *[lɛkd], *[vɪgt], and so on could not be words of English. This restriction can be described as a contextually limited contrast: while obstruents in English generally do contrast for voicing, there is no contrast (for example "[mips]/[mipz]") in word-final position after an obstruent; rather, the only possible voicing value is the one that agrees with the voicing of the preceding obstruent.

The fact that the voicing contrast is limited in this way gives rise to phonological alternations. The past tense suffix, which is analyzed as underlying /-d/, is actively devoiced (surfacing as [-t]) whenever this is necessary to avoid a disagreement in voicing between two obstruents. Here are representative data:

/-d/ *remains voiced after a sonorant.*		/-d/ *remains voiced after a voiced obstruent.*		/-d/ *is devoiced to* [-t] *after a voiceless obstruent.*	
paid	[peɪ-d]	*rubbed*	[ɹʌb-d]	*picked*	[pɪk-t]
filled	[fɪl-d]	*eased*	[iz-d]	*tapped*	[tæp-t]
barred	[bɑɹ-d]	*dragged*	[dɹæg-d]	*missed*	[mɪs-t]
slammed	[slæm-d]	*lived*	[lɪv-d]	*laughed*	[læf-t]

The usual analysis given for this pattern is to assume that a phonological rule of Voicing Assimilation (similar to Russian, but applying in the opposite direction) changes the voicing of the /d/ where necessary to avoid a voicing conflict. This rule can be written as follows:

Voicing Assimilation

$$[-\text{sonorant}] \rightarrow [\alpha\text{voice}] \ / \begin{bmatrix} -\text{sonorant} \\ \alpha\text{voice} \end{bmatrix} \underline{\quad}]_{\text{word}}$$

An obstruent in word-final position takes on the same voicing as a preceding obstruent.

Here are derivations for representative past tenses that illustrate Voicing Assimilation.

pay	*rub*	*pick*	
/peɪ/	/rʌb/	/pɪk/	lexical entries
			Morphology:
peɪ-d	ɹʌb-d	pɪk-d	Past Tense Formation (p. 112)
			Phonology:
/peɪd/	/ɹʌbd/	/pɪkd/	underlying forms
—	—	t	Voicing Assimilation
[peɪd]	[ɹʌbd]	[pɪkt]	surface forms

Voicing Assimilation also accounts for the completely parallel alternation [-z] ~ [-s] in the plural suffix (*bays* [beɪ-z], *tubs* [tʌb-z], *tacks* [tæk-s]) and in the third singular present verbal ending (*pays* [peɪ-z], *rubs* [ɹʌb-z], *picks* [pɪk-s]).

Under this analysis, Voicing Assimilation is a case of dynamic neutralization; in the context of the rule the general contrast of voicing in obstruents is suspended, and underlying forms that would violate the principle of voicing disagreement are actively "repaired" by changing the voicing of the rightmost obstruent.

Consider now a case of static neutralization, also from English.

Alveolar Place Enforcement

$$\begin{bmatrix} -\text{sonorant} \\ -\text{continuant} \end{bmatrix} \rightarrow \begin{bmatrix} +\text{coronal} \\ +\text{anterior} \end{bmatrix} / \begin{bmatrix} -\text{sonorant} \\ -\text{continuant} \end{bmatrix} \underline{\quad\quad}]_\text{word}$$

Word-final stops following a stop must be alveolar.

According to this rule, no final stop clusters may end in anything other than [t] or [d]. Thus, words like *concept* ['kansɛpt] or *bagged* [bægd] are possible in English, but speakers will consider hypothetical words like *['kansɛtp], *['kantætk], *[mɪlkp], *[bædg], or *[ɹʌdb] to be phonologically impossible.

The difference between Voicing Assimilation and Alveolar Place Enforcement is that for the latter there are *no cases of repair*. We can easily imagine what such a case would look like if it existed. For instance, there could be a suffix /-b/ whose place of articulation is changed to alveolar just in case this is necessary to avoid violating the "only alveolars second" restriction. Attached to *pay*, the suffix would appear as [-b], but attached to (say) *lag*, it would be changed to [-d], to conform to the restriction. Obviously, English has no such suffix.

In conclusion, both Voicing Assimilation and Alveolar Place Enforcement express true patterns about English phonology, involving the suspension of a contrast (voicing or place) that exists elsewhere. But while Voicing Assimilation imposes its neutralization dynamically (altering the form of morphemes), Alveolar Place Enforcement is entirely static, imposing no actual changes. Phonologists generally use the word "neutralization" to refer to either static or dynamic neutralization.

Phonological theories differ in whether they treat dynamic neutralization differently from static neutralization. In the remainder of this book, I will assume that there is no real difference: we set up rules to specify the neutralizations, and consider it more or less an accident whether a language happens to have any underlying forms that get repaired by the rules – the rules for static neutralization are needed in any event, to characterize (for example) that *['kansɛtp], *['kantætk] and so on are not possible words of English.

6.4 Near-Neutralization

An intriguing pattern in some phonological systems is **near-neutralization**. This occurs when the rules map distinct underlying forms into surface forms that are distinct – but just barely so. The distinction may be so small that it cannot reliably be detected by ear. For this reason it is useful for phonologists to learn to make phonetic measurements, and to do simple experiments to determine whether the neutralizations they encounter are near or complete.

Here is an example of a near neutralization. If one listens to the following two sentences, spoken fluently:

Let's help Russ Schuh to the head of the line.
Let's help rush Schuh to the head of the line.

it is quite plausible to suppose that they are homophonous. The /s/ at the end of *Russ* /ɹʌs/ sounds like an /ʃ/, and therefore the same as the last sound of underlying *rush* /ɹʌʃ/. If the two are truly identical, we would be justified in writing a rule of phonological neutralization, along the following lines:

/s/ Assimilation

s → ʃ / ___ ʃ   (optional)[4]

Russ Schuh	*rush Schuh*	
/ɹʌs ʃu/	/ɹʌʃ ʃu/	underlying forms
ɹʌʃ ʃu	—	/s/ Assimilation
[ɹʌʃ ʃu]	[ɹʌʃ ʃu]	surface forms

However, phonetic measurements suggest that the phonemic /s/ of *Russ* typically is *not* realized as [ʃ], but rather as a dynamic sound that starts out like [s] and ends up like [ʃ]: [s͡ʃ]. /s/ Assimilation is thus more properly stated as a near-neutralizing rule:

/s/ Assimilation

s → s͡ʃ / ___ ʃ (optional)

To give a representative case, the spectrogram in figure 6.1 shows the acoustic result when the author said, in fairly fluent speech, *Russ, Russ Schuh, rush Schuh*. The circled region shows the region where the assimilated sequence [s͡ʃʃ] shows spectral characteristics similar to the [s] of *Russ*. The assimilated [s͡ʃʃ] is subtly but noticeably different from the [ʃʃ]. The difference is noticeable to the ear as well, but only with very careful listening.

Thus, careful phonological analysis checks, where possible, the neutralizations that it hypothesizes, to make sure that they are really neutralizing. For instance, experimental work (see Further reading, below) has confirmed that Korean Stop Nasalization, described above in §6.2.1, is a truly neutralizing rule.

---

[4]   In features, and suitably generalized: [+strident] → $\begin{bmatrix} -\text{ant} \\ +\text{front} \end{bmatrix}$ / ___ $\begin{bmatrix} +\text{strid} \\ +\text{cont} \\ -\text{ant} \end{bmatrix}$.

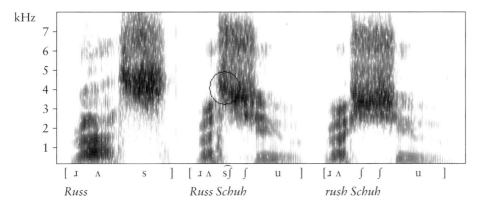

Figure 6.1 Spectrogram: Russ Schuh

Exercises

1 *Lango II: Alternations*

This problem builds on the Lango problem given in chapter 2, exercise 2, which should be done first. The present problem pursues Lango phonology a bit further by examining how the phonological rules of Lango interact with the morphology. Note that tones and [Advanced Tongue Root] are omitted in this problem, which covers only consonant phonology. Phonetic symbols: [t͡ɕ] and [d͡ʑ] are alveolopalatal affricates, [ɕ] an alveolopalatal fricative, and [ɾ̥] a voiceless tap.

In Lango, there are suffixes that specify the possessor of a noun. Consider the following paradigms:

[pala]	'knife'	[le]	'ax'
[palana]	'my knife'	[lena]	'my ax'
[palani]	'your knife'	[leni]	'your ax'
[palameɾe]	'his/her knife'	[lemeɾe]	'his/her ax'
[palawa]	'our knife'	[lewa]	'our ax'
[palawu]	'your-plural knife'[5]	[lewu]	'your-pl. ax'
[palagi]	'their knife'	[legi]	'their ax'

---

[5] Like many languages, Lango distinguishes a singular from a plural in the second person. This is seen in dialects of English in which "you" is used to refer to just one person and "y'all" to more than one.

[boŋo]	'dress'	[gulu]	'pot'
[boŋona]	'my dress'	[guluna]	'my pot'
[boŋoni]	'your dress'	[guluni]	'your pot'
[boŋomeɾe]	'his/her dress'	[gulumeɾe]	'his/her pot'
[boŋowa]	'our dress'	[guluwa]	'our pot'
[boŋowu]	'your-pl. dress'	[guluwu]	'your-pl. pot'
[boŋogi]	'their dress'	[gulugi]	'their pot'

a.   Write morphological rules to attach these possessive suffixes, following the format given in chapter 5. You may assume that [plural] is a morphological feature, and that the person feature takes the values [1person], [2person], and [3person].

When we attach these *same suffixes* to stems ending in a consonant, we obtain underlying consonant sequences (the first consonant from the stem, the second from the suffix). Such sequences are often altered by phonological rules.

b.   Examine the data below and provide an analysis. The analysis should follow the method given in this chapter: the morphological rules are simple, and attach affixes in their underlying forms. These underlying forms are then altered by the phonological rules. You will want to include two phonological rules to handle the alternations.

[alop]	'buck'	[it͡ɕok]	'sweet potato'
[aloppa]	'my buck'	[it͡ɕokka]	'my sweet potato'
[aloppi]	'your buck'	[it͡ɕokki]	'your sweet potato'
[aloppeɾe]	'his/her buck'	[it͡ɕokkeɾe]	'his/her sweet potato'
[alopwa]	'our buck'	[it͡ɕokwa]	'our sweet potato'
[alopwu]	'your-plural buck'	[it͡ɕokwu]	'your-pl. sweet potato'
[alobgi]	'their buck'	[it͡ɕoggi]	'their sweet potato'

[ot]	'house'	[pig]	'juice'
[otta]	'my house'	[pigga]	'my juice'
[otti]	'your house'	[piggi]	'your juice'
[otteɾe]	'his/her house'	[piggeɾe]	'his/her juice'
[otwa]	'our house'	[pigwa]	'our juice'
[otwu]	'your-plural house'	[pigwu]	'your-pl. juice'
[odgi]	'their house'	[piggi]	'their juice'

Here is a traditional notation to handle total assimilation:

A	B	→		
1	2		2	2

(Assume that A and B are bundles of features, as in normal rules.) The notation means, "If you have an A followed by a B, replace it with a sequence of two B's." Adapt this notation to the particular rule seen in Lango.

c. Is the rule that changes the final consonant of the stem an allophonic rule or a neutralizing rule? Explain your answer, giving appropriate examples to demonstrate your point.
d. Provide underlying forms and derivations for [otta] and [odgi].

The next batch of morphology to be considered involves an additional set of possessive suffixes. A bit of background on possession is needed here. In many languages, Lango included, we find a distinction between **inalienable** possession and **alienable** possession. Inalienable possession is for things you possess on a permanent or near-permanent basis, like body parts and relatives. Alienable possession is for things you possess as a more accidental matter, like household objects or money. Body parts are particularly interesting here, because when you own the leg of an animal (say, to roast and eat), the possession is alienable, whereas your own leg is possessed inalienably.

The inalienable/alienable distinction in Lango is made only in the singular. In the plurals the same suffix is used no matter what kind of possession is involved.

[ɾep]	'liver'			
[ɾeppa]	'my (animal) liver'		[ɾeɸa]	'my (own) liver'
[ɾeppi]	'your (animal) liver'		[ɾeɸi]	'your (own) liver'
[ɾeppeɾe]	'his/her (animal) liver'		[ɾeɸe]	'his/her (own) liver'
[ɾepwa]	'our (animal or own) liver'			
[ɾepwu]	'your-plural (animal or own) liver'			
[ɾebgi]	'their (animal or own) liver'			

[leb]	'tongue'			
[lebba]	'my (animal) tongue'		[leba]	'my (own) tongue'
[lebbi]	'your (animal) tongue'		[lebi]	'your (own) tongue'
[lebbeɾe]	'his/her (animal) tongue'		[lebe]	'his/her (own) tongue'
[lebwa]	'our (animal or own) tongue'			
[lebwu]	'your-plural (animal or own) tongue'			
[lebgi]	'their (animal or own) tongue'			

[lem]	'cheek'			
[lemma]	'my (animal) cheek'		[lema]	'my (own) cheek'
[lemmi]	'your (animal) cheek'		[lemi]	'your (own) cheek'
[lemmeɾe]	'his/her (animal) cheek'		[leme]	'his/her (own) cheek'
[lemwa]	'our (animal or own) cheek'			
[lemwu]	'your-plural (animal or own) cheek'			
[lemgi]	'their (animal or own) cheek'			

[jit]   'ear'
[jitta]   'my (animal) ear'   [jiɾa]   'my (own) ear'
[jitti]   'your (animal) ear'   [jiɾi]   'your (own) ear'
[jitteɾe]   'his/her (animal) ear'   [jiɾe]   'his/her (own) ear'
[jitwa]   'our (animal or own) ear'
[jitwu]   'your-plural (animal or own) ear'
[jidgi]   'their (animal or own) ear'

[bad]   'arm'
[badda]   'my (animal) arm'   [bada]   'my (own) arm'
[baddi]   'your (animal) arm'   [badi]   'your (own) arm'
[baddeɾe]   'his/her (animal) arm'   [bade]   'his/her (own) arm'
[badwa]   'our (animal or own) arm'
[badwu]   'your-plural (animal or own) arm'
[badgi]   'their (animal or own) arm'

[tjen]   'leg'
[tjenna]   'my (animal) leg'   [tjena] 'my (own) leg'
[tjenni]   'your (animal) leg'   [tjeni] 'your (own) leg'
[tjenneɾe]   'his/her (animal) leg'   [tjene] 'his/her (own) leg'
[tjenwa]   'our (animal or own) leg'
[tjenwu]   'your-plural (animal or own) leg'
[tjengi]   'their (animal or own) leg'

[lak]   'tooth'
[lakka]   'my (animal) tooth'   [laxa]   'my (own) tooth'
[lakki]   'your (animal) tooth'   [laxi]   'your (own) tooth'
[lakkeɾe]   'his/her (animal) tooth'   [laxe]   'his/her (own) tooth'
[lakwa]   'our (animal or own) tooth'
[lakwu]   'your-plural (animal or own) tooth'
[laggi]   'their (animal or own) tooth'

[dog]   'mouth'
[dogga]   'my (animal) mouth'   [doga]   'my (own) mouth'
[doggi]   'your (animal) mouth'   [dogi]   'your (own) mouth'
[doggeɾe]   'his/her (animal) mouth'   [doge]   'his/her (own) mouth'
[dogwa]   'our (animal or own) mouth'
[dogwu]   'your-plural (animal or own) mouth'
[doggi]   'their (animal or own) mouth'

[t͡ɕoŋ]   'knee'
[t͡ɕoŋŋa]   'my (animal) knee'   [t͡ɕoŋa] 'my (own) knee'
[t͡ɕoŋŋi]   'your (animal) knee'   [t͡ɕoŋi] 'your (own) knee'
[t͡ɕoŋŋeɾe]   'his/her (animal) knee'   [t͡ɕoŋe] 'his/her (own) knee'
[t͡ɕoŋwa]   'our (animal or own) knee'
[t͡ɕoŋwu]   'your-plural (animal or own) knee'
[t͡ɕoŋgi]   'their (animal or own) knee'

[del]   'skin'
[della]   'my (animal) skin'   [dela]   'my (own) skin'
[delli]   'your (animal) skin'   [deli]   'your (own) skin'
[delleɾe]   'his/her (animal) skin'   [dele]   'his/her (own) skin'
[delwa]   'our (animal or own) skin'
[delwu]   'your-plural (animal or own) skin'
[delgi]   'their (animal or own) skin'

e. What should be the phonological underlying form for each of the three
    inalienable-possession suffixes?
f. Now add whatever rule or rules you need so that your analysis derives all
    the forms in the problem set. You may want to review your answer to the
    earlier Lango problem, chapter 2, exercise 2.
g. Find an instance of neutralization and provide an arrow diagram similar to
    that on p. 130.
h. Provide phonological underlying forms and derivations for the following forms:
    [ɾep], [ɾeppa], [ɾeɸa], [jit], [jitti], [jiɾ̥i].

Further reading

The issue of how to analyze neutralization has a long history in phonology. The
approach taken in the text is an adaptation of the "Richness of the Base" theory,
apparently first suggested in Morris Halle (1962) "Phonology in generative
grammar," *Word* 18: 54–72, and developed extensively in Alan Prince and Paul
Smolensky's *Optimality Theory: Constraint Interaction in Generative Grammar*
(2004, Blackwell). For an approach that permits constraints on the underlying
representations themselves, see Chomsky and Halle, *The Sound Pattern of English*
(1968, Harper and Row).

   A general discussion of near-neutralization appears in Daniel Dinnsen (1985)
"A re-examination of phonological neutralization," *Journal of Linguistics* 21:
265–79; see also Robert F. Port and Penny Crawford (1989) "Incomplete
neutralization and pragmatics in German," *Journal of Phonetics* 17: 257–82.

   Russian voicing assimilation: Daniel Jones and Dennis Ward, *The Phonetics of
Russian* (1969, Cambridge University Press), pp. 197–8. Iambic Lengthening in
Choctaw: Pamela Munro and Charles Ulrich (1984) "Structure preservation and
Western Muskogean rhythmic lengthening," *West Coast Conference on Formal
Linguistics* 3: 191–202; and Thurston Dale Nicklas, "Choctaw morphopho-
nemics," in James M. Crawford, ed., *Studies in Southeastern Indian Languages*
(1975, University of Georgia Press). Stop Nasalization in Korean: Sun-Ah Jun,
*The Phonetics and Phonology of Korean Prosody: Intonational Phonology and
Prosodic Structure* (1996, Garland).

7 Phonological Alternation II

7.1 Phonemic Environments and Rule Ordering

An interesting aspect of phonological systems is that some rules evidently apply in environments that are defined *phonemically,* rather than phonetically. Such a rule looks like it is applying in the wrong environment, if one examines only the phonetic data, but deeper analysis shows the true context. The crucial mechanism for analyzing such cases is to apply the phonological rules in a particular order.

Our discussion of this phenomenon will be based on two phonological rules of North American English. One is found in a large number of dialects, especially in the northeastern US and throughout Canada.

/aɪ/ Raising

$$\text{aɪ} \rightarrow \text{ʌɪ} / \underline{\quad} \begin{bmatrix} -\text{syllabic} \\ -\text{voice} \end{bmatrix}$$

/aɪ/ *is realized as* [ʌɪ] *when it precedes a voiceless consonant.*

As a result of this rule, we find the following distribution of data.

tripe	/tɹaɪp/	[tɹʌɪp]	*tribe*	/tɹaɪb/	[tɹaɪb]
right	/ɹaɪt/	[ɹʌɪt]	*ride*	/ɹaɪd/	[ɹaɪd]
hiker	/haɪkɚ/	[hʌɪkɚ]	*tiger*	/taɪgɚ/	[taɪgɚ]
life	/laɪf/	[lʌɪf]	*live*	/laɪv/	[laɪv]
rifle	/ɹaɪfəl/	[ɹʌɪfəl]	*rival*	/ɹaɪvəl/	[ɹaɪvəl]
rice	/ɹaɪs/	[ɹʌɪs]	*rise*	/ɹaɪz/	[ɹaɪz]
			rye	/ɹaɪ/	[ɹaɪ]
			ion	/aɪɑn/	[aɪɑn]

The other rule we will need is the rule of Tapping, previously discussed on p. 142. There, we formulated the rule to apply only to /t/. But in fact, Tapping also affects /d/, converting it as well into a tap. The data below demonstrate this. The left column shows instances of phonemic /d/ that fit the environment for

Tapping; namely, they follow a vowel and precede a stressless vowel. The right column shows instances of phonemic /d/ in various other environments.

	Phonemic	Phonetic		Phonemic	Phonetic
Ada	/ˈeɪdə/	[ˈeɪɾə]	*Dan*	/ˈdæn/	[ˈdæn]
ladder	/ˈlædɚ/	[ˈlæɾɚ]	*adept*	/əˈdɛpt/	[əˈdɛpt]
reading	/ˈɹidɪŋ/	[ˈɹiɾɪŋ]	*Camden*	/ˈkæmdən/	[ˈkæmdən]
edify	/ˈɛdɪˌfaɪ/	[ˈɛɾɪˌfaɪ]	*Hilda*	/ˈhɪldə/	[ˈhɪldə]
sediment	/ˈsɛdɪmənt/	[ˈsɛɾɪmənt]	*Ogden*	/ˈagdən/	[ˈagdən]
adolescent	/ˌædəˈlɛsənt/	[ˌæɾəˈlɛsənt]	*Edgar*	/ˈɛdgɚ/	[ˈɛdgɚ]
			pad	/ˈpæd/	[ˈpæd]

This is the same pattern as was seen for /t/.

The generalized version of Tapping can be stated as follows. The material to the left of the arrow uses the features of chapter 4 to characterize the natural class of alveolar stops:

Tapping (revised)

$$\begin{bmatrix} +\text{anterior} \\ -\text{continuant} \end{bmatrix} \rightarrow ɾ \;/\; [-\text{consonantal}] \;\underline{\quad}\; \begin{bmatrix} +\text{syllabic} \\ -\text{stress} \end{bmatrix}$$

An alveolar stop is realized as [ɾ] *when it is preceded by a vowel or* /ɹ/, *and followed by a stressless vowel.*

Since Tapping converts both /t/ and /d/ to [ɾ], it converts distinct underlying forms to identical surface forms, and thus counts as a rule of neutralization (for the definition of neutralization, see p. 130). We can see the neutralization in a pair like *heating* vs. *heeding*. The underlying forms are justified by the stems *heat* [hit] and *heed* [hid]. But when the *-ing* suffix is added, Tapping applies, and neutralizes the underlying /t/ and /d/ as [ɾ]:

heating	*heeding*	
/ˈhit/	/ˈhid/	lexical entries
ˈhit-ɪŋ	ˈhid-ɪŋ	Morphology: Present Participle Formation (p. 132)
ˈhiɾɪŋ	ˈhiɾɪŋ	Phonology: Tapping
[ˈhiɾɪŋ]	[ˈhiɾɪŋ]	surface forms

At least in fluent speech, for most speakers of North American English *heating* and *heeding* do appear to be pronounced identically, so the example constitutes a true neutralization. Similar examples are given below:

bet	*betting*	*bed*	*bedding*
/ˈbɛt/	/ˈbɛt-ɪŋ/	/ˈbɛd/	/ˈbɛd-ɪŋ/
[ˈbɛt]	[ˈbɛɾɪŋ]	[ˈbɛd]	[ˈbɛɾɪŋ]

wet	*wetting*	*wed*	*wedding*
/'wɛt/	/'wɛt-ɪŋ/	/'wɛd/	/'wɛd-ɪŋ/
['wɛt]	['wɛɾɪŋ]	['wɛd]	['wɛɾɪŋ]

butt	*butted*	*bud*	*budded*
/'bʌt/	/'bʌt-əd/	/'bʌd/	/'bʌd-əd/
['bʌt]	['bʌɾəd]	['bʌd]	['bʌɾəd]

With the two rules of /aɪ/ Raising and Tapping in hand, we can now see how they might interact. Crucial words that would bear on the question are the following, which for the moment we give in spelled and phonemic form only:

write	*writing*	*ride*	*riding*
/'ɹaɪt/	/'ɹaɪt-ɪŋ/	/'ɹaɪd/	/'ɹaɪd-ɪŋ/

cite	*cited*	*side*	*sided*
/'saɪt/	/'saɪt-əd/	/'saɪd/	/'saɪd-əd/

white	*whiter*	*wide*	*wider*
/'waɪt/	/'waɪt-ɚ/	/'waɪd/	/'waɪd-ɚ/

The crucial point is that /aɪ/ Raising depends on the voicing of the following consonant, and Tapping changes the voicing of a /t/. We can ask: <u>will the allophone of /aɪ/ ([aɪ] vs. [ʌɪ]) that emerges depend on the voicing seen in the</u> *phonemic* form of the following consonant (/t/ vs. /d/), or will it depend on its *phonetic* form ([ɾ])? If /aɪ/ Raising depends on a phonemic environment, then we would expect to get [ʌɪ] just in case the following consonant is /t/, even though that consonant actually gets pronounced as [ɾ]. On the other hand, if /aɪ/ Raising depends on the *phonetic* form of the following consonant, it will not apply, since a tap is voiced, and we will get [aɪ] across the board.

It would be nice if we could establish some general principle of phonology that would predict the correct outcome. But this turns out to be impossible: *both* outcomes can be found, depending on the dialect of English one is examining.

For millions of speakers, /aɪ/ Raising depends on the *phonemic* voicing of the following consonant. Because of this, the crucial pairs come out distinct, with [ʌɪ] appearing whenever the following sound is a phonemic /t/:

write	*writing*	*ride*	*riding*
/'ɹaɪt/	/'ɹaɪt-ɪŋ/	/'ɹaɪd/	/'ɹaɪd-ɪŋ/
['ɹʌɪt]	['ɹʌɪɾɪŋ]	['ɹaɪd]	['ɹaɪɾɪŋ]

cite	*cited*	*side*	*sided*
/'saɪt/	/'saɪt-əd/	/'saɪd/	/'saɪd-əd/
['sʌɪt]	['sʌɪɾəd]	['saɪd]	['saɪɾəd]

white	*whiter*	*wide*	*wider*
/'waɪt/	/'waɪt-ɚ/	/'waɪd/	/'waɪd-ɚ/
['wʌɪt]	['wʌɪɾɚ]	['waɪd]	['waɪɾɚ]

There are also millions of speakers who have both /aɪ/ Raising and Tapping, for whom Tapping depends on the *phonetic* voicing of the following consonant. Since a tap is voiced, this means that whenever Tapping is applicable the outcome in these words is [aɪ]:

write	*writing*	*ride*	*riding*
/ˈɹaɪt/	/ˈɹaɪt-ɪŋ/	/ˈɹaɪd/	/ˈɹaɪd-ɪŋ/
[ˈɹʌɪt]	[ˈɹʌɪɾ-ɪŋ]	[ˈɹaɪd]	[ˈɹaɪɾɪŋ]

cite	*cited*	*side*	*sided*
/ˈsaɪt/	/ˈsaɪt-əd/	/ˈsaɪd/	/ˈsaɪd-əd/
[ˈsʌɪt]	[ˈsʌɪɾ-əd]	[ˈsaɪd]	[ˈsaɪɾ-əd]

white	*whiter*	*wide*	*wider*
/ˈwaɪt/	/ˈwaɪt-ɚ/	/ˈwaɪd/	/ˈwaɪd-ɚ/
[ˈwʌɪt]	[ˈwʌɪɾ-ɚ]	[ˈwaɪd]	[ˈwaɪɾ-ɚ]

Most other dialects of English lack either /aɪ/ Raising or Tapping or both, and therefore do not bear on the question.

A widely employed method of analyzing differences such as the one just shown is to suppose that phonological rules must be *ordered*. We can imagine phonology as an "assembly line" that takes in phonemic forms, applies phonological rules in a particular order, and outputs phonetic forms. Under such a theory, the difference between the two dialects just described is a difference of rule ordering. In the dialect in which *writing* and *riding* are pronounced distinctly ([ˈɹʌɪɾɪŋ] vs. [ˈɹaɪɾɪŋ]), /aɪ/ Raising is order before Tapping; and in the dialect in which *writing* and *riding* are pronounced the same, Tapping is ordered before /aɪ/ Raising.

Here are derivations using both orderings:

/aɪ/ Raising precedes Tapping

write	*writing*	*ride*	*riding*	
/ˈɹaɪt/	/ˈɹaɪt-ɪŋ/	/ˈɹaɪd/	/ˈɹaɪd-ɪŋ/	underlying forms
ˈɹʌɪt	ˈɹʌɪtɪŋ	—	—	/aɪ/ Raising
—	ˈɹʌɪɾɪŋ	—	ˈɹaɪɾɪŋ	Tapping
[ˈɹʌɪt]	[ˈɹʌɪɾ-ɪŋ]	[ˈɹaɪd]	[ˈɹaɪɾɪŋ]	surface forms

Tapping precedes /aɪ/ Raising

write	*writing*	*ride*	*riding*	
/ˈɹaɪt/	/ˈɹaɪt-ɪŋ/	/ˈɹaɪd/	/ˈɹaɪd-ɪŋ/	underlying forms
—	ˈɹaɪɾɪŋ	—	ˈɹaɪɾɪŋ	Tapping
ˈɹʌɪt	—	—	—	/aɪ/ Raising
[ˈɹʌɪt]	[ˈɹaɪɾ-ɪŋ]	[ˈɹaɪd]	[ˈɹaɪɾɪŋ]	surface forms

Analytically, it is usually fairly easy to determine how two rules must be ordered. One simply tries both possibilities, seeing which one outputs the observed phonetic forms. Often, both will, in which case the ordering doesn't matter.

7.1.1 Rule ordering and minimal pairs

The *writing/riding* example is a case in which a minimal pair (['ɹʌɪɾɪŋ]/['ɹaɪɾɪŋ]) does not prove a phonemic distinction. Because the phonological rule system manifests the contrast of underlying /t/ vs. /d/ as phonetic [ʌɪ] vs. [aɪ], the minimal pair is misleading with respect to the actual phonemic forms. Such cases are sometimes called displaced contrasts – here, the underlying contrast of /t/ vs. /d/ is displaced to surface [ʌɪ] vs. [aɪ].

The general lesson is that the results of any pre-established analytical recipe in phonology should be taken as provisional. An analyst confronting the ['ɹʌɪɾɪŋ]/['ɹaɪɾɪŋ] data for the first time would probably be wise to consider /ʌɪ/ vs. /aɪ/, at least at first, as separate phonemes. Subsequently, when further facts are considered, they would be reanalyzed as allophones.[1] The subsequent facts that force a revision are two: that [ʌɪ] and [aɪ] contrast only before tap, and that the pattern of alternation shows that there is an underlying environment (/ ___ t vs. / ___ d) that conditions the contrast.

7.2 Phonological Alternation and Rule Ordering in Chimwiini

To summarize what we have so far: morphology and syntax string together morphemes in their underlying forms, and phonology then applies to the resulting sequences. Since the morphology and syntax can place phonemes in different environments, different rules will be applicable, often resulting in phonological alternation, including neutralization. Often, we find that the phonological rules must be applied in a particular order, which can create effects like the "pseudo-minimal pairs" of the preceding section.

With this basic analytical scheme, a great deal can be accomplished in analyzing complex phonological and morphological systems. Quite a few languages have numerous morphemes that alternate predictably. The pattern in such languages can often be explicated with just a few phonological rules.

A good example is the phonology of Chimwiini, a language of the Bantu family. Chimwiini is indigenous to Brava, a city in southern Somalia, and can be understood (but only with difficulty) by speakers of Swahili dialects spoken nearby in Kenya. The data and essential generalizations reported here come from research by Charles Kisseberth and Mohammed Abasheikh, who draw on earlier work by Morris Goodman.

---

[1] Allophones of a particular kind, that is, derived at a "deep" level.

7.2.1   *Chimwiini morphology*

Chimwiini has a morphological system similar to that of Swahili, which we saw on p. 115. Here are a few affixes of Chimwiini and the rules that attach them.

Chimwiini verbal infinitives are formed with the prefix /ku-/, by the following rule:

Infinitive Formation
V → kuV   when [+infinitive]

For example, the infinitive of the verb stem /reːb/ 'stop' is [ku-reːb-a].[2]

The form [ku-reːb-a] ends in the suffix [-a]. This is the so-called "final vowel," found in verbs throughout the Bantu language family. The final vowel doesn't really mean anything, but occurs in a verb that would otherwise end in a consonant (either because its stem ends in a consonant and there are no suffixes, or because its rightmost "real" suffix ends in a consonant). Following traditional Bantuist analytic practice, we can express the rule as a morphological insertion rule general to verbs:

Final Vowel Attachment
XC → XCa   in verbs
If a verb would otherwise end in a consonant, add /-a/.[3]

/-eɺ/ is the applicative suffix. It means that the action of the verb is done on behalf of someone. ([ɺ] is the IPA symbol for a lateral flap.)

Applicative Formation
V → Veɺ   when [+applicative]

The applicative form of [ku-reːb-a] is [ku-reːb-eɺ-a], which means 'to stop for someone'.

The applicative suffix must be attached to the stem before the final vowel; in terms of rule ordering, this means that Applicative Formation must precede Final Vowel Attachment.

/-an/ is the reciprocal suffix. It means that the entities doing the action of the verb do the action to each other.

Reciprocal Formation
V → Van   when [+reciprocal]

---

[2]   When the following stem begins with a voiceless consonant, /ku/ is realized as [x-]; this is due to a phonological rule we will not cover here; it is discussed in Kenstowicz and Kisseberth (1977, 101), cited at the end of this chapter.
[3]   A possibility to consider is that this is not really morphology but phonology (epenthesis); we will ignore this here, as it is not crucial.

For example, [ku-ḍirk-a] means 'to reach', and [ku-ḍirk-an-a] means 'to reach one another.' Like Applicative Formation, Reciprocal Formation must be applied before Final Vowel Attachment.

/-oːw/ is the passive suffix; its meaning is "to be Verbed."

Passive Formation
V → Voːw   when [+passive]

For example, [ku-big-a] means 'to hit', and [ku-big-oːw-a] means 'to be hit'. Passive Formation must also precede Final Vowel Attachment.

With this morphology in hand, we can now begin examining some phonological alternations.

7.2.2 *Preantepenultimate Shortening*

Minimal and near-minimal pairs, of which the following are examples, show that vowel length in Chimwiini is phonemic.

[x-kuːl-a]	'to extract'	[x-kul-a]	'to grow'
[x-teːk-a]	'to load (an animal)'	[x-tek-a]	'to fetch'
[x-peːlek-a]	'to be able to be swept'	[x-pelek-a]	'to send'
[ku-baːram-a]	'to talk'	[ku-balam-a]	'to promise'

However, this phonemic length contrast is subject to contextual neutralization. In particular, there is no contrast in positions that are more than three syllables from the end of a phrase (for phrases, see §7.2.4). All vowels occurring in such positions must be short, and when a phonemic long vowel is placed there by morphological processes, it is shortened.

Here is an example. [ku-reːb-a] 'to stop' has a phonemic long vowel, which is phonologically legal, being only two syllables from the end. The applicative form of [ku-reːb-a] is [ku-reːb-eḷ-a] 'to stop for someone'. This, too, is phonologically legal, because the long vowel comes only three syllables from the end. But now consider the reciprocal form of [ku-reːb-eḷ-a], which is [ku-reb-eḷ-an-a] 'to stop for one another'. The outcome that we would expect, all else being equal, would be *[ku-reːb-eḷ-an-a], retaining the long vowel of /reːb/. The reason we get [ku-reb-eḷ-an-a] instead is the application of a shortening rule, stated informally as follows:

Preantepenultimate Shortening
Shorten a vowel when at least three vowels follow it.[4]

---

[4] Formalizable as [+syllabic] → [−long] / ___ C_0 V C_0 V C_0 V. For the notation C_0, see p. 154 below.

The name of the rule is based on standard phonological terminology:

ultimate = final
penultimate = second to last
antepenultimate = third to last
preantepenultimate = anything before third to last

To understand [ku-reb-eɹ-an-a] fully, we can build it up step by step, applying morphological, then phonological rules:

/reːb/	lexical entry for 'stop'
	Morphological component:
reːb-eɹ	Applicative Formation
reːb-eɹ-an	Reciprocal Formation
reːb-eɹ-an-a	Final Vowel Attachment
ku-reːb-eɹ-an-a	Infinitive Formation
	Phonological component:
/ku-reːb-eɹ-an-a/	Output of morphology = phonological underlying form
e	Preantepenultimate Shortening
[kurebeɹana]	surface form

In these derivations, the morphological rules attaching suffixes must be applied in the order shown. Infinitive Formation could apply anywhere, since just a single prefix is involved. The crucial point for phonological purposes is that when the morphology adds enough material following the root /reːb/, then the long vowel of this root gets phonologically shortened.

Preantepenultimate Shortening does not depend on any particular suffixes being present, but applies quite generally to vowels more than three syllables from the end, irrespective of what morphological processes cause these syllables to be present. The following examples illustrate this point.

[boːz-eɹ-e]	'he stole'	[boz-eɹ-en-i]	'what did he steal?'
[dʒoːhari]	'jewel'	[dʒohari-je]	'her jewel'
[x-faːɲ-a]	'to do'	[x-faɲ-iɹiz-a]	'to do with'
[x-saːmeh-a]	'to forgive'	[x-sameh-an-a]	'to forgive one another'

7.2.3 *Justifying underlying forms*

The original researchers cited here, Kisseberth and Abasheikh, when presenting the evidence for Preantepenultimate Shortening, take care to *justify their underlying forms*. For Preantepenultimate Shortening, it is not sufficient merely to note that vowels are always short when more than three from the end. One must show further, if possible, that vowels that one would expect on other grounds to be long show up as short. It is for this reason that the authors give not just forms like [kurebeḻana], but also [ku-reːb-a] and [ku-reːb-eḻ-a]. Under the assumption that a morpheme normally has a single representation throughout its paradigm,[5] the latter two forms show that [kurebeḻana] must be underlyingly /ku-reːb-eḻ-an-a/. Were it not for the existence of these paradigmatically related forms, we could take the path of least resistance and assume that [kurebeḻana] is simply underlying /kurebeḻana/.

Careful authors justify their underlying forms whenever they are different from the surface forms. The two kinds of justification that are most commonly given are as follows:

- The underlying form is needed to account for other forms in the paradigm ([kurebeḻana] must be /ku-reːb-eḻ-an-a/ because of forms like [kureːba]).
- The underlying form is needed to unify a group of allophones into a single phoneme (see chapters 2 and 3).

Occasionally, one finds analyses in which the author appeals to spelling to justify the underlying form, or to historically earlier stages of the language. Such forms of evidence are generally considered not legitimate. In the case of spelling, we can note that not all speakers of a language are necessarily literate, particularly at the age when the phonological system is acquired. And children certainly do not have access to historical data about their language. Assuming that the goal of analysis is to describe the system of rules that develops in children on exposure to language data, the analysis must be based on the same kind of data that children get. For further discussion, see chapter 10.

7.2.4 Phrase-Final Shortening and Word-Final Lengthening

We can now continue the analysis with an additional shortening rule. To express this rule, we must briefly cover the idea of phrases in phonology. A phrase is, informally, a phonologically cohering sequences of words. The exact nature of the phrases of Chimwiini will be explored in chapter 10; for the moment we will assume that every utterance given in this chapter (for the moment we will be considering only very short ones) consists of one single phrase. Therefore, "at the end of a phrase" is for present purposes the same as "before a pause."

With this in mind, we can note that every phrase-final vowel in Chimwiini is short. The relevant shortening rule can be expressed as follows:

---

[5] For the exceptions to this principle, see §3.5 and §9.9.

Phrase-Final Shortening
[+syllabic] → [−long] / ___]$_{Phrase}$
Vowels become short at the end of a phrase.

There is also an environment in which Chimwiini vowels show up as long: when-ever they are final in a word, but *not* final in the phrase. This can be seen in the following forms:

[na]	'by'	[naː noka]	'by a snake'
[kolko]	'than'	[kolkoː mi]	'than me'
[kama]	'like'	[kamaː mpʰaka]	'like a cat'
[hudʒo]	'the one who eats'	[hudʒoː mbele]	'the one who eats first'

There are various ways to capture this pattern. The analysis here assumes a very simple rule that requires all vowels to be long at the end of a word:

Word-Final Lengthening
[+syllabic] → [+long] / ___]$_{word}$

We will order this rule before Phrase-Final Shortening, which means that its effects get undone in phrase-final position. Therefore, only the non-final words of a phrase will show the effect of the rule in surface forms.

Here is a representative derivation. It assumes that the syntax has formed a complete phrase, /kama mpʰaka/ 'like' + 'cat', that is, 'like a cat'.

/kama mpʰaka/		output of syntax = underlying form of phonology
aː	aː	Word-Final Lengthening
	a	Phrase-Final Shortening
—		Preantepenultimate Shortening
[kamaː mpʰaka]		surface form

If Phrase-Final Shortening were (wrongly) ordered before Word-Final Lengthening, the derivation would give the wrong output, as follows:

/kama mpʰaka/		output of syntax = underlying form of phonology
—		Phrase-Final Shortening
aː	aː	Word-Final Lengthening
—		Preantepenultimate Shortening
*[kamaː mpʰakaː]		surface form

Indeed, under this ordering there would be no evidence that Phrase-Final Shortening even existed.

7.2.5 Ordering Word-Final Lengthening and Preantepenultimate Shortening

Here is another ordering: Word-Final Lengthening can be shown to precede Preantepenultimate Shortening. The crucial cases arise when we have a two-word phrase, with the second word trisyllabic or longer. Here is an example of the relevant type:

[kuna]   'to drink'
[kahawa]   'coffee'
[kuna kahawa]   'to drink coffee'

Here, even though [kuna] is a word that is non-final in its phrase, its final vowel does not surface as lengthened. The reason is that the word [kahawa] has three syllables. Therefore, the last vowel of [kuna] is more than three syllables from the end, and is eligible for Preantepenultimate Shortening – which, as it turns out, counts the syllables of the whole phrase, and not just of single words.

The following derivation, with Preantepenultimate Shortening ordered after Word-Final Lengthening, produces the correct output:

/kuna kahawa/   underlying form
   aː   aː   Word-Final Lengthening
   a   Preantepenultimate Shortening
           a   Phrase-Final Shortening
[kuna kahawa]   surface form

If Word-Final Lengthening were ordered after Preantepenultimate Shortening, we would get the wrong result, as follows:

/kuna kahawa/   underlying form
   —   Preantepenultimate Shortening
   aː   aː   Word-Final Lengthening
           a   Phrase-Final Shortening
*[kunaː kahawa]   predicted surface form

The form [kuna kahawa] is just one of a large number of similar examples, which according to Kisseberth and Abasheikh work in just the same way. Here are three further cases.

[maji malaḍa]   'water' + 'fresh'   = 'fresh water'
[tʃisu tʃihaba]   'knife' + 'small'   = 'small knife'
[kubola tʃiwovu]   'to steal' + 'wallet' = 'to steal a wallet'[6]

---

[6]   The words for 'water' and 'to steal' have underlying long vowels, as their isolation forms show us: [maːji], [kuboːla]. In the examples above, these long vowels are shortened, just as we would expect, by Preantepenultimate Shortening.

These may be compared to the forms [naː noka], [kolkoː mi], [kamaː mpʰaka], and [hudʒoː mbele], given earlier. In these forms, the fact that the second word has only two vowels means that the effect of Word-Final Lengthening survives intact, as it is not overridden by the subsequent application of Preantepenultimate Shortening.

Kisseberth and Abasheikh give a number of phrases containing the verb [ku-big-a] 'hit', which is found in many idiomatic expressions in Chimwiini:

[kubigaː luti]	'to hit with a stick'
[kubigaː ŋgoma]	'to strike a drum'
[kubigaː zita]	'to make war'
[kubiga ŋkʰeŋgele]	'to ring a bell'
[kubiga maʔipi]	'to slap'
[kubiga rasaːsi]	'to pull the trigger of a gun'

As expected, the length of its final vowel depends on the number of syllables in the following word. Other words alternate similarly.

7.2.6   Illustrating rule order with Hasse diagrams

As we accumulate data and rule orderings, it is useful to keep track of the orderings, in part to make sure that they are mutually consistent. A method commonly used is to lay out the rule names and connect with arrows the rule pairs for which there is ordering evidence. The resulting graph is sometimes called a **Hasse diagram**. For the analysis so far, with just three rules and two orderings, the Hasse diagram is very simple:

Word-Final Lengthening

Preantepenultimate Shortening   Phrase-Final Shortening

Where there is no evidence concerning ordering, as with Preantepenultimate Shortening and Phrase-Final Shortening, no arrow is drawn.

7.2.7   Pre-Long Shortening

There is one more rule of Chimwiini to be discussed here. Its basic pattern is this: whenever morphology or syntax sets up two long vowels in consecutive syllables, the first of them is shortened. Here are some representative alternations:

[x-siːb-a]   'to afflict'
[x-sib-oːw-a]   'to be afflicted'
[sib-iːl-e]   'afflicted'

[x-ṭuːf-a]   'to go around the *ka'aba*'
[x-ṭuf-oːw-a]   'to be gone around'
[ṭuf-iːl-e]   'went around the *ka'aba*'

[x-saːjḍ-a]   'to help'
[x-sajḍ-oːw-a]   'to be helped'
[sajḍ-iːl-e]   'helped'

The rule that is needed can be stated as follows:

Pre-Long Shortening

$$[\text{+syllabic}] \rightarrow [\text{−long}] \; / \; \underline{\hspace{2em}} \; C_0 \begin{bmatrix} \text{+syllabic} \\ \text{+long} \end{bmatrix}$$

Shorten a vowel if the next vowel is long.

Here, C_0 is a conventional notation that means "any number of consonants." When it appears in a rule, it can be matched to a consonant string of any length, including no consonants at all. C_0 is one way of writing rules in which vowels influence vowels in neighboring syllables.[7] The following is a representative derivation involving Pre-Long Shortening.

/siːb/   lexical entry for 'afflict'

                      Morphological component:
/siːb-oːw/   Passive Formation (p. 148)
/siːb-oːw-a/   Final Vowel Attachment (p. 147)
/x-siːb-oːw-a/   Infinitive Formation (/ku/ → [x] by phonological rules
                      not covered here)

                      Phonological component:
/x-siːb-oːw-a/   underlying form
            aː   Word-Final Lengthening
        —   Preantepenultimate Shortening
            a   Phrase-Final Shortening
      i   Pre-Long Shortening
[xsiboːwa]   surface form

Pre-Long Shortening, like Preantepenultimate Shortening, is a neutralizing rule. This is illustrated by a case in which it creates an ambiguous form (§6.2.1): the

---

[7] In the original proposal for the C_0 notation, the notation was specified as C_n^m, meaning "at least *n* consonants and at most *m*." Other than C_0, the C_n^m scheme is seldom employed today in phonological rule writing.

verbs [x-kul-a] 'to grow' and [x-kuːl-a] 'to extract', cited earlier as a minimal pair, have identical passive forms (both [xkuloːwa]),[8] due to the effect of Pre-Long Shortening on underlying /x-kuːl-oːw-a/.

The ordering of Pre-Long Shortening with respect to the other rules must be established. The following forms suffice to show that Pre-Long Shortening must follow Word-Final Lengthening. The derivations are given as exercise 1 below.

[kubiga paːsi]	'to iron clothes'
[kuḍara leːmbe]	'to sharpen a razor'
[x-tʃimbil-a siːmba]	'to run from a lion'

Pre-Long Shortening must also be ordered after Phrase-Final Shortening, as can be determined from the following data. The derivations are left as exercise 2.

[kolko]	'than'	[mi]	'me'	[kolkoː mi]	'than me'
[kama]	'if'	[we]	'you'	[kamaː we]	'if you'

The following forms will be derived differently, depending on how the shortening rules are ordered with respect to one another. All orderings that put Word-Final Lengthening first will work for these forms, but you might want to try out the various possibilities to make sure you have a solid understanding of the system.

[nuːmba]	'house'	[numbaː nkulu]	'large house'
[sanḍuːxu]	'box'	[sanḍuxuː nzito]	'heavy box'
[miṭaːna]	'rooms'	[miṭana miwiḷi]	'two rooms'
[ziḷaːtu]	'shoes'	[ziḷatu zizito]	'heavy shoes'

7.2.8 Chimwiini summary

In Chimwiini, alternations between long and short vowels are numerous. But the system they follow is regular, being reducible to phonological rules. For the part of the Chimwiini system we have covered here, the four rules must be ordered according to the following Hasse diagram:

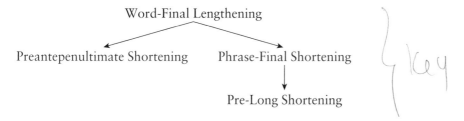

Word-Final Lengthening

Preantepenultimate Shortening   Phrase-Final Shortening

Pre-Long Shortening

---

[8] More precisely, [xkuḷoːwa], due to a minor phonological rule not discussed here; see Kisseberth and Abasheikh (2004, p. xxix). The point about neutralization is not affected.

The alternations follow from these four rules as applied to the output of Chimwiini syntax and morphology.

Exercises

1 *Chimwiini rule ordering I*

Justify the Chimwiini rule order of Word-Final Lengthening before Pre-Long Shortening (p. 155) with two derivations, one correct and one incorrect.

2 *Chimwiini rule ordering II*

Same as above, except for Phrase-Final Shortening preceding Pre-Long Shortening (p. 155).

3 *Chimwiini rule ordering III*

Provide all derivations of /nuːmba nkulu/ → [numbaː nkulu] 'large house' that are compatible with the Hasse diagram on p. 155.

4 *Displaced contrast and pseudo-minimal pairs*

On p. 93 are given some "pseudo-minimal pairs" similar to the [ˈɹaɪɾɚ]/[ˈɹʌɪɾɚ] pair discussed in §7.1. Reread the discussion on p. 00 and consider the examples *safe* [sĕɪf] vs. *save* [seɪf] (the latter can also surface as [seɪv], which you may ignore). Produce the rules that are needed to cover these cases, state the ordering needed, and give derivations for both *safe* and *save*. Then explain why they are not a true minimal pair for vowel length.

5 *Rule ordering in* Vancouver

In the speech of many English speakers there is an allophonic rule whereby the phoneme /æ/ is diphthongized to [æ͡ɪ] before /ŋ/

/æ/ Diphthongization
/æ/ → [æ͡ɪ] / ___ ŋ

The effects of the rule can be seen in pairs such as the following:

pan	/pæn/	[pæn]	*pang*	/pæŋ/	[pæ͡ɪŋ]
fan	/fæn/	[fæn]	*fang*	/fæŋ/	[fæ͡ɪŋ]
gander	/ˈgændɚ/	[ˈgændɚ]	*anger*	/ˈæŋgɚ/	[ˈæ͡ɪŋgɚ]

In the same dialect there is an optional rule of /n/ Assimilation, as given below (for the notation [place$_i$] see p. 89).

/n/ Assimilation:

$$n \rightarrow [place_i] / \underline{\quad} \begin{bmatrix} -syllabic \\ place_i \end{bmatrix} \quad \text{(in casual speech)}$$

Assimilate /n/ in place of articulation to a following consonant.

Among the effects of this rule is the shifting of /n/ to [ŋ], as seen in the last four items below.

input	[ˈɪnˌpʊt] or [ˈɪmˌpʊt]
unprepared	[ˌʌnpɹəˈpeɹd] or [ˌʌmpɹəˈpeɹd]
unbelievable	[ˌʌnbəˈlivəbəl] or [ˌʌmbəˈlivəbəl]
I live in Minnesota	[aɪ ˈlɪv ɪn ˌmɪnəˈsoʊɾə] or [aɪ ˈlɪv ɪm ˌmɪnəˈsoʊɾə]
phone call	[ˈfoʊn ˌkɔl] or [ˈfoʊŋ ˌkɔl]
concourse	[ˈkanˌkɔɹs] or [ˈkaŋˌkɔɹs]
con game	[ˈkanˌgeɪm] or [ˈkaŋˌgeɪm]
in college	[ɪn ˈkalɪd͡ʒ] or [ɪŋ ˈkalɪd͡ʒ]

a. Assess the implications of the following forms for the relative ordering of /æ/ Diphthongization and /n/ Assimilation. Pick a representative form from each of the two groups below, and work out the predictions of *both* orderings.

Word	**Phonemic Form**	
pancake	/ˈpænˌke͡ɪk/	
Vancouver	/vænˈkuvɚ/	
Dan Gurney	/ˈdæn ˈgɚni/	
sank	/ˈsæŋk/	
anchor	/ˈæŋkɚ/	
Rangoon	/ɹæŋˈgun/	
pang cake	/ˈpæŋˌke͡ɪk/	'cake eaten to assuage pangs of hunger'

b. Assess your own English concerning these forms (possible answers: "I have both rules, with X ordered before Y," "I only have Rule X," "I have neither rule," etc.). Justify your answer with data from your own speech.

For reference, it can be noted that the author of this book says the seven words under (a) as [ˈpænˌke͡ɪk], [vænˈkuvɚ], [ˈdæŋ ˈgɚni], [ˈsæŋk], [ˈæ͡ɪŋkɚ], [ɹæ͡ɪŋˈgun], and [ˈpæ͡ɪŋˈke͡ɪk]. I'm not sure what dialect variation occurs here.

6 *Toba Batak consonant alternations*

Toba Batak is an Austronesian language spoken in northern Sumatra (Indonesia). This language has several processes which modify consonants in various contexts. Here is an example:

Ex. 1. [halak]   'person'   Ex. 2. [tuak]   'palm wine'
       [an]   'that'   [i]   'the'
       [halah an] 'that person'   [tuah i] 'the palm wine'

These forms illustrate a rule of /k/ Weakening, which requires that whenever /k/ is placed before a vowel, it becomes [h]. (This process will not, however, be crucial for this rest of the problem.)

Here are some other data illustrating additional rules. These rules apply to the consonant clusters that arise when words are combined into phrases or sentences.

1. [maŋan]   'is eating'   2. [baoa an]   'that man'
   [baoa an]   'that man'   [pɛddɛk]   'short'
   [maŋab baoa an]   'that man   [baoa ap   'that man
                is eating'   pɛddɛk]   is short'

3. [lɛan]   'give'   4. [soŋon]   'as'
   [lali]   'hen-harrier'   [gottina]   'replacement'
   [lɛal lali]   'give a   [soŋog gottina]   'in exchange'
              hen-harrier'

5. [maɲinum]   'drink'   6. [holom]   'somewhat'
   [tuak]   'palm wine'   [saɔtik]   'dark'
   [maɲinup tuak]   'drink palm   [holop saɔtik]   'somewhat dark'
              wine'

7. [mananɔm]   'bury'   8. [manaŋ]   'or'
   [piɾiŋ]   'dish'   [pulpen]   'pen'
   [mananɔp piɾiŋ]   'bury a dish'   [manak pulpen]   'or a pen'

9. [daŋ]   'not'   10. [maɾisap]   'smoke'
   [tibbo]   'tall'   [hita]   'we'
   [dak tibbo]   'not tall'   [maɾisap pʰita]   'let us smoke'

11. [dɔhɔt]   'and'   12. [manipak]   'kick'
   [halak]   'person'   [haɾaɟɟan i]   'the basket'
   [dɔhɔt tʰalak]   'and a person'   [manipak   'kick the basket'
                       kʰaɾaɟɟan i]

13. [modom] 'sleeping'
    [halah i] 'the man'
    [modop pʰalah i] 'the man
    is sleeping'

14. [ibɛɾɛŋ] 'saw'
    [halah i] 'the man'
    [ibɛɾɛk kʰalah i] 'the man saw'

15. [ganup] 'every'
    [taɔn] 'year'
    [ganuʔ taɔn] 'every year'

16. [dɔhɔt] 'and'
    [lali i] 'the hen-harrier'
    [dɔhɔʔ lali i] 'and the
    hen-harrier'

17. [halak] 'person'
    [batak] 'Batak'
    [halaʔ batak] 'Batak person'

18. [lap] 'wipe off'
    [piŋgol] 'ear'
    [laʔ piŋgol] 'wipe off an ear'

19. [maɲihut] 'following'
    [taɔn] 'year'
    [maɲihuʔ taɔn] 'according to
    the year'

20. [maɲan] 'is eating'
    [halah i] 'the person'
    [maɲak kʰalah i] 'the person
    is eating'

Rather than give examples for all of the logical possibilities, this problem simply expresses them in table 7.1, which works as follows. To find out what happens when you put a /p/-initial word after an /n/-final word, you examine where the row for /n/ intersects the column for /p/; thus phonemic /np/ sequence appears phonetically as [pp]. (There is an actual example of this change under (2) above.)

Gray cells are the ones that involve no change. The overlapping outlines are meant to help: look inside them to see the rules that are applying.

Table 7.1 Toba Batak consonant alternations

Rows: last sound of first word.
Columns: first sound of second word.

	p	t	h	s	b	d	ɟ	g	m	n	ŋ	ɾ	l	Vowel
p	ʔp	ʔt	ppʰ	ʔs	ʔb	ʔd	ʔɟ	ʔg	ʔm	ʔn	ʔŋ	ʔɾ	ʔl	pV
t	ʔp	ʔt	ttʰ	ʔs	ʔb	ʔd	ʔɟ	ʔg	ʔm	ʔn	ʔŋ	ʔɾ	ʔl	tV
k	ʔp	ʔt	kkʰ	ʔs	ʔb	ʔd	ʔɟ	ʔg	ʔm	ʔn	ʔŋ	ʔɾ	ʔl	hV
s	sp	st	ssʰ	ss	sb	sd	sɟ	sg	sm	sn	sŋ	sɾ	sl	sV
n	pp	tt	kkʰ	ss	bb	dd	ɟɟ	gg	mm	nn	ŋŋ	ɾɾ	ll	nV
ŋ	kp	kt	kkʰ	ks	ŋb	ŋd	ŋɟ	ŋg	ŋm	ŋn	ŋŋ	ŋɾ	ŋl	ŋV
m	pp	pt	ppʰ	ps	mb	md	mɟ	mg	mm	mn	mŋ	mɾ	ml	mV
ɾ	ɾp	ɾt	ɾh	ɾs	ɾb	ɾd	ɾɟ	ɾg	ɾm	ɾn	ɾŋ	ɾɾ	ɾl	ɾV
l	lp	lt	lh	ls	lb	ld	lɟ	lg	lm	ln	lŋ	lɾ	ll	lV

Determine what rules, other than /k/ Weakening, are applying in the Batak data. How must the rules be ordered with respect to each other? For each case of ordering, provide a derivation to illustrate it. Show both correct and incorrect orders, indicating how only the correct order will work.

Further reading

The rule-ordered analysis of ['ɹʌɪɾɪŋ] vs. ['ɹaɪɾɪŋ] given in §7.1 was first proposed in Morris Halle (1962) "Phonology in generative grammar," *Word* 18: 54–72. It is not clear that the analysis works for all dialects that have ['ɹʌɪɾɪŋ] vs. ['ɹaɪɾɪŋ]. Subsequent research has located dialects in which [aɪ] and [ʌɪ] have evolved into two separate phonemes, which can be diagnosed by straightforward, monomorphemic minimal pairs. See Timothy Vance (1987) " 'Canadian Raising' in some dialects of the Northern United States," *American Speech* 62: 195–210. An interesting question that this work raises is just how diachronically stable cases of displaced contrast are – does the displaced contrast tend to be reanalyzed by new learners as a straight phonemic contrast?

Chimwiini phonology: Morris Goodman (1967) "Prosodic features of Bravanese, a Swahili dialect," *Journal of African Languages* 6: 278–84; Charles W. Kisseberth and Mohammad Imam Abasheikh "Vowel length in Chi-Mwi:ni: A case study of the role of grammar in phonology," in Anthony Bruce, Robert A. Fox, and Michael L. LaGaly, eds., *Papers from the Parasession on Natural Phonology* (1974, Chicago Linguistic Society); Michael Kenstowicz and Charles Kisseberth, *Topics in Phonological Theory* (1977, Academic Press); Kisseberth and Abasheikh's *The Chimwiini Lexicon Exemplified* (2004, Tokyo University of Foreign Studies).

8   Morphophonemic Analysis

Morphophonemic analysis designates the analytic procedure whereby paradigms with phonological alternations are reduced to underlying representations and phonological rules. The Chimwiini example from the previous chapter is one instance of morphophonemic analysis. This chapter lays out a general method for morphophonemic analysis and illustrates it with an extended example.

8.1   A Method for Morphophonemic Analysis

When we conduct morphophonemic analysis, we seek to establish a connection between data and theory. The theory in question is the one given in the previous chapter: that morphemes are stored in the lexicon in an invariant phonemic form, are strung together by morphological and syntactic rules, and are then converted to their surface forms by a sequence of phonological rules (often neutralizing), applied in a particular order. The purpose of morphophonemic analysis is to discover a set of underlying forms and ordered rules that is consistent with the data; and the payoff is that seemingly complex patterns are often reduced to simplicity.

Morphophonemic analysis may be contrasted with phonemic analysis, covered in chapter 2. Phonemic analysis is a more limited form of phonological analysis that seeks only to discover the non-neutralizing (allophonic) rules of the phonology. In phonemic analysis, only the distribution and similarity of the phones is examined. Therefore, the data need not be grouped in paradigms, but need only comprise a sufficiently large and representative set of words.[1]

---

[1]   The term "morphophonemic analysis" has a now obscure origin. In the 1940s and 1950s, many phonologists worked with a theory in which (roughly) all neutralizing rules were assumed to apply before all allophonic rules. This in effect divided the phonology into two components: a neutralizing component, whose units were called "morphophonemes," and a non-neutralizing component, which dealt with phonemes and allophones. This bifurcated-phonology theory is widely considered untenable today, but "morphophonemics" remains a useful term for characterizing the study of neutralizing phonological rules as they apply in paradigms.

Like phonemic analysis, morphophonemic analysis can be pursued with a systematic method, which is laid out in the sections that follow. Here is the method in broadest outline:

Procedure for Morphophonemic Analysis
- Examine the data, consulting the glosses, and make a provisional division of the forms into morphemes.
- Find each morpheme that alternates, and locate all of its allomorphs.
- Within each allomorph, locate the particular segment or segments that alternate.
- Considering the logical possibilities, set up the underlying representations so that all the allomorphs of each morpheme can be derived from a single underlying representation by general phonological rules.

This overall scheme is elaborated step by step below.

8.1.1 Pre-processing the data: phonemicization

It is almost always easier to do morphophonemic analysis with data that are already expressed as phonemes, so if this has not already been done, it is advisable first to reduce the data to phonemes, using the method laid out in chapter 2.

8.1.2 Morpheme division

The next step is to break up the forms into their component morphemes. A potential complication is that phonological alternations may obscure this division. In the hard cases, one must try more than one possibility for "placing the hyphens," ultimately selecting the choice that yields a working analysis. As the words are divided into morphemes, it is usually also possible to state and order the rules of morphology that are active.

8.1.3 Setting up underlying representations

As with morpheme division, the problem of choosing underlying representations often involves considering more than one hypothesis, with the final choice defended by its leading to a working analysis. The following strategy is often helpful. Suppose segment A alternates with segment B in the data. In such a case, the analyst should consider two possibilities:

1   Segments showing A ~ B alternation are underlyingly /A/, which is converted to [B] in certain contexts by one or more phonological rules.

2 Segments showing A ~ B alternation are underlyingly /B/, which is converted
to [A] in certain contexts by one or more phonological rules.

In other words, always consider both directions.

To give a concrete example: if we were analyzing Chimwiini (as in the previous chapter), we would find many instances of long vowels alternating with
short, as in

[x-soːm-a]	'to read'
[x-som-oːw-a]	'to be read'

We would consider the possibility that such cases are underlyingly long vowels
('read' = /soːm/), and consider shortening rules (this turns out to be correct), as
well as the possibility that these are underlyingly short vowels ('read' = /som/),
and consider lengthening rules (this turns out to fail; see §8.1.6 below).

8.1.4 Constructing underlying representations under a particular hypothesis

Assuming that you have picked a particular direction for the rules (/A/ → [B],
or /B/ → [A]) and are trying it out, the next step is to construct underlying
representations. Here is a recommended procedure.

- Segments that do not alternate can (normally) be assumed to be phonemically
  identical in their underlying representation to their surface representation. (This
  presupposes, as already noted, that phonemic analysis is already accomplished,
  so any positional allophones will already appear in their underlying form.)
- For segments that alternate, follow the hypothesis you made about underlying forms, implementing it consistently through the data. Thus if you are
  assuming that an alternation A ~ B, found in a particular context, is underlain
  by A, you should set up /A/ in the underlying representation for all such
  alternations in that context.
- Be sure that the underlying representation of each morpheme is uniform
  throughout its paradigm – this is a basic hypothesis of the theory you are
  assuming.

In our example of [x-soːm-a] ~ [x-som-oːw-a], under the hypothesis that the
rule is a shortening rule, these principles force us to set up the underlying representations /soːm/ for the root, and /-oːw/ for the invariantly long passive suffix.[2]

---

[2] The final vowel /-a/ turns out to be a special case: its surface length is actually non-distinctive,
being determined entirely by the phonological rules. Our grammar will work no matter what underlying length is assigned to this suffix.

8.1.5   *Working out the rules*

When you have a suitable set of hypothesized underlying forms, it is helpful to arrange them in a row, aligning their corresponding surface forms underneath them, as follows:

'to read' (p. 153)	'to be read' (p. 153)	'to stop for one another' (p. 148)	
/x-soːm-a/	/x-soːm-oːw-a/	/ku-reːb-eɭ-an-a/	underlying forms
. . .	. . .	. . .	*add rules here*
[xsoːma]	[xsomoːwa]	[kurebeɭana]	surface forms

It is then a matter of coming up with a rule system that will derive the bottom row from the top. If you get stuck doing this, you can try collecting the **local environments** for the sounds that change, as described above for phonemic analysis (§2.10.3).

8.1.6   *A clue for choosing underlying representations*

When you are deciding whether to set up underlying A and derive B from it, or vice versa (see §8.1.4), there is often a clue in the data to guide you, namely, a contextually limited contrast (§3.6; §6.3). In the present case, note that while vowel length is phonemic in Chimwiini, only short vowels are allowed when more than three syllables from the end of a phrase, or when a long vowel follows. Such limitations are a strong clue that there must be a rule that wipes out the contrast in these environments.[3]

   Another way of saying the same thing is: *don't analyze in a direction opposite to that of a neutralization*. When we analyze Chimwiini with shortening, our analysis fits in well with the contextually neutralized distribution of long and short vowels in the language. If, however, we try to analyze Chimwiini with lengthening, the phonological distribution will stymie us. The following quadruplet of forms should make this point clear.

[x-kuːl-a]	'to extract'	[x-kul-oːw-a]	'to be extracted'
[x-kul-a]	'to grow'	[x-kul-oːw-a]	'to be grown'

   The top row of forms shows an alternation between [uː] and [u], which we earlier analyzed assuming underlying /uː/ and the neutralizing rule of Pre-Long

---

[3]   Indeed, under one approach to contextually limited contrast (see §3.6), something like the rules of Preantepenultimate Shortening and Pre-Long Shortening would have to be assumed for Chimwiini, even if the language had no alternations at all.

Shortening (p. 154). It is plain that Pre-Long Shortening is neutralizing, since the passive form of [x-kuːl-a], [x-kul-oːw-a], is identical to the passive of [x-kul-a], meaning 'to grow'. If we had wrongly chosen underlying /u/ for the root meaning 'extract', we would be defeated: no matter what lengthening rule we tried, it would be unable to derive [x-kuːl-a] for 'extract' and [x-kul-a] for 'grow', since these two forms would have the same underlying representation.

8.2   The Isolation Form Shortcut and Why It Sometimes Fails

When one is looking for underlying forms, it is tempting to appeal to a "shortcut" that finds them with great speed:

The Isolation Form Shortcut
"The underlying form of a stem is simply the way that the stem appears in isolation (taking away the effects of any allophonic rules)."

This strategy particularly suggests itself for languages like English, where stems frequently appear alone. Hearing an alternation like ['plænt] ~ ['plænɪŋ] (*plant ~ planting*; see §6.2.2), we are tempted to take the evidence of the isolation form ['plænt] as evidence sufficient in and of itself to justify the underlying form /'plænt/. This turns out to work fine for this particular case, and it also suffices for the Chimwiini example of the previous chapter.

However, the Isolation Form Shortcut does not work in general. The reason for this lies in how the system is set up, and simple logic: it is certainly possible that neutralization rules could apply *just in case no affix is added to a stem*. We would say that in such cases, the affix "protects" the stem from the neutralizing rule, serving as a kind of buffer.

To make this more precise: neutralizing phonological rules are often conditioned by word edge; that is, they have environments like / ___]$_{word}$. When an affix is present, a stem will be buffered by the affix, and the crucial rule won't apply. Indeed, the rule will apply in *only those members of the paradigm where there is no affix*, so that the buffering effect is absent.

Phonologies that have this kind of phenomenon are quite common, occurring in Korean, Japanese, English, German, Russian, and many other languages. The next section gives a fairly elaborate example from a less familiar language. We will develop the analysis systematically, showing how following the method laid out in §8.1 above can locate the right underlying forms, even where the isolation form shortcut fails.

8.3 Lardil

Lardil is an Australian aboriginal language, spoken on Mornington Island just off the northern coast of the continent in the Bay of Carpinteria. The description and analysis below are taken from the work of the late Kenneth Hale, with additional ideas taken from later researchers who combed through Hale's data seeking further improvements in the analysis. Lardil is of particular interest here because it is a fairly dramatic instance of a language in which the underlying form of a stem cannot be determined from its isolation form.

8.3.1 *Segment inventory*

As the following chart shows, Lardil has four contrasting vowel qualities, each occurring in short and long versions:

	$\begin{bmatrix} +\text{front} \\ -\text{back} \end{bmatrix}$	$\begin{bmatrix} -\text{front} \\ -\text{back} \end{bmatrix}$	$\begin{bmatrix} -\text{front} \\ +\text{back} \end{bmatrix}$
$\begin{bmatrix} +\text{high} \\ -\text{low} \end{bmatrix}$	i, iː		u, uː
$\begin{bmatrix} -\text{high} \\ +\text{low} \end{bmatrix}$	æ, æː[4]	a, aː	

The consonant system of Lardil is more elaborate, with four different types of coronal consonant. The four types form a symmetrical inventory, with apical (tongue tip) and laminal (tongue blade) consonants both in front of and behind the alveolar ridge.

	Labial	Apico-alveolar	Apico-palatal (=retroflex)	Lamino-dental	Lamino-palatal	Velar
Voiceless stops	p	t	ʈ	t̪	tʲ	k
Nasals	m	n	ɳ	n̪	nʲ	ŋ
Tap		ɾ				
Approximants:						
lateral		l				
central	w		ɻ			j

In features, the coronals of Lardil will be classified here as in table 8.1.

---

[4] A minority of Lardil speakers use [e] or [ɛ] in place of [æ]; for these speakers, the phonological rules would have to be stated slightly differently.

Table 8.1   Features for coronal consonants in Lardil

[−distributed]		[+distributed]	
[+anterior]	[+anterior]	[+anterior]	[−anterior]
t, n	ʈ, ɳ	t̪, n̪	tʲ, nʲ

8.3.2 *Data and beginning analysis*

The paradigm data that suffice to get us started consist of uninflected noun stems and two of their inflected forms: the accusative nonfuture, and the accusative future (remarkably, Lardil nouns inflect for tense, in agreement with the verb). In the data, morpheme breaks are marked with hyphens:

Uninflected	Acc. Nonfuture	Acc. Future	Gloss
[kæntapal]	[kæntapal-in]	[kæntapal-uɻ]	'dugong'
[ʈuɳal]	[ʈuɳal-in]	[ʈuɳal-uɻ]	'tree'
[kæʈaɾ]	[kæʈaɾ-in]	[kæʈaɾ-uɻ]	'river'
[tʲumuɾ]	[tʲumuɾ-in]	[tʲumuɾ-uɻ]	'coolimon (a container)'
[mijaɻ]	[mijaɻ-in]	[mijaɻ-uɻ]	'spear'

A reasonable preliminary hypothesis for these data is as follows: there is no ending for the uninflected noun, the accusative nonfuture form takes the suffix /-in/, and the accusative future form takes the suffix /-uɻ/. We can write the morphological rules as follows:

Accusative Nonfuture Formation
X   →   Xin   when [Noun, +accusative, −future]

Accusative Future Formation
X   →   Xuɻ   when [Noun, +accusative, +future]

Here are more data:

Uninflected	Acc. Nonfuture	Acc. Future	Gloss
[mæla]	[mæla-n]	[mæla-ɻ]	'sea'
[wanka]	[wanka-n]	[wanka-ɻ]	'arm'
[kuŋka]	[kuŋka-n]	[kuŋka-ɻ]	'groin'
[ʈawa]	[ʈawa-n]	[ʈawa-ɻ]	'rat'
[taɽŋka]	[taɽŋka-n]	[taɽŋka-ɻ]	'barracuda'
[tʲæmpæ]	[tʲæmpæ-n]	[tʲæmpæ-ɻ]	'mother's father'
[wiʈæ]	[wiʈæ-n]	[wiʈæ-ɻ]	'interior'

We see here two new allomorphs of the accusative nonfuture and the accusative future suffixes: [-n] and [-ɽ]. These allomorphs apparently are what we get after stems that end in a vowel (for the moment, these stem vowels are limited to /a/ and /æ/; further cases will appear below).

Let us now follow the analytical procedure laid out earlier in this chapter. We have the alternation [-in] ~ [-n] in the accusative nonfuture suffix and [-uɽ] ~ [-ɽ] in the accusative future. According to the principle that tells us to consider both directions, we should think about two possibilities: namely, that the underlying representations are [-in] and [-uɽ], with deletion of vowels, or that the underlying representations are [-n] and [-ɽ], with insertion of vowels.

Consider first the hypothesis that the underlying forms are /-in/ and /-uɽ/. We would set up representative underlying and surface forms as follows, and suppose that mediating between them is a "Rule X," whose nature we have not yet determined:

/kæntapal-in/	/kæntapal-uɽ/	/mæla-in/	/mæla-uɽ/	underlying forms
—	—	mælan	mælaɽ	Rule X
[kæntapalin]	[kæntapaluɽ]	[mælan]	[mælaɽ]	surface forms

In fact, this looks straightforward: Lardil, like many other languages, forbids consecutive vowels (a configuration often called **hiatus**), and alters the underlying forms whenever such configurations arise. The hiatuses that are avoided in the above examples are shown in boldface. Apparently, Rule X must be something like this:

Vowel Deletion
[+syllabic] → ∅ / [+syllabic] ___
Delete a vowel after a vowel.

This successfully derives the outputs above from the inputs. In passing, we can note that it also fits what phonologists have learned in language surveys of hiatus resolution: very often, languages avoid hiatus by sacrificing an affix vowel rather than a stem vowel.

Now consider the alternative hypothesis mentioned above: that the vowel ~ zero alternations result from underlying zero, with *insertion* of vowels:

/kæntapal-n/	/kæntapal-ɽ/	/mæla-n/	/mæla-ɽ/	underlying forms
kæntapalin	kæntapaluɽ	—	—	Rule Y
[kæntapalin]	[kæntapal-uɽ]	[mæla-n]	[mæla-ɽ]	surface forms

This doesn't look promising: while we would have no trouble in determining *where* the epenthetic (= inserted) vowel should go (it breaks up word-final consonant sequences), we are basically stuck in determining *which* vowel should be inserted: is it [i] or [u]? There seems to be no principled basis for making this prediction. A reasonable conclusion, then, is that Rule Y simply doesn't exist, and that this approach is not the right one. We choose instead (at least tentatively) to adopt our earlier hypothesis, that the suffix vowels are underlyingly present but deleted in hiatus.

Our choice represents a use of the principle given in §8.1.6 above, whereby we make use of the patterns of restricted contrast in the language to guide us in the choice of underlying representations: since Lardil makes no contrast of vowel vs. consonant in the position after a vowel (only consonants are legal), the Vowel Deletion analysis, which is based on this pattern, will work. In contrast, any analysis that tried to insert the alternating vowels would be working against the direction of neutralization, since Lardil neutralizes (for example) underlying /a+i/ and /a+u/ as surface [a].

Summing up, the analysis so far includes the two morphological rules of Accusative Nonfuture Formation and Accusative Future Formation, and one phonological rule of Vowel Deletion.

8.3.3   *Alternations of vowel quality*

A more pervasive alternation is seen in the following forms:

Uninflected	Acc. Nonfuture	Acc. Future	Gloss
[ŋuka]	[ŋuku-n]	[ŋuku-ɻ]	'water'
[kaʈa]	[kaʈu-n]	[kaʈu-ɻ]	'child'
[ŋawa]	[ŋawu-n]	[ŋawu-ɻ]	'wife'
[pulpa]	[pulpu-n]	[pulpu-ɻ]	'mound, hill'
[muɳa]	[muɳu-n]	[muɳu-ɻ]	'elbow'

To start, we must first make decisions about the morphological composition of the data. The presentation of the data above, with hyphens, indicates a particular decision on this point: the two suffixes that are underlyingly /-in/ and /-uɻ/ are shown as just [-n] and [-ɻ], under the assumption that these five stems are vowel-final stems and that Vowel Deletion has removed underlying vowels after them. Another possibility to consider is that (say) [ŋukuɻ] should be divided as [ŋuk-uɻ], treating [ŋuk] as a consonant stem. However, under this view we would expect *[ŋuk-in], not [ŋukun], for the accusative nonfuture. For this reason, it appears that these stems must be treated as ending in [u].

In light of this, we must deal with the alternation [a] ~ [u]: the uninflected forms have [a] in the location corresponding to [u] in the suffixed forms, appearing in boldface above. We can as usual consider two analyses.

First, the underlying forms of these stems might simply be the same as the isolation forms, and thus end in /a/ (/ŋuka/, /kaʈa/, /ŋawa/). We then need to figure out just why the /a/s should show up as /u/ when a suffix is present. This turns out to pose insuperable problems. The difficulty is that while the forms just given do alternate in this way, an earlier set of stems (three of them are repeated below) also end in /a/ and fail to alternate, keeping /a/ across the board.

Uninflected	Acc. Nonfuture	Acc. Future	Gloss
[mæla]	[mæla-n]	[mæla-ɻ]	'sea'
[wanka]	[wanka-n]	[wanka-ɻ]	'arm'
[kuŋka]	[kuŋka-n]	[kuŋka-ɻ]	'groin'

The dilemma is made clearest if we give charts showing the sort of derivations that we would want, if this were a workable analysis:

/ŋuka/	/ŋuka-in/	/wanka/	/wanka-in/	underlying forms
—	ŋukan	—	wankan	Vowel Deletion
—	**u**	—	**NO**	Rule X
[ŋuka]	[ŋukun]	[wanka]	[wankan]	surface form

The failure of this account should be clear: Rule X, whatever it is, must somehow convert /ŋukan/ to [ŋukun], but not convert /wankan/ to *[wankun]. The number of preceding consonants cannot matter, since /mæla-(i)n/ keeps its /a/: [mælan], just like /wanka/. Unless there is some environment no one has yet noticed that turns out to work, we are exploring a dead end.

Faced with failure from the /a/ → [u] direction for our rule, we can continue by trying the /u/ → [a] direction. What this means is that for those stems that alternate [u] and [a], we set up underlying /u/ in the relevant position. Doing this for the same cases, and setting up the underlying forms, we have the following:

/ŋuku/	/ŋuku-in/	/wanka/	/wanka-in/	underlying forms
—	ŋukun	—	wankan	Vowel Deletion
a	—	—	—	Rule X
[ŋuka]	[ŋukun]	[wanka]	[wankan]	surface form

What is this Rule X that converts /u/ to [a]? Plausibly, its environment is simply word-final position. I will state it tentatively as follows:

Final Lowering (tentative version)

u → a / ___]$_{\text{word}}$

Lower /u/ to [a] if it occurs at the end of a word.

Does this rule work? Plainly, it does account for the data we are looking at right now, as we have seen no instances of surface [u] in final position. But if it is to count as a valid rule, it must be correct for the language as a whole, because under the theory assumed all words are submitted to the same set of phonological rules. Therefore, to check the analysis properly, we must search the whole language, to see if word-final /u/'s actually exist: if they do, then our rule cannot work, and we are back at square one.

In actual fact, the rule does work. There *are* some final /u/s, but they have an independent explanation based on rule ordering. This will be given in §8.3.10 below, once we have examined additional data.

8.3.4 Underlying forms are not always isolation forms

The portion of the analysis just established is our first illustration of the inadequacy of the Isolation Form Shortcut (p. 165). It is tempting, from knowing that the stem for 'water' in Lardil pronounced alone is [ŋuka], to assume that the underlying representation of this stem is simply /ŋuka/. However, we need to account not just for this plain-stem form, but for the whole paradigm, and for this purpose the more remote underlying representation /ŋuku/ is needed.

The other lesson that emerges is that a word edge can act as a crucial phonological environment. This is actually quite common in phonology, particularly for the edge that comes at the end of a word. Right word edges, though not audible and not physically articulated, induce a great variety of phonological changes: devoicing (German, Polish, Quiché), vowel lengthening (Chimwiini), glottal stop insertion (Japanese), consonant loss (Catalan), and vowel loss (Latvian, and as we will shortly see, Lardil). The phonological effects of word edges are discussed further in chapter 10.

8.3.5 Generalizing Final Lowering to front vowels

The hypothesis that Final Lowering is a rule of Lardil phonology is further supported when we look at other data:

Uninflected	Acc. Nonfuture	Acc. Future	Gloss
[kæɳʈæ]	[kæɳʈi-n]	[kæɳʈi-wuɻ]	'wife'
[ɲinæ]	[ɲiɲi-n]	[ɲiɲi-wuɻ]	'skin'
[papæ]	[papi-n]	[papi-wuɻ]	'father's mother'
[tʲimpæ]	[tʲimpi-n]	[tʲimpi-wuɻ]	'tail'
[nʲæɾwæ]	[nʲæɾwi-n]	[nʲæɾwi-wuɻ]	'place'

These involve an alternation between a low and a high vowel, [æ] ~ [i], which parallels the alternation we saw earlier of [a] ~ [u]. There is, moreover, another alternation, with [w] appearing in the Accusative Future suffix; more on this shortly.

For the height alternation, the same considerations seen earlier show that the alternation must be due to lowering, not raising: there are stems (repeated below) that have final [æ] throughout the paradigm.

Uninflected	Acc. Nonfuture	Acc. Future	Gloss
[tʲæmpæ]	[tʲæmpæ-n]	[tʲæmpæ-ɹ]	'mother's father'
[wiʈæ]	[wiʈæ-n]	[wiʈæ-ɹ]	'interior'

As before, the underlying stem-final vowels must be the ones that appear in the contextual allomorphs: thus [tʲæmpæ] is underlyingly /tʲæmpæ/, while [papæ] is underlyingly /papi/.

The fact that both show up with final [æ] in their isolation forms will follow from a generalized version of Final Lowering, which lowers not just /u/ to [a], but also /i/ to [æ]. To make both changes in one rule, we can use features as follows:

Final Lowering

$$[\text{+syllabic}] \rightarrow \begin{bmatrix} -\text{high} \\ +\text{low} \\ -\text{back} \\ -\text{round} \end{bmatrix} / \underline{\quad} \,]_{\text{word}}$$

This rule changes [round], so that /u/ will become unrounded, and it also changes [back], so that /u/ will become central [a] rather than back [ɑ]. These changes are vacuous (harmless) in the case of /i/, which is already [−round, −back].

Here are sample derivations for representative stems ending in /i/ and /æ/:

/papi /	/papi-in/	/witæ/	/witæ-in/	underlying forms
—	papin	—	witæn	Vowel Deletion
æ	—	—	—	Final Lowering
[papæ]	[papin]	[wiʈæ]	[wiʈæn]	surface forms

There is one further detail: recall that after stems ending underlyingly in /i/ (data on p. 171), the accusative future ending /-uɹ/ shows up with the allomorph /-wuɹ/, as in [kænʈæ] ~ [kænʈi-n] ~ [kænʈi-wuɹ]. While various analyses are possible, it seems at least reasonable to suppose that this is due to epenthesis of /w/, by the following rule:

/w/ Epenthesis
$\varnothing \rightarrow w / i \underline{\quad} u$
Insert [w] *between* [i] *and* [u].

This can be seen, like Vowel Deletion, as a hiatus-resolving rule. It is fairly common for languages to resolve high-vowel hiatus by inserting a glide that is **homorganic** (shares the same articulatory position) with one of the two adjacent vowels; here, [w] is homorganic with [u]. Some varieties of English have such glides; they appear in emphatic speaking style and are homorganic with a preceding high vowel: /'suɚ/ → ['suwɚ] *sewer*, /'bi-ɪŋ/ → ['bijɪŋ] *being*.

/w/ Epenthesis must be ordered before Vowel Deletion. Both "try" to resolve hiatus. In cases where the hiatus is /iu/, /w/ Epenthesis gets the first chance, resolving it as [iwu]. The hiatus being resolved, Vowel Deletion is blocked. Vowel Deletion does get to apply, however, in all other cases.

Putting this all together, we can now give a fairly complete analysis of the vowel-final stems. Here are derivations for each of four vowel phonemes of Lardil, /i/, /æ/, /u/, and /a/:

/papi/	/papi-in/	/papi-uɻ/	/witæ/	/witæ-in/	/witæ-uɻ/	underlying forms
—	—	papiwuɻ	—	—	—	/w/ Epenthesis
—	papin	—	—	witæn	witæɻ	Vowel Deletion
æ	—	—	—	—	—	Final Lowering
[papæ]	[papin]	[papiwuɻ]	[witæ]	[witæn]	[witæɻ]	surface forms

/ŋuku/	/ŋuku-in/	/ŋuku-uɻ/	/wanka/	/wanka-in/	/wanka-uɻ/	underlying forms
—	—	—	—	—	—	/w/ Epenthesis
—	ŋukun	ŋukuɻ	—	wankan	wankaɻ	Vowel Deletion
a	—	—	—	—	—	Final Lowering
[ŋuka]	[ŋukun]	[ŋukuɻ]	[wanka]	[wankan]	[wankaɻ]	surface forms

8.3.6 A minor phenomenon

The following sections will cover the most important phonological rules of Lardil. However, to make the presentation as clear as possible it will be useful first to dispose of a minor corner of the system. The following data are paradigms of stems that end in a nasal consonant.

Uninflected	Acc. Nonfuture	Acc. Future	Gloss
[jaɾaman]	[jaɾaman-in]	[jaɾaman-kuɻ]	'horse'
[piɾŋæn]	[piɾŋæn-in]	[piɾŋæn-kuɻ]	'woman'
[kaɳtʲin]	[kaɳtʲin-in]	[kaɳtʲin-kuɻ]	'wallaby'
[tupalan]	[tupalan-in]	[tupalan-kuɻ]	'road'
[maːɳ]	[maːɳ-in]	[maːɳ-kuɻ]	'spear'

The accusative nonfuture forms are just as we would expect (no phonology applies), but the accusative future, normally /-uɻ/, shows a curious and unexpected [k]. Various analyses of this /k/ are possible; for now we assume that it is inserted by a rule of epenthesis. Inspection suggests that to get this to work will require a rather complicated and arbitrary-seeming rule:

/k/ Epenthesis
Ø → k / [+nasal] ___ uɻ
Insert [k] *between a nasal sound and a following* /uɻ/ *sequence.*

Here is a sample derivation:

/piɾŋæn-uɹ/	underlying form
k	/k/ Epenthesis
[piɾŋænkuɹ]	surface form

No rule ordering is required. /k/ Epenthesis will serve our purposes for now, deriving the correct Accusative Future forms for nasal stems. However, as it is rather suspect due to its complexity, we will explore an alternative approach in §9.9.

8.3.7 *Some more dramatic alternations*

The following stems show a pattern of alternation we have not previously seen.

Uninflected	Acc. Nonfuture	Acc. Future	Gloss
[jalul]	[jalulu-n]	[jalulu-ɹ]	'flame'
[majaɾ]	[majaɾa-n]	[majaɾa-ɹ]	'rainbow'
[wiwal]	[wiwala-n]	[wiwala-ɹ]	'bush mango'
[puʈuɹmaɾ]	[puʈuɹmaɾa-n]	[puʈuɹmaɾa-ɹ]	'native companion'
[kaɾikaɾ]	[kaɾikaɾi-n]	[kaɾikaɾi-wuɹ]	'butterfish'
[kaŋkaɹi]	[kaŋkaɹi-n]	[kaŋkaɹi-wuɹ]	'father's father'
[jilijil]	[jilijili-n]	[jilijili-wuɹ]	'species of oyster'

The suffix allomorphs we see ([-n], [-ɹ], [-wuɹ]) are what we would expect, given the preceding stem vowels. However, the stem vowels alternate with zero in the uninflected form, an alternation not previously seen. We must therefore consider two hypotheses, deletion and insertion.

Insertion doesn't look promising, because there is no straightforward basis for determining which vowel should be inserted – it can be [u], [i], or [a] (the absence of cases with [æ] appears to be accidental).

Deletion looks more promising. Examine in particular the following partial derivation, for the paradigm of the stem /kaɾikaɾi/:

/kaɾikaɾi/	/kaɾikaɾi-in/	/kaɾikaɾi-uɹ/	underlying forms
—	—	—	/k/ Epenthesis
—	—	kaɾikaɾiwuɹ	/w/ Epenthesis
—	kaɾikaɾin	—	Vowel Deletion
kaɾikaɾ	—	—	**Rule X**
[kaɾikaɾ]	[karikarin]	[karikariwuɾ]	surface forms

An encouraging thing to notice, even before we try to figure out Rule X, is that the underlying form, under this analysis, is an "inherently reduplicated" stem, that is, two copies of /kaɾi/. Many other cases of this type are found in Lardil; for example /jilijili/ and others given below. While /kaɾi/ is apparently not in itself a meaningful morpheme of Lardil, it remains true that quite a few languages (e.g. Ilokano, Toba Batak, Arabic, Hebrew) employ this kind of stem frequently. So this gives the deletion analysis some plausibility, even before we've got the relevant rule worked out.

As for the rule: it appears to delete vowels in final position, a common phonological process (seen also in Menomini, French, Ponapeian, and Middle English). The hard part is to determine why final vowel drop should occur in the forms presently under consideration, but not in the data we saw earlier – which also include underlying final vowels. You may find it useful to look over the data again and try to figure out the answer before going on. The relevant earlier cases to compare are on pp. 167, 169, and 171.

The answer is that vowel drop depends on the underlying length of the stem. Specifically, no stem ever loses its final vowel if it has just two vowels to start with. This restriction can be formalized in the deletion rule, which is stated below. The name of the rule, Apocope ([əˈpɑkəpi]), is a traditional phonological term meaning "deletion in final position":

Apocope
$$V \rightarrow \varnothing \; / \; V \; C_0 \; V \; C_0 \; \underline{\quad} \;]_{word}$$
Delete the final vowel of the word if at least two vowels precede it.

The formalism of the rule is explained as follows. C_0, introduced on p. 154, means "any number of consonants." Thus, to apply the rule to a form like /puṯuɻmaɾa/ 'native companion-uninflected', the matchup between rule and form would be as follows:

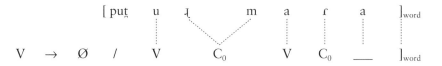

With the rule of Apocope in place, we can compare the derivations of a short and a long stem. Apocope only applies to /puṯuɻmaɾa/, where enough underlying vowels are present; /papi/ lacks the required three vowels.

/papi/	/papi-in/	/papi-uɻ/	/puṯuɻmaɾa/	/puṯuɻmaɾa-in/	/puṯuɻmaɾa-uɻ/	underlying forms
—	—	papiwuɻ	—	—	—	/w/ Epenthesis
—	—	—	—	—	—	/k/ Epenthesis
—	papin	—	—	puṯuɻmaɾan	puṯuɻmaɾaɻ	Vowel Deletion
æ	—	—	—	—	—	Final Lowering
NO	—	—	puṯuɻmaɾ	—	—	Apocope
[papæ]	[papin]	[papiwuṯ]	[puṯuɻmaɾ]	[puṯuɻmaɾan]	[puṯuɻmaɾaɻ]	surface forms

8.3.8   *Cluster Reduction*

Consider next the following forms.

Uninflected	Acc. Nonfuture	Acc. Future	Gloss
[jukaɾ]	[jukaɾpa-n]	[jukaɾpa-ɻ]	'husband'
[wulun]	[wulunka-n]	[wulunka-ɻ]	'species of fruit'
[wuṭal]	[wuṭaltʲi-n]	[wuṭaltʲi-wuɻ]	'meat'
[panṭʲipan]	[panṭʲipanṭʲi-n]	[panṭʲipanṭʲi-ɻ]	'hat'
[kantukan]	[kantukantu-n]	[kantukantu-ɻ]	'red'
[kaɾwakaɾ]	[kaɾwakaɾwa-n]	[kaɾwakaɾwa-ɻ]	'species of wattle'
[jaɾpajaɾ]	[jaɾpajaɾpa-n]	[jaɾpajaɾpa-ɻ]	'bird species'

Like the previous ones, these show vowel ~ zero alternations, but also consonant ~ zero alternations. For example, in [jukar], both the /p/ and the /a/ seen in [jurkarpa] are missing. As before, it is unlikely that the consonants could be derived by insertion, since there are several different consonants that alternate ([p, t, tʲ, k, w] in these forms), and the environment for inserting different consonants would be impossible to state.

Often when the analysis has reached a certain state of development, the best analytic procedure is to set up the most likely underlying forms, run them through the rules developed so far, and see in what way the result diverges from the actual outcomes. At this stage, we have a fairly clear notion that we should not be looking to the uninflected forms, but rather to the suffixed forms, to give us the underlying forms. If we set up our underlying forms and derivations on this basis, we obtain the following set of predicted output forms:

/jukaɾpa/	/jukaɾpa-in/	/jukaɾpa-uɻ/	underlying forms
—	—	—	/k/ Epenthesis
—	—	—	/w/ Epenthesis
—	jukaɾpan	jukaɾpaɻ	Vowel Deletion
—	—	—	Final Lowering
jukaɾp	—	—	Apocope
*[jukaɾp]	[jukaɾpan]	[jukaɾpaɻ]	predicted surface forms

The analysis works except where it generates *[jukaɾp] instead of the correct [jukaɾ]. It would likewise also generate the incorrect *[wulunk], *[wuṭaltʲ], *[paṭʲipanṭʲ], *[kantukant], *[kaɾwakaɾw], and *[jaɾpajaɾp] for the forms given above. This problem is not hard to fix, provided one notices that no word in Lardil ever ends with a sequence of consonants. What seems to be happening is this: Apocope applies freely to words of sufficient length, and when it creates a final consonant cluster, a further rule eliminates the cluster by deleting its second member.

The rule may be formulated as follows:

Cluster Reduction

$C \rightarrow \emptyset \: / \: C \underline{\hspace{2em}} \:]_{\text{word}}$

Delete a word-final consonant when it is preceded by a consonant.

This leads to the correct outcome, as follows:

/jukaɾpa/	/jukaɾpa-in/	/jukaɾpa-uɽ/	underlying forms
—	—	—	/k/ Epenthesis
—	—	—	/w/ Epenthesis
—	jukaɾpan	jukaɾpaɽ	Vowel Deletion
—	—	—	Final Lowering
jukaɾp	—	—	Apocope
jukaɾ	—	—	Cluster Reduction
[jukaɾ]	[jukaɾpan]	[jukaɾpaɽ]	surface forms

Plainly, Cluster Reduction must be ordered after Apocope, since it is Apocope that exposes the consonant cluster to word-final position.

Cluster Reduction also applies in a few forms that end *underlyingly* in clusters, such as the following:

Uninflected	Acc. Nonfuture	Acc. Future	Gloss
[makaɾ]	[makaɾk-in]	[makaɾk-uɽ]	'anthill'
[waŋal]	[waŋalk-in]	[waŋalk-uɽ]	'boomerang'
[tanʲiɾ]	[tanʲiɾk-in]	[tanʲiɾk-uɽ]	'hip'

Here are derivations for the paradigm of /makaɾk/ 'anthill'.

/makaɾk/	/makaɾk-in/	/makaɾk-uɽ/	underlying forms
—	—	—	/k/ Epenthesis
—	—	—	/w/ Epenthesis
—	—	—	Vowel Deletion
—	—	—	Final Lowering
—	—	—	Apocope
makaɾ	—	—	Cluster Reduction
[makaɾ]	[makaɾkin]	[makaɾkuɽ]	surface forms

8.3.9 Another deletion rule

There is one more rule to be covered whose effects can be seen in the following forms:

Uninflected	Acc. Nonfuture	Acc. Future	Gloss
[putu]	[putuka-n]	[putuka-ɹ]	'short'
[muɾkuni]	[muɾkunima-n]	[muɾkunima-ɹ]	'nullah'[5]
[ŋawuŋa]	[ŋawuŋawu-n]	[ŋawuŋawu-ɹ]	'termite'
[pukatʲi]	[pukatʲija-n]	[pukatʲija-ɹ]	'scavenger hawk'
[tipiʈi]	[tipiʈipi-n]	[tipiʈipi-wuɹ]	'species of rock cod'
[ʈaɾawu]	[ʈaɾawuʈa-n]	[ʈaɾawuʈa-ɹ]	'trousers' (< English)
[ʈapu]	[ʈaputʲi-n]	[ʈaputʲi-wuɹ]	'older brother'
[jaːku]	[jaːkuwa-n]	[jaːkuwa-ɹ]	'blue-tongued lizard'
[ŋunʲiŋu]	[ŋunʲiŋunʲi-n]	[ŋunʲiŋunʲi-wuɹ]	'message stick'[6]

The uninflected forms are the apparent exceptions to Final Lowering alluded to above in §8.3.4 and §8.3.5. These final high vowels will be explained shortly.

The forms look somewhat like the Cluster Reduction forms of the previous section. Plainly, the final vowels of the stems get deleted, and there is also a consonant ~ zero alternation, but this time not in a cluster. Assuming as before that the underlying forms can be read off the suffixed forms, we want the derivation to do the following:

/putuka/	/putuka-in/	/putuka-uɹ/	underlying forms
—	—	—	/k/ Epenthesis
—	—	—	/w/ Epenthesis
—	putukan	putukaɹ	Vowel Deletion
—	—	—	Final Lowering
putuk	—	—	Apocope
—	—	—	Cluster Reduction
putu	—	—	**Rule X**
[putu]	[putukan]	[putukaɹ]	surface forms

A crucial fact is that no word of Lardil ever ends in /k/, which suggests that any /k/ that is placed at the end of a word by Apocope gets deleted by Rule X. Thus, the analytic strategy that makes sense here is to sort out the consonants of Lardil according to whether they delete, and see if the deletable consonants constitute a natural class.

Before we do this, some further data will be helpful. These are rather simpler forms, in which a consonant deletes, but it is underlyingly final rather than being exposed to final position by Apocope:

---

[5] According to the *Oxford English Dictionary*, "A watercourse, river-bed, or ravine."
[6] Hale gives only an underlying represention (/ŋunʲiŋunʲi/) for this form; the paradigm given is constructed using his rules.

Uninflected	Acc. Nonfuture	Acc. Future	Gloss
[t̪uɾaɾa]	[t̪uɾaɾaŋ-in]	[t̪uɾaɾaŋ-kuɻ]	'shark'
[ŋalu]	[ŋaluk-in]	[ŋaluk-uɻ]	'story'
[kumpu]	[kumpuŋ-in]	[kumpuŋ-kuɻ]	'anus'
[milwaɾkaɻu]	[milwaɾkaɻuŋ-in]	[milwaɾkaɻuŋ-kuɻ]	'shovelnose shark'

The underlying representations here would be /t̪uɾaɾaŋ/, /ŋaluk/, and so on.

With these data in hand, we can now sort the consonants of Lardil into those which delete finally and those which do not. In Lardil in general, the following consonants are permitted word-finally:

[t]	as in [ŋawit] 'stomach'[7]		
[n]	as in [pirɲæn]	[ɳ]	as in [maːɳ]
[l]	as in [jalul]	[ɻ]	as in [mijaɻ]
[ɾ]	as in [majaɾ]		

The following consonants are not observed finally, and indeed are observed to disappear when they would otherwise be expected to occur in final position:

[p]	([tipit̪i], not *[tipit̪ip])
[m]	([muɾkuni], not *[muɾkunim])
[w]	([ŋawuɲa], not *[ŋawuɲaw])
[t̪]	([t̪aɾawu], not *[t̪aɾawut̪])
[tʲ]	([t̪apu], not *[t̪aputʲ])
[nʲ]	([ɲunʲiɲu], not *[ɲunʲiɲunʲ])
[j]	([pukatʲi], not *[pukatʲij])
[k]	([putu], not *[putuk])
[ŋ]	([t̪uɾaɾa], not *[t̪uɾaɾaŋ])

Consulting the phonetic chart for Lardil (p. 166) it can be seen that the crucial class consists of apicals; that is, only apical consonants can survive in final position. With the features assumed here (p. 167), the apicals are [–distributed], so that the deletion rule can be stated informally as follows:[8]

Non-Apical Deletion
C → Ø / ___]₍word₎ unless C = [–distributed]

[7] The phonology of /t/-stems in Lardil involves complexities treated in the sources (see Further reading) but not covered here. Underlying /t/ is converted in various contexts to [t̪], [tʲ], or [ɾ].

[8] Here is the fine print concerning Non-apical Deletion. (1) The rule predicts that [t] should be legal at the end of a word, which is not true. The absence of final [t] is due to an additional rule of Sonorantization: /t/ → [ɻ] / ___]₍word₎, as in /kit̪ikit̪i/ → kit̪ikit → [kit̪ikiɻ] 'moon' (compare Acc. Nonfut. [kit̪ikit̪i-n]). (2) There are apparently no stems that have underlying /ɳ/ in a deletable position; the prediction made by the analysis is that if such stems did exist, their final consonants would alternate with zero.

Below are derivations that illustrate the rule. Underlying /putaka/ has a non-apical in the crucial position, which succumbs to Non-Apical Deletion. /jilijili/ has an apical in the analogous location, which survives. The crucial comparison is in boldface.

/putuka/	/putuka-in/	/putuka-uɹ/	/jilijili/	/jilijili-in/	/jilijili-uɹ/	underlying forms
—	—	—	—	—	—	/k/ Epenthesis
—	—	—	—	—	jilijiliwuɹ	/w/ Epenthesis
—	putukan	putukaɹ	—	jilijilin	—	Vowel Deletion
—	—	—	—	—	—	Final Lowering
putuk	—	—	jilijil	—	—	Apocope
—	—	—	—	—	—	Cluster Reduction
putu	—	—	**NO**	—	—	Non-Apical Deletion
[putu]	[putukan]	[putukaɹ]	[jilijil]	[jilijilin]	[jilijiwuɹ]	surface forms

Like Cluster Reduction, Non-Apical Deletion must apply after Apocope, for the same reason: Apocope exposes the deletable consonant to word-final position.

There is another reason why Non-Apical Deletion has to follow Apocope. Suppose we start out with a quadrisyllabic stem like /murkunima/, from p. 181. Apocope removes the final vowel: /murkunim/, and Non-Apical Deletion removes the /m/: /murkuni/. We have exposed a new vowel to word-final position. Now, observe that the resulting word is trisyllabic, but it doesn't undergo Apocope again! That is, we get [murkuni], not *[murkun]. This follows from the analysis, which already is formulated (for independent reasons) so that Apocope precedes Non-Apical Deletion.

This looks like it is a result that comes "for free"; but in fact it depends on a particular assumption about rule ordering, namely that rules have to be applied in a strict order. In a theory where rules were allowed to reapply freely whenever they were applicable, this would not be so.

For roots which end underlying in a non-apical, like /ʈuraraŋ/ (p. 179), the derivations are simpler, involving only Non-Apical Deletion in the uninflected form:

/ʈuraraŋ/	/ʈuraraŋ-in/	/ʈuraraŋ-uɹ/	underlying forms
—	—	ʈuraraŋkuɹ	/k/ Epenthesis
—	—	—	/w/ Epenthesis
—	—	—	Vowel Deletion
—	—	—	Final Lowering
—	—	—	Apocope
—	—	—	Cluster Reduction
ʈurara	—	—	Non-Apical Deletion
[ʈurara]	[ʈuraraŋin]	[ʈuraraŋkuɹ]	surface forms

8.3.10 Some further rule orderings

To complete the Lardil analysis, we must establish all relevant rule orderings.

The following forms suffice to show that Cluster Reduction precedes Non-Apical Deletion:

Uninflected	Acc. Nonfuture	Acc. Future	Gloss
[muŋkumu]	[muŋkumuŋku-n]	[muŋkumuŋku-ɻ]	'wooden axe'
[tʲumputʲu]	[tʲumputʲumpu-n]	[tʲumputʲumpu-ɻ]	'dragonfly'

That is, for underlying /muŋkumuŋku/, first Apocope deletes the final vowel (/muŋkumuŋk/), then Cluster Reduction deletes the second member of the resulting cluster (/muŋkumuŋ/). Then (and only then) can Non-Apical Deletion delete the word-final /ŋ/, yielding [muŋkumu].

Here is another ordering argument. Review the following forms, which all have been considered earlier when we were setting up the rules of Apocope, Cluster Reduction, and Non-Apical Deletion:

Uninflected	Acc. Nonfuture	Acc. Future	Gloss
[murkuni]	[murkunima-n]	[murkunima-ɻ]	'nullah'
[tipiti]	[tipitipi-n]	[tipitipi-wuɻ]	'species of rock cod'
[putu]	[putuka-n]	[putuka-ɻ]	'short'
[ʈapu]	[ʈaputʲi-n]	[ʈaputʲi-wuɻ]	'older brother'
[ŋalu]	[ŋaluk-in]	[ŋaluk-uɻ]	'story'
[muŋkumu]	[muŋkumuŋku-n]	[muŋkumuŋku-ɻ]	'wooden axe'
[tʲumputʲu]	[tʲumputʲumpu-n]	[tʲumputʲumpu-ɻ]	'dragonfly'

In all of these forms, the uninflected surface stem ends in a high vowel. But earlier in the analysis, we claimed that word-final high vowels were illegal, and wrote a rule of Final Lowering (p. 172) to eliminate them by lowering in final position. The resolution of the problem comes from the observation that final high vowels are well-formed provided that they are not *underlyingly* final, but rather final by virtue of Non-Apical Deletion. That is, all of the final high vowels shown immediately above are in words that expose a final high vowel by deleting a consonant. It is these vowels, and only these, that survive as high.

Analytically, we can get this by ordering Final Lowering before Non-Apical Deletion. This will work, for representative examples, as follows:

/putuka/	/ŋuku/	underlying forms
—	—	/k/ Epenthesis
—	—	/w/ Epenthesis
—	—	Vowel Deletion
—	ŋuka	Final Lowering
putuk	—	Apocope
—	—	Cluster Reduction
putu	—	Non-Apical Deletion
[putu]	[ŋuka]	surface forms

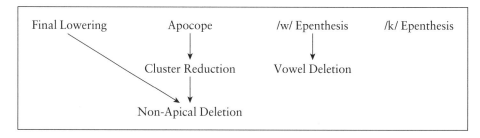

Figure 8.1 Hasse diagram illustrating the ordering of three rules of Lardil

As can be seen, Non-Apical Deletion "applies too late" for the resulting final vowel to be lowered.

The Hasse diagram in figure 8.1 depicts all of the necessary orderings in the analysis. Any arrangement of the rules in a strict linear order that is compatible with the arrows in the diagram will work.

8.3.11   Concluding remarks on Lardil

This completes the analysis of Lardil, insofar as it is covered here (for more, see Further reading). The general lessons that emerge are as follows.

First, Lardil stems alternate in a fairly drastic way, but the system is fundamentally a simple one: the pattern of alternation reduces to a set of phonological rules applied to the output of the morphological component.

Second, Lardil is a classic illustration of the fact that the Isolation Form Shortcut (§8.2) does not always work. Lardil isolation forms are subjected to remarkable processes of right-edge erosion. It is only when a suffix protects the stem from this erosion that the base form of a stem can be seen plainly.

Lastly, although the Lardil facts are complex, they yield to systematic procedures of analysis – something which is useful to remember when you get stuck while doing analytical work. These procedures invoke the following questions: what are the patterns of alternation among morphemes? If these patterns are to be reduced to rule, what is the full set of possibilities for choosing the underlying representations? Considering *each* of these hypotheses, what would the underlying forms look like, and what rules (if any) would suffice to derive the surface forms? Where does there appear to be neutralization (which usually forces a choice as to the "direction" in which the rules apply)? What natural classes are evident in the data pattern? The answers to these questions often will lead to a working analysis.

8.4   Rule-Ordering Terminology

Rule ordering clearly plays a major role in the Lardil analysis. Thus, Lardil is a useful example for learning four terms about rule ordering that are commonly used by phonologists. These terms are **feeding**, **bleeding**, **counterfeeding**, and **counterbleeding**.

8.4.1   *Feeding*

Observe that Apocope, when it exposes a consonant cluster at the end of a word, thereby *makes it possible* for Cluster Reduction to apply. The following abbreviated derivation (see p. 176 for the original) shows this:

/jukaɾpa/	underlying form
jukaɾp	Apocope
jukaɾ	Cluster Reduction
[jukaɾ]	surface form

This is said to be a case of **feeding**: Apocope "feeds" Cluster Reduction. The term is defined in general as follows.

Rule A **feeds** rule B when:

- A is ordered before B, and
- A creates novel configurations to which B may apply.

8.4.2   *Bleeding*

Consider next the interaction of /w/ Epenthesis and Vowel Deletion, shown in the following abbreviated derivation (see p. 173 for the original):

/papi-uɻ/	underlying form
papiwuɻ	/w/ Epenthesis
—	Vowel Deletion
[papiwuɻ]	surface form

It is clear that *if /w/ Epenthesis had not applied*, then Vowel Deletion would have had an additional chance to apply, creating *[papiɻ]. Thus, we might say that /w/ Epenthesis, in this particular derivation, "blocks" or "pre-empts" Vowel Deletion. The standard term used, however, is **bleeding**; /w/ Epenthesis bleeds Vowel Deletion. More generally:

Rule A **bleeds** rule B when:

- A is ordered before B, and
- A removes configurations to which B could otherwise have applied.

8.4.3   Counterfeeding

Rule ordering terminology also includes two terms that are useful but tricky: they both mean "is ordered too late to do X." Consider first the derivation of the Lardil form [ŋalu] 'story-uninflected', from underlying /ŋaluk/ (the justification for the underlying form can be seen in the accusative nonfuture [ŋaluk-in]). The relevant stages are these:

/ŋaluk/	underlying form
—	Final Lowering
ŋalu	Non-Apical Deletion
[ŋalu]	surface form

Evidently, Non-Apical Deletion *applies too late to feed* Final Lowering (whose action is seen elsewhere in simple derivations like /ŋuku/ → [ŋuka] 'water', p. 170). The term normally used to describe this situation is **counterfeeding**; specifically, Non-Apical Deletion counterfeeds Final Lowering. In general terms:

Rule A **counterfeeds** rule B when:

- A is ordered after B, and
- A creates novel configurations to which B could have applied, if A had been applied before B.

It is useful to think of "counterfeed" as meaning "fails to feed," or "arrives too late to feed." "Counterfeed" is by no means the same as "bleed."

8.4.4   Counterbleeding

The last term of ordering commonly used is **counterbleed**, which means "is ordered too late to bleed." The derivation for [papiwuɻ], already given as an example of bleeding, also illustrates counterbleeding. In particular, Vowel Deletion counterbleeds /w/ Epenthesis.

/papi-uɻ/	underlying form
papiwuɻ	/w/ Epenthesis (p. 172)
—	Vowel Deletion (p. 168)
[papiwuɻ]	surface form

If Vowel Deletion had (counter to fact) applied first, deriving *[papiɻ], it would have bled /w/ Epenthesis. This can be seen most clearly if we provide an incorrect derivation with this opposite order:

/papi-uɻ/	underlying form
papiɻ	Vowel Deletion
—	/w/ Epenthesis
*[papiɻ]	incorrect surface form

In the incorrect derivation Vowel Deletion bleeds /w/ Epenthesis. Therefore, in the correct derivation, with the opposite order, Vowel Deletion counterbleeds /w/ Epenthesis. A definition of counterbleeding is as follows:

Rule A **counterbleeds** rule B when:

- A is ordered after B, and
- A would have removed configurations to which B applies, had A applied first.

8.4.5 Summary

These four terms, though tricky to learn to use accurately, continue to be employed by phonologists because they provide a clear classification of the reasons why rules have to be ordered. Table 8.2 may be of help in studying these terms.

Table 8.2   Summary of rule ordering terminology

		Rule Ordering	
		A precedes B	A follows B
Does Rule B apply?	B succeeds in applying	A **feeds** B (creates a location where B can apply)	A **counterbleeds** B (ordered too late to remove a location where B can apply)
	B fails to apply	A **bleeds** B (removes a location where B could have applied)	A **counterfeeds** B (ordered too late to create a location where B could apply)

The Hasse diagram for Lardil rule ordering, from p. 182, can be annotated with the reason for each ordering:

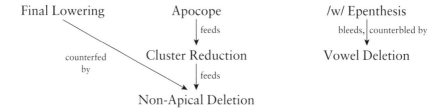

Exercises

1 *Lardil rule ordering*

a. Give an incorrect derivation for Lardil /jukarpa/ 'husband-uninflected', showing what output is obtained if Cluster Reduction is ordered before Apocope (for correct derivation, see p. 177).

b. Give an incorrect derivation for Lardil /putuka/ 'short-uninflected', showing what output is obtained if Apocope is ordered after Non-Apical Deletion (for correct derivation, see p. 180).

c. Give an incorrect derivation for Lardil /muŋkumuŋku/ 'wooden axe-uninflected' (p. 181), showing what output is obtained if Non-Apical Deletion is ordered before Cluster Reduction.

2 *Yidiɲ*

This problem concerns the phonological alternations that arise in the nominal paradigms of Yidiɲ, an aboriginal language of Queensland, Australia.

Hints: It is probably best to consider the different batches of data in order, rather than trying to solve the problem all at once. If you get stuck, count the number of syllables in all of the words in part (b).

a. Make a phonetic chart for all the sounds in the data.

b. What are the phonemic forms of the stems and case suffixes below? In order to derive the observed phonetic forms, what phonological rules must apply? (You will find one of these rules difficult to formalize; it is all right just to express it clearly in words.) Make sure that your rules predict when vowels will be long. If your rules must be ordered, what is the required ordering?

Absolutive	Comitative	Genitive	Comitative + Genitive	gloss
buɲa	buɲaːj	buɲaːn	buɲajini	'woman'
manu	manuːj	manuːn	manujini	'treetop'
wuda	wudaːj	wudaːn	wudajini	'shark'
wugu	wuguːj	wuguːn	wugujini	'work'
biniːr	biniriji	binirini	binirijiːn	'money'
wajiːl	wajiliji	wajilini	wajilijiːn	'red bream'
mindiːr	mindiriji	mindirini	mindirijiːn	'salt-water centipede'
gambiːɻ	gambiɻaji	gambiɻani	gambiɻajiːn	'tablelands'
gubuːm	gubumaji	gubumani	gubumajiːn	'black pine'
gumaːl	gumalaji	gumalani	gumalajiːn	'stage in the development of grubs'
gindaːn	gindanuji	gindanuni	gindanujiːn	'moon'
jaguːɲ	jaguɲuji	jaguɲuni	jaguɲujiːn	'echidna'
gujuːɻ	gujuɻuji	gujuɻuni	gujuɻujiːn	'storm'
ŋunaŋgara	ŋunaŋgaraːj	ŋunaŋgaraːn	ŋunaŋgarajini	'whale'
bugamugu	bugamuguːj	bugamuguːn	bugamugujini	'daylight'
ɟulugunu	ɟulugunuːj	ɟulugunuːn	ɟulugunujini	'black myrtle'
ɟilibiɻi	ɟilibiɻiːj	ɟilibiɻiːn	ɟilibiɻijini	'lungfish'

c. Unlike the set of stems previously given, the following stems may appear in odd-syllabled surface forms. They nonetheless show vowel length alternations. You may wish to revise your analysis from the preceding section, or you can write up questions (b) and (c) as one answer.

Absolutive	Comitative	Genitive	Comitative + Genitive	gloss
ŋumbuːbu	ŋumbubuji	ŋumbubuni	ŋumbubujiːn	'new-born baby'
waɻaːba	waɻabaji	waɻabani	waɻabajiːn	'wide creek'
gujŋgiːlbi	gujŋgilbiji	gujŋgilbini	gujŋgilbijiːn	'Moreton Bay tree'
gawuːda	gawudaji	gawudani	gawudajiːn	'coat'
guluːdu	guluduji	guluduni	guludujiːn	'dove'
bunbuːɻa	bunbuɻaji	bunbuɻani	bunbuɻajiːn	'(spinning) top'
gabuːɻu	gabuɻuji	gabuɻuni	gabuɻujiːn	'white clay'
baɻiːnɟi	baɻinɟiji	baɻinɟini	baɻinɟijiːn	'sutton bird'
giɻaːrɟi	giɻarɟiji	giɻarɟini	giɻarɟijiːn	'policeman'
guruːŋga	guruŋgaji	guruŋgani	guruŋgajiːn	'kookaburra'
ɟaraːga	ɟaragaji	ɟaragani	ɟaragajiːn	'step-relative'
ɟumbaːgi	ɟumbagiji	ɟumbagini	ɟumbagijiːn	'tobacco'
ɲuruːgu	ɲuruguji	ɲuruguni	ɲurugujiːn	'sound of talking far off'

d. Explain how your analysis can account for these additional inflected forms, providing underlying forms for the suffixes. The stems are the same as those given already.

Dative	*Accusative*	*Purposive*	*Comitative +* *Apprehensive*	*"Another"*
buɲaːnda	buɲaːɲ	buɲaːgu	buɲajida	buɲaːbi
manuːnda	manuːɲ	manuːgu	manujida	manuːbi
wudaːnda	wudaːɲ	wudaːgu	wudajida	wudaːbi
wuguːnda	wuguːɲ	wuguːgu	wugujida	wuguːbi
binirinda	biniriɲa	binirigu	binirijiːda	biniribi
wajilinda	wajiliɲa	wajiligu	wajilijiːda	wajilibi
mindirinda	mindiriɲa	mindirigu	mindirijiːda	mindiribi
gambiɭanda	gambiɭaɲa	gambiɭagu	gambiɭajiːda	gambiɭabi
gubumanda	gubumaɲa	gubumagu	gubumajiːda	gubumabi
gumalanda	gumalaɲa	gumalagu	gumalajiːda	gumalabi
gindanunda	gindanuɲa	gindanugu	gindanujiːda	gindanubi
jaguɲunda	jaguɲuɲa	jaguɲugu	jaguɲujiːda	jaguɲubi
gujuɭunda	gujuɭuɲa	gujuɭugu	gujuɭujiːda	gujuɭubi
ŋunaŋgaraːnda	ŋunaŋgaraːɲ	ŋunaŋgaraːgu	ŋunaŋgarajida	ŋunaŋgaraːbi
bugamuguːnda	bugamuguːɲ	bugamuguːgu	bugamugujida	bugamuguːbi
ɟulugunuːnda	ɟulugunuːɲ	ɟulugunuːgu	ɟulugunujida	ɟulugunuːbi
ɟilibiɭiːnda	ɟilibiɭiːɲ	ɟilibiɭiːgu	ɟilibiɭijida	ɟilibiɭiːbi
ŋumbubunda	ŋumbubuɲa	ŋumbubugu	ŋumbubujiːda	ŋumbububi
waɭabanda	waɭabaɲa	waɭabagu	waɭabajiːda	waɭababi
gujŋgilbinda	gujŋgilbiɲa	gujŋgilbigu	gujŋgilbijiːda	gujŋgilbibi
gawudanda	gawudaɲa	gawudagu	gawudajiːda	gawudabi
guludunda	guluduɲa	guludugu	guludujiːda	guludubi
bunbuɟanda	bunbuɟaɲa	bunbuɟagu	bunbuɟajiːda	bunbuɟabi
gabuɟunda	gabuɟuɲa	gabuɟugu	gabuɟujiːda	gabuɟubi
baɟinɟinda	baɟinɟiɲa	baɟinɟigu	baɟinɟijiːda	baɟinɟibi
giɟarɟinda	giɟarɟiɲa	giɟarɟigu	giɟarɟijiːda	giɟarɟibi
guruŋganda	guruŋgaɲa	guruŋgagu	guruŋgajiːda	guruŋgabi
ɟaraganda	ɟaragaɲa	ɟaragagu	ɟaragajiːda	ɟaragabi
ɟumbaginda	ɟumbagiɲa	ɟumbagigu	ɟumbagijiːda	ɟumbagibi
ɲurugunda	ɲuruguɲa	ɲurugugu	ɲurugujiːda	ɲurugubi

Here is some background information on Yidiɲ:

- Absolute forms are used for the subjects of intransitive verbs and the objects of transitive verbs. A noun would normally be said in isolation in its absolutive form.
- The comitative suffix means essentially 'with' and forms adjectives from nouns.
- The genitive suffix means essentially 'of'.

- The purposive suffix means essentially 'for'; e.g. [ŋaju galiŋ miɲaː-gu] 'I'm going-out for-meat'.
- A noun marked *comitative+apprehensive* means 'for fear of N'.
- Glosses: the echidna is the marsupial porcupine; a kookaburra is a kind of kingfisher; a bream is a kind of fish.

Further reading

Lardil phonology: Kenneth Hale, "Deep-surface canonical disparities in relation to analysis and change: an Australian example," in Thomas Sebeok, ed., *Current Trends in Linguistics 11* (1973: Mouton), pp. 401–58. Further data and close analysis can be found in Terry J. Klokeid's 1976 MIT PhD dissertation *Topics in Lardil grammar*, available at https://dspace.mit.edu. For information on how Lardil phonology has changed in subsequent years, see Norvin Richards (1997) "Old and New Lardil," *MIT Working Papers in Linguistics* 13, available at http://web.mit.edu/norvin/www/papers/Leerdil.pdf.

Later work on Lardil has focused on increasing the generality of the analysis by uniting as many phenomena as possible under a single system. For an analysis that links Non-Apical Deletion to Lardil syllable structure, see Junko Ito's *Syllable Theory in Prosodic Phonology* (1988, Garland). For an analysis that relates Apocope to the length requirements seen in Lardil words, see Karina Wilkinson (1988) "Prosodic structure and Lardil phonology," *Linguistic Inquiry* 19: 325–34. Ito and Wilkinson's ideas are pursued further in Alan Prince and Paul Smolensky's *Optimality Theory: Constraint Interaction in Generative Grammar* (2004, Blackwell), which pursues generality even further with a theory that uses only constraints, and no rules.

For a survey of hiatus resolution (§8.3.2) in a number of languages, see Roderic Casali (1997) "Vowel elision in hiatus contexts: Which vowel goes?," *Language* 73: 493–533. Casali's findings support the general pattern mentioned in the text, whereby stem material is preferentially preserved in hiatus resolution.

For the arguments against the theory of fn. 1, in which all neutralization rules must precede all allophonic ones, see §7.1 (a direct counterexample), as well as Morris Halle's *The Sound Pattern of Russian* (1959, Mouton). Halle's example shows that the same rule is sometimes neutralizing, sometimes allophonic.

The standard terminology for rule ordering (feeding, bleeding, counterfeeding, counterbleeding) was first published in an article by Paul Kiparsky, "Linguistic universals and linguistic change," in Emmon Bach and Robert Harms, eds., *Universals in Linguistic Theory* (1968, Holt, Rinehart and Winston).

9 Productivity

Productivity was defined above (§5.8) as the capacity of a rule to apply in novel circumstances. Phonological rules, just like the morphological rules discussed earlier, can be evaluated and classified according to their productivity. The most productive phonological rules are iron-clad, applying automatically whenever their conditions are met. A native speaker can override such rules only with conscious effort, and often only with training and practice. But many phonological rules are less productive. Lowered productivity is often associated with the presence of **lexical exceptions**, which are particular stems or other morphemes that idiosyncratically fail to undergo a rule.

What follows is a survey of phonological rules with varying degrees of productivity, with discussion of their lexical exceptions. A theme that will recur is the idea that the existence of exceptions does not (necessarily) imply the non-existence of the rule. People can tacitly learn, and even productively extend, rules that have lexical exceptions.

9.1 Vowel Nasalization – A Fully Productive Rule

Vowel Nasalization in English (p. 50, repeated below) is a good example of a fully productive phonological rule.

Vowel Nasalization
[+vowel] → [+nasal] / ___ [+nasal]

It applies readily in novel contexts (for example, the context *Hello, my name is Plen* [plɛ̃n]). To say [plɛn] here, without nasality, would be quite unnatural in English. Indeed, it is difficult for native speakers to suppress Vowel Nasalization, a clear diagnostic of its productivity.

9.2 Postnasal /t/ Deletion – An Almost Fully Productive Rule

Postnasal /t/ Deletion was discussed in §6.2.2, and is repeated below.

Postnasal /t/ Deletion

$$t \rightarrow \varnothing \: / \: n \:\underline{}\: \begin{bmatrix} +\text{syllabic} \\ -\text{stress} \end{bmatrix}$$

We saw earlier that this rule is responsible for phonological alternations in which /t/ is lost from stem-final /nt/ clusters, whenever a suffix beginning with a stress-less vowel is added. For example, when the suffix *-ing* is added to the stem /ˈplænt/ *plant* (yielding the underlying form /ˈplænt-ɪŋ/), Postnasal /t/ Deletion derives the surface form [ˈplænɪŋ] *planting*.

The earlier discussion can be refined a bit: it appears that for most speakers who have this rule, it applies optionally, so that, for example, *planting* can also be pronounced [ˈplæntɪŋ]. As with many other optional phonological rules, the output where the rule is suppressed is judged as appropriate for more careful speaking styles, whereas the output where the rule applies is judged as more casual. Moreover, while in our earlier examples the environment for the rule was set up by suffixation, there are also cases where the rule applies entirely within a morpheme, as we can tell by the free variation in words like *center* [ˈsɛ̃nɚ, ˈsɛ̃ntɚ], *Santa* [ˈsæ̃nə, ˈsæ̃ntə], or *intellectual* [ˌĩnəˈlɛktʃəwəl, ˌĩntəˈlɛktʃəwəl].

In my own speech, Postnasal /t/ Deletion has a single exception: the word *intonation* has a phonemic /nt/ sequence in the appropriate context for Postnasal /t/ Deletion, and thus ought to allow the variant [ˌĩnəˈneɪʃ̃n]. However, I (and quite a few speakers like me) judge this pronunciation to be deviant, and allow only [ˌĩntəˈneɪʃ̃n]. In some idiolects similar to mine there are *two* exceptions, namely *intonation* and *intuition*, pronounced [ˌĩntəˈwɪʃ̃n] and never *[ˌĩnəˈwɪʃ̃n]. (I, and some other speakers, find [ˌĩnəˈwɪʃ̃n] to be acceptable.) Thus idiolects differ in their set of lexical exceptions to this rule.

There is evidence that even though Postnasal /t/ Deletion has exceptions, it is nonetheless a productive phonological rule. When new words are encountered that are eligible for Postnasal /t/ Deletion, they undergo it. The same holds true for completely made-up words: for example, "*truntiply*" doesn't exist, but the judgment seems clear that if it did, it could be pronounced either [ˈtɹĩnəˌplaɪ] or [ˈtɹĩntəˌplaɪ]. A real-life example is the word *Pentium*, made up in the early 1990s by Lexicon Branding, Inc. for the Intel Corporation. I remember clearly that when this word was new, it felt "proper" to pronounce it as [ˈpɛ̃ntiəm] – because careful speech is commonly used in pronouncing words that might not be familiar to one's interlocutor. But as the Pentium processor chip became widely distributed, and thus familiar, the pronunciation [ˈpɛ̃niəm], with Postnasal /t/ Deletion, came to seem fully acceptable. The point that emerges is that exceptions do not necessarily falsify rules or their productivity.[1]

9.3   Polish /n/ Weakening

Here is a similar example, taken from Polish. The Polish phoneme /n/ shows a curious allophone, nasalized [w̃], when it appears before fricatives. Here is the rule:

Polish /n/ Weakening

$$n \rightarrow \tilde{w} \ / \ \underline{\hspace{1cm}} \begin{bmatrix} -\text{sonorant} \\ +\text{continuant} \end{bmatrix}$$

The weakening of nasals to glides before fricatives is a fairly common rule type in languages, also found, for instance, in Japanese.

/n/ Weakening applies to the great bulk of the Polish vocabulary, as in the following examples.

/venx/	[vew̃x]	'sense of smell'
/vons/	[võw̃s]	'moustache'
/pensja/	[pew̃sja]	'salary'
/parkinʒek/	[parkiw̃ʒek]	'parking-diminutive'

The exceptions come in when one examines words from the borrowed vocabulary. They appear to be exceptional because of an attempt to imitate the pronunciation of the source word; thus German [kʊnst] 'art' is rendered into Polish as [kunʃt],[2] and the pan-European word *institute* as [instɨtut]. From the viewpoint of Polish phonology, they must both be treated as exceptions to /n/ Weakening.

Again, the existence of such exceptions does not imply that there is no rule; in fact, there is ample evidence for the productivity of /n/ Weakening. In particular, words which are exceptions to /n/ Weakening *lose their exceptional status* in unguarded speech, as shown below.

---

[1]   Before going on, I should mention that it is unlikely that the exceptional status of *intonation* and (for some) *intuition* is arbitrary. Rather, the lack of /n/ Deletion in these forms probably has something to do with their base forms *intone* [ɪn'toʊn] and *intuit* [ɪn'tuɪt], where Postnasal /t/ Deletion is blocked by the stress on the following vowel. The treatment of these peculiar relations requires theoretical notions that go beyond the scope of this text. I think the example remains a valid one, however, since there are speakers who say [ˌɪntə'neɪʃən] for *intonation* but [ˌɪnə'wɪʃən] for *intuition* – the distinction between the two appears to be truly a lexical idiosyncrasy, since their morphological composition is so similar.

[2]   The reason for the /s/ → /ʃ/ shift is unknown to me. Polish has /s/ in its phonemic inventory.

	Careful Speech	Unguarded Speech
'institute'	[institut]	[iw̃stɨtut]
'art'	[kunʃt]	[kuw̃ʃt]

Moreover, /n/ Weakening is found as a transfer effect (§3.2.3) in English spoken by (certain) Polish speakers as a second language. Such errors include, for example, [siw̃s] for *since*. Both of these observations support the view that /n/ Weakening is highly productive.

The facts also indicate that the notion of "exception-hood" is itself somewhat variable. English *intonation* is a consistent exception to /n/ Deletion, but Polish [institut] is only a "part-time" exception to /n/ Weakening.

9.4   Lesser Degrees of Productivity

There are rules that are less productive than Postnasal /t/ Deletion or /n/ Weakening, but nevertheless still have a fairly clear status as rules. Consider the following English data.

knife	[naɪf]	*knives*	[naɪvz]	*half*	[hæf]	*halves*	[hævz]
wife	[waɪf]	*wives*	[waɪvz]	*calf*	[kæf]	*calves*	[kævz]
life	[laɪf]	*lives*	[laɪvz]	*elf*	[ɛlf]	*elves*	[ɛlvz]
leaf	[lif]	*leaves*	[livz]	*shelf*	[ʃɛlf]	*shelves*	[ʃɛlvz]
sheaf	[ʃif]	*sheaves*	[ʃivz]	*wolf*	[wʊlf]	*wolves*	[wʊlvz]
thief	[θif]	*thieves*	[θivz]	*scarf*	[skɑɹf]	*scarves*	[skɑɹvz]
loaf	[loʊf]	*loaves*	[loʊvz]	*wharf*	[wɔɹf]	*wharves*	[wɔɹvz]
hoof	[hʊf]	*hooves*	[hʊvz]				

These forms are all nouns showing a voicing alternation: the /f/ that appears in the singular corresponds to a /v/ in the plural. The alternation seems to be specific to plurals, as we don't find it in 3rd sing. pres. verbs (*I loaf around* [loʊf] ~ *he loafs around* [loʊfs], *[loʊvz]), nor in possessives (*wife's* [waɪfs], *[waɪvz]). For this reason it is stated below in a form that includes morphological features, so that it will only apply in noun plurals:

/f/ Voicing

$$f \rightarrow [+\text{voice}] / \_\_ z]_{\left[\begin{smallmatrix} \text{Noun} \\ +\text{plural} \end{smallmatrix}\right]}$$

/f/ Voicing applies to most of the common words to which it is eligible. However, there are also some exceptions:

trough	troughs	[tɹɔfs]	*[tɹɔvz]
oaf	oafs	[oʊfs]	*[oʊvz]
chief	chiefs	[tʃifs]	*[tʃivz]
reef	reefs	[ɹifs]	*[ɹivz]
fief	fiefs	[fifs]	*[fivz]
gaffe	gaffes	[gæfz]	*[gævz]
motif	motifs	[moʊˈtif]	*[moʊˈtivz]
spoof	spoofs	[spufs]	*[spuvz]

Given that there are quite a few of these, it is worth asking if /f/ Voicing is a rule at all. An alternative hypothesis would be to say that we simply memorize all the plurals that change /f/ to /v/ and store them in the mental lexicon. Under this hypothesis, lexical entries would look like figure 9.1. This may be compared to the lexical entries for doublet forms like *envelope* (p. 59).

It is uncontroversial that *some* inflected forms have listed lexical entries. This is proven by the existence of so-called **suppletive** forms, which are inflected forms that have no phonological connection at all to the related forms of their paradigm. For instance, the past tense form for *go* in English is *went*. (For more on suppletion, see §9.9.1 below.) The analysis just suggested, in which /f/ Voicing is not a rule, is saying in a sense that all of {['naɪvz], ['waɪvz], ['ʃivz], etc.} are suppletive: speakers just memorize them as wholes, and establish no systematic linguistic relationship between them and their bases – despite the strong phonological similarity of the singular and plural forms.

Opinions in this area differ, but my own view is that /f/ Voicing does exist as a rule and indeed is still moderately productive.

First, there have been productive extensions of this rule to new forms. As a result of complex historical processes, the word *dwarf* once had the plural *dwarrows*. This form, being extremely irregular, eventually disappeared, to be replaced by *dwarfs*. But many people now say *dwarves* instead,[3] and the form appears in literature.

Figure 9.1   Lexical entry for "knife"

---

[3]   Google hit counts on December 27, 2006: *dwarfs* 5,870,000; *dwarves* 3,800,000.

Second, individual speakers create, or are at least moderately comfortable with, new forms. For example, people have told me they like *gulves* as the plural of *gulf* or *chieves* as the plural of *chief*. I find I don't seriously object to ['ɛpə,tævz] as the plural of *epitaph*.

Third, the claim that /f/ Voicing is not a rule should be evaluated not against the rather crude formulation of the rule above, but against the best version of the rule we can come up with. While we will not take on this project in detail, we can notice first that /f/ Voicing does not apply to forms with certain lax stem vowels: thus never with [ʌ] *cuff, earmuff*; with [ɪ] *stiff, tiff*; or with [ɛ] *F, chef*. Similarly, the rule never affects /f/ in stressless syllables: *sheriff, bailiff, midriff, plaintiff, serif, Conniff*. It also never applies to nouns that are derived from other parts of speech by rules of morphological conversion (see p. 104):

Base form	Noun singular	Noun plural	Transcription
[believe]ᵥ	[[belief]ᵥ]ₙ	*beliefs*	[bə'lifs]
[safe]₋Adj.	[[safe]₋A]ₙ	*safes*	['seɪfs]
[prove]ᵥ	[[proof]ᵥ]ₙ	*proofs*	['pɹufs]
[brief]₋Adj.	[[brief]₋A]ₙ	*briefs*	['bɹifs]
[goof]ᵥ	[[goof]ᵥ]ₙ	*goofs*	['gufs]

If the rule were reformulated in various ways to exclude these cases, we would find that it has a rather better "performance record" among the words that truly fit its requirements.

Lastly, /f/ Voicing in some form is supported by experimental evidence, discussed below in §9.8.

I would conclude two things. First, it seems right to say that there really is an /f/ Voicing rule of some sort in English, but that it is complicated, has quite a few exceptions, and is not fully productive. Second, this conclusion is independent of the question of whether forms like *knives* are lexically listed. In fact, I believe it likely that *knives* and similar forms *are* memorized. /f/ Voicing characterizes a pattern among memorized forms that is apprehended, and occasionally extended, by native speakers. In this respect, forms like *knives* are similar to the outputs of semi-productive morphological rules, as with forms like *paradoxical*, discussed in §5.8.

For more on /f/ Voicing, see §11.7.

9.5 A Possible Case of a Non-Rule

There are a few pairs in English that show a phonological alternation between [g] and [dʒ]:

fungus	['fʌŋgəs]	*fungi*	['fʌndʒaɪ]
alga	['ælgə]	*algae*	['ældʒi]
regal	['ɹigəl]	*regicide*	['ɹɛdʒɪ,saɪd]
ichthyophagous	[ˌɪkθi'ɑfəgəs]	*ichthyophagy*	[ˌɪkθi'ɑfədʒi][4]

The dutiful phonologist noticing these data might write a rule that converts /g/ to /dʒ/ in certain environments. But here, productivity seems really low. In particular, speakers of English quite often pronounce words from the right column with [g], as if they were somehow "resisting" the [g] ~ [dʒ] alternation: forms like ['fʌŋgaɪ] and ['ælgi] are often heard.

The term **leveling** is used to describe changes in a language that eliminate phonological alternation; in the present case, one would say here that the [g] ~ [dʒ] alternation in English is gradually being leveled. The existence of leveling is often taken as evidence for the non-productivity – or even non-existence – of the rule responsible for the alternation. In other words, a possible explanation for the leveling we see here is that speakers of English do not apprehend the [g] ~ [dʒ] alternation as a systematic pattern, and the few cases of alternation found in the language are indeed just lexically listed.[5]

9.6 Major and Minor Rules

There is little consensus within the field of phonology about how semiproductive or unproductive phonology is to be analyzed. Here is one approach that has been proposed.

A **minor rule** is a rule that applies only when the stem to which it applies bears a special **diacritic feature**, which is often written as [+Rule X], where X is the name of the rule. For instance, under an analysis in which /f/ Voicing is a minor rule, then the English lexicon would be assumed to contain entries like these:

loaf	*oaf*
/loʊf/	/oʊf/
[+/f/ Voicing]	

The word *loaf*, because it bears the diacritic feature, will undergo /f/ Voicing in instances where the morphological rule for plurals has applied, adding the /z/

---

[4] *Ichthyophagous*: "Said of one that characteristically eats fish"; *ichthyophagy* "the practice of eating fish."

[5] A parallel alternation in English replaces /k/ with [s] (as in *critical ~ criticize, specific ~ specificity, reciprocal ~ reciprocity, focus ~ foci*) and is perhaps slightly more productive. The two alternations are often referred to together under the name Velar Softening.

mentioned in the rule (p. 193) and setting up the appropriate structural description. *Oaf* lacks the feature [+/f/ Voicing] and therefore does not undergo the rule
in the plural.

Opposed to the minor rule is the **major rule**, which is just a normal, productive
phonological rule. Major rules apply unless a diacritic feature, [–Rule X], is
present in the input that **blocks** application. Here are two sample underlying forms
from both the English and the Polish examples given above:

intonation	*center*
/ɪntəneɪʃən/	/sɛntɚ/
[–Postnasal /t/ Deletion]	
art	*sense of smell*
/kunʃt/	/venx/
[–/n/ Weakening]	

In this view, what distinguishes utterly productive rules such as English Vowel
Nasalization is that there exists no exception feature for them.

In sum, this simple theory recognizes just three degrees of productivity, encom-
passing minor rules, major-but-exceptionful rules, and exceptionless rules. These
are rules that (respectively) apply only with a [+Rule X] feature present, apply if
there is no [–Rule X] feature present, and lack any such feature.

9.7   Exceptions in Lardil and Chimwiini

Some analyses given earlier in this text also involve exceptions.

In Lardil (§8.3), the stem meaning 'spear-thrower' has the following unusual
paradigm:

Uninflected	Acc. Nonfuture	Acc. Future
[muɾuku]	[muɾuku-n]	[muɾuku-ɻ]

From the second two forms we know that the underlying form must be
/muɾuku/, and thus we would expect the uninflected form to be *[muɾu] following
the rules of Apocope (p. 175) and Non-Apical Deletion (p. 179). Assuming that
Apocope is a major rule in Lardil, the stem /muɾuku/ must therefore be assigned
the feature [–Apocope] in the lexicon. In addition, /muɾuku/ must be assigned
[–Final Lowering] (p. 172), in order to avoid the illegal output *[muɾuka].

In Chimwiini (§7.2), the form [dʒaːsuːsi] 'spy' (borrowed from Arabic) is an
exception to the rule of Pre-Long Shortening (p. 154). Assuming that this is a
major rule, /dʒaːsuːsi/ must bear the feature [–Pre-Long Shortening] in its lexical
entry, or else it will surface as *[dʒasuːsi].

9.8   Experiments with Productivity

The most systematic way to assess the productivity of a phonological rule is to conduct a phonological experiment, of the kind sometimes called a **nonce-probe study**. Such experiments were pioneered in the 1950s by Jean Berko Gleason, an expert in language acquisition.

The idea of a nonce-probe study is to teach one's consultant a hypothetical new word of the language – the nonce probe – then arrange a sentence fill-in task that requires the consultant to provide an appropriately inflected form of the probe. Figure 9.2 shows an example, taken from Gleason's work. By answering [wʌgz], the consultant shows awareness of both morphological and phonological rules: the morphological rule is the one that suffixes /-z/ to form the plural (p. 112), and the phonological rule is the one that forces sequences of obstruents in final position to agree in voicing (p. 134). This particular example is sufficiently familiar among linguists that tests of this kind are often referred to informally as **wug tests,** and I will use this term here.

The purpose of wug testing is to force the consultant to apply the rules of his or her language in order to come up with an answer. Since the consultant has never heard the nonce probe before, there is no possibility that he or she could be answering on the basis of memorized forms, as might occur if one tested with real words.

Here is another item from Berko's 1958 wug test.

Linguist: (*shows picture of one insect*) "This is a [hif]."
                  (*shows picture of two such insects*) "Now there is another one. There are two of them. There are two . . ."

Berko found that of her adult subjects, 58 percent answered [hifs] and 42 percent [hivz]. Thus, the assertion given in §9.4 that /f/ Voicing is partly productive is

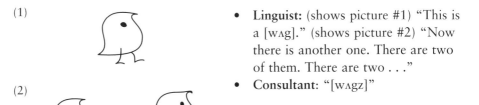

(1)

(2)

- Linguist: (shows picture #1) "This is a [wʌg]." (shows picture #2) "Now there is another one. There are two of them. There are two . . ."
- **Consultant:** "[wʌgz]"

Figure 9.2   Nonce-probe study. From J. Berko (1958) "The child's learning of English morphology." *Word,* 14: 150–77. © Jean Berko Gleason

given at least tentative support by Berko's data. Her experimental subjects who were preschoolers or first graders generally answered [hifs], which suggests that /f/ Voicing tends to be acquired rather late, as we might expect given its irregularity.

Quite a few phonological patterns, even in well-known languages, have never been submitted to wug testing, a gap that is now slowly being closed.

The following are a few hints here on how to wug-test, based on the research literature and my own experience. First, languages often have special phonological/morphological strategies for dealing with foreign words. Thus, it is probably wise to use frame sentences that suggest to the consultant that the word is *native but unknown to them*. Possible topics of this kind for frame sentences include farming technology, history, daily life in the past, and so on. Second, the rules of a language often are such that for a particular question there is more than one plausible answer, as with *heaf* above. Wug tests are thus sometimes designed to have the consultants not just give one answer, but rate various possibilities on a scale, for instance one in which 1 is the lowest and 7 is the highest rating. Lastly, wug words should be selected carefully so that they do not closely resemble any particular existing word, to rule out the possibility that the wug word will be inflected on a direct analogy with that particular word.

9.9 Alternations Specific to Single Morphemes

Rather often, languages have alternations that are productive, but *productive for only one morpheme*. Here is an example of such alternation, from Yidiɲ, an Australian aboriginal language (see chapter 8, exercise 2 for Yidiɲ phonology). Yidiɲ has a morphological category called the **ergative** case. It is used on the subject of a sentence, when there is also an object present. The Yidiɲ ergative has two allomorphs: [-ŋgu] is attached to bases that end in a vowel and [-du] to bases that end in a consonant.[6]

Base form	Ergative form	Gloss
[waguɟa]	[waguɟa-ŋgu]	'man'
[mulari]	[mulari-ŋgu]	'initiated man'
[gudaga]	[gudaga-ŋgu]	'dog'
[gujgal-ni]	[gujgal-ni-ŋgu]	'bandicoot (adjectival form)'
[wagal]	[wagal-du]	'wife'
[maŋgumbar]	[maŋgumbar-du]	'leaf grub'
[bulijiɻ]	[bulijiɻ-du]	'chicken hawk'
[warabal]	[warabal-du]	'flying squirrel'

[6] The transcriptions have been simplified to focus attention on the problem at hand. In fact, all trisyllabic words have long penultimate vowels, due to rules studied in the problem set just mentioned.

Following the method of morphophonemic analysis given in chapter 8, we might in principle try out two underlying forms for the ergative (/-ŋgu/ and /-du/), and formulate phonological rules in each case that can derive the other allomorph. If the ergative is underlyingly /-ŋgu/, we will need a rule converting /ŋg/ to [d] following a consonant. If, on the other hand, the ergative is underlyingly /-du/, we will need a rule converting /d/ to [ŋg] following a vowel.

However, neither of these phonological rules has much plausibility. The sequence [ŋg] occurs rather frequently after a consonant in Yidiɲ, and so does [d] after a vowel. The following examples illustrate this.

[ŋg] after Consonant		**[d] after Vowel**	
[guralŋgan]	'curlew'	[gadil]	'very small'
[wulŋgu]	'female song-style'	[mada]	'soft'
[darŋgidarŋgi]	'old woman'	[bida]	'bark canoe'
[murŋgal]	'short feather'	[jidiɲ]	'language name'
[bajŋga]	'hot stone used in cooking'	[gudaɻ]	'cold'
[ɟajŋgaɻ]	'rapids in river'	[wuda]	'shark'

Therefore, neither a phonological rule changing /ŋg/ to [d] after a consonant, nor a rule changing /d/ to [ŋg] after a vowel, would have any validity for Yidiɲ *other than for accounting for ergative suffix allomorphy*. Moreover, for either of these rules there is a further objection: the rule would not just change a few features, as with most phonological rules, but would carry out a wholesale change involving both place of articulation and number of segments. For these reasons an analysis with phonological rules seems implausible for the Yidiɲ ergative.

An alternative is to assign the alternation to the morphological component. To do this, we would set up a morphological rule for forming the ergative that includes two different affixation processes, as shown below:

Yidiɲ Ergative Formation

When [+ergative], $\left\{ \begin{array}{l} X[-\text{syllabic}] \to X[-\text{syllabic}] \ \text{ŋgu} \\ X[+\text{syllabic}] \to X[+\text{syllabic}] \ \text{du} \end{array} \right\}$

Such an approach claims that there is no *phonological* connection between the allomorphs [-ŋgu] and [-du]; only the morphological connection that they both serve to realize the ergative case.

A data pattern in which a morpheme has multiple allomorphs, but not because of the rules of the phonology, is often called **allomorphy**. Allomorphy can be productive (that is, novel words always take the expected allomorph), but it is not *phonologically* productive, because the pattern of alternation is confined to a single morpheme.

9.9.1 Stem allomorphy

Allomorphy occurs in stems as well as in affixes, notably in instances of suppletion, already mentioned (*go/went*) on p. 194. Here is another example of suppletive stem allomorphy. In Persian, the verb meaning 'see', has two completely different stems, with /bin/ used for present tense forms and /did/ for past tense forms. This is illustrated in the following paradigms.

Category	Present	Past	Gloss
1st person singular	mi**bin**æm	**did**æm	'I see/saw'
2nd person singular	mi**bin**i	**did**i	'you see/saw'
3rd person singular	mi**bin**æd	**did**	'he/she sees/saw'
1st person plural	mi**bin**im	**did**im	'we see/saw'
2nd person plural	mi**bin**id	**did**id	'you-plural see/saw'
3rd person plural	mi**bin**ænd	**did**ænd	'they see/saw'

These suppletive paradigms contrast with those for the regular verb /xæɾ/ 'buy', which forms its past stem from the present stem in the normal way for Persian, namely suffixation of the regular past tense ending /-id/:

Category	Present	Past	Gloss
1st person singular	mi**xæɾ**æm	**xæɾid**æm	'I buy/bought'
2nd person singular	mi**xæɾ**i	**xæɾid**i	'you buy/bought'
3rd person singular	mi**xæɾ**æd	**xæɾid**	'he/she buys/bought'
1st person plural	mi**xæɾ**im	**xæɾid**im	'we buy/bought'
2nd person plural	mi**xæɾ**id	**xæɾid**id	'you-plural buy/bought'
3rd person plural	mi**xæɾ**ænd	**xæɾid**ænd	'they buy/bought'

For stem allomorphy, the usual analysis is to place both allomorphs in the lexicon. In the Persian case, the stem meaning 'see' would have two listed allomorphs, along the following lines:

Lexical entry for Persian verb meaning "see":

> Syntax: verb
> Meaning: (to see)
> Phonemic forms:
> /bin/$_{[-past]}$
> /did/$_{[+past]}$

9.9.2 Cases that are hard to diagnose

When allomorphs are phonologically very dissimilar, as in Yidiɲ /-ŋgu/ ~ /-du/ or Persian /did/ ~ /bin/, it is reasonable to assume allomorphy, and therefore assign the alternation to the morphological rules (in the case of affixes) or to the lexicon (for stems). However, when the alternation is morpheme-specific but the allomorphs in question are phonologically similar, the analysis is often not so clear.

Here is an example, involving the accusative future suffix of Lardil, seen in §7.3.6. There, a rather complicated rule of /k/ Epenthesis was proposed:

/k/ Epenthesis (from p. 173)

$\emptyset \to k$ / [+nasal] ___ uɻ

Insert [k] *between a nasal sound and a following* /uɻ/ *sequence.*

By this rule, the underlying form /piɻŋæn-uɻ/ 'woman-acc. fut.', with the underlying form of the acc. future suffix /-uɻ/, surfaces as [piɻnænkuɻ], with epenthetic [k]. In fact, the only function of the rule is to account for the variation in this particular suffix – calling into question the claim that the rule expresses a general phonological principle of the language. An alternative would be to express this alternation as allomorphy, in the morphological rule for the Accusative Future:

Lardil Accusative Future Formation (with allomorphy)

When $\begin{bmatrix} +\text{accusative} \\ +\text{future} \end{bmatrix}$,

	X[+nasal]	$\to$	X[+nasal]kuɻ
else	X	$\to$	Xuɻ

An advantage of this analysis is that it would eliminate a complex phonological rule of very limited scope. The drawback is that the similarity of the allomorphs [uɻ] and [-kuɻ] is no longer captured. The data of the language itself cannot decide between these two analyses, and indeed I believe that advances in linguistic theory and methodology will be needed before we can confidently advocate one or the other.

9.9.3   *When a phonological account is favored*

Not all cases are ambiguous in this way. An analytical choice favoring phonological rules sometimes is quite clear, whenever we find cases in which a speaker utters a new allomorph that she has never heard before.

For instance, in a wug test on English carried out by Albright and Hayes, many of the experimental subjects spoke casually enough to apply Tapping (p. 143) to inflected wug words. For wug stems like [flɛt] or [glɪt], they offered present participles like ['flɛɾɪŋ] and ['glɪɾɪŋ]. Allomorphs like [flɛɾ] and [glɪɾ] are the expected result of applying Tapping to the new underlying representations /flɛt-ɪŋ/ and /glɪt-ɪŋ/. They offer firm evidence against the view that the Tapping alternations are due to some kind of (massive) lexical allomorphy: since the speakers had never heard [flɛɾ] or [glɪɾ] before, they could not possibly be listed in the lexicon. These novel allomorphs must be created "on the fly" by the productive application of phonological rules.

Summing up, it seems that (1) a morphological or lexical account is required when an alternation is morpheme-specific and there is no phonological relationship between the allomorphs; (2) a phonological analysis is called for when the alternation is productively extended to new morphemes; (3) there are intermediate cases (morpheme-specific, with phonologically similar allomorphs) where we cannot determine the correct analysis with our current knowledge.

Exercises

1 Suppletion

Find a suppletive adjectival comparative in English (comparatives are forms like *taller* or *redder*). Find a suppletive noun plural.

2 Productivity of /f/ Voicing

Use an internet search engine to test the following: (a) Stems where Standard English has /f/ Voicing (p. 193) but the webpage "hit" does not. Suggested cases: *knifes, wifes, sheafs, wolfs, scarfs*. Search also on *knives, wives*, etc., and record the counts. (b) Stems where Standard English does not have /f/ Voicing and the webpage "hit" does; suggested cases *gulves, oaves, chieves*. Search also on *gulfs, oafs*, etc. and record the counts. If you're having trouble getting plurals, try searching for "two X," using the quotation marks to search for the whole string.

Questions: does frequency make a difference in whether a stem is likely to shift from [+F Voicing] to [−F Voicing]? Do stems ever shift from [−F Voicing] to [+F Voicing]? What sort of hits are found in searches of this kind that should be discounted as observations?

3 Wug testing

Invent a small wug test that will assess the productivity of the following two rules:

Aspiration (p. 122)   as in *occu*[p]*ant ~ occu*[pʰ]*ation*

/i/ Lowering

i → ɛ / ___ lt]ᵥₑᵣᵦ   as in *deal ~ dealt, feel ~ felt*

List (in IPA) the stimuli you would employ, and the sentence frames in which you would elicit them. Describe some possible answers you might expect to get, and how they would bear on the productivity of the rules.

Further reading

The psycholinguist Steven Pinker and his colleagues have undertaken a number of experiments that bear on the question of productivity. Pinker takes an interestingly radical view of the subject, claiming that only extremely general and systematic rules can be productive; less productive phenomena are attributed to a kind of analogy. See his *Words and Rules* (1999, Basic Books) for an overview of this research.

A discussion of how rule exceptions work in various languages is found in chapter 2 of Michael Kenstowicz and Charles Kisseberth's book *Topics in Phonological Theory* (1977, Academic Press).

The question of whether inflected forms are listed in the lexicon (§9.4) has occupied the attention of many psycholinguists. Recent research has led to the conclusion that even completely regular forms can be lexically listed if they are of high frequency (it is this finding that leads me to be rather confident that less regular forms like *knives* are also listed; p. 195.) A good reference, which cites other work, is Harald Baayen, Robert Schreuder, Nivja De Jong, and Andrea Krott, "Dutch inflection: The rules that prove the exception," in Sieb Nooteboom, Frank Wijnen, and Fred Weerman, eds., *Storage and Computation in the Language Faculty* (2002, Kluwer).

The reference for the original wug test by Jean Berko Gleason is Jean Berko (1958) "The child's learning of English morphology," *Word* 14: 150–77. A wug-testing study of the phonological alternations in Japanese verb stems is reported in chapter 12 of Timothy Vance's *An Introduction to Japanese Phonology* (1987, State University of New York Press). Another source that reports phonological experiments is John Ohala, ed., *Experimental Phonology* (1986, Academic Press). The wug test mentioned in §9.9.3 was published in Adam Albright and Bruce Hayes (2003) "Rules vs. analogy in English past tenses: a computational/experimental study," *Cognition* 90: 119–61 (www.linguistics.ucla.edu/people/hayes/rulesvsanalogy/.

/n/ Weakening in Polish: Jerzy Rubach, *Cyclic and Lexical Phonology: The Structure of Polish* (1984, Foris Publications). Yidiɲ phonology: Robert M. W. Dixon, *A Grammar of Yidiɲ* (1977, Cambridge University Press). History of English *dwarves*: see the entry for *dwarf* in the monumental *Oxford English Dictionary*, found in research libraries and as a fee service (often paid for by universities) at http://oed.com/.

10 The Role of Morphology and Syntax

10.1 Introduction

The sounds of a language, themselves meaningless, exist in order to make audible the higher-level structural units that do bear meaning: morphemes, words, phrases, sentences. It should not be surprising that phonology is closely connected with morphology and syntax, the two components of grammar that create these higher-level units. No adequate phonological description of a language is possible without reference to morphology and syntax.

This chapter will cover two mechanisms that have been suggested as playing a central role in mediating between grammar and phonology: **bounding domains** and **edge-sensitive rules**.

10.2 Bounding Domains

A rule has a **bounding domain** if, when it scans an input, it only applies when all the segments that it analyzes fall in the same domain. Such domains can include the word, the stem, and various types of phrases.

Here is some terminology that will help clarify the concept of bounding domain. A phonological rule normally has a **focus**, which is the segment that gets changed, and one or two **environment strings**, on the left and/or on the right. This is shown below for the generic rule A → B / P ___ Q.

A	→	B	/	P	___	Q
Focus		*change*		*left environment string*		*right environment string*

A **word-bounded** rule applies to a particular configuration only if the focus, all of the left environment string (if there is one), and all of the right environment string (if there is one) are contained within the same word. Stem-bounded and phrase-bounded rules are defined analogously.

Here is an example of a word-bounded rule. /aɪ/ Raising, from p. 142, accounts for the [ʌɪ] allophone of /aɪ/ that appears in many English dialects before voiceless consonants. The rule is repeated below:

/aɪ/ Raising

$$ \text{aɪ} \quad \rightarrow \quad \text{ʌɪ} \ / \ \underline{\quad} \ \begin{bmatrix} -\text{syllabic} \\ -\text{voice} \end{bmatrix} $$

/aɪ/ *is realized as* [ʌɪ] *when it precedes a voiceless consonant.*

For instance, the rule derives the [ʌɪ] allophone heard in *tripe* ([tɹʌɪp]), which may be compared with the [aɪ] of *tribe* ([tɹaɪb]), where there is no voiceless consonant to trigger the rule.

For present purposes, /aɪ/ Raising needs to be formulated a bit more carefully than before in order to show the focus and environment strings clearly:

/aɪ/ Raising (restated)

a   →   [–low] / ___ ɪ [–voice]   Bounding domain: Word

In the terminology just given, the focus of this rule is /a/, there is no left environment string, and the right environment string is ɪ [–voice]. Moreover, the rule is now stated with a bounding domain, the word. This means that the rule will apply only if the focus segment /a/ and all the segments matched up with the right environment string fall within the same word.

A case where the bounding requirement is not met, so the rule is blocked, is the phrase *buy potatoes*. This utterance is phonemically /baɪ pəteɪtoʊz/. If we include labeled brackets to indicate the word division, it is represented as follows:

[baɪ]~word~ [pəteɪtoʊz]~word~

The word *buy* contains a match for the focus of /aɪ/ Raising, namely the segment [a]. Moreover, the next two sounds, [ɪ] and [p], form a match for the right environment string of /aɪ/ raising, which is ɪ [–voice]. However, to obtain this match, we have "spilled over" into the next word; thus, not all of the sounds analyzed by the rule are in the same word. Since /aɪ/ Raising is a word-bounded rule, it cannot apply here, and the phonetic output is the unaltered [baɪ pəteɪtoʊz].

A way to visualize the blocking effect of domains is to line up the parts of the rule with the parts of the linguistic form they analyze:

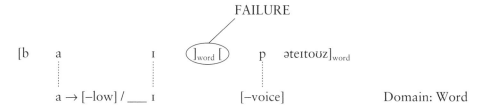

FAILURE

[b a ɪ]ₗₒᵣₐ [p əteɪtoʊz]ₗₒᵣₐ

a → [−low] / ___ ɪ   [−voice]   Domain: Word

The appearance of word brackets within the string of analyzed material in the case of a word-bounded rule means that the rule cannot apply. The juncture of two words, annotated with the expression circled above, is sometimes called a **word boundary**. In some phonological writings it is notated not with the double-bracket string][but rather with symbol #, as in /baɪ # pəteɪtoʊz/, or sometimes /# baɪ # pəteɪtoʊz #/, with boundaries at the beginning and end.

Buy potatoes may be contrasted with the similar form *wipe a table*, underlyingly [waɪp]ₗₒᵣₐ [ə]ₗₒᵣₐ [teɪbəl]ₗₒᵣₐ. As with *buy potatoes*, the focus of /aɪ/ Raising, [a], is contained in the first word *wipe*. The right environment string [ɪp], matched up in the rule to ɪ [−voice], is likewise entirely within the word *wipe*. Therefore, /aɪ/ Raising can match to this form, the requirements of word bounding being satisfied, and the rule applies, creating [wʌɪp ə teɪbəl]. The complete matchup is shown below:

[w a ɪ p]ₗₒᵣₐ [ə]ₗₒᵣₐ [teɪbəl]ₗₒᵣₐ

a → [−low] / ___ ɪ [−voice]   Domain: Word

10.3 Bounding Creates Pseudo-Minimal Pairs

Minimal pairs (§2.10.1) are the fundamental basis for establishing contrast in phonology. However, the existence of bounding creates additional minimal pairs of a secondary kind, which could fairly be called **pseudo-minimal pairs**. The basis of such pairs is as follows: they contain exactly the same phonemes in the same order, but differ in their boundary locations, in such a way that when the rules apply to them, different outcomes are derived.

Here is an example. The underlying representation /[ɹaɪs]ₗₒᵣₐ[eɪlz]ₗₒᵣₐ/ (*rice ales*, 'ales brewed from rice') has an /aɪ/ that precedes a voiceless consonant within the same word. Hence the word-bounded rule of /aɪ/ Raising can apply, yielding [ɹʌɪs eɪlz]. The rule matchup is shown below:

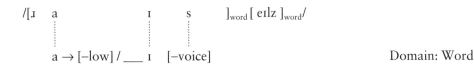

a → [–low] / ___ ɪ [–voice]   Domain: Word

The underlying representation /[ɹaɪ]_{word}[seɪlz]_{word}/ (*rye sales*, 'sales of rye') has an /aɪ/ that precedes a voiceless consonant in the next word. Hence the word-bounded rule of /aɪ/ Raising is blocked, and the output is [ɹaɪ seɪlz]. The rule matchup is shown below:

FAILURE

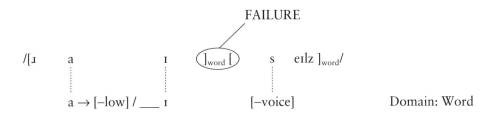

a → [–low] / ___ ɪ   [–voice]   Domain: Word

The phonetic transcriptions given above for these two forms, [ɹʌɪs eɪlz] and [ɹaɪ seɪlz], follow the standard convention of placing spaces where the word boundaries fall. Yet what the linguist normally hears in eliciting these forms is in fact [ɹʌɪseɪlz] and [ɹaɪseɪlz]; speakers do not ordinarily place pauses between words when they speak. If you heard the pair [ɹʌɪseɪlz], [ɹaɪseɪlz] without knowing its linguistic structure, you could easily arrive at an erroneous conclusion, namely that /ʌɪ/ and /aɪ/ constitute separate phonemes of English.

Thus, *rice ales* and *rye sales* contain the same phonemes in the same order, but have different surface representations because of the grouping of the phonemes into words. The minimal pair proves that we have encountered different *structures*, but in the present case it does not prove that we have encountered different phonemes. The different structures are summarized below:

/[ɹʌɪs]_{word} [eɪlz]_{word} /   *rice ales*
/[ɹaɪ]_{word} [seɪlz]_{word} /   *rye sales*

In the discussion of minimal pairs in chapter 2, it was claimed that minimal pairs diagnose differences of phonemes. This is only an approximation of the truth. In fact, *minimal pairs diagnose distinct underlying representations.* Underlying representations can be distinct in ways other than the phonemes that they contain, since they can also differ in their grammatical structure.

The existence of pseudo-minimal pairs created by grammatical structure has implications for elicitation, during the phase of analysis where the phoneme inventory of a language is being worked out. At this stage, it may be best to employ **monomorphemic** minimal pairs (composed of just one morpheme each), to the extent that this is possible. The reason is that all monomorphemic utterances have the same (trivial) bracketing structure. This strategy avoids possible confusion from grammatical effects during the initial analysis. Once the basic phonemic system is in hand, the analyst can move on to examining prefixed forms, suffixed forms, and multi-word utterances, and locate the allophones that arise from bounding effects.

10.4   An Example of a Non-Bounded Rule

Not all rules are word-bounded. Some apply whenever their structural descriptions are met. Consider for instance a rule of /ɹ/ Epenthesis found in Standard British English. This rule inserts /ɹ/ between a schwa and a following stressless vowel (there are other environments, but we will concentrate on this one):

/ɹ/ Epenthesis

$$\varnothing \to \text{ɹ} / \text{ə} \underline{\hspace{1em}} \begin{bmatrix} -\text{syllabic} \\ -\text{stress} \end{bmatrix}$$

You can see the inserted /ɹ/ in the following examples:

Kafka	['kæfkə]		
Kafka is . . .	['kæfkəɹɪz . . .]		
Kafka election	['kæfkəɹə'lɛkʃən]	*Kafka elephants*	['kæfkə'ʔɛləfənts]
Kafka-ish	['kæfkəɹɪʃ]	*Kafkaesque*	[ˌkæfkə'ʔɛsk]

The examples in the right column are included to demonstrate that when the vowel that follows the schwa is stressed, one does not get an /ɹ/. Instead, a different epenthesis rule applies, inserting a glottal stop.

It can be seen that this rule applies across word boundaries: in order to insert the /ɹ/ in *Kafka election*, it has to be able to "see" both the schwa of *Kafka* and the initial stressless vowel of *election*.

In fact, one can even get epenthesis at locations that seem intuitively to involve a kind of "phonological break", where in writing an utterance down we would be inclined to punctuate with a comma. Consider the sentence that begins:

Once we have completed our study of Kafka, an important further goal will be . . .

For the native speakers I have queried, this sentence has two variants. Provided speaking actually *ceases* (a brief silence) at the point following *Kafka*, then no /ɹ/ is inserted:

[. . . 'kæfkə . . . ənɪm'pɔːtənt . . .]

But if there is no pause between *Kafka* and *an important*, then the /ɹ/ is inserted:

[. . . 'kæfkəɹənɪm'pɔːtənt . . .]

We can prove that it really is the same rule applying here, by checking to make sure that it is blocked by a following stress. For example, in the following sentence, the sequence *Kafka, everything* shows up as [. . . 'kæfkə'ʔɛvɹɪθɪŋ . . .], no matter what the speaking rate.

Once we have completed our study of Kafka, everything will be different.

Thus, /ɹ/ Epenthesis appears to be an "across-the-board" rule: it is blocked only by the actual cessation of speech. Another way to put this is that /ɹ/ Epenthesis is **utterance-bounded**. The phonological Utterance consists of the maximum sequence of speech falling between two pauses.

10.5   A Stem-Bounded Rule

Bounding effects can also be found in the interior of words. For studying such effects, it is useful to set up a linguistic unit which I will refer to as the **stem**. Although the word *stem* has multiple meanings in linguistics, for purposes of this discussion I will assume that it is the minimal constituent within a word that can stand as an independent word. Thus, in *jumping* [[dʒʌmp]ᵥ ɪŋ]ₙ, the stem is [dʒʌmp]ᵥ. In *identifier* [[[aɪdɛnt] ɪfaɪ]ᵥ ɚ]ₙ, the stem is [aɪdɛntɪfaɪ]ᵥ. Although we can recognize a smaller root morpheme [aɪdɛnt] within this word (compare *identity*, *identical*), we will not consider it to be the stem, since it cannot occur as an independent word. This definition of stem is only an approximation, but will serve for present purposes.

Consider now an example of a stem-bounded rule. The following rule occurs in some version in a number of English dialects:

Pre-/l/ Monophthongization
o͡ʊ → o / ___ l

We can see the effects of the rule in the following data:

/oʊ/ before /l/: [o]				/oʊ/ in other environments: [o͡ʊ]			
pole	[pol]	*Coltrane*	[koltʃɹeɪn]	*Poe*	[po͡ʊ]	*propane*	[pɹo͡ʊpeɪn]
hole	[hol]	*told*	[told]	*hope*	[ho͡ʊp]	*toad*	[to͡ʊd]
mole	[mol]	*fold*	[fold]	*moat*	[mo͡ʊt]	*phone*	[fo͡ʊn]
poultry	[poltʃɹi]	*mold*	[mold]	*Oakley*	[o͡ʊkli]	*most*	[mo͡ʊst]

The above are all simple, monomorphemic forms. The more subtle effects occur when we add suffixes to stems that end in /o͡ʊ/ or in /o͡ʊ/ plus /l/.

First, if we add a suffix or compound member starting with /l/ to a stem that ends in /o͡ʊ/, we get [o͡ʊ], contrary to what we might have expected:

lowly ['lo͡ʊli]
slowly ['slo͡ʊli]
lowlands ['lo͡ʊləndz]
toeless ['to͡ʊləs]

There is nothing about suffixation per se that produces this result. Thus, if we add a vowel-initial suffix to a stem that ends in /o͡ʊ/ plus /l/, then the monoph-thongal allophone appears:

goalie ['goli]
hole-y ['holi]
rolling ['ɹolɪŋ]
Pol-ess ['poləs] 'a female Pole'

These facts can be accounted for if we assume that Pre-/l/ Monophthongization is a stem-bounded rule. Below, I have labeled the stem morphemes within the full words.

lowly | *goalie* |
[[lo͡ʊ]stem li] word | [[go͡ʊl]stem i] word | underlying forms
BLOCKED | o | Pre-/l/ Monophthongization
lo͡ʊli | goli | surface forms

It can be seen that underlying /oʊ/ gets monophthongized only if it is in the same stem as the immediately following /l/. The blocking effect can be seen more clearly in the following diagram:

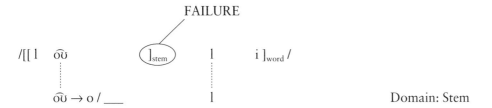

FAILURE

/[[l o͡ʊ   ]stem   l   i]word /

o͡ʊ → o / ___   l   Domain: Stem

Another rule that seems to be stem-bounded in English is Vowel Nasalization (p. 50), which converts underlying oral vowels to their nasal counterparts before a nasal consonant. I find that many English speakers have near-minimal pairs for nasality of the following type:

Venus	['vīnəs]	*freeness*	['fɹinəs]
bonus	['bo͠ʊnəs]	*slowness*	['sloʊnəs]
Uranus	[jʊ'ɹe͠ɪnəs]	*greyness*	['gɹeɪnəs]
Linus	['lãɪnəs]	*dryness*	['dɹaɪnəs]

These distinctions can be derived under the assumption that the rule that derives nasalization is stem-bounded:

Vowel Nasalization (refined)
[+syllabic] → [+nasal] / ___ [+nasal]   Domain: Stem

A stem-bounded rule will match up to an underlying representation like /[[vinəs]ₛₜₑₘ]word/ but not to /[[fɹi]ₛₜₑₘ nəs]word/.

10.6   Word-Bounding is Still Necessary

At this point it is worth returning to our earlier example (§10.2) of /aɪ/ Raising. The claim made earlier was that this rule cannot apply to *rye sales* because the /aɪ/ and the voiceless /s/ are in separate words. But maybe this is wrong: perhaps the rule is really bounded within stems; this would get exactly the same result as before, since *rye* is both a stem and a word.

Some further data supports the original analysis. In the derivation of *height* below, /aɪ/ Raising applies before a voiceless consonant that is not part of the stem (but is not in a separate word either):

height
[[haɪ]ₛₜₑₘ t]word   underlying form
    ʌ   /aɪ/ Raising
   hʌɪt   surface form

Thus, at least as far as we can tell from this example, the bounding domain of /aɪ/ Raising really does seem to be the word.

10.7   The Hierarchy of Domains and How Rules Respect It

In the derivation for *height* just given, we see a word-bounded rule matched up against a representation that includes an internal stem domain. The precise matchup of rule to form in such a case deserves further scrutiny. Here is the crucial diagram:

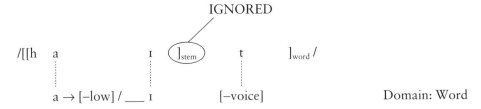

IGNORED

$$/[[h \quad a \qquad \iota \quad]_{stem} \quad t \qquad]_{word} /$$

$$a \rightarrow [-low] / \underline{\quad} \iota \qquad [-voice] \qquad \text{Domain: Word}$$

In this derivation, it seems that we are running up against a fundamental principle governing how rules are matched up against forms, given on p. 73: if two elements in a rule are adjacent, they may only be matched up against elements in forms that are also adjacent. The derivation here seems to go against this principle, since the bracket defining the stem edge (sometimes called the "stem boundary") intervenes between the /ɪ/ and /t/.

A common view of how to deal with this issue is to suppose that the domains of phonological rules form a **hierarchy**, such as the following:

Utterance > Phrase > Word > Stem

The idea is that when we match up a word-bounded rule, we may ignore stem boundaries occurring in the form. When we match up a phrase-bounded rule, we may ignore both stem and word boundaries in the form, and when we match up an utterance-bounded rule, we may ignore phrase, word, and stem boundaries in the form. Thus, with a complication to be covered below, each kind of rule only "sees" the brackets defined for its level or above. In the case just given, a stem boundary is invisible to a word-level rule.

10.8   Rules Bounded by Phonological Phrases

There are bounding domains that are larger than a word, but smaller than the whole utterance. These domains are typically related to the syntactic structure of the sentence. They are often called **phonological phrases**, though other terminology is used as well.

Chimwiini (§7.2), is a language whose phonology is strongly influenced by phonological phrasing. Consider the following sentence of Chimwiini:

mwaːrabu	vete	tʃiɺeːmbe
Arab	has put on	turban

'An Arab has put on a turban.'

This sentence is a Chimwiini riddle, whose answer is [ɖaːŋkʰu], meaning 'popcorn'. The phonological underlying form of this sentence is /mwaːrabu veːte tʃiɺeːmbe/. We know this because *vete*, 'has put on' when pronounced alone is [veːte].

The sentence offers an interesting puzzle relating to the rule of Preantepenultimate Shortening (p. 148), which, it will be recalled, shortens any long vowel that is four or more syllables from the end of its phrase. The long vowel of [mwaːrabu] is eight syllables from the end of the sentence, yet it fails to shorten. However, the long vowel of /veːte/, which is five syllables from the end of the sentence, does shorten.

What is needed to get the rules to work is an analysis of phonological phrasing in Chimwiini. The analysis given here assumes that any sentence in Chimwiini consists of a sequence of one or more phonological phrases. Rules that have been proposed for forming phonological phrases in Chimwiini on the basis of syntax are given below.

Chimwiini Phonological Phrase Formation
1. Locate the *right edge* of every syntactic phrase (Noun Phrase, Verb Phrase, Sentence, etc.).
2. The material occurring before the first such right edge, and between consecutive right edges, forms a Phonological Phrase.

The application of these rules for the sentence given above is shown in the following diagrams. First, we examine the syntactic structure of the sentence, and find all of the right edges of phrases, as indicated.

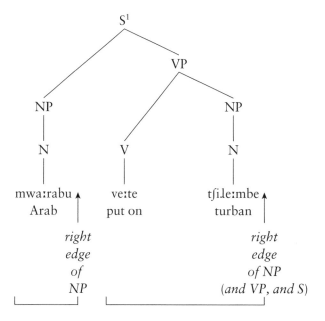

---

[1] Abbreviations used here in trees: S = Sentence, NP = Noun Phrase, VP = Verb Phrase, N = Noun, V = Verb, P = Preposition, C = Conjunction. You may have encountered different terminology or structures in your prior study of syntax; the differences are unlikely to be important for present purposes.

Then, following the rules just provided, we form Phonological Phrases out of the material preceding the first right edge, and between all right edges, as indicated by the brackets at the bottom of the tree. The phrasing rules produce the following structure:

[mwaːrabu]ₚₕᵣₐₛₑ [veːte tʃiɺeːmbe]ₚₕᵣₐₛₑ

Now it can be seen that the long /aː/ of [mwaːrabu] is only antepenultimate in its phonological phrase, and thus is preserved. The long /eː/ of /veːte/, fifth from the end of its phrase, undergoes Preantepenultimate Shortening.

A more precise representation for the output of the phrasing rules would include the word bracketing as well:

[[mwaːrabu]word]phrase [[veːte]word [tʃiɺeːmbe]word]phrase

However, by the principle given in the previous section, the word boundaries are treated as invisible to phrasal rules.

Here is a full derivation for this form, involving all four of the length-affecting rules developed in chapter 7:

[[mwaːrabu]word]phrase [[veːte]word [tʃiɺeːmbe]word]phrase	underlying form (phrased)
– uː – eː eː	Word-Final Lengthening
– – e e –	Preantepenultimate Shortening
– u – – e	Phrase-Final Shortening
– – – – –	Pre-Long Shortening
[[mwaːrabu]word]phrase [[vete]word [tʃiɺeːmbe]word]phrase	surface form

From this derivation it can be seen that the phonological phrases of Chimwiini play two roles in the phonology. First, as just noted, they form the bounding domain for Preantepenultimate Shortening. The long /aː/ of [mwaːrabu] doesn't shorten, because only two vowels, not seven, follow it within the bounding domain of the rule. Second, the phrasing determines the locations where Phrase-Final Shortening will apply: the last vowel of [mwaːrabu] surfaces as short because it is phrase-final.

Here is a second example of how phonological phrasing works in Chimwiini. In this case, we have a Noun Phrase that gets divided into two Phonological Phrases:

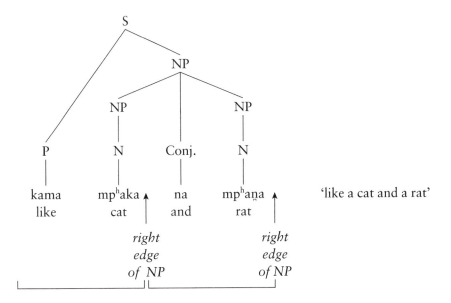

'like a cat and a rat'

With the phrasing that results, [kama mpʰaka]ₚₕᵣₐₛₑ [na mpʰaɲa]ₚₕᵣₐₛₑ, the phono-logical derivation will work as shown below. For clarity, the word divisions are shown only with spaces, not brackets.

[kama mpʰaka]phrase [na mpʰaɲa]phrase				Underlying form, phrased
aː	aː	aː	aː	Word-Final Lengthening
–	–	–	–	Preantepenultimate Shortening
–	a	–	a	Phrase-Final Shortening
–	–	–	–	Pre-Long Shortening
[kamaː mpʰaka]phrase [naː mpʰaɲa]phrase				Surface form

In some languages, there is evidence for two nested levels of phonological phrasing. Thus, in Korean, there is a rather small kind of phrase, usually about two or three words long and roughly corresponding to the phonological phrases of Chimwiini, plus a larger domain containing one or more phrases of the smaller type. In analytical work on Korean, these are usually called the Accentual Phrase and the Intonational Phrase, respectively. The Intonational Phrase is the domain of the Stop Nasalization rule discussed above in §6.2.1.

10.9   Edge-Sensitive Rules

As noted at the beginning of this chapter, bounding is not the only way that morphology and syntax influence phonology. It is also common to find cases where particular edges are themselves part of the structural requirements of rules. Rules of this kind can be termed **edge-sensitive**.

A common type is found where the edge involved is a word edge, particularly a right-side word edge. Lardil (§8.3) includes four edge-sensitive rules (Final Lowering, Apocope, Cluster Reduction, and Non-Apical Deletion), all of which refer to the right edge of the word by including in their formulations the material shown below:

$$/ \underline{\quad}]_{word}$$

In Chimwiini, Word-Final Lengthening and Phrase-Final Shortening are sensitive to word and phrase edge, respectively. English Final Fricative Devoicing (p. 94) applies at utterance edge.

Polish has a rule that is sensitive to the edges of stems. It converts alveolar /s/ into alveolopalatal [ɕ] before a front vowel, as follows:[2]

Polish /s/ Palatalization

$$s \rightarrow \varsigma / \underline{\quad}]_{stem} \begin{bmatrix} +\text{syllabic} \\ +\text{front} \end{bmatrix}$$

The presence of the labeled bracket: $]_{stem}$ in the formulation make the rule edge-sensitive: it applies only when a suffix is attached to a stem. This holds true in the following examples:

$[[pas]_{stem}]_{word}$	'belt'	$[[pa\varsigma]_{stem} e]_{word}$	'belt-locative'
$[[servis]_{stem}]_{word}$	'auto repair place'	$[[servi\varsigma]_{stem} e]_{word}$	'auto repair place-locative'
$[[silos]_{stem}]_{word}$	'silo'	$[[silo\varsigma]_{stem} e]_{word}$	'silo-locative'
		$[[silo\varsigma]_{stem} ik]_{word}$	'silo-diminutive'

In the simple forms on the left, there is only one morpheme; the stem is coextensive with the word. The forms on the right involve a stem to which a suffix has been added to form the word; the suffix has a front vowel, so /s/ Palatalization applies.

The examples *servis* and *silos* are especially informative: notice that they contain /s/'s (the initial ones) which precede front vowels but are not palatalized. The reason is that these particular /s/'s are not found at the right edge of a stem. The

---

[2] Using the features from ch. 3, this is:

$$\begin{bmatrix} +\text{continuant} \\ -\text{voice} \\ +\text{anterior} \end{bmatrix} \rightarrow \begin{bmatrix} -\text{anterior} \\ +\text{distributed} \\ +\text{dorsal} \\ +\text{high} \\ +\text{front} \end{bmatrix} / \underline{\quad} \begin{bmatrix} +\text{syllabic} \\ +\text{front} \end{bmatrix}$$

As analyzed in my reference, Rubach (1984, ch. 4), this rule applies to the full class of coronals; the text here focuses solely on /s/ to avoid some irrelevant complications.

crucial matchups of rule and form are illustrated in the figure below, which shows how /s/ Palatalization achieves a matchup for the second /s/ of /[[serviç]ₛₜₑₘ e]_word/, but not the first:

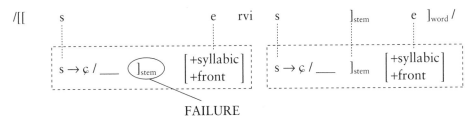

FAILURE

It should be clear from the example that bounding and edge-sensitivity are not the same thing: Polish /s/ Palatalization is sensitive to stem edges, but it is not stem-bounded; in fact, it crucially refers to material falling outside the stem.

Cases like Polish /s/ Palatalization also lead us to define more carefully the "visibility" of edges to phonological rules, discussed above in §10.7. When a rule is bounded, it is permitted to ignore edges in the form if they are of lower rank than the bounding domain of the rule. For example, the example in §10.7 was one in which a stem boundary in the form was ignored in achieving a match with a word-bounded rule. In the present case, however, the stem edge is given *in the rule itself*. This being so, it cannot be ignored. More generally, in the theory assumed here so far, all material in a rule must find a match in the form if the rule is to apply.

10.10   The Functions of Bounding and Edge-Sensitivity

Phonologists have on occasion speculated about why phonology should refer to morphology and syntax in the ways that are observed. At least two "purposes" have been suggested.

First, bounding cuts down on the amount of alternation. By removing from consideration any material outside the domain of a rule, it cuts off contexts, and thus reduces the number of context-sensitive rule applications. Since this is the usual origin of alternation (§6.1), the total amount of alternation will be less. This may be a help to the listener. When there is less alternation, the listener can consider fewer possibilities in trying to recognize morphemes from the continuous stream of incoming speech.

Second, when rules are either bounded or edge-sensitive, the allophones or contextually limited contrasts that result can serve as a signal to the listener about how the speech signal is to be divided up into words (recall that normally there are no pauses between words in speech). For example, in the dialect of English discussed above in §10.2, the phonetic difference between [ɹʌɪseɪlz] and [ɹʌɪseɪlz] can serve as a clue that the sequence should be divided as *rice ales* or *rye sales*, depending. In particular, given the word-bounded rule of /aɪ/ Raising, [ɹaɪseɪlz] can only exist if there is a word boundary after [ɹaɪ]. Moreover, the sequence [ɹʌɪs] can exist only if there is *no* word boundary after [ɹʌɪ].

A term sometimes used by phonologists for this idea is **Grenzsignal** ['gʁɛnt͡szɪgnal], German for 'boundary signal'. In the present case, the context / aɪ __ [–voice] is a *positive* Grenzsignal. The listener can infer that a word boundary must be present in this location since, if it were not, /aɪ/ Raising would have applied. The context / ʌɪ __ is a *negative* Grenzsignal. The listener can infer that there is no word boundary in this location, because otherwise there would be no way to derive [ʌɪ]. In Lardil (chapter 8), any non-apical consonant preceding a vowel is a negative Grenzsignal for word boundary; if it were word-final the rule of Non-Apical Deletion (p. 179) would have removed it.

Exercises

1   Bounding domains in English

In dialects of English spoken in the coastal cities of the northeastern United States one finds minimal pairs for [ɛə] vs. [æ], of the following type:

banner   ['bænɚ]   'flag'
banner   ['bɛənɚ]   'one who bans (books, or whatever)'

Despite the minimal pair, these two vowels are largely predictable in their distribution. But to make the prediction, you have to refer to boundaries.

The particular data examined here are from a dialect spoken on Long Island, in the eastern suburbs of New York City.

Forms with [ɛ͡ə]		Forms with [æ]	
		cat	['kæt]
		tap	['tæp]
		tack	['tæk]
		batch	['bæt͡ʃ]
mass	['mɛəs]	*Massachusetts*	[ˌmæsə'tʃusəts]
massing	['mɛəsɪŋ]		
pass	['pɛəs]	*Pasadena*	[ˌpæsə'dinə]
passing	['pɛəsɪŋ]		
plan	['plɛən]	*planet*	['plænət]
planning	['plɛənɪŋ]		
planner	['plɛənə]		
class	['klɛəs]	*placid*	['plæsɪd]

classing	['klɛəsɪŋ]		
graph	['gɹæf]	*cafeteria*	[ˌkæfə'tʰɹɪiə]
graphable	['gɹæfəbəl]		
clam	['klɛəm]	*Amadeus*	[ˌæmə'deɪəs]
clammy	['klɛəmi]		
trash	['tɹɛəʃ]	*passion*	['pæʃən]
trashy	['tɹɛəʃi]		
laugh	['lɛəf]	*affable*	['æfəbəl]
laughable	['lɛəfəbəl]		
grab	['gɹɛəb]	*rabble*	['ɹæbəl]
grabber	['gɹɛəbə]		
mad	['mɛəd]	*Madeleine*	['mæɾəˌlaɪn]
madder	['mɛəɾə]		
maddest	['mɛəɾəst]		
man	['mɛən]	*manifold*	['mænəˌfold]
mannish	['mɛənɪʃ]		

a. Formulate an analysis using bounding domains that accounts for the surface distribution of [æ] and [ɛə]. Here are two hints.

1 [ɛə] is found only before one of the segments [m, n, v, z, f, θ, s, ʃ, b, d, dʒ, g]; whereas [æ] can occur before these or any other segments. The set [m, n, v, z, f, θ, s, ʃ, b, d, dʒ, g] forms a counterexample to the general principle (see §2.10.4) that phonological rules apply to natural classes. Try to reduce the set to just two natural classes, connecting them with curly brackets, as in $\left\{\begin{matrix}[\ ]\\[\ ]\end{matrix}\right\}$ (for more on curly brackets see p. 259), or just write two rules. For an English consonant chart see p. 21.

2 The distribution has nothing to do with suffixes *as such*. A form like *planets* would come out ['plænəts], and similarly for the other forms in the right column.

b. What does the phonology tell us about how native speakers of this dialect morphologically relate the following forms?

graph	['gɹæf]	*graphic*	['gɹæfɪk]
psychopath	['sʌɪkouˌpɛəθ]	*pathological*	[ˌpæθə'lɑdʒɪkəl]

c. Given *madder* ['mɛəɾɚ] vs. *fatter* ['fæɾɚ], how must /æ/ Diphthongization be ordered with respect to Tapping (p. 143) in this dialect? Justify your answer with derivations.

2 *Phonological phrasing in Chimwiini*

Consider the underlying representation /kama mpʰaka na mpʰana/ on p. 216. Write down every *logically possible* phrasing (other than the one given in the text, which you can skip, there are seven), apply the phonological rules, and determine what would be the outcome.

3   *Boundary signals*

a. Multiple choice:

[plẽɪneɪl]: ___ *plain ale*   ___ *play nail*
[pleɪneɪl]: ___ *plain ale*   ___ *play nail*

Justify your answers. For simplicity, you may assumed that Vowel Nasalization (p. 212) is word-bounded, not stem-bounded.

b. For every arrow shown below, specify whether a word boundary *must* occur at the location, *must not* occur, or *may* occur. Explain your answer, in terms of the rules and ideas included in this chapter, particularly §10.5. You should give a phonological answer, not one based on what actual words occur in English. Assume that these are isolation utterances; no other words precede or follow them.

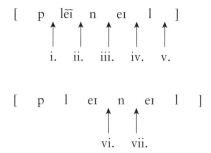

Sample answer for (i): "No word boundary could occur here, because there is no such thing as an English word that consists of a single consonant, like [p]."

Further reading

For the idea of a hierarchy of phrases in phonology, see James McCawley, *The Phonological Component of a Grammar of Japanese* (1968, Mouton), pp. 52–8; also pp. 201–20 of Bruce Hayes, "The Prosodic Hierarchy in Meter," in Paul Kiparsky and Gilbert Youmans, eds., *Rhythm and Meter* (1989, Academic Press); www.linguistics.ucla.edu/people/hayes/Papers/Hayes_ProsodicHierarchy.pdf.

The idea that phonological phrasing in Chimwiini and other languages can be determined by looking at the edges of syntactic phrases was proposed by Elisabeth O. Selkirk in her paper "On derived domains in sentence phonology," *Phonology Yearbook* 3: 371–405 (1986).

The idea of the phonological Grenzsignal is associated with the phonologist Nikolai S. Trubetzkoy, and appears in his 1939 book *Grundzüge der Phonologie* (English translation *Principles of Phonology*, Christiane Baltaxe, 1969, University of California Press).

Polish /s/ Palatalization: Jerzy Rubach, *Cyclic and Lexical Phonology: The Structure of Polish* (1984, Foris). Phrasal bounding domains in Korean: Sun-Ah Jun, *The Phonetics and Phonology of Korean Prosody: Intonational Phonology and Prosodic Structure* (1996, Garland Press).

11 Diachrony and Synchrony

11.1 Historical Change

Languages change over time, in an interesting and paradoxical way. The speakers of a language often don't notice the language changing. They can communicate with their grandparents in childhood and with their grandchildren in old age. These conversations cover a total of five generations. But consider a translation of a biblical verse into the English of about 40 generations ago (Old English, about 1000 CE; IPA transcription is a conjecture).

urne	gedæghwamlican	hlaf	syle	us	to dæg
['urnɛ	gɛ'dæɣwamlikan	'l̥af	'sylɛ	us	to 'dæɣ]
our	daily		bread	give	us	today

'Give us this day our daily bread'

This would be unintelligible to a speaker of Modern English who had not studied Old English, and many of the morphemes have evolved so as to be only faintly recognizable (e.g. [dæɣ] = *day*, ['l̥af] = *loaf*, [lik] = *-ly*). Somehow, a series of changes that were little noticed as they were happening have gradually converted English into an entirely different language.

The field of **historical linguistics** attempts to understand the process of linguistic change, and to use this understanding to provide an account of the ancestry and history of the world's languages.

11.2 Sound Change

One of the major areas of language change is **sound change**. For example, the voiceless [l̥] in Old English ['l̥af] 'bread', given above, has become voiced [l] in Modern English *loaf*. This change happened not just to this particular instance of voiceless [l̥], but to *every* [l̥] of Old English; for example, the words *loud* and *laughter* once had initial voiceless [l̥]'s and now have plain [l]'s just like *loaf*. As a language evolves, it is subjected to dozens or even hundreds of sound changes, until it takes on a form that would be unintelligible to the original speakers.

Sound change is connected in a curious way to phonology. Basically, sound change results from the fact that throughout its history, a language has a large number of phonological rules.

The rules are the *seeds* of sound change; but they are not the same thing as sound change. A sound change is a historical event. For example, if all the words that in 1300 were pronounced with voiceless [l̥] are pronounced with voiced [l] in 1500, then we say that during this time the language has undergone a sound change taking [l̥] to [l]. A phonological rule, on the other hand, is something in the mind of a native speaker; it is part of a speaker's unconscious mental grammar.

Some terminology: **diachrony** ([daɪˈækɹəni]) is the study of language evolving through time. **Synchrony** ([ˈsɪŋkɹəni]) is the study of language as it exists at a particular point in time. In modern linguistics, the object of synchronic study is the linguistic knowledge internalized by the native speaker. Using these terms, we can say that *sound change* is a diachronic concept, and *phonological rule* is a synchronic concept.

11.3   Restructuring

A naïve and false conception of the relation of phonological rules and sound change is that the phonology of a language at any one time is simply the accumulation of the sound changes that have happened in the past. The reason this is not true is a phenomenon called **restructuring**. To understand restructuring, it will help to do an example in detail.

The sound change we will examine is a fairly recent one. American English is divided into a minority dialect that has an extra phoneme /ʍ/ (the voiceless labial-velar approximant) and a majority dialect that lacks this phoneme. I will call the dialect that has /ʍ/ Conservative American English, and the dialect that lacks it Innovating American English. In Conservative American English, the word *which* is pronounced [ʍɪt͡ʃ] and *witch* is pronounced [wɪt͡ʃ]; whereas in Innovating American English, both words are pronounced [wɪt͡ʃ].[1] In fact, Innovating American English has /w/ in all of the morphemes where Conservative American English has /ʍ/. /ʍ/ is not attested, and is phonologically impermissible, in Innovating American English.

It can be argued that Conservative American English is a continuation of the original state of the language, and that Innovating American English has

---

[1] For the (rather erratic) geographic distribution of these two dialects, see www.ling.upenn.edu/phono_atlas/maps/Map8.html, from the TELSUR project at the University of Pennsylvania.

undergone a sound change whereby [ʍ] has been replaced by [w] in all environments. The evidence for this is that the old written documents from past centuries spell out the [w]–[ʍ] distinction as *w* vs. *wh* (or earlier, *hw*). We can only explain this if the distinction is an ancient one. The medieval scribes who invented English spelling must have been hearing *something*.[2]

What could have given rise to this sound change? The place to look would be in the English that existed shortly before Innovating American English came into being. In fact, we can do this, since Conservative American English plausibly is a direct continuation of this older state. The idea, then, is to look within Conservative American English to find the roots of the sound change that Innovating American English has undergone. The basic idea is conveyed by this diagram:

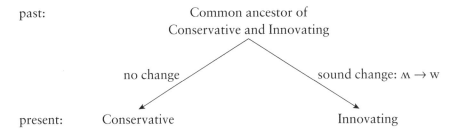

past: Common ancestor of
              Conservative and Innovating

     no change   sound change: ʍ → w

present: Conservative   Innovating

11.4 The Phonology of Conservative American English

Conservative American English, at least as I and others speak it, has the following phonological rule:

/ʍ/ Voicing
ʍ → [+voiced] in all environments, optionally (applies in casual or rapid speech)

That is, while the /w/–/ʍ/ distinction is part of the phonological system of Conservative American English, the distinction is obliterated in rapid or casual speech, since the voicing rule applies. The following data illustrate this:

The whale is over there = [ðə'ʍeɪlɪz͡ˌoʊvɚ'ðɛɹ]   (normal)
                      [ðə'weɪlɪz͡ˌoʊvɚ'ðɛɹ]   (casual speech)

Consider now the sequence of events that might have led to the transition from Conservative to Innovating American English. First of all, when a language has an optional rule, it often comes to be applied more and more often through time. Just why this happens, and why it happens for some rules and not others, is not known. Let us assume, however, that we are dealing with a rule that has come to apply far more often than not; say, 95 percent of the time.

The next step involves the introduction of a new generation of speakers. As young children, these speakers face the task of learning the phonemic system of their language. In the present case, the task is a very difficult one. The older speakers, who supply the data, have stored in their mental lexicons a phonemic distinction between /w/ and /ʍ/. However, in their actual pronunciations /ʍ/ is rare, because (by hypothesis) 95 percent of the time, they are applying the rule of /ʍ/ Voicing to it. The new generation thus has very little information from which to learn the /ʍ/ phoneme.

It is easy to see how this situation will turn out. The younger generation is likely not to notice the [ʍ]'s at all, and they will acquire a different phonological system. Here are the old and new phonological systems compared:

Older Speakers
two phonemes, /w/ and /ʍ/
Phonological rule of /ʍ/ Voicing: ʍ → [+voice] in all but careful speech

Younger Speakers
one phoneme: /w/
no /ʍ/ Voicing rule

The crucial point is that while the speech of the older and younger generations is almost the same (5% vs. 0% [ʍ] in the relevant set of words), they have quite different phonologies.

This phenomenon is an instance of **restructuring**, which may be defined as a major shift in a linguistic system induced by reinterpretation of the older generation's output by a younger, language-acquiring generation. Innovating American English probably arose from a restructuring by younger speakers of the phonological system of the ancestor dialect, a dialect which is still preserved in the form of Conservative American English.

In general, quite a few sound changes are the result of the following process:

1 A new phonological rule is introduced into a language.
2 The rule is applied with increasing frequency.
3 A new generation restructures the system: they acquire no rule, but a different set of underlying representations.

We can now consider the question raised earlier: why don't we notice language changing? Part of the answer is we *can* notice it; whenever you examine an optional rule, you may well be looking at a sound change in progress. The other part concerns the more drastic changes, the restructurings: these occur less frequently, and are subtle in their observable effects. Hence restructuring has seldom been observed in progress.

11.5   Phoneme Creation

Before going on, I will address a peripheral though interesting problem in diachrony. Notice that /ʍ/ Voicing eliminated a phoneme: where once there was /ʍ/ and /w/, there later was only /w/. A similar sound change in progress, /ɔ/ Unrounding, has wiped out the /ɑ/–/ɔ/ distinction (§3.2.1) from numerous North American dialects.[3] In fact, sound changes eliminate distinctions rather often. If this is so, why don't the phonemic inventories of the world's languages steadily shrink, until we are reduced to a pitiable, infantile [bababba . . .]?

One answer is that languages sometimes borrow phonemes from neighboring languages. For example, English borrowed the phoneme /v/ from French (it had a [v] before, but only as an allophone of /f/, not as a separate phoneme). The ongoing expansion of the Japanese phoneme inventory through borrowing is discussed in §3.4.2.

However, it is also possible for a language to create a new phoneme entirely on its own. To give a schematic example, imagine that a language has the vowel system /i, e, a, o, u/, has disyllabic words (such as, say, /tuti/) and monosyllabic words like /tut/. Suppose further a sequence of sound changes: vowels become front when a front vowel follows in the next syllable ([tuti] → [tyti], with high front rounded [y]) and then final vowels are dropped (tyti > tyt). Assuming that the changes are restructured, this sequence of changes will have *created a new phoneme*, namely /y/, which will occur in minimal pairs like [tyt], [tut].

This is actually a fairly common historical event: former allophones (like [y] at the [tyti] stage above) become phonemes when the environment that formerly conditioned them is lost to sound change. The scheme just given is, for instance, an outline account of how German acquired its front rounded vowel phonemes /yː, ʏ, øː, œ/. Similarly, certain consonants produce allophonic differences of pitch on neighboring vowels. When the consonants are lost or neutralized in sound change, the pitch differences can remain behind as phonemic tone ("tonogenesis").

---

[3]   See www.ling.upenn.edu/phono_atlas/maps/Map2.html for a map showing which dialects have undergone the merger.

11.6   The Fate of Rules

What are the possible fates of phonological rules? We are particularly interested in what happens when an originally optional rule comes to apply with 100 percent frequency. There are three cases to consider.

11.6.1   *Non-neutralizing rules*

Suppose a rule applies to all instances of a phoneme, and is non-neutralizing. An example of this is a rule that came to affect various dialects of Dutch in recent centuries:

/ɾ/ Uvularization
ɾ → ʁ

The status of this rule varies among Dutch dialects. There are some dialects (call them Class I) that have nothing but /ɾ/. These dialects lack [ʁ] entirely, and likewise lack /ɾ/ Uvularization. Other dialects, to be called Class II, have /ɾ/ Uvularization as an *optional rule*; speakers of these dialects produce words containing underlying /ɾ/[4] with either [ɾ] or [ʁ], in free variation. Lastly, there are dialects, which we will call Class III, where the only rhotic sound is [ʁ]. Here is a summary:

Class I: [ɾ] only
Class II: free variation, [ɾ] ~ [ʁ]
Class III: [ʁ] only

The history of this situation seems to be as follows. Probably all Dutch dialects were Class I at some time in the past. With the appearance of /ɾ/ Uvularization (perhaps as a prestigious import from France), the Class II dialects came into being, and they too continue to exist to this day. Finally, and crucially for our present point, in some Class II dialects, the application of /ɾ/ Uvularization became so common that it triggered restructuring: the possibility of saying [ɾ] disappeared in the innovating generation, and [ʁ] became obligatory. This created the Class III dialects.

The crucial point is this: for a speaker of a Class III dialect, who always says [ʁ], there is no justification for supposing that [ʁ] is anything other than underlying /ʁ/. Nor is there any justification for positing [ɾ] Uvularization as a

---

[4]   The underlying form could also be assumed to be /ʁ/, with a rule converting /ʁ/ to [ɾ].

phonological rule for the Class III dialects. If this point is not clear, bear in mind that a child growing up in a monodialectal Class III environment never hears [ɾ] at all.

This is restructuring, but unlike the restructuring in English /ʍ/ → /w/, there is no loss of contrast. The system of contrasting phonemes in Class III dialects can be straightforwardly mapped onto the system of phonemes in Class I dialects: the slot in the phonemic system that was formerly filled by /ɾ/ is now filled by /ʁ/.

11.6.2 *Neutralizing rules that create alternations*

Consider now a rule that neutralizes, just like our earlier case of /ʍ/ Voicing. But this time, let us suppose that the morphology of the language in question is such that the rule creates alternations, applying in some but not all of the various forms of a given morpheme.

Here is an example. In Standard Italian, there are seven vowel phonemes:

i		u
e		o
ɛ		ɔ
	a	

However, these seven vowels appear only in syllables that bear stress. Elsewhere, there is just a five-vowel system:

i		u
e		o
	a	

The process of reduction takes underlying /ɛ, ɔ/ to [e, o] in stressless syllables, as in the following alternations:

['lɛtto]	'bed'	[let'tino]	'bed-diminutive'
['kɔɾo]	'choir'	[ko'ɾale]	'choral'

The rule is neutralizing, since there are also stems with underlying /e, o/ that do not alternate under changes of stress:

['bene]	'good'	[be'nino]	'sort of good'
['oɾa]	'hour'	[o'ɾetta]	'about an hour'

Synchronically, we can write a rule of Vowel Reduction, which works as follows:

Italian Vowel Reduction

$$\begin{bmatrix} +\text{syllabic} \\ -\text{low} \\ -\text{stress} \end{bmatrix} \rightarrow [+\text{tense}]$$

Stressless /ɛ/ and /ɔ/ become [e] *and* [o].

Vowel Reduction can be considered also as a sound change, part of the history of Standard Italian. In fact, historically, the rule had a somewhat broader scope. It is known that words like [ele'fante] 'elephant' and others once had lax vowels: [ɛlɛ'fante]. We can tell this because we know essentially the entire phonological history of Italian, with Classical Latin as its starting point (Latin: [elefantus], where former [e] evolved into Italian [ɛ]). But here is the crucial part: the vowel [e] in modern Italian [ele'fante] *does not alternate*: it has no allomorph in which it bears stress. As far as phonemicization goes, there seems no reason not to take the straightforward approach "what you hear is what you get," phonemicizing [ele'fante] as /ele'fante/.

Considering now the history of this situation, we get a divided result. First, insofar as Vowel Reduction still creates alternations, there has been no restructuring. Modern Standard Italian [let'tino] 'bed-diminutive' is still underlyingly /let'tino/, because morphologically it is derived from /'lɛtto/ 'bed'.[5] The Vowel Reduction rule applies within the modern-day grammar, just as it did historically, to derive the surface form [let'tino]. On the other hand, where the historical change of Vowel Reduction did *not* create alternations, restructuring has taken place, shifting what was once /ɛlɛ'fante/ to /ele'fante/.

11.6.3 Neutralizing rules that create no alternations

What we've just seen is that the pattern of alternation in a language can, as it were, "freeze" the underlying representations in a historically prior state. The relevant sound change continues as a productive part of the phonology of the language, precisely because the presence of alternations blocks the restructuring process. It is only where alternating forms happen to be lacking that the restructuring occurs.

With this in mind, we can return to our original example, the /ʍ/ Voicing change in English. The crucial fact about this sound change is that it applied to *all* instances of /ʍ/, irrespective of environment. As a result, there never arose any morphemes that alternated by context. From this it follows that there were never any alternating forms that could have preserved the old underlying representations. As a result, restructuring occurred across the board.

---

[5] A note on morphology: the [-o] suffix is (approximately) a gender marker for masculines, so the morphological structures involved are /lɛtt-o/, /lɛtt-in-o/. Italian morphology attaches the diminutive suffix directly to the stem, not to the [stem+gender marker] combination.

11.7   Restructuring of Rules

Restructuring can affect not just the underlying representations, but also the phonological rules. Consider the [f] ~ [v] alternations seen in the singulars and plurals
of English nouns, discussed above (§9.4) in connection with productivity. A few
examples are repeated below.

knife	[naɪf]	*knives*	[naɪvz]
wife	[waɪf]	*wives*	[waɪvz]
life	[laɪf]	*lives*	[laɪvz]
leaf	[lif]	*leaves*	[livz]
sheaf	[ʃif]	*sheaves*	[ʃivz]
thief	[θif]	*thieves*	[θivz]
self	['sɛlf]	*selves*	[sɛlvz]

These pairs may be said to justify a rule – only partly productive – of /f/ Voicing,
formulated above on p. 193. For present purposes it will be helpful to give the
rule a more specific name than before:

/f/ Voicing in Plurals
f → [+voice] / ___ z]$_{\begin{bmatrix} \text{Noun} \\ \text{+plural} \end{bmatrix}}$

A curious aspect of this rule is that it was never a sound change. Instead, it is
itself the result of restructuring, induced by a whole sequence of historical developments. The voicing alternation dates from a time when the English plural suffix
had a vowel everywhere, not just after sibilants as it does today. In Old English,
[v] was simply an allophone of /f/, occurring between voiced sounds. Around the
year 1200, the forms *self* and *selves* would have been something like this:

	Phonemic	Phonetic
self	/sɛlf/	[sɛlf]
selves	/sɛlf-əs/	[sɛlvəs]

The rule of Old English that derived the [v] allophone would have been something like the following:

Intervoiced /f/ Voicing[6]
f → [+voice] / [+voice] ___ [+voice]

---

[6]   In fact, *all* the fricatives of Old English had voiced allophones in this environment, but this will
not be crucial here.

There were several later historical developments. (1) /v/ became an independent phoneme, as a result of borrowings from French (like *vine*) and from regional English dialects (like *vat*). (2) Borrowings led to instances of [f] (not [v]) in the intervoiced environment, like *muffle*. (3) /s/ was voiced to [z] in final position after schwa. (4) The plural suffix lost its vowel in all environments except when a [+strident] consonant preceded it (as in *horses* [ˈhɔɹsəz]). Combined, these created the modern data pattern. The historical sequence is shown below (again, note that this is a description of language history, not a phonological derivation):

self	*selves*	
sɛlf	sɛlv-es	Old English, with [v] allophone of /f/
—	sɛlv-əs	reduction of stressless vowels to schwa
—	sɛlv-əz	voicing of fricatives after stressless vowels
sɛlf	sɛlvz	loss of schwa in inflectional endings

However, the data pattern that we have today can only be sensibly analyzed using the rule of /f/ Voicing in Plurals, *not* with Intervoiced /f/ Voicing. This is because of various changes that have happened since Old English times that make the Intervoiced /f/ Voicing analysis unworkable. In particular, today, /f/ freely occurs in the intervoiced environment (in words like *muffin*, *offer*, *muffle*, and so on). Moreover, the plural suffix has a vowel only in one special environment (after sibilants), and not across the board as it did in Old English. Faced with such a data pattern, a child encountering Modern English could not arrive at the view that her language has a rule of Intervoiced /f/ Voicing; rather, she would analyze the data as they are today and set up a rule along the lines of /f/ Voicing in Plurals.

The upshot is that /f/ Voicing in Plurals is a restructured rule; a rule that was never a sound change, but is the restructured consequence of a whole sequence of sound changes.[7]

11.8 Restructuring: Summary

All the complications involving the relation of historical change to synchronic phonology reduce fundamentally to the fact that children can only learn the phonology of their language on the basis of the data that they actually hear. These

---

[7] The ancient rule of Intervoiced /f/ Voicing has other restructured historical descendents in Modern English, notably the voicing alternations between nouns and verbs seen in cases like: *half ~ halve*, *proof ~ prove*, *belief ~ believe*, *shelf ~ shelve*, *grief ~ grieve*, *calf ~ calve*. These forms are plausibly analyzed with a semi-productive rule of /f/ Voicing In Verbs: /f/ → [+voice] / ___]$_{Verb}$. Historically, they arose from Intervoiced /f/ Voicing, applying in the presence of former vowel-initial verbal endings that are now lost.

data include the phonetic forms of words, the patterning of free variation, and the alternations that appear in different forms of the same morpheme. In many cases, these data suffice for the child to construct a grammar that is the same as that as the preceding generation. But when optional rules apply with great frequency, with the crucial conservative variants too rare to notice, the child will create a grammar on her own which may diverge dramatically from the form of the adult grammar.

The child's new grammar will resemble the old one to the extent that the factor of alternations makes it so. Alternations tend to preserve archaic underlying representations, because an older allomorph is preserved in some particular context which serves as evidence for the underlying form. Where there is no alternation, the child will restructure, setting up underlying forms that are the same as the surface data. That is, the child takes the data she hears at face value, there being no reason not to do so.

We now restate why phonology is not the same thing as historical linguistics: because language is handed down from generation to generation, there is ample opportunity for the system to be restructured by new learners. Thus, it is very seldom the case that the synchronic underlying representations of Language X are simply the surface forms of X as it was spoken a thousand years ago. The odds are high that restructuring will have occurred along the way.

Exercises

1 Hypercorrection

In West Indian English, spoken in Jamaica and elsewhere in the Caribbean, words that in other dialects have [t], [θ], [d], and [ð] are often pronounced differently. Here are some examples. In Jamaican English, *thing* is normally pronounced [tɪŋ] and *father* is normally pronounced ['faːda]. These differences are the result of a sound change that was neutralizing, so that (for instance) both *thin* and *tin* are pronounced with [t], both *faith* and *fate* are pronounced with [t]; both *though* and *dough* are pronounced with [d], and both *breathe* and *breed* are pronounced with [d].

However, on occasion, some speakers of this dialect are heard to produce variant pronunciations, saying [θɪŋ] for *thing*, [θɪn] for *tin* (as well as for *thin*), ['faːða] for *father*, [θʌŋ] for *tongue*, [fʊθ] for *foot*, and [bɛð] for *bed*.

a. Does this mean that these speakers have a phonemic distinction between [t] and [θ], and between [d] and [ð]?
b. Give a historical explanation for the origin of pronunciations like [θɪn] for *tin*, [θʌŋ] for *tongue*, and [bɛð] for *bed*.

2 Restructuring

A dialect of English spoken in Indiana has undergone a sound change:

$$l \rightarrow \emptyset \, / \, \mathtt{ɔ} \, \underline{\quad} \,]_{word}$$

In this dialect, *maul* and *maw* are homophones ([mɔ]), as are *Saul* and *saw* [sɔ]. *Saul* and *haul* rhyme ([sɔ], [hɔ]). *Pauley* is still ['pɔli], *mauling* is still ['mɔlɪŋ], and *hauling* is still ['hɔlɪŋ]. The sound change is complete, and speakers of this dialect consider [sɔl] to be difficult to pronounce.

Consider the *synchronic* phonology of this dialect.

a.   Has the word *Saul* undergone restructuring? In other words, should its underlying form still be /sɔl/?

b.   Have the words *maul* and *haul* undergone restructuring? (Hint: consider what their paradigms would be.)

Further reading

The biblical text at the opening of this chapter is from Rolf Kaiser, *Medieval English* (1958).

The concept of restructuring is laid out in the textbook *Historical Linguistics* by Theodora Bynon (1977, Cambridge University Press), and in the context of English dialects by John Wells in his *Accents of English* (1982, Cambridge University Press). Some intriguing cases of restructuring are analyzed in Paul Kiparsky in his *Explanation in Phonology* (1992, Foris Publications).

History of /f/ Voicing in English: Otto Jespersen, *A Modern English Grammar on Historical Principles. Part I: Sounds and Spellings* (1909, Allen and Unwin); Karl Luick, *Historische Grammatik der Englischen Sprache* (1921, reprinted 1964, Blackwell).

12 Abstractness

12.1 Abstractness Defined

Chapters 6–8 covered a standard method of phonological analysis capable of reducing complex arrays of data to rule. The core ideas are that each morpheme has a unique underlying phonological representation, and that alternation in paradigms is the result of concatenating the underlying forms with simple morphological rules, followed by the ordered application of a set of phonological rules.

This theory provides no explicit method for extracting the underlying forms from the data. Although it is possible to formulate heuristic strategies (such as those in §8.1), in the end, the theory simply assumes that we will choose *whatever works*. Once we have arrived at a suitable set of underlying forms (by whatever means), it is possible to justify that choice by showing that all the surface forms can be derived from them by means of phonological rules. But the original choice of underlying forms is free.

The fact that the theory does not impose any constraints on the choice of underlying forms has led various phonologists at times to propose analyses in which the underlying representations depart radically from what appears in surface forms. Analyses have been proposed whose underlying representations include sounds that never occur in surface representations at all. Such representations are usually proposed to facilitate the analysis of difficult, irregular-seeming paradigms.

When a phonological analysis uses underlying elements that are very different from surface forms – especially, segments that appear nowhere on the surface – it is often called an **abstract** analysis. In what follows, I will present the outlines of a well-known abstract analysis, then discuss its implications.

12.2 Polish Vowel ~ Zero Alternations

Below are some extracts from the noun paradigms of Polish. This language has a rather complicated morphology. Nouns come in three genders (masculine, feminine, neuter) and are inflected for number (singular vs. plural) as well as case (nominative, accusative, dative, genitive, instrumental, locative, vocative). Different genders can take different endings for the various combinations of number and case. For present purposes, all that matters is that nouns normally occur in at least one *unsuffixed* allomorph (usually the nominative singular or genitive plural) as well as a variety of *suffixed* allomorphs. The crucial thing to look for in the data is the difference between the form of a stem when it is suffixed vs. when it is not; the particular suffix does not matter.

For instance, a portion of the paradigm of the word for 'sweater' is as follows:

	Singular	*Plural*
Nominative	[sveter]	[svetr-ɨ]
Accusative	[sveter]	[svetr-ɨ]
Dative	[svetr-ovi]	[svetr-om]
Instrumental	[svetr-em]	[svetr-ami]
Genitive	[svetr-a]	[svetr-uf]

In the two unsuffixed forms, the nominative and accusative singular, the stem shows up with an extra [e] vowel which is missing in the suffixed forms. There are hundreds of Polish noun stems that also show this alternation between [e] and ∅, of which the following are examples.

Polish stems with [e] ~ ∅ alternations

a. *Longer stems*

[sveter]	'sweater-nom sg.'	[svetr-ɨ]	'sweater-nom. pl.'
[holender]	'Dutchman-nom sg.'	[holendr-a]	'Dutchman-gen. sg.'
[koper]	'fennel-nom. sg.'	[kopr-u]	'fennel-gen. sg.'
[kaliber]	'caliber-nom. sg.'	[kalibr-a]	'caliber-gen. sg.'
[dʲabew]	'devil-nom. sg.'	[dʲabw-a]	'devil-gen. sg.'
[perew]	'pearl-gen. pl.'	[perw-a]	'pearl-nom. sg.'
[knebel]	'gag-nom. sg.'	[knebl-a]	'gag-gen. sg.'
[dizel]	'diesel car-nom. sg.'	[dizl-a]	'diesel car-gen. sg.'
[sosen]	'pine-gen. pl.'	[sosn-a]	'pine-nom. sg.'
[vojen]	'war-gen. pl.'	[vojn-a]	'war-nom. sg.'

b. *Short stems*

[den]	'bottom-gen. pl.'	[dn-o]	'bottom-nom. sg.'
[mex]	'moss-nom. sg.'	[mx-u]	'moss-gen. sg.'
[len]	'flax-nom sg.'	[ln-u]	'flax-gen. sg.'
[veʃ]	'louse-nom. sg.'	[vʃ-ɨ]	'louse-gen. sg.'
[wez]	'tear-gen. pl.'	[wz-a]	'tear-nom. sg.'
[tew]	'background-gen.pl.'	[tw-o]	'background-nom. sg.'

Not all stems that have [e] as their last vowel show this kind of alternation, however. An almost equal number show the [e] throughout their paradigms:

Non-alternating Polish stems with [e]

a. *Longer stems*

[krater]	'crater-nom. sg.'	[krater-ɨ]	'crater-nom. pl.'
[order]	'order-nom. sg.'	[order-u]	'order-gen. sg.'
[papʲer]	'paper-nom. sg.'	[papʲer-u]	'paper-gen. sg.'
[numer]	'number-nom. sg.'	[numer-u]	'number-gen. sg.'
[skalpel]	'scalpel-nom. sg.'	[skalpel-a]	'scalpel-gen. sg.'
[karmel]	'caramel-nom. sg.'	[karmel-u]	'caramel-gen. sg.'
[basen]	'basin-nom. sg.'	[basen-u]	'basin-gen. sg.'
[omen]	'omen-nom. sg.'	[omen-u]	'omen-gen. sg.'

b. *Short stems*

[ren]	'reindeer-nom. sg.'	[ren-a]	'reindeer-gen. sg.'
[ser]	'cheese-nom. sg.'	[ser-a]	'cheese-gen. sg.'
[ʃef]	'boss-nom. sg.'	[ʃef-a]	'boss-gen. sg.'
[kres]	'end-nom. sg.'	[kres-u]	'end-gen. sg.'
[ʒer]	'food-nom. sg.'	[ʒer-u]	'food-gen. sg.'
[sketʃ͡]	'sketch-nom. sg.'	[sketʃ͡-u]	'sketch-gen. sg.'

Let us pursue the method of phonological analysis given in §8.1. If there is a vowel ~ zero alternation, as in the first data set, we should consider hypotheses with both insertion and deletion.

Hypothesis I: Syncope[1]
What underlies the [e] ~ ∅ alternation is /e/. There is a rule of Syncope (environment to be determined) which deletes underlying /e/ from stems when a suffix is added.

Hypothesis II: Epenthesis
What underlies the [e] ~ ∅ alternation is ∅. There is a rule of Epenthesis (environment to be determined) which inserts [e] into word-final consonant clusters.

Hypothesis I, the syncope hypothesis, appears from the facts to be untenable. Whatever Syncope rule we wrote to handle (for example) /sveter-ɨ/ → [svetrɨ] would wrongly delete the vowel of /krater-ɨ/, yielding *[kratrɨ], and similarly for the other non-alternating forms. But Hypothesis II, the epenthesis hypothesis, looks more promising. We suppose that the underlying forms are basically what one sees in

---

[1] "Syncope" (['sɪŋkəpi]) is the usual term for any process that deletes vowels in medial position.

the second column of the data sets, for example /svetr/ and /krater/. These underlying forms show a fundamental contrast (final / . . . CeC/ vs. final / . . . CC/), which is neutralized by the insertion of [e] into certain final clusters. This Epenthesis rule would convert underlying /svetr/ to [sveter], thus neutralizing it in the crucial respects with underlying /krater/.

The actual environment for Epenthesis is not generally agreed upon; inspection of earlier research (see references below) and my own Polish data set[2] suggests that there are at least two Epenthesis rules in Polish. The first such rule splits up final consonant clusters just in case the second consonant is a sonorant:

Sonorant Cluster Epenthesis

$$\varnothing \rightarrow e \,/\, C \underline{\quad} \begin{bmatrix} -\text{syllabic} \\ +\text{sonorant} \end{bmatrix}]_{\text{word}}$$

Split up an underlying word-final C + sonorant *cluster with an epenthetic* [e].

You should examine the "*sveter*" data on p. 236 above to verify that the limitation to sonorant-final stems is indeed correct.

The other rule needed applies to *vowelless* underlying forms. If, as we are assuming, the underlying form of a stem is the allomorph that appears before a suffix, then the underlying form for an alternation like [den] ~ [dn-o], seen above, must be /dn/. The vowelless representation /dn/ can be converted to the correct surface form [den] by epenthesizing [e] with the following rule:

Monosyllabic Epenthesis

$$\varnothing \rightarrow e \,/\, [\, C_0 \underline{\quad} C \,]_{\text{word}}$$

If a word would otherwise have no vowels at all, place [e] *before its final consonant.*

It should be recalled (p. 154) that C_0 is an abbreviation meaning "any number of consonants." The left word bracket is needed to show that the rule inspects the entire word, and therefore applies only if the word has no vowels at all (you can think of the rule as saying: $[\, C_0 C \,]_{\text{word}} \rightarrow [\, C_0 e C \,]_{\text{word}}$).

To sum up the analysis, here are the two rules applying in sample derivations. In each case, a form with epenthesis is compared with an analogous form with underlying /e/.

'sweater nom. sg.'	'sweater nom. pl.'	'crater nom. sg.'	'crater nom. pl.'	
/svetr/	/svetr-i/	/krater/	/krater-i/	underlying forms
sveter	—	—	—	Sonorant Cluster Epenthesis
—	—	—	—	Monosyllabic Epenthesis
[sveter]	[svetri]	[krater]	[krateri]	surface forms

---

[2] This is a set of about 1500 noun paradigms, entered into a spreadsheet and checked by two native speakers of Polish. The stems to be included were a complete selection of the stem types discussed here, taken from R. Grzegorczykowa and J. Puzynina *Indeks a tergo* (1973, Państwowe Wydawnictwo Naukowe), a reverse-alphabetical dictionary.

'bottom- gen. pl.'	'bottom- nom. sg.'	'reindeer- nom. sg.'	'reindeer- gen. sg.'	
/dn/	/dn-o/	/ren/	/ren-a/	underlying forms
—	—	—	—	Sonorant Cluster Epenthesis
den	—	—	—	Monosyllabic Epenthesis
[den]	[dno]	[ren]	[rena]	surface forms

It may be added that both Sonorant Cluster Epenthesis and Monosyllabic Epenthesis would be accepted by most phonologists as sensible phonological rules. It is quite common for languages to avoid *consonant + sonorant* clusters at the ends of words; as noted above in §4.4.1, languages tend to arrange the consonants of syllables so that the more sonorous segments are adjacent to the vowel, and epenthesis rules that add vowels so that sonorant consonants will be vowel-adjacent can be found in, for instance, Turkish and Modern Hebrew. It is arguable that English has such a process: if alternations like *cyclic* ['saɪkl-ɪk] ~ *cycle* ['saɪkəl] are underlain by a phonemic form /saɪkl/, then the isolation form is indeed derived by a process of epenthesis similar to that posited here for Polish. Moreover, the plausibility of Monosyllabic Epenthesis is manifest: it is very unusual for languages to tolerate vowelless words, and Monosyllabic Epenthesis is expressly set up to avoid them.

12.2.1 Some further Polish facts

From the data given so far, the epenthesis analysis of Polish looks feasible. However, the rule of Sonorant Cluster Epenthesis on which it depends turns out to suffer from a great number of exceptions – in fact, in my database there are about as many exceptions as undergoers. Here are representative examples of stems that have final C [+*son*] clusters and would be expected to undergo Sonorant Cluster Epenthesis, but do not.

Exceptions to Sonorant Cluster Epenthesis

[katedr]	'cathedral-gen. pl.'	[katedr-a]	'cathedral-nom. sg.'
[zebr]	'zebra-gen. pl.'	[zebr-a]	'zebra-nom. sg.'
[algebr]	'algebra-gen. pl.'	[algebr-a]	'algebra-nom. sg.'
[filtr]	'filter-nom. sg.'	[filtr-a]	'filter-gen. sg.'
[miçl]	'thought-nom. sg.'	[miçl-ax]	'thought-loc. pl.'
[konstabl]	'constable-nom. sg.'	[konstabl-a]	'constable-gen. sg.'
[tç'vikw]	'red beet sauce-gen. pl.'	[tç'vikw-a]	'red beet sauce-nom. sg.'
[blizn]	'scar-gen. pl.'	[blizn-a]	'scar-nom. sg.'
[himn]	'hymn-nom. sg.'	[himn-u]	'hymn-gen. sg.'
[kombajn]	'combine-nom. sg.'	[kombajn-a]	'combine-gen. sg.'

If the rule of Sonorant Cluster Epenthesis is to be considered valid, every one of these words must be marked with the rule feature (§9.6) [–Sonorant Cluster Epenthesis]. At least at first blush, this seems a rather high price to pay.

This, then, is the dilemma. If we assume that the [CC] ~ [CeC] alternations of Polish are underlain by /CC/, then the Sonorant Cluster Epenthesis rule that is needed will have many exceptions. On the other hand, if we assume that these alternations are underlain by /CeC/, then the Syncope rule that would be needed would likewise have many exceptions. Neither alternative offers a clean analysis.

12.2.2   The abstract analysis – general approach

The problem just seen in Polish can be characterized in a general way:

Not enough underlying forms

- There are forms where [A] alternates with [A].
- There are forms where [B] alternates with [B].
- There are forms where [A] alternates with [B].

In the Polish example, [A] is [CeC] and [B] is [CC]. In such cases, no matter whether we select /A/ or /B/ as the underlying form, there will be counterexamples to any rule we propose. This is because there are only two underlying forms, but three patterns of alternation.

For some time, phonologists have pondered dilemmas of this kind, which arise in other languages as well. No consensus approach has emerged, but there is one analytical option that is often pursued. The idea is that for the cases in which A alternates with B, we should set up some *third* underlying entity, /C/, like this:

Surface alternation	*Underlying form*
[A] ~ [A]	/A/
[B] ~ [B]	/B/
[A] ~ [B]	/C/

In the phonology, we set up a rule that converts /C/ to [B] in the appropriate environments. Then a second rule converts any leftover /C/'s that didn't become [B] into [A] – thus, no /C/'s at all survive on the surface. Together, these rules create the cases of [A] ~ [B] alternation. Invariant [A] and invariant [B] undergo no rules and thus surface identically with their underlying forms. This analysis is *abstract*, in the sense given above (p. 235), because /C/ never appears on the surface; it is an abstract segment.

12.2.3   The abstract approach applied to Polish

Let us consider the abstract approach as it has been applied to Polish. Polish is normally thought of as being a six-vowel language, with the following inventory:

/i/   /ɨ/   /u/
/e/   /o/
       /a/

In the abstract analysis, we suppose that there are actually more vowels in the system underlyingly than there are on the surface. For present purposes all we need is one extra vowel, which (following some but not all earlier proposals) we will assume to be the lax high front unrounded vowel /ɪ/:[3]

/i/   /ɨ/   /u/
/ɪ/
/e/   /o/
       /a/

"Hidden" vowels like the proposed /ɪ/ are commonly known in Slavic linguistics as **jers** (pronunciation: [jeɹ]). The analytical device of the jer vowel has been invoked for the analysis of a number of the modern Slavic languages, including Russian, Slovak, and Serbo-Croatian.

Under the jer approach, we set up the underlying representations as follows:

Pattern	UR	Examples
Non-alternating [e]:	/e/	[krater] ~ [krater-ɨ], [ren] ~ [ren-a]
Non-alternating [Ø]:	/Ø/	[filtr] ~ [filtr-a]
[e] alternating with [Ø]:	/ɪ/	[sveter] ~ [svetr-ɨ], [den] ~ [dn-o]

The phonological rules that are needed are these. (The rules would be refined somewhat in a full analysis of Polish, but the basic idea can be put across with these simple versions.)

Jer Lowering
/ɪ/ → e / ___ C₀]word
If a jer is the last vowel of the word, lower it to a mid vowel.

Jer Deletion
/ɪ/ → Ø
Delete jers.

Plainly, Jer Lowering and Jer Deletion must apply in the order given, else no jer would ever get a chance to surface.

It can be seen from these rules that if there is an underlying jer in a word, it will survive, altered to [e], when no suffix is present. If a suffix *is* present, then

---

[3] To cover finer details of Polish not discussed here, phonologists pursuing this approach sometimes adopt a second abstract vowel, which is high, lax, and back.

its vowel will block Jer Lowering (the jer no longer being the last vowel of its word), and Jer Deletion will then remove the jer. Here are derivations for the five stems given above.

'sweater nom. sg.'	'sweater nom. pl.'	'crater nom. sg.'	'crater nom. pl.'	'filter- nom. sg.'	'filter- gen. sg.'	
/svetɪr/	/svetɪr-i/	/krater/	/krater-ɨ/	[filtr]	[filtr-a]	underlying forms
e	—	—	—	—	—	Jer Lowering
—	∅	—	—	—	—	Jer Deletion
[sveter]	[svetrɨ]	[krater]	[kraterɨ]	[filtr]	[filtr-a]	surface forms

'bottom- gen. pl.'	'bottom- nom. sg.'	'reindeer- nom. sg.'	'reindeer- gen. sg.'	
/dɪn/	/dɪn-o/	/ren/	/ren-a/	underlying forms
e	—	—	—	Jer Lowering
—	∅	—	—	Jer Deletion
[den]	[dno]	[ren]	[rena]	surface forms

It can be seen that for the forms with jers ('sweater' and 'bottom'), the rules of Jer Lowering and Jer Deletion derive the [e] ~ ∅ alternation. The remaining forms are essentially inert, lacking jers, and do not alternate.

12.2.4   Assessment

By using abstract segments, this analysis reduces an otherwise rather intractable data pattern to the application of automatic rules. The function of the underlying jers is not to represent a surface phonetic distinction, but rather to encode a pattern of phonological alternation, whose overt elements belong to the observable phoneme inventory of Polish. In the jer analysis, we need not assume that hundreds of Polish stems are marked as exceptions to rules.

Let us now consider the abstract analysis in more detail. Phonological theory is intended by most of its participants as a realist theory: a correct phonological description is held to embody the knowledge that is internalized (for the most part, unconsciously) by language learners during language acquisition. To take the abstract analysis seriously, we interpret it to mean that when Polish-learning children encounter the data conundrum that we have just encountered, they respond to it by expanding their underlying vowel systems to include jers. In a sense, Polish children are claimed to *invent the jers* intuitively as a means of handling the data, just as clever phonologists have done in their consciously guided analytical work.

This claim is potentially problematic. One might be wary, for instance, of a theory in which the right answer must come from a lively act of the imagination – for what happens to the language acquirer who through bad luck or inferior skill happens never to arrive at the right inspiration?[4] Further, if the language acquirer is expected (under the theory) to be willing to entertain fairly radical hypotheses about the underlying representations, then the *number of hypotheses* that she must consider in figuring out the underlying forms of her language becomes much larger. Given the finite time during which language acquisition must take place, the proposal for abstract vowels may or may not prove to be compatible with an explicit theory of phonological acquisition – though any serious theory of this sort remains mostly in the future.

It would be intriguing to find that Polish speakers intuitively "feel" the presence of jers. When I have queried speakers on this point, they generally tell me that they do not intuitively sense that their vowel phoneme inventories contain /ɪ/. Yet this consideration seems not particularly helpful as evidence against abstractness. Much experience tells us that a great deal of linguistic knowledge is unconscious (§2.7), and it is quite possible that knowledge of abstract representations falls into this category.

My conclusion is that at the present time, the field is not yet adequately equipped to assess the truth or falsehood of abstract analyses. I anticipate that such an assessment *will* be possible someday, but some of the crucial evidence is likely to come from psycholinguistic experimentation rather than just further sifting of the phonological data.

12.2.5 The abstract analysis of Polish and language history

There is a reason why the abstract analysis of Polish [e] ~ ∅ alternations works: it recapitulates the history of the Polish language over the last few centuries. It is indeed the case that Proto-Slavic had an extra vowel whose quality was more or less [ɪ], and that this vowel was historically lowered and deleted in (roughly speaking) the environments specified in the rules above. Thus, it was the events of history that set up the difficult data pattern analyzed here. However, as I hope to have made clear in discussing the synchrony/diachrony distinction (chapter 11), these historical facts cannot be made to bear on the synchronic analysis of Polish, because Polish children learning the complex phonology of their language have no access to historical information.

In fact, the historical data might give a certain comfort to jer-skeptics: such a skeptic might say, "Of course the jer analysis works; it works because the data pattern got to be the way it is by virtue of linguistic changes that completely

---

[4] In principle, one might comb through the population of Polish-speaking children, seeking out the ones for whom vowel ~ zero alternations are terribly difficult because they have never hit upon the crucial idea. To my knowledge such cases have not yet been found (or, for that matter, even searched for).

parallel the proposed analysis. But that doesn't mean that children really learn the proposed analysis, since what they do has no necessary connection with history."

12.2.6 *Some factual arguments*

The epenthesis analysis given at the start of §12.2 above seems to constitute a minority view among phonologists of Polish, but in fact it has some virtues worth noticing. In particular, because it attributes the alternating vowels to epenthesis, rather than to the underlying representations, it makes more precise predictions than the jer analysis does about *what kind* of [e] ~ Ø alternations may occur in Polish.

First, because both Sonorant Cluster Epenthesis and Monosyllabic Epenthesis insert [e] only before the *last* consonant of a word, the epenthesis analysis predicts that [e] ~ Ø alternations for final triple clusters can only take the form [CCC] ~ [CCeC], and never *[CCC] ~ [CeCC]. This prediction is by and large true, but under the jer analysis it is a complete accident: there is no reason not to have stems ending underlyingly in /C₁CC/, from which the non-occurring alternation could be derived.

Second, Sonorant Cluster Epenthesis is stated to require that the last consonant of a stem must be a sonorant, thus making a prediction about possible alternations that likewise is not made by the jer analysis; that is, except in the stems covered by Monosyllabic Epenthesis, only C + [+*son*] stems will exhibit [e] ~ Ø alternation. This prediction turns out to be not quite true, but it comes rather close. The epenthesis analysis will work if it is supplemented with two further epenthesis rules, as follows. (1) There must be an epenthesis rule that applies before *single-consonant suffixes*, even when they are obstruents, such as the diminutive suffix [-k] ([kot-k-a] 'cat-dim.-nom. pl. ~ [kot-ek] 'nom. sg.'). (2) There must also be a minor rule (in the sense of §9.6) epenthesizing [e] in the simple context / C ___ C], to cover the small handful of stems that end in an obstruent but nevertheless show [e] ~ Ø alternation (an example is [ovʲes] 'oats' ~ [ovs-a] 'gen. sg.').

With these adjustments in place, the epenthesis analysis is as accurate as the jer analysis and offers, I think, a more nuanced characterization of the data, albeit at the cost of attaching the rule exception feature [–Sonorant Cluster Epenthesis] to hundreds of stems like [filtr]. It should be noted, however, that the question of which mechanism – abstract segments or exception features – should be considered more costly in phonological analysis is an open one.

The "jer debate" concerning Polish (and other Slavic) phonology is likely to continue. My own opinion concerning this question is that advocates of jers need to find ways to refine the jer analysis so that it captures the more subtle distinctions captured by the epenthesis analysis. Advocates of the epenthesis analysis need to develop a more complete theory of exceptions in phonology, including how a rule with hundreds of exceptions might be learned by language-acquiring children.

12.3   Abstractness Elsewhere

As noted above, what motivates the hypothesis of jer vowels in Polish is the fact that there are more patterns of alternation present than there are surface phonemes available to serve as underlying forms for these patterns. This phenomenon is not all that uncommon, and wherever it has arisen, phonologists have proposed abstract analyses. Here are two further examples:

- Yawelmani Yokuts, a Penutian language of Northern California, has two kinds of surface long [oː]. One of them patterns (in vowel harmony and other phenomena) similarly to the short /o/ of the language. The other [oː] patterns similarly to the short /u/ of Yawelmani Yokuts. The latter type is often analyzed as an abstract vowel, underlyingly /uː/, with a late lowering rule that converts it to [oː].
- Turkish has three contrasting stop series. One appears as voiceless [ptk] in all environments, the second appears as voiced [bdg] in all environments, and the third appears as voiced before a vowel but voiceless otherwise. It has been suggested that these three patterns are underlain by (1) /ptk/, (2) /bdg/ and (3) abstract /PTK/. The latter are segments that lack an underlying specification for voicing (unlike the "don't care" segments discussed in §4.8, which are underspecified on the surface). Underspecified /PTK/ undergo special rules making them fully voiced or voiceless in particular contexts.

12.4   Abstractness in English: Is Stress Predictable?

English does not have any robust instances of the pattern (that is to say, more alternation types than available concrete underlying forms) that has been taken as evidence for abstractness in Polish, Yawelmani Yokuts, and Turkish. Yet there are other patterns in English phonology for which abstract analyses have been proposed. One notable instance is the suggestion made by Chomsky and Halle (1968) that with suitable abstract underlying representations, the position of stress in English words is predictable. Their strategy is to set up stress rules that cover the bulk of the cases in straightforward fashion, then set up abstract representations to account for the rest.

Chomsky and Halle's English stress analysis is quite intricate and cannot be briefly summarized. However, we can get a sense of the strategy they employ by considering just a few cases, starting with the fact that the great majority of English disyllabic nouns have initial stress, as in the following examples:

turnip	['tɚnɪp]	*olive*	['ɑlɪv]	*filbert*	['fɪlbɚt]
seraph	['sɛrəf]	*table*	['teɪbəl]	*tennis*	['tɛnɪs]
Jerry	['dʒɛɹi]	*tiger*	['taɪgɚ]	*duffel*	['dʌfəl]
banner	['bænɚ]	*possum*	['pɑsəm]	*dollop*	['dɑləp]

For this reason, Chomsky and Halle set up their stress rules so that, ordinarily, disyllabic nouns will receive initial stress. (For more on English stress, see chapter 14.)

There are, however, a small minority of disyllabic nouns that have final stress.

giraffe	[dʒə'ɹæf]	*baton*	[bə'tɑn]
gazelle	[gə'zɛl]	*canal*	[kə'næl]
lacrosse	[lə'kɹɔs]	*cassette*	[kə'sɛt]
guitar	[gə'tɑɹ]	*hotel*	[hoʊ'tɛl]

These words might be taken as evidence that English stress is unpredictable, so that it would have to be included in the underlying phonological representations of words. However, abstract phonology offers an alternative. Suppose that *giraffe* (to work with just one example) underlyingly contains two abstract segments: there is a final /ɛ/ that is absent in the surface form; and the surface [f] actually derives from an underlying double (geminate) consonant /ff/. The full underlying form is thus /dʒɹæffɛ/, from which the surface form [dʒə'ɹæf] can be derived by rules worked out below.

Observe first that when an English noun contains *two consonants following the second-to-last vowel*, it generally receives stress on the penultimate syllable. This can be seen in many words, of which the following are a sample.

agenda	[ə'dʒɛndə]	*synopsis*	[sə'nɑpsɪs]	*jujitsu*	[dʒu'dʒɪtsu]
referendum	[ɹɛfə'ɹɛndəm]	*amalgam*	[ə'mælgəm]	*dialectal*	[daɪə'lɛktəl]
Columbus	[kə'lʌmbəs]	*fandango*	[fæn'dæŋgoʊ]	*contingent*	[kən'tɪndʒənt]
consensus	[kən'sɛnsəs]	*embargo*	[ɛm'baɹgoʊ]	*abysmal*	[ə'bɪzməl]

These forms can be compared with analogous forms that have just one consonant after the penultimate vowel, which usually get antepenultimate stress:

regiment	['ɹɛdʒɪmənt]	*Canada*	['kænədə]	*A'merica*	[ə'mɛɹəkə]
accident	['æksɪdənt]	*Los Angeles*	[lɔs 'ændʒələs]	*animal*	['ænəməl]
capital	['kæpəɾəl]	*Sheraton*	['ʃɛɹəɾən]	*cannibal*	['kænəbəl]
halibut	['hæləbət]	*therapy*	['θɛɹəpi]	*cholera*	['kɑləɹə]

For more on this data pattern, see §14.6.8.

The crucial point is that if we set up [dʒə'ɹæf] as underlying /dʒɹæffɛ/, and apply the stress rules early, then they would derive the intermediate form [dʒə'ɹæffɛ], with stress in the right location, due to the extra underlying vowel and the double consonant sequence.

Next we turn to the rules that have the effect of "cleaning" up the abstract segments on the surface. First, it can be observed that no word in English can end in [ɛ]. This provides a rationale for an obligatory rule of /ɛ/ Drop that deletes /ɛ/ in final position: ɛ → ∅ / __]_word_. Moreover, English stems (as defined in §10.5) never permit geminates (though they are allowed in compounds and certain affixed forms, such as *bookcase* [bʊkkeɪs] or *unknown* [ʌnnoʊn]). Thus, there is a rationale for a rule of Degemination, which would be stem-bounded and would reduce all geminates to the corresponding singletons.

By ordering the stress rule before the "cleanup" rules, it is possible to derive the stress pattern of *giraffe*, as follows:

/dʒəɹæffɛ/	underlying form
dʒəˈɹæffɛ	Stress Assignment (penultimate, due to double consonant)
dʒəˈɹæfɛ	Degemination
dʒəˈɹæf	/ɛ/ Drop
[dʒəˈɹæf]	surface form

There are other forms that can be derived using just one abstract segment instead of two; thus *eclipse* [iˈklɪps] needs only the abstract final /ɛ/, and *vanilla* needs only the abstract underlying geminate (without the geminate it would be stressed like *Canada*).

eclipse	*vanilla*	
/iklɪpsɛ/	/vənɪllə/	underlying forms
iˈklɪpsɛ	vəˈnɪllə	Stress Assignment
—	vəˈnɪlə	Degemination
iˈklɪps	—	/ɛ/ Drop
[iˈklɪps]	[vəˈnɪlə]	surface forms

First appearances to the contrary, this analysis is hardly an "anything goes" system; in fact, there are plenty of stress patterns that it cannot describe and are largely absent from English, such as preantepenultimate stress. Moreover, the rules needed are ordinary – degemination rules and final vowel drop rules are quite common in the world's languages. However, it seems reasonable to show some skepticism over the virtuosity that the analysis evokes. In effect, the analysis states that English-learning children, confronted with what looks like phonemic stress, do not interpret the data as such, but instead assign abstract structures, of a rather ingenious sort, to much of the vocabulary. It is not easy to specify what mechanisms of phonological acquisition there might be that could automatically make such clever devices available to the language learner. Finally, it can be noted that languages with phonemic stress are quite common: no principle of phonology tells us that stress has to be predictable, so it is not unreasonable to suppose that English language learners might simply assume that stress is phonemic, albeit with important positional restrictions.

Exercises

1   Abstract analysis of English stress

Assuming the abstract analysis of English stress given in §12.4, provide the underlying forms that would be needed for the following forms. Do not include more abstract segments than are necessary under the analysis.

a.   *cassette*   [kə'sɛt]
b.   *baton*   [bə'tɑn]
c.   *antenna*   [æn'tɛnə]
d.   *Dupont*   [du'pɑnt]

2   Spanish diphthongization

[sen't-amos]	'we sit'	['sjent-o]	'I sit'
[ten'd-emos]	'we stretch'	['tjend-o]	'I stretch'
[po'ð-emos]	'we can'	['pweð-o]	'I can'
[kon't-amos]	'we count'	['kwent-o]	'I count'
[ren't-amos]	'we rent'	['rent-o]	'I rent'
[ben'd-emos]	'we sell'	['bend-o]	'I sell'
[po'ð-amos]	'we prune'	['poð-o]	'I prune'
[mon'tamos]	'we mount'	['mont-o]	'I mount'
[alje'n-amos]	'we alienate'	[a'ljen-o]	'I alienate'
[frekwen't-amos]	'we frequent'	[fre'kwent-o]	'I frequent'

Assume for Spanish that there is a rule assigning stress to the penultimate vowel of the word; this is only a rough approximation, but will suffice here. Also, assume that the choice of [-amos] vs. [-emos] for the first person plural suffix is *not* due to phonology; in fact, the choice represents a completely arbitrary morphological property of Spanish: what are called "first conjugation" verbs take [-amos], and second conjugation verbs take [-emos].

These data involve the conundrum observed in this chapter: there is A ~ A alternation; A ~ B alternation, and B ~ B alternation. Propose two analyses: an abstract analysis, with abstract underlying segments, and a concrete analysis with exception features (as in §9.6). State your rules and name them; and give sample derivations for the paradigms of the stems meaning 'sit', 'rent', and 'alienate'.

Further reading

Theodore Lightner's original proposal for underlying jer vowels in a Slavic language (Russian) may be read in his *Problems in the Theory of Phonology* (1972, Linguistic Research, Inc.). Two studies which worked out the jer analysis for Polish are *Studies in Abstract Phonology* (1980, MIT Press) by Edmund Gussmann and *From Cyclic to Lexical Phonology* by Jerzy Rubach (1984, Foris Publications). Since then there have appeared a great number of further jer-based analyses; these often make a different choice than /ɪ/ for the underlying form of the jer.

The epenthesis analysis given in this chapter is a restatement of a proposal made in a 1988 paper by Alicja Gorecka. This article was never published, but it is quoted and partially endorsed in Christina Bethin's book *Polish Syllables: The Role of Prosody in Phonology and Morphology* (1992, Slavica Publishers). Bethin's study also offers thorough coverage of the Polish data and of the theoretical debate up to the time.

For the three-way contrast in Turkish, see Ellen Kaisse (1986) "Locating Turkish devoicing," *West Coast Conference on Formal Linguistics* 5: 119–28. A brief summary, with supporting data, is Stephen M. Wilson (2003), "A phonetic study of voiced, voiceless and alternating stops in Turkish," *Center for Research in Language Newsletter* 15.1, online at http://crl.ucsd.edu/newsletter/15-1/15-1.pdf.

Predictable word stress in English using abstractness: Chomsky and Halle's *The Sound Pattern of English* (1968, Harper and Row).

A variety of work has expressed skepticism, in varying degrees, about abstractness: Nigel Love's *Generative Phonology: A Case Study from French* (1981, John Benjamins); Joan B. Hooper's *An Introduction to Natural Generative Phonology* (1976, Academic Press); and Paul Kiparsky's article "How Abstract is Phonology?" (1968, reprinted in P. Kiparsky, *Explanation in Phonology*, 1982, Foris Publications).

Turkish epenthesis: Charles Pyle (1974) "Why a conspiracy?" in *Papers from the Parasession on Natural Phonology* (Chicago Linguistic Society); Modern Hebrew epenthesis: Ruth Berman, *Modern Hebrew Structure* (1978, Tel-Aviv: University Publishing Projects). Slovak jers: Michael Kenstowicz and Jerzy Rubach (1987) "The phonology of syllabic nuclei in Slovak," *Language* 63: 463–97. Abstractness in Yawelmani Yokuts: a good starting point is to read the discussion in Michael Kenstowicz and Charles Kisseberth's *Generative Phonology: Description and Theory* (1979, Academic Press), and follow the references cited there.

13   Syllables

13.1   Syllables in Phonological Theory

Among phonological entities, syllables are unusual in the degree to which they stand out to the native speaker at the conscious level. It is relatively easy for people to count the syllables of a word – much easier than counting the segments. People also find it intuitive to count out syllables and arrange them in time whenever they use them in verse, chant, and song.

Looking within phonology itself, we find that syllables frequently appear in environments of phonological rules, both for deriving allophones and in morphophonemic alternation. Syllables also are the units that bear stress (chapter 14) and serve as the "anchor points" for tones in tonal systems and in intonation (chapter 15). It is hardly surprising that phonologists have often made use of syllables in phonological theory.

13.2   Representation

Various means are used to depict syllables formally. In the International Phonetic Alphabet, syllables are shown by separating them with a boundary symbol, specifically a period; thus, *connective* is represented with its syllabification as [kə.nɛk.tɪv]. Another approach, followed here, eschews boundary symbols and assumes instead that syllables are *phonological constituents*. For representing such constituency, the clearest notation is tree structure. In the representation for *connective* below, the syllable constituents are labeled with /σ/ (Greek sigma, for "syllable"):

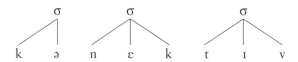

A more concise notation uses brackets, annotated with σ: [$_\sigma$ kə]$_\sigma$ [$_\sigma$ nɛk]$_\sigma$ [$_\sigma$ tɪv]$_\sigma$ or, still more concisely, [kə]$_\sigma$[nɛk]$_\sigma$[tɪv]$_\sigma$. The full tree notation will be used here for phonological derivations in which segments get added to or removed from syllables, or for cases where brackets must be reserved for morphological or syntactic structure.

In discussing syllables, it is useful to be able to refer to certain substrings of them. The **onset** of a syllable is defined as the consonant or sequence of consonants at the beginning of a syllable. The **coda** is the consonant or sequence of consonants at the end of a syllable. The **nucleus** of a syllable is the vowel or diphthong found at the syllable's core and functioning as its sonority peak (sometimes **peak** is used instead of nucleus). It is obligatory for a syllable to have a nucleus, very common for a syllable to lack a coda, and less common for it to lack an onset.

In some theories, the onset, nucleus, and coda are described as constituents (they are daughters of the syllable node σ, and dominate segments). This book will use "onset," "nucleus," and "coda" merely as useful descriptive terminology. The representations used will be the simple structures shown above in which σ dominates segments directly.

13.3 Syllabification

In principle, syllabification could be part of the phonemic representation of forms. Where this is so, we would be able to detect it in the form of minimal pairs (chapter 2) that differ only in syllabification. Thus, we could imagine a language in which there is a word judged by native speakers to be syllabified [at]$_\sigma$[ra]$_\sigma$, which means (say) 'sheep', and a different word judged to be syllabified [a]$_\sigma$[tra]$_\sigma$, which means 'goat'. This would be a minimal pair for syllabification. Such distinctions have in fact been suggested, but only for a very few languages (see Further reading). In most languages, however, syllabification is predictable: starting out from the string of segments, one can predict the syllabification (or multiple syllabifications, in cases of free variation). Just as a complete phonological description seeks to derive all of the predictable allophones of the language by rule, it should also derive the syllabification.

The basis on which syllabification is derived must be (partly) language-specific: every language has its own principles of syllabification. We can see this by looking at very similar segmental strings that get syllabified differently in different languages. The word for 'four' in Spanish is syllabified [kwa]$_\sigma$[tɾo]$_\sigma$. But in Ilokano, where the same word occurs as a borrowing, it is syllabified [kwat]$_\sigma$[ɾo]$_\sigma$.[1]

---

[1]   The question arises of how we know this. First, native speakers of both languages intuit these syllabifications. Second, the distribution of allophones supports it: for instance, the /t/ of Ilokano [kwat]$_\sigma$[ɾo]$_\sigma$ is the preglottalized [ʔt] allophone that we generally find in syllable-final position, not the plain [t] found syllable-initially. In addition, vowels are typically shorter when they are followed by a consonant in their syllable, and the Ilokano [a] vowel is noticeably shorter than the Spanish.

13.3.1   *General principles of syllabification*

Such interlinguistic differences, however, are usually modest; it is the cross-linguistic resemblances that are perhaps more striking. It is possible to state a set of "garden-variety" principles of syllabification that give at least an approximation to syllabification in most languages; and this task is addressed in the following sections.

13.3.1.1   Finding the syllable nucleus

The nucleus of the syllable is normally a vowel or diphthong, though in some languages other segments with lower sonority (liquids and nasals) can be syllabic and form syllable nuclei; this is discussed in §4.4.3.

Definitionally (see §4.4.3), there is a one-to-one correspondence between [+syllabic] sounds and syllables; every [+syllabic] sound is the nucleus of its own syllable. However, the questions of what sounds count as [+syllabic] is an analytic one and cannot be determined by merely listening to the data. Cases that often need to be addressed are whether a particular sequence should count as [aa] (two [+syllabic, –long] segments) or [aː] (one [+syllabic, +long] segment, §3.4.1); or whether the [l] of a word-final sequence like [abl] has a [+syllabic] [l̩] or a [–syllabic] [l]; the syllabification will depend on this decision.

13.3.1.2   Syllabic affiliations of consonants

Assuming that the choice of [+syllabic] segments has been correctly made, the main task in syllabification is determining to which syllable the consonants belong.

It is generally true that when a consonant immediately precedes a vowel, it must belong to the same syllable as the vowel. As a consequence, VCV is normally syllabified $[V]_\sigma[CV]_\sigma$, not $*[VC]_\sigma[V]_\sigma$. Moreover, while VCCV is sometimes syllabified as $[VC]_\sigma[CV]_\sigma$ and sometimes as $[V]_\sigma[CCV]_\sigma$, it would be very unlikely for it to be syllabified as $*[VCC]_\sigma[V]_\sigma$.

This leaves two choices ($[V]_\sigma[CCV]_\sigma$ and $[VC]_\sigma[CV]_\sigma$) for biconsonantal clusters and three ($([V]_\sigma[CCCV]_\sigma$, $[VC]_\sigma[CCV]_\sigma$, and $[VCC]_\sigma[CV]_\sigma$) for triconsonantal clusters. To choose among these, we will assume that languages have ordered rules that affiliate consonants either to the following or to the preceding syllable. Such rules can be complex, and we will only give some outline analyses here. Before proceeding, however, it is useful to consider a heuristic principle that guides many analyses.

This heuristic, the **Maximal Onset Principle**, states that we can often predict the syllabification of intervocalic clusters by observing *the set of consonant clusters that may begin a word*: VC_1C_2V will be syllabified $[V]_\sigma[C_1C_2V]_\sigma$ if a word can begin C_1C_2V (and similarly, $VC_1C_2C_3V$ will be syllabified $[V]_\sigma[C_1C_2C_3V]_\sigma$ if a word can begin $C_1C_2C_3V$, and so on).

Here is an example: in English, *approve* is syllabified as [ə]$_\sigma$[pɹuv]$_\sigma$ because English words can begin with /pɹ/; but *Wheatley* is syllabified [wit]$_\sigma$[li]$_\sigma$, because no word can begin with /tl/. In Persian, the maximal consonant sequence at the beginning of a word is just one, so a word like /æbɾu/ 'eyebrow' must be syllabified [æb]$_\sigma$[ɾu]$_\sigma$, not *[æ]$_\sigma$[bɾu]$_\sigma$.

The Maximal Onset Principle often can predict syllabification in languages, but is not infallible. For example, in Ilokano, *kwatro* is syllabified [kwat]$_\sigma$[ɾo]$_\sigma$ even though there are words that can begin with /tɾ/, for example *tres* 'three'. The principle also produces incorrect results when applied with certain English onsets. /dw/ is a possible (though rare) onset in English (*dwell*), but *Edwardian* seems to be syllabified [ɛd]$_\sigma$['waɹ]$_\sigma$[di]$_\sigma$[ən]$_\sigma$, not *[ɛ]$_\sigma$['dwaɹ]$_\sigma$[di]$_\sigma$[ən]$_\sigma$. (We can tell this from allophone evidence: [d] shows up in *Edwardian* with the coda allophone heard in *Ed* [ɛd], not the slightly affricated [dˢ] onset allophone heard in *dwell*.)

The Maximal Onset Principle, though useful, is only a heuristic; it is not really specific enough to be part of a phonological analysis. The reason is that a full grammar of a language should say what the word-initial onsets are; for example that [bl] is a possible onset of English and that *[bn] is not. *[bnɪk] is an impossible word of English, because it begins with an impossible onset. For a language with a syllable onset inventory as complex as that of English, the establishment of a set of rules that can derive all and only the possible onsets involves fairly extensive analysis, which will not be attempted here. The usefulness of the Maximal Onset Principle is that it predicts, correctly in most cases, that if there is a choice between syllabifying a consonant as an onset or as a coda, it will be syllabified as an onset.

13.3.1.3 An outline scheme for syllabification

With this background in place, we can set up an outline version of how syllabification works, sufficiently detailed to serve in the discussion that follows. There are three rules, which apply in the order shown.

σ Assignment
Assign syllable nodes (σ) to be in one-to-one correspondence with [+syllabic] sounds.

Onset Formation
Join consonants to the following syllable, provided the resulting cluster can occur at the beginning of a word (Maximal Onset Principle).

Coda Formation
Join any consonants not yet syllabified to the preceding syllable.

These rules can be illustrated with the English word *contract* (/kɑntɹækt/). First, to enforce the one-to-one correspondence of [+syllabic] sounds and syllables, σ Assignment must affiliate a syllable node with the vowels /ɑ/ and /æ/.

k   ɑ   n   t   ɹ   æ   k   t   underlying form

          σ   σ

k   ɑ   n   t   ɹ   æ   k   t   σ Assignment

Next, Onset Formation attaches /k/ to the first syllable and /tɹ/ to the second; thus respecting the Maximal Onset Principle (compare *track*, *try*, *tree*, but no words like *[ntɹæk]):

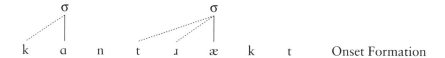

k   ɑ   n   t   ɹ   æ   k   t   Onset Formation

The remaining consonants are syllabified by Coda Formation:

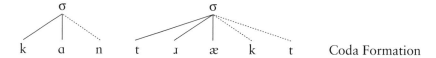

k   ɑ   n   t   ɹ   æ   k   t   Coda Formation

This analysis implements the Maximal Onset Principle through rule ordering: Coda Formation follows Onset Formation and applies only to unsyllabified consonants; hence it syllabifies only the consonants that were not already syllabified by Onset Formation. Where the Maximal Onset Principle does not hold true, as in cases like *Edwardian*, it would be necessary to limit certain cases of Onset Formation to word-initial position.

13.4   Syllables and Phonological Derivations

Syllabification is complicated by the fact that the rules of the phonology often rearrange the sequence of consonants and vowels, through deletion, insertion, and other processes. How does syllabification respond to such changes? More generally, what is the place of syllabification in the phonological derivation?

One widely held view, adopted here, is that the rules of syllabification are **persistent**. This means that underlying phonological representations are syllabified by the syllabification rules at the outset of the derivation, and that whenever a phonological rule applies, the syllabification rules reapply if applicable. We will see evidence that bears on this claim later on; for now, I will simply give an example to illustrate the concept of persistence.

In Tonkawa, an extinct American Indian language once spoken in Texas, there is a Syncope rule that deletes the second vowel of a word when it is not adjacent to a consonant cluster or final consonant:

Tonkawa Syncope
V → Ø / [_word_ CVC ___ CV

The underlying representation /notoxo-n-o-ʔ/ 'he hoes it' ('hoe-progressive-declarative-3 person present'), would be initially syllabified as shown below:

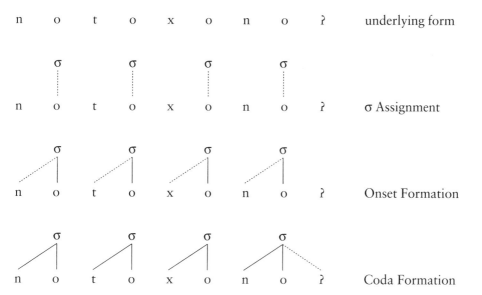

n   o   t   o   x   o   n   o   ʔ   underlying form

n   o   t   o   x   o   n   o   ʔ   σ Assignment

n   o   t   o   x   o   n   o   ʔ   Onset Formation

n   o   t   o   x   o   n   o   ʔ   Coda Formation

Once the form is syllabified, it is submitted to the phonological rules. Syncope removes the second vowel, creating the following representation:

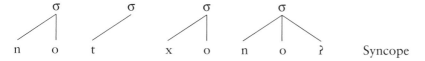

n   o   t   x   o   n   o   ʔ   Syncope

The syllable nodes are now no longer in one-to-one correspondence with the [+syllabic] segments, [t] being [−syllabic]. Therefore, the persistent rule of σ Assignment is applicable. I assume that what this means is that the σ which is not affiliated with a [+syllabic] sound is removed:

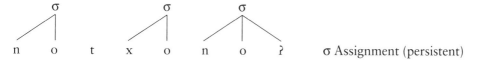

n   o   t   x   o   n   o   ʔ   σ Assignment (persistent)

This restores the one-to-one correspondence specified in the rule, but it also "liberates" a [t] which must be syllabified. Onset Formation, in the version appropriate to Tonkawa, is not applicable, as the language tolerates only single consonants at the beginning of a syllable. But Coda Formation is applicable, and it reaffiliates the stranded [t]:

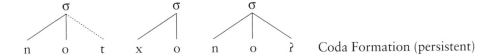

Coda Formation (persistent)

Thus, according to the persistent-syllabification approach, [t] is a syllable-initial segment at the outset of the phonology, but ends up as syllable-final.

The underlying representation given here can be justified by other forms in the paradigm. For instance, [wentoxono?] 'he hoes them', is derived from underlying /we-notoxo-n-o-?/ 'them-hoe-prog.-declar.-3 pres.' by Syncope, applying to a different vowel of the stem.

13.5 Word Boundaries and Syllables

Just like other phonological rules (chapter 10), syllabification rules often "respect word boundaries"; that is, Onset Formation and Coda Formation are often word-bounded. Consider for instance the following sentence of German:

Das ist ein alter Ochs.
[das ɪst aɪn ˈaltəʁ ˈɔks]
'That is an old ox.'

The final consonants of *das* [s], *ist* [t], *ein* [n], and *alter* [ʁ] all precede vowels, so that, in principle, Onset Formation could affiliate them with the σ nodes attached to these vowels. Under the assumption of a word-bounded Onset Formation rule for German, however, no such affiliation is possible. Instead, these consonants must undergo Coda Formation, and are syllabified within their own word. The resulting alignment of words and syllables is shown below.

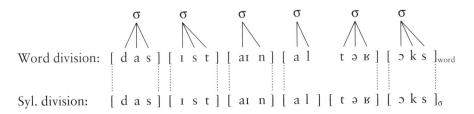

Whether Onset Formation is word-bounded or not is evidently language-specific, however. Spanish is an example of a language where Onset Formation applies phrasally: if Word₁ ends in a consonant, and Word₂ begins in a vowel, then the last consonant of Word₁ will be syllabified in the first syllable of Word₂:

Los otros estaban en el avion.
[los 'otɾos es'taβan en el a'βjon]
'The others were on the airplane.'

Syl. division:

Word div.: [l o s] [o t ɾ o s] [e s t a β a n] [e n] [e l] [a β j o n]_word

The dotted lines above show the syllable memberships that cross word boundaries.

13.6   The Onset/Coda Distinction and Its Consequences

The remainder of this chapter covers some of the ways in which syllable structure influences segmental phonology. One of these involves an important distinction between onset and coda position: the segments of onsets and the segments of codas show strikingly different phonological behavior. Onsets are often obligatory, articulated more forcefully, and the locus of rich phonemic contrasts. Codas are often optional or even forbidden, they are articulated less forcefully, and they are the locus of phonological neutralization, including deletion. The following survey illustrates these patterns.

13.6.1   *Obligatory onsets, optional codas, forbidden codas*

In many languages (e.g. Arabic, Ilokano), every syllable must begin with an onset; that is, no syllable may begin with a vowel. Moreover, onsets are never forbidden; there is no such thing as an onsetless language. For codas, the typology is the opposite. In many languages (e.g. Samoan, Zulu), codas are forbidden. Moreover, there are apparently no languages that require every syllable to have a coda. Thus, the only "universal syllable," present in every language, is CV.

The preference for syllables to have onsets can be seen in German. In the example given earlier, the vowel-initial syllables undergo a rule of Glottal Epenthesis in careful speech, so that they will surface with a /ʔ/ onset.

Glottal Epenthesis

$\varnothing \rightarrow ʔ / [_\sigma \underline{\hspace{1.5em}} V$

Insert a glottal stop at the beginning of a vowel-initial syllable.

This rule would apply to the example given earlier to derive the following output:

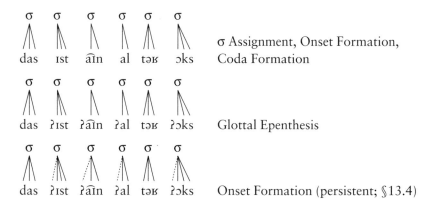

English has the same rule, mentioned above in §10.4. The English rule probably applies less frequently than its German counterpart and is found more often in clear or emphatic speech. Examples include cases like *three apples* /θɹi æpəlz/ → [θɹi ʔæpəlz], with an epenthetic glottal stop at the beginning of the second word, as well as the case of *Kafkaesque* (/kæfkə-ɛsk/ → [ˌkæfkəˈʔɛsk]) mentioned on p. 209.

There are apparently no epenthesis rules that apply in coda position (such a rule would ensure that every syllable will have a coda).

13.6.2 *Neutralization in codas*

Coda position is often the location of *neutralization*. There are many examples; we will cover one here from the Cibaeño dialect of Spanish, spoken in the Dominican Republic.

In Cibaeño, as in all Spanish dialects, there is a contrast between the liquids /l/ and /ɾ/. In certain positions, an optional rule of Liquid Gliding applies converting /l/ and /ɾ/ to [j]. /j/ is also a phoneme of this dialect ([rej] 'king'), so this is a triple neutralization. Here are representative data.

Forms with /ɾ/		Forms with /l/	
['kaɾta], ['kajta]	'letter'	['alɣo], ['ajɣo]	'something'
['pweɾko], ['pwejko]	'pig'	[almo'aða], [ajmo'aða]	'pillow'
[mu'xeɾ], [mu'xej]	'woman'	[pa'pel], [pa'pej]	'paper'
['paɾke], ['pajke]	'park'	[a'sul], [a'suj]	'blue'
[bol'βeɾ], [boj'βej]	'to return'	[bol'βeɾ], [boj'βej]	'to return'

In all cases in which Liquid Gliding applies, the /l/ or /ɾ/ occurs before a consonant or word finally. When these sounds occur before a vowel, they are unaffected:

[koɾa'son] (only)   'heart'   [ala'meða] (only)   'poplar cove'
['paɾe] (only)   'stop'   ['limite] (only)   'limit'[2]

Liquid Gliding creates alternations whenever a vowel-initial suffix is attached to a stem ending in /l/ or /ɾ/, as in the following cases:

[mu'xeɾ], [mu'xej]   'woman'
[mu'xeɾ-es] (only)   'women'

[tɾaβaxa'ðoɾ], [tɾaβaxa'ðoj]   'worker'
[tɾaβaxa'ðoɾ-es] (only)   'workers'

The question at hand is how to formulate a rule that applies both preconsonantally and finally. An analysis occasionally proposed uses so-called **curly brackets**. These are a notational device that denotes the logical notion "or":

Cibaeño Liquid Gliding (with curly brackets)

$$
\begin{bmatrix} +\text{sonorant} \\ +\text{consonantal} \\ +\text{continuant} \end{bmatrix} \rightarrow j \: / \: \underline{\quad} \begin{Bmatrix} C \\ ]_{word} \end{Bmatrix}
$$

Liquids are converted to [j] *if they precede a consonant or are word-final.*

Many linguists have expressed the view that curly brackets offer little or no insight into linguistic phenomena, since they evade the question of what the two listed environments might have in common. For the many cases like Cibaeño Liquid Gliding, a widely adopted alternative solution is to suppose that the environment is *syllable-final*, as follows.

Cibaeño Liquid Gliding (syllable-based version)

$$
\begin{bmatrix} +\text{sonorant} \\ +\text{consonantal} \\ +\text{continuant} \end{bmatrix} \rightarrow j \: / \: \underline{\quad}]_{\sigma}
$$

Liquids are converted to [j] *in syllable-final position.*

In other words, the neutralization of liquids occurs in codas.

---

[2] No examples of initial [ɾ] are given because this phoneme is excluded from initial position in Spanish; only the trill [r] may occur in this location.

Here are derivations for the relevant forms.

/bolbeɾ/		/limite/	/koɾason/	underlying forms
[bol]σ[beɾ]σ		[li]σ[mi]σ[te]σ	[ko]σ[ɾa]σ[son]σ	syllabification
[boj]σ[bej]σ	—	—	—	Liquid Gliding (optional)
[boj]σ[βej]σ	[bol]σ[βeɾ]σ	—	—	Spirantization (see pp. 33, 42 above)
[boj]σ[βej]σ	[bol]σ[βeɾ]σ	[li]σ[mi]σ[te]σ	[ko]σ[ɾa]σ[son]σ	surface forms

The syllabification analysis treats the two cases of gliding in a unified way. In /bolbeɾ/, the first liquid /l/ is made syllable-final because it cannot form an onset with the following syllable (no Spanish syllable begins with [lC]), and of course the utterance final consonant /ɾ/ is necessarily syllable-final as well.

The Cibaeño case is one of many in which a phonemic distinction is "dynamically" neutralized in codas, resulting in alternation. There are also many cases where the restriction is static (for the dynamic/static distinction, see §6.3). In Mandarin Chinese, about 20 distinct consonants are allowed in onsets, but only two or three (/n/, /ŋ/, and in some dialects /ɻ/) are permitted in codas. There are no alternations, because Mandarin underlying forms already conform to these restrictions.

13.6.3 *Fortition and lenition*

Phonological rules often alter onset consonants so that they have a tighter constriction in the vocal tract. Such changes are often described as **fortition**, literally "becoming stronger." In some cases, fortition is a small effect that produces only subtle allophones. For example, in an English word like *none*, the first (onset) /n/ is given tighter articulatory closure than the second (coda) /n/, but the difference is so small there is no standard way to depict it in IPA transcription. A similar example mentioned above concerns the English phoneme /d/, which has a very slightly affricated allophone [dʒ] before /w/ – but only when it is in onset position: compare *Duane* [dʒweɪn]σ with *Edward* [ɛd]σ[wɚd]σ.

In other languages, onset fortition can be most noticeable. In the Porteño dialect of Spanish (Buenos Aires), the glide /j/ in onset position is realized as a fricative [ʒ]; that is, it retains the same general place of articulation, but acquires a much tighter closure. In coda, [j] appears.

Porteño Spanish Glide Fortition
j → ʒ / [σ ___ (= syllable-initially)
Realize /j/ as [ʒ] when it is syllable-initial.

Glide Fortition gives rise to alternations in nominal paradigms. The plural suffix /-es/, attached to the end of a consonant-final noun, causes the noun-final consonant to become an onset, following the rule of Onset Formation. As a result of these syllabifications, Glide Fortition applies in the plural but not the singular, producing alternations like the following.

/lej/ → [lej]	'law'	/lej-es/ → [leʒes]	'laws'
/komboj/ → [komboj]	'convoy'	/komboj-es/ → [komboʒes]	'convoys'
/uɾugwaj/ → [uɾuɣwaj]	'Uruguay'	/uɾugwaj-o/ → [uɾuɣwaʒo]	'Uruguayan'
/bwej/ → [bwej]	'ox'	/bwej-eɾo/ → [bweʒeɾo]	'ox driver'
/rej/ → [rej]	'king'	/rej-eswelo/ → [reʒeswelo]	'king-diminutive'

The application of Glide Fortition in the paradigm of "law" is shown below.

The crucial aspect of these derivations is that syllabification applies to the output of morphology, just like the rest of phonology does. Thus the /j/ alternates between coda and onset position, and therefore between surface [j] and [ʒ].

Contrariwise, coda consonants often are modified to achieve a looser degree of closure. Thus in English casual speech, coda /l/ can optionally lose its alveolar closure in codas, but not in onsets; e.g. in *tell* or *helping*, but not in *let*. (In IPA this might be transcribed with the symbol [ɤ]; hence ['tɛɤ], ['hɛɤpɪŋ] vs. ['lɛt].) This process also creates alternations; the /l/ of *tell* can be non-alveolar, but the /l/ of *telling* ['tɛlɪŋ] must have alveolar closure.

Weakening of closure, which is the opposite of fortition, is called **lenition**. It occurs commonly in codas.[3]

13.6.4 Deletion in codas

A natural extension of lenition is deletion, which, as we would by now expect, often targets coda consonants but leaves onset consonants intact. A well-known example is found in the phonology of French, where nasal consonants delete in codas, but not in onsets. This produces nasal ~ zero alternations such as the following.

---

[3] Lenition is also common in intervocalic position. Examples from this book are Maasai Spirantization (p. 42), Spanish Spirantization (p. 42), and English Tapping (p. 143).

'good-masc.'	'goodness'	'good-fem.'	
/bɔn/	/bɔn-te/	/bɔn-ə/	underlying forms
[bɔn]σ	[bɔn]σ[te]σ	[bɔ]σ[nə]σ	syllabification
[bɔ̃n]σ	[bɔ̃n]σ[te]σ	—	**Nasalization:**

$$V \rightarrow \text{[+nasal]} / \underline{\quad} \begin{bmatrix} -\text{syllabic} \\ +\text{nasal} \end{bmatrix}]_\sigma$$

| [bɔ̃]σ | [bɔ̃]σ[te]σ | — | **Nasal Deletion:** |

$$\begin{bmatrix} -\text{syllabic} \\ +\text{nasal} \end{bmatrix} \rightarrow \varnothing / \underline{\quad}]_\sigma$$

—	—	[bɔn]σ	**Schwa Deletion:**
			$ə \rightarrow \varnothing / \underline{\quad}]_{word}$
[bɔ̃]σ	[bɔ̃]σ[te]σ	[bɔn]σ	surface form

It should be noted that the underlying forms above are rather abstract, and are controversial; see Further reading. However, at the very least the derivation above represents how the alternations originally arose, so the basic point about deletion in codas vs. onsets holds in any event.

13.6.5 A general pattern in syllable-based alternation

The alternations treated in the previous three sections have a similar character. Here is a description of this pattern in general terms. Suppose that a language has stems that end in consonants and suffixes that begin with vowels. In such a situation, a stem-final consonant will have a special status, namely of *alternating in its syllable position*. Where the stem stands alone ((a) below), or followed by a consonant-initial affix ((b)), then Coda Formation will normally place that consonant in coda position. But when the stem precedes a vowel-initial suffix, as in (c), Onset Formation will normally apply. In the diagrams, the crucial stem-final consonant is shown in bold.

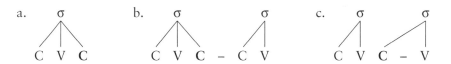

If there is a rule of lenition, deletion, or neutralization that applies in codas, it will affect segments marked with an arrow in the diagrams below. The application of any such rule is shown with lower case:

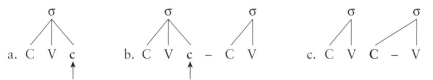

The result will be that the stem alternates, the two allomorphs being [CVc] and [CVC].

An instance of "CVc" from the Cibaeño example above would be [mu'xej], "CVC" being [muxer(-es)]. Here, "c" stands for the neutralization of distinctions among liquids and [j]. In French, "CVc" is /bɔn/ → [bɔ̃], "CVC" is [bɔn(ə)], and "c" stands for deletion. The pattern also occurs, in slightly different form, in the Porteño Spanish example of §13.6.2. The Porteño rule is a fortition rule that affects only onsets; but the data pattern that results is the essentially the same.

This pattern is the basis of phonological alternations in a great many languages.

13.7   Syllables and Derivations: Vocalic Epenthesis

Many rules that epenthesize vowels can be analyzed in terms of the syllable structure of the language they occur in. Vocalic epenthesis often makes it possible to syllabify consonants that otherwise could not be syllabified.

Consider the following data from Yawelmani Yokuts, a Penutian language of Northern California. The first row gives four partial verb paradigms, and the second gives the same stems in the form of unaffixed verbal nouns (for morphological conversion processes of this sort, see §5.2).

'Might V'	'Future II'	Nonfuture	'Having V'ed'	'Future I'	
[pʰaʔtʰ-al]	[pʰaʔtʰ-ɛn]	[pʰaʔitʰ-hin]	[pʰaʔitʰ-mi]	[pʰaʔitʰ-nitʰ]	'fight'
[ʔilkʰ-al]	[ʔilkʰ-ɛn]	[ʔilikʰ-hin]	[ʔilikʰ-mi]	[ʔilikʰ-nitʰ]	'sing'
[lihm-al]	[lihm-ɛn]	[lihim-hin]	[lihim-mi]	[lihim-nitʰ]	'run'
[ʔajj-al]	[ʔajj-ɛn]	[ʔajij-hin]	[ʔajij-mi]	[ʔajij-nitʰ]	'pole a boat'

Verbal nouns
[pʰaʔitʰ]	'fighting'
[ʔilikʰ]	'singing'
[lihim]	'running'
[ʔajij]	'poling a boat'

These verb stems alternate: an allomorph of the form CVCC occurs before vowel-initial suffixes such as [-al] and [-ɛn], and an allomorph of the form CVCiC occurs before consonant-initial suffixes such as [-hin], [-mi], and [-nitʰ], as well as word-finally as in the verbal nouns. In general, all vowel ~ zero alternations of this type in Yawelmani involve the vowel /i/, which suggests that the alternation is due to epenthesis, not syncope; if it were syncope, we would expect all of the Yawelmani vowels to participate.

Using curly brackets, as in the Cibaeño example above (p. 259), an epenthesis rule can be formulated that derives the correct pattern:

Yawelmani Epenthesis (first version)

$$\emptyset \rightarrow i \: / \quad C \underline{} C \begin{Bmatrix} C \\ ]_{word} \end{Bmatrix}$$

Insert the vowel [i] *in second position in a triple consonant cluster, or between two word-final consonants.*

This would apply as shown below:

/pʰaʔtʰ+al/	/pʰaʔtʰ+hin/	/pʰaʔtʰ/	underlying forms
—	pʰaʔitʰhin	pʰaʔitʰ	Epenthesis
[pʰaʔtʰal]	[pʰaʔitʰhin]	[pʰaʔitʰ]	surface forms

There are two reasons why rules formulated in this way have struck many phonologists as unsatisfactory. First, as with the Cibaeño Liquid Gliding case, the rule makes no connection between the two cases listed in the curly brackets. Second, the rule does not take account of Yawelmani syllable structure. In fact, all Yawelmani syllables begin with a single consonant, and end with up to one consonant. The underlying representations that undergo Epenthesis are precisely the ones that *could not be syllabified*, under these limitations.

An alternative is to let the principles of syllabification do most of the work for us. The idea is that syllabification incorporates whatever it can, then Epenthesis provides a vowel to permit syllabification of the remainder.

To do this, we must state proper rules of Onset Formation and Coda Formation for Yawelmani, which forms onsets and codas of just one consonant.

Onset Formation (Yawelmani)
Join a single consonant to the following syllable.

Coda Formation (Yawelmani)
Join a single unaffiliated consonant to the preceding syllable.

As before, Onset Formation must precede Coda Formation, forcing the syllabification [V]σ[CV]σ for /VCV/. Assuming these rules, the forms under examination would be syllabified as follows.

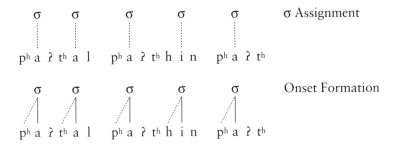

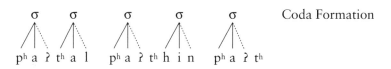

Coda Formation

The result is that there are still consonants (the [tʰ] in the second and third forms), that are as yet unaffiliated with any syllable; such consonants are normally referred to as **stray**.

We now suppose that Epenthesis is formulated to repair any consonants that are left stray following the initial application of syllabification. The rule that is needed can be expressed as follows; the notation C′ indicates an unsyllabified consonant.

Yawelmani Epenthesis (syllabic version)
$\varnothing \rightarrow i \, / \underline{\quad} C'$
Insert [i] *before a stray consonant.*

Since only the last two representations above include unsyllabified consonants, only they trigger Epenthesis:

Epenthesis

Since syllabification rules are persistent, they will reapply as shown below, establishing the normal syllabification on the surface:

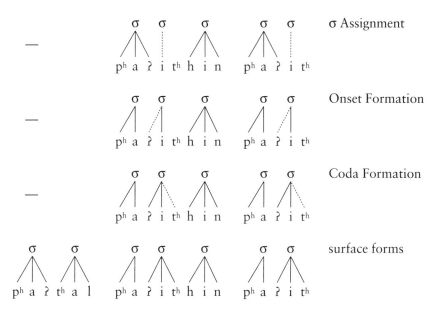

σ Assignment

Onset Formation

Coda Formation

surface forms

It is claimed here that the revised version of Epenthesis is an improvement, for two reasons. First, it unifies the two separate environments of the earlier rule into a single environment. Second, it establishes a connection between the syllabification principles of Yawelmani and the epenthesis pattern – epenthesis renders consonants syllabifiable if they would otherwise not be.

Other epenthesis processes in other languages further support the claimed connection between syllable structure and epenthesis. For instance, both Turkish and Modern Hebrew (chapter 12, Further reading, p. 249) have epenthesis processes that are more complex than that of Yawelmani: they apply only where they produce a well-formed sonority profile, in line with the sonority sequencing restrictions (§4.4.1) observed in these languages.

13.8   Other Remedies for Unsyllabifiable Consonants

The requirement that every consonant belong to some syllable drives other phonological processes as well.

A close relative of vocalic epenthesis is the family of rules that change [–syllabic] sounds to the corresponding [+syllabic] sounds. Such rules can apply to glides (**glide vocalization**; j → i, w → u), as well as to liquids (l → ļ, r → ṛ) and nasals (m → m̩, n → n̩). Thus in English, alternations like *central* ~ *center* ['sɛntɹəl] ~ ['sɛntɹ̩] plausibly reflect an underlying form /sɛntɹ/, which is retained intact in *central*, where the result can be syllabified ([sɛn]σ[tɹəl]σ), but replaces the /ɹ/ with its [+syllabic] counterpart [ɹ̩] (usual IPA transcription: [ɚ]) when the result would not form a legal syllable (*[sɛntɹ]).

In other cases, a language actually sacrifices a consonant where it would not fit into the syllabic pattern. For example, in Spanish the verb *esculpir* [eskul'piɾ] 'to sculpt' consists of the stem /eskulp/ plus the third conjugation infinitive ending /-iɾ/. With the suffix *-tura*, this stem would produce the underlying form /eskulp-tuɾa/, which means 'sculpture'. However, the corresponding surface form is actually [eskultuɾa], with loss of the underlying /p/. This can be understood as the loss of a segment that cannot be incorporated into either neighboring syllable: /lp/ is not a legal coda of Spanish, nor is [pt] a possible onset. The rule that would be needed is something like the following:

Stray Erasure
C′ → ∅
Delete a stray consonant.

Here is a schematic derivation for [eskultuɾa]:

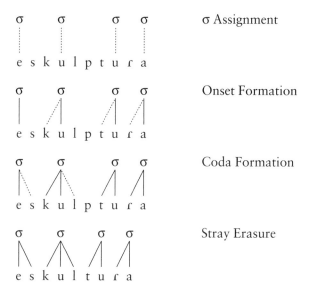

This can only be considered a schematic derivation, since in a full version we would have to provide versions of Onset Formation and Coda Formation that produced all and only the legal onsets and codas of Spanish. The general point at hand is that the loss of /p/ in [eskultuɾa] is related to the general principles of syllable well-formedness in Spanish.

In sum, a frequently followed course in phonological analysis is to set up the syllabification system as an overarching set of well-formedness principles, expressed here through the persistent application of σ Assignment, Onset Formation, and Coda Formation. The segmental rules of the language shoehorn the underlying forms, by means of insertion, vocalization, and deletion, into the legal syllabic forms.

Exercises

1 *English /ʌl/ coalescence*

In some English dialects the sequence /ʌl/ is optionally realized as syllabic [l̩] in certain environments. Here are relevant data.

dull	['dʌl] or ['dl̩]		*Culver*	['kʌlvɚ] or ['kl̩vɚ]
null	['nʌl] or ['nl̩]		*Mulholland*	[mʌl'halənd] or [ml̩'halənd]
hull	['hʌl] or ['hl̩]		*bulky*	['bʌlki] or ['bl̩ki]

color	['kʌlɚ] only
Cullen	['kʌlən] only
Tuller	['tʌlɚ] only

a. Apply the rules given in the readings to syllabify all the underlying forms above.
b. State a rule for /ʌl/ → [l̩]. To write a rule that is undergone by two segments, merging them into one, use the numerical subscripts shown in fn. 9, p. 101, and let one of the sounds become zero.
c. Give derivations, including the initial syllabification stage, of *dull*, *Culver*, and *color*.

2 Distribution of English Consonants

English /w/ may occur in onsets but not codas, as shown by the following examples:

- Onsets: *will* [wɪl], *twin* [twɪn], *away* [ə.weɪ]
- Not codas: no words like *[piw], *[ˈpiw.lə][4]

Examine all of the English consonants (see chart on p. 21) and assess each for whether it can occur in onsets, codas, or both. Give examples in the same format as just given. You should be able to find three consonants (including /w/) that are limited to onsets, and one consonant that is limited to codas.

3 Allophones of German /ʁ/

In one variety of German, the voiced uvular fricative [ʁ] is in complementary distribution with a voiced uvular approximant, which will be described with the IPA symbol [ʌ]. For the features of [ʁ] see p. 96; you may assume that [ʌ] differs from [ʁ] in being [−consonantal, +sonorant, +approximant].

a. Produce a phonemic analysis for these two sounds, following the method given in chapters 2 and 3. Your analysis should make use of syllable structure, as discussed in this chapter. Include derivations for the forms [ˈʁoːt], [paʁaˈdiːs], [ˈɪʌ], [ˈfyːʌ-t], and [ˈaʌbaɪt].

In the data, hyphens are included to help with the meanings; they can be ignored for purposes of syllabification and the allophone environments.

---

[4] Some textbooks use /w/ as a transcription for the second part of the diphthongs [oʊ] and [aʊ], as in "ow" or "aw." It is assumed here that this is not a phonologically valid transcription, since if /w/ were generally able to occur in codas we would expect there to be cases like *[iw], *[ew], *[ɛw], etc.

Forms with [ʁ]		*Forms with* [ʌ̯]	
[ˈʁoːt]	'red'	[ˈɪʌ̯]	'delusion'
[ˈɪʁ-ə]	'be mistaken-1 sg. pres.'	[ˈɪʌ̯-t]	'be mistaken-3 sg. pres.'
[ˈleːʁ-ə]	'empty-fem./plur.'	[ˈleːʌ̯]	'empty'
[ˈbɛsəʁ-ə]	'better-fem./plur.'	[ˈfiːʌ̯]	'four'
[ˈʁaʊx]	'smoke'	[ˈfyːʌ̯]	'for'
[ˈbɪtəʁ-ə]	'bitter-fem./plur.'	[ˈoːʌ̯]	'ear'
[ˈvandəʁ-ə]	'wander-1 p. sing.'	[ˈfyːʌ̯-t]	'lead-3 sg. pres.'
[ˈʁuːə]	'rest'	[ˈfyːʌ̯-tə]	'lead-3 sg. past'
[ˈʁaɪn]	'Rhine'	[ˈvaʌ̯t-ə]	'wait-1 sg. pres.'
[ˈdʁai]	'three'	[ˈvɛʌ̯k-ə]	'work-plur.'
[paʁaˈdiːs]	'paradise'	[paʌ̯ˈtaɪ]	'party'
[ˈeːʁa]	'era'	[ˈaʌ̯baɪt]	'work'
[ˈbʁaɪt]	'broad'	[ˈɔʌ̯dnʊŋ]	'order'
[ˈfyːʁ-ə]	'lead-1 sg. pres.'		
[leoˈnoːʁə]	'Leonore'		
[maˈʁiːnə]	'navy'		

b. Add an additional rule to cover these data. The clue is to look for the same stems above as they appear with vowel-initial suffixes.

[ˈbɛsʌ̯]	'better'
[ˈbɛsʌ̯-t]	'make better-3 sg. pres.'
[ˈbɪtʌ̯]	'bitter'
[ˈvandʌ̯-t]	'wander-3 sg. pres.'

Further reading

The account of syllabification based on ordered rules of consonant adjunction is taken from Daniel Kahn (1976) "Syllable-based generalizations in English phonology," MIT PhD thesis (https://dspace.mit.edu). A set of rules needed to form English onsets can be found in George N. Clements and S. Jay Keyser, *CV Phonology: A Generative Theory of the Syllable* (1983, MIT Press).

The idea that syllabification rules syllabify what they can, letting further rules deal with stray consonants, is from James Harris, *Syllable Structure and Stress in Spanish* (1983, MIT Press). The *escultura* example is taken from this source. The general idea that phonological processes have the goal of making underlying representations conform to general structural principles on the surface (§13.7, §13.8) has been extensively elaborated in Optimality Theory; for readings in this area see p. 68.

Barra Gaelic (phonemic syllable division): George N. Clements, "Syllabification and epenthesis in the Barra dialect of Gaelic," in K. Bogers, H. van der Hulst and M. Mous, eds., *The Phonological Representation of Suprasegmentals* (1986, Foris). Cibaeño Spanish Liquid Gliding: Rafael Nuñez-Cedeño (1997) "Liquid gliding in Spanish and feature geometry theories," *Hispanic Linguistics* 9: 143–64. Efik (phonemic syllable division): William E. Welmers, *African Language Structures* (1973, University of California Press). French nasal vowels: Sanford Schane, *French Phonology and Morphology* (1968, MIT Press); Bernard Tranel *Concreteness in Generative Phonology: Evidence from French* (1981, University of California Press). Ilokano syllabification: Bruce Hayes and May Abad (1989) "Reduplication and syllabification in Ilokano," *Lingua* 77: 331–74. Porteño Spanish fortition: James Harris and Ellen Kaisse (1999) "Palatal vowels, glides and obstruents in Argentinian Spanish," *Phonology* 16: 117–90. Tonkawa syncope: Harry Hoijer "Tonkawa," in Harry Hoijer et al., eds., *Linguistic Structures of Native America* (1946, Viking Fund). Yawelmani epenthesis: Stanley Newman, *Yokuts Language of California* (1944, Viking Fund).

14 Stress, Stress Rules, and Syllable Weight

14.1 Introduction

Stress is generally taken to involve the force or intensity with which a syllable is uttered. Stress is also detectable from the many effects it has on segments, since it appears so often in the environment of segmental rules. The influence of stress on segments has been treated already in several locations in this text. The present chapter covers the rules that determine the position of the stress, relating these rules to syllables and to syllable structure.

14.2 Some General Properties of Stress

14.2.1 Culminativity

In most stress languages, every word has exactly one main stress. This observation is sometimes stated by saying that stress is **culminative**; each word "culminates" in one main-stressed syllable. By the principle of culminativity, ['dɔg], ['kæt], and ['hɔɹs] are possible words in English, but a stressless form like *[bə] would not be.

There is one apparent exception to the principle of culminativity: grammatical words, such as articles, pronouns, prepositions, and auxiliary verbs, are often stressless, as in the word *the* in *the book* [ðə 'bʊk]. The evident reason why some grammatical words can be stressless is that they are typically used in the presence of a stressed content word. The grammatical word "leans on" (more formally: is **clitic** to) the content word, and in a sense forms a part of the content word for phonological purposes. When such a grammatical word is used by itself, it receives an artificially imposed stress (['ðʌː] or ['ðiː]), and thus satisfies the principle of culminativity.

14.2.2   No syllable-internal contrasts

Up to now we have treated stress as a property of vowels and other [+syllabic] segments; one speaks of "stressed vowels," "unstressed vowels," and so on. But it is probably more accurate to consider stress as a property of syllables; that is, the units that can be stressed or stressless are syllables, and not segments. Thus when we speak of a "stressed vowel," this can be seen as an informal way of designating the vowel of a stressed syllable.

The reason for saying this is that there are apparently no *contrasts* of stress within the syllable. For example, if we have a syllable containing a diphthong, it is apparently impossible for a language to have a contrast involving stressing the first half vs. the second half of the diphthong. Thus, there are four logically possible ways (assuming culminativity) of stressing a hypothetical word like [pa.ta.ki.ma]: ['pa.ta.ki.ma], [pa.'ta.ki.ma], [pa.ta.'ki.ma], and [pa.ta.ki.'ma]. But there are only three ways of stressing the trisyllable [pa.tai.ma]: ['pa.tai.ma], [pa.'tai.ma], and [pa.tai.'ma]. The stressing [pa.ta'i.ma] is not possible unless there are actually four syllables: [pa.ta.'i.ma].

One way to account for this contrast limitation is to adopt representations in which the feature [stress] is attached to syllables rather than to vowels. In this view, [pa.tai.ma] does indeed have only three possibilities for stress, shown below.

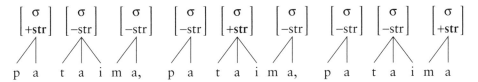

We will see that attaching stress to syllables also offers advantages in formulating stress assignment rules.

14.2.3   Fixed vs. free stress

Stress can be phonemic, by which is meant that it cannot be predicted; there are minimal or near-minimal pairs, as in Spanish ['saβana] 'bedsheet' vs. [sa'βana] 'savanna'. English, Russian, Ilokano, and many other languages have phonemic stress. Stress can also be predictable, as in Polish (penultimate stress; see next section) or French (final stress). One occasionally encounters the terms **free stress**, which means phonemic stress; and **fixed stress**, which means predictable stress.

Even in languages where stress is phonemic, there are almost always tendencies and limitations in stress placement. Spanish observes the limitation that stress must go on one of the last three syllables of the word (the "trisyllabic window"), and shows a strong tendency toward penultimate stress. English likewise has a three-syllable window (violated only rarely in words like '*hesitancy*), and various other limitations discussed in §14.5.3.

14.3 Stress Rules

Where stress is predictable, we can characterize this by deriving it with phonological rules. We will start with a simple case from Polish, where stress is almost entirely predictable. Here are some typical data, illustrating the penultimate stress pattern of this language.

[tele'vizor]   'TV'
[televi'zor-ek]   'little TV'
[televizo'r-etʃ-ek]   'tiny little TV'   (k → tʃ / ___ e)

The way we write this rule depends on our approach to representing stress phonologically. Under our earlier approach, with the feature [stress] attached to vowels, the rule would be written to count off the vowels from the end of the word, using the notation /C_0/ (p. 154) to skip over the consonants:

Penultimate Stress (vowel-counting version)
V → [+stress] / ___ C_0 V C_0]$_{word}$
Assign stress to the second-to-last vowel in the word.

Since vowels and syllables are in one-to-one correspondence, such a rule will have the desired effect.

On the other hand, we just saw that in order to limit possible contrasts, it is appropriate to assign stress to syllables, not to vowels. This idea also permits us to simplify the stress rule somewhat:

Penultimate Stress (syllabic version; preliminary)
σ → [+stress] / ___ σ]$_{word}$
Assign stress to the second to last syllable in the word.

In formulating stress rules, we will assume that syllables always surface as stressless unless they are assigned stress by rule. This will follow if the syllabification algorithm (p. 253) automatically assigns the value [−stress] to syllables when they are created; this can be changed by the later application of the stress rule. Thus the derivation for /televizor/ starts out like this:

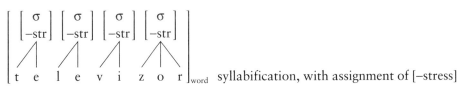

[t   e   l   e   v   i   z   o   r]$_{word}$ underlying form

syllabification, with assignment of [−stress]

The Penultimate Stress Rule is matched up to this form as follows, deriving the correct result:

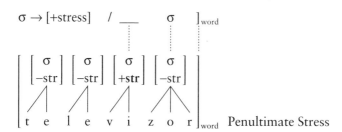

$$\sigma \to [+\text{stress}] \quad / \underline{\quad} \quad \sigma \quad]_{\text{word}}$$

Penultimate Stress

Consider now some additional facts. Polish has monosyllabic words, which get stressed:

['sen]   'dream'
['stax]   'Stan' (dimin. of *Stanislaw*)

This is not what our stress rule predicts; since these words don't have a penultimate syllable, they don't match up to the rule and thus shouldn't get stressed at all.

Intuitively, what is happening is that since penultimate stress is impossible, the language "settles for" final stress. We will see more complicated examples of this pattern later on – for example, Macedonian aims for antepenultimate stress in words of at least three syllables, and settles for penultimate stress in disyllabic words and final stress in monosyllables.

Within phonological theory, we need to provide a device for characterizing this pattern. Of the various proposals that have been made, we will adopt one that involves a special use of **parenthesis notation**. In this approach, the Polish rule is written as follows:

Polish Stress (final version)
$$\sigma \to [+\text{stress}] / \underline{\quad} (\sigma)]_{\text{word}}$$

When a parenthesized rule is written out both including and excluding the parenthesized material, we obtain what are called its **expansions**:

Polish Stress: Expansions
$$\sigma \to [+\text{stress}] / \underline{\quad} \sigma]_{\text{word}}$$
$$\sigma \to [+\text{stress}] / \underline{\quad}]_{\text{word}}$$

It should be clear that the longer expansion can be used to assign penultimate stress to words with two or more syllables, whereas the shorter expansion will be used to derive stress on monosyllables.

What is needed to complete the analysis is a set of general principles that determine which expansion is applicable to any given form. These are stated below.

Conventions on Application of Stress Rules Containing Parentheses

a. *Longest first*
   If a stress rule includes an expression in parentheses, the longest expansions must be tried first.
b. *Blockage*
   When a stress rule is applied under some expansion, all remaining expansions are skipped.
c. *Completeness*
   If a stress rule cannot apply in a longer expansion, then the longest available remaining expansion must be tried next.

In the Polish case, the first expansion given above is longest and therefore must be tried first. The representations below leave out the feature [−stress] for the sake of legibility.

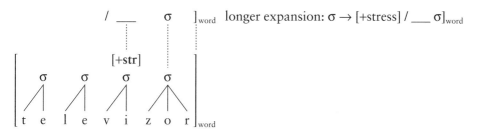

longer expansion: σ → [+stress] / ___ σ]word

At this point the Blockage provision is crucial – it terminates the application of the stress rule. If Blockage were not in effect, we would go on to derive a second, erroneous stress on polysyllabic words, like this:

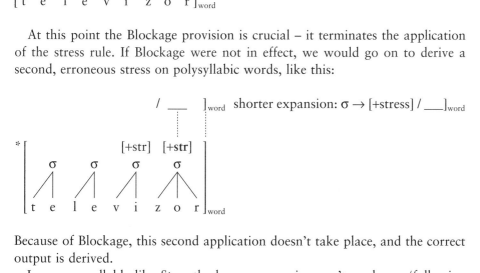

shorter expansion: σ → [+stress] / ___]word

Because of Blockage, this second application doesn't take place, and the correct output is derived.

In a monosyllable like *Stax*, the longer expansion can't apply, so (following the Completeness principle) the shorter version is applicable, giving the right result.

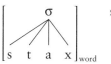

syllabification

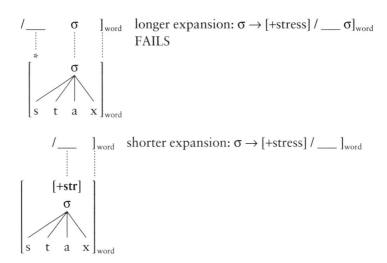

14.3.1 Stress rules with multiple parentheses

The conventions on the use of parentheses in stress rules can be applied for multiple parentheses as well. Consider the stress pattern of Macedonian (Slavic, Macedonia), where stress goes three syllables from the end (that is, on the **antepenult**), and on the initial syllable in words shorter than three syllables:

Three syllables and up		Two syllables		One syllable	
['beseda]	'lecture'	['ʒena]	'woman'	['den]	'day'
[vo'denitʃar]	'miller'	['vide]	'sees'	['rid]	'hill'
[be'sedata]	'the lecture'				
[vode'nitʃari]	'millers'				
[vodeni'tʃarite]	'the millers'				

A possible rule for deriving this pattern is given below.

Macedonian Stress
σ → [+stress] / ___ ((σ) σ)]word

To apply this rule to a form, it is necessary first to determine its expansions. The longest expansion is σ → [+stress] / ___ σ σ]word, with nothing omitted. Leaving out the inner set of parentheses yields σ → [+stress] / ___ σ]word, and leaving out the outer set yields σ → [+stress] / ___]word. If these are applied following the conventions to words of length three (or more), two, and one, the appropriate expansion will assign stress correctly; this is given as exercise 1 below.

A detail of the Macedonian analysis is that within limits, it does not matter where the parentheses are placed. Two other versions of the rule that would work just as well would be σ → [+stress] / ___ (σ) (σ)]word and σ → [+stress] / ___ (σ (σ))]word. They work identically because they have the same expansions.

The general pattern that the theory predicts is that stress often goes a certain distance from a particular word boundary (this can be either the left or the right boundary, depending on the language). The substance of the theory is that if the word is too short for stress to go the maximum distance, it is placed as far from the boundary as possible. Thus, if the theory is correct, we would not expect to find a language that was like Macedonian but placed stress in disyllables on the final syllable instead of the initial. Of the dozen or so languages I'm aware of that place stress up to three syllables from the end, all work like Macedonian in stressing disyllabic words initially.

14.4   Alternating Stress

In many languages stress can fall on several syllables of a word: one primary (strongest) stress and also (in longer words) one or more secondary stresses. Frequently one finds a pattern in which every other syllable is stressed; this is called **alternating stress**. Warao, a language of Venezuela, is an example:

[ˌjapuˌɾukiˌtaneˈhase]	'verily to climb'	(8 syllables)
[ˌnahoˌɾoaˌhakuˈtai]	'the one who ate'	(8 syllables)
[jiˌwaraˈnae]	'he finished it'	(5 syllables)
[eˌnahoˌɾoaˌhakuˈtai]	'the one who caused him to eat'	(9 syllables)

Here, there is penultimate main stress, and a train of alternating secondary stresses going from right to left (orthographically speaking) across the word.

To analyze this pattern, we must first amplify the feature system to accommodate the distinction between primary and secondary stress. This can be done by adding the feature [main]: primary stressed (also called "main stressed") syllables are [+main, +stress], secondary stressed syllables are [−main, +stress], and stressless syllables are [−main, −stress]. Just as with [stress], we will assign the feature [main] to syllable nodes.

Let us first handle the Warao primary stress pattern. In real Warao, there are various complications to the pattern not treated here; for present purposes we will simply write the penultimate stress rule needed for the data at hand; it is essentially the same as the rule in Polish.

Warao Primary Stress

$$\sigma \;\rightarrow\; \begin{bmatrix} +\text{main} \\ +\text{stress} \end{bmatrix} / \underline{\quad} (\sigma) \;]_{\text{word}}$$

Turning to secondary stress, the task at hand is to write a rule that can in principle lay down an unlimited number of secondary stresses, constrained only by the length of the word to which it applies. This can be done with **iterative rules**. An iterative rule is assumed to apply to its own output, and it keeps on applying until it can no longer be matched to the input. The basis for iteration normally is that the rule creates new environments for itself; that is, it is **self-feeding** (see §8.4).[1]

The iterative secondary stress rule for Warao can be stated as follows:

Warao Secondary Stress

$$\sigma \;\rightarrow\; [\text{+stress}] \;/\; \underline{\quad}\; \sigma \begin{bmatrix} \sigma \\ \text{+stress} \end{bmatrix} \qquad \text{(iterative)}$$

Note that the change specifying [+stress] will create secondary stress, not primary, under the assumption that all syllables start out as [−main].

Here is an example of how the rules would work:

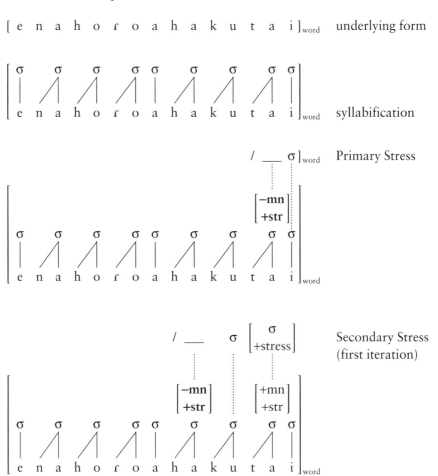

₁ The other possibility is self-bleeding; see Further reading.

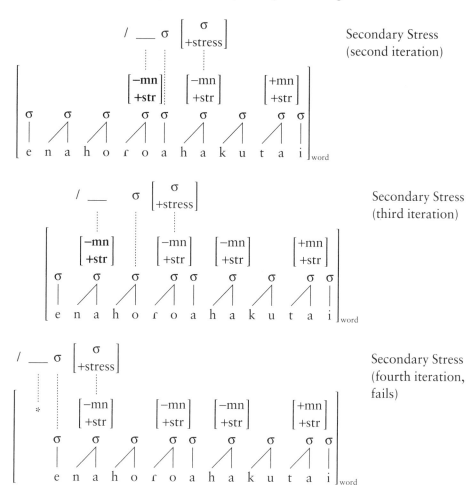

Here, the Primary Stress rule assigns the penultimate stress, and the Secondary Stress rule then iterates leftward to assign the remaining stresses. It can be seen that Secondary Stress is self-feeding because it assigns the feature value [+stress], which appears in its own environment. At the last attempt to apply Secondary Stress, no stress can be assigned. The Secondary Stress rule has no parenthesized material, and hence does not have a shorter expansion.

Alternating secondary stress is found in many languages, including English, where it is heard in long words such as ˌreconˌciliˈation, ˌonoˌmataˈpoeia, ˌirreˌtrievaˈbility.

14.5 Syllable Weight

In many stress languages, stress is sensitive to a distinction called **syllable weight**. In a simple weight distinction, there are heavy and light syllables, defined as follows:

Heavy syllable: syllable that either
- ends in a consonant or
- has a long vowel or diphthong

Light syllable: syllable that ends in a short vowel

We will use the symbol /ˉ/, called a **macron**, to denote a heavy syllable, and the symbol /˘/, called a **breve**, to denote a light syllable.

A **closed** syllable is one that ends in a consonant; an **open** syllable one that ends in a short vowel or diphthong. Thus we can restate the definition above: short-voweled open syllables are light, all others are heavy. Other weight distinctions exist, but here we will limit ourselves to languages that use the distinction just given.

Intuitively, heavy syllables are intrinsically more prominent than lights, and in stress systems they tend to be stress-attracting. This is only a tendency, however; as we will see there are cases in which the stress rules of a language will stress a light syllable even when a heavy one is available.

Formally, we must identify just what is meant by /ˉ/ and /˘/. For present purposes, it suffices to assume a feature [+heavy] attached to syllable nodes, and assigned its value by the syllabification rules, using the definition just given. Thus a hypothetical word /pa.tap.tai͡.maː/ would be represented as follows.

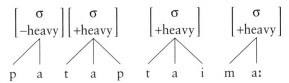

The symbols /ˉ/ and /˘/, when they appear in rules, can thus be interpreted as [+heavy] and [–heavy].

14.5.1 Quantitative meter

The linguistic relevance of heavy vs. light syllables can be shown independently of their role in stress rules. The phenomenon at hand is **meter**, which can be defined as the use of phonological material to embody conventionalized rhythmic patterns in poetry. Meter in English and many other languages is based on stress. However, this is not the only possible kind of meter: in other languages, the basis of meter is an arrangement of the syllables of a line according to their weight.

An example is given below from classical Persian verse (*Golestan*; Saʾdi, *c*.1250). First, I give just the transcription and its stress pattern.

d͡ʒæˈhɑːn,	ˈej	ˈbæɾɑːdær,	ˈnæmɑːnæd	be	ˈkæs
world	O	brother	waits	for	no one

"The world, O brother, waits for no one,"

ˈdel	ændær	d͡ʒæˈhɑːn	ɑːfæˈɾiːn	ˈbænd	o	ˈbæs
heart	to	world-	creator	tie	and	enough

"Set thy heart on the creator of the world and it is enough."

The stress patterns of these lines are not rhythmic in any way (σ 'σ 'σ 'σ σ σ 'σ σ σ 'σ / 'σ σ σ σ 'σ σ σ 'σ 'σ σ 'σ), and could not be the basis of the meter. However, if we syllabify these utterances and classify them into heavies and lights, a clear pattern emerges.

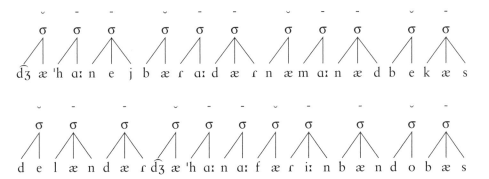

The pattern common to these lines (and indeed to all the thousands of lines of Persian verse written in this meter, called *motaqareb*) is as follows:

˘ ¯ ¯ ˘ ¯ ¯ ˘ ¯ ¯ ˘ ¯

Clearly, this is a rhythm, consisting of the periodic sequence ˘ ¯ ¯, truncated to just ˘ ¯ in its fourth appearance.

It can be noted that to get the weights right, we must assume that classical Persian resembled Spanish (§13.5) in allowing syllabification to cross word boundaries freely. Were this not so, the word [del] in the second line would retain its coda and wrongly count as heavy. This principle of syllabification holds fairly generally in the corpus of Persian verse.

Meter that makes use of heavy vs. light syllable is called **quantitative meter** ("quantity" being a synonym for "weight" in this context). It is found in many languages, both dead and living. The principle of quantity apparently comes naturally and intuitively to speakers of such languages; for example, many speakers of Berber and of Hausa are able to compose quantitative verse as a form of oral improvisation. The quantitative verse best known to Westerners is found in Greek and Latin. The following example is the first line of Virgil's *Aeneid* (1st century BCE) written in Classical Latin.[2]

| 'arma | wi'rumkʷe | 'kanoː | 'troːjãe͡ | kʷiː | 'priːmus | ab | 'oːris |
| of-arms | man-and | I-sing | from-Troy | who | first | from | place |

"I sing of arms and the man, who first from the place of Troy . . ."

---

[2] Original spelling *arma uirumque cano Troiae qui primus ab oris*. For how scholars make informed inferences about Latin phonemes and syllables, see the reference by W. S. Allen in Further reading.

Here, the rhythm becomes obvious only when one generalizes over many lines to determine the free variation allowed. The full version of the pattern turns out to be the following repeating sequence:

$$ - \left\{ \begin{smallmatrix} \smile\smile \\ - \end{smallmatrix} \right\} - \left\{ \begin{smallmatrix} \smile\smile \\ - \end{smallmatrix} \right\} - \left\{ \begin{smallmatrix} \smile\smile \\ - \end{smallmatrix} \right\} - \left\{ \begin{smallmatrix} \smile\smile \\ - \end{smallmatrix} \right\} - \left\{ \begin{smallmatrix} \smile\smile \\ - \end{smallmatrix} \right\} - - $$

This pattern is called **dactylic hexameter**. It consists of six units ("feet"), usually taking the form $- \left\{ \begin{smallmatrix} \smile\smile \\ - \end{smallmatrix} \right\}$. Feet of this type (maximally trisyllabic, with the long element first) are traditionally called "dactyls." It can be seen that the dactyls permit free variation in how they are realized: instead of two lights, a single heavy may be used instead, and this substitution is obligatory for the last dactyl in the line.

Summing up, quantitative meter forms an argument for the psychological reality of syllable weight. In languages that have a clear quantity distinction, speakers find it natural to arrange the heavies and lights in rhythmic patterns when they create poetry and song.

14.5.2 *Stress based on syllable weight*

Let us now consider how the heavy vs. light distinction plays a role in stress assignment. The following data illustrate the stress pattern of Classical Arabic as it is rendered by speakers in Palestine and Lebanon:

Antepenultimate		Penultimate		Final	
a.	['kassarat] 'she smashed'	n.	[ka'sartu] 'I broke'	u.	['lan] 'not'
b.	[kas'sartuhu] 'I smashed it'	o.	[saː'fartu] 'I traveled'		
c.	[ka'sartuhu] 'I broke it'	p.	[kassa'ruːhu] 'they smashed it'		
d.	['kaːtibun] 'a writer'	q.	[kasar'naːhu] 'we broke it'		
e.	['saːfara] 'he traveled'	r.	[kaːti'biːna] 'writers'		
f.	[mali'katuhu] 'his queen'	s.	['qabla] 'before'		
g.	[ma'likatun] 'a queen'	t.	['faqatˤ] 'only'		
h.	[mak'tabatun] 'a library'				
i.	[makta'batuhu] 'his library'				
j.	[taf'tatiħu] 'he opens ceremoniously'				
k.	[tastaq'biluhu] 'he receives him (as guest)'				
l.	[d͡ʒaː'warahu] 'it bordered it'				
m.	[jud͡ʒaː'wiruhu] 'it borders it'				

In reducing this pattern to rule, the first step is to syllabify and retranscribe as sequences of syllable weight. The one aspect of Classical Arabic syllabification one needs to know is that VCCV is always divided as VC.CV, even for sequences like /abla/ where V.CCV is a plausible candidate. Thus, for example, (o) [saːˈfartu] is syllabified and weighted thus:

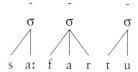

and would appear in a data list as ˉ ˈˉ ˇ. Reduced to weight sequences in this way, and right-justified, the data look like this:

Antepenultimate		Penultimate		Final
a. ˈˉ ˇ ˇ	h. ˉ ˈˇ ˇ ˉ	n. ˇ ˈˉ ˇ		u. ˈˉ
b. ˉ ˈˉ ˇ ˇ	i. ˉ ˇ ˈˇ ˇ ˇ	o. ˉ ˈˉ ˇ		
c. ˇ ˈˉ ˇ ˇ	j. ˉ ˈˇ ˇ ˇ	p. ˇ ˇ ˈˉ ˇ		
d. ˈˉ ˇ ˉ	k. ˉ ˉ ˈˇ ˇ ˇ	q. ˇ ˉ ˈˉ ˇ		
e. ˈˉ ˇ ˇ	l. ˉ ˈˇ ˇ ˇ	r. ˉ ˇ ˈˉ ˇ		
f. ˇ ˇ ˈˇ ˇ ˇ	m. ˇ ˉ ˈˇ ˇ ˇ	s. ˈˉ ˇ		
g. ˇ ˈˇ ˇ ˉ		t. ˈˇ ˉ		

In this format, the crucial generalizations become easy to spot: if the *penult* is light, then (assuming enough syllables are present), the *antepenult* gets the stress, as in examples (a)–(m). If the penult is heavy (examples (n)–(s)), or there are only two syllables (examples (s)–(t)), then the penult gets stressed, and in the remaining case (monosyllables like (u)), the final syllable is stressed.

In searching for rule that can assign these stresses, a useful way to start is to state its longest expansion, given below:

Classical Arabic Stress: longest expansion
σ → [+stress] / ___ ˇ σ]_word   (for (a)–(m))

This will skip one syllable at the end of a word, and also a light penult, covering the items of (a)–(m) above.

The two shorter expansions must assign penultimate stress and final stress; we have already seen rules of this sort for Polish and Warao.

Classical Arabic Stress: shorter expansions
σ → [+stress] / ___ σ]_word   (for (n)–(t))
σ → [+stress] / ___]_word   (for (u))

Once we have all three expansions, we can collapse them together into a single rule covering all three cases, as follows:

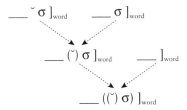

Thus the final form of the rule is as follows.

Classical Arabic Stress

$$\sigma \rightarrow [+stress] \ / \ \underline{\quad} \ ((\breve{\ }) \ \sigma) \ ]_{word}$$

The Classical Arabic case illustrates a general principle involving syllable weight: heavy syllables tend to attract stress, even though they are not invariably stressed. Thus, heavy penults always attract stress, but in a word like (j) [taf'tatiħu] (¯ ᷆ ˘ ˘), the initial heavy syllable cannot be stressed. The stress rule specifies a three-syllable window within which stress must fall, and the requirements of this window override the tendency to stress heavy syllables.

The Classical Arabic rule also illustrates the simplification in stress rules we can obtain by using syllable weights. Stated in segments, the same rule would be:

Classical Arabic Stress (segmental version)

$$[+syllabic] \quad \rightarrow \quad [+stress] \ / \ \underline{\quad} \ C_0 \ ((\begin{bmatrix} +syllabic \\ -long \end{bmatrix} C \ ) \ V \ C_0 \ ) \ ]_{word}$$

And it is this simple only because Classical Arabic has a very simple syllable structure. As we will see, in a language that has the same rule, but divides VCCV as VC.CV or V.CCV according to the consonants included, the statement of the rule becomes far more complex.

The Classical Arabic rule is a surprisingly common stress rule among the languages of the world. In various forms it is found in Latin and some modern Romance languages, Klamath (Penutian, Oregon), the historical ancestor of Chimwiini (chapter),[3] and various modern Arabic dialects.

---

[3] Specifically, it appears that at one time Chimwiini stressed its words as in Latin, then shortened all stressless vowels. Later, the language adopted a new stress system (see ch. 11, Further reading). The rules of Phrase-Final Shortening, Pre-Long Shortening, and Preantepenultimate Shortening are historical restructurings (§11.7), the residue of this history.

14.5.3 *Main stress in English*

In fact, it appears that the rule σ → [+stress] / ___ ((˘) σ)]$_{word}$ has seeped into English, probably as a result of the massive influx of Latin loan words. The rule also works when applied to the native words, because the native words are so short (one or two syllables). We see this below.

Where the penult is a light syllable, we normally get antepenultimate stress in words of at least three syllables:

'*regiment*, '*Canada*, *A*'*merica*, '*accident*, *Los* '*Angeles*, '*animal*, '*capital*
 [d͡ʒə]   [nə]   [ɹɪ]   [sɪ]   [d͡ʒə]   [nɪ]   [pɪ]

Where the penult is closed, and thus is heavy, it attracts the stress:

ap'*pendix*, ˌ*dia*'*lectal*, *Co*'*lumbus*, ˌ*conso*'*nantal*, *e*'*jective*, *sus*'*pension*
 [pɛn]   [lɛk]   [lʌm]   [næn] [d͡ʒɛk]   [pɛn]

Likewise when the penult has a long vowel or diphthong, and is therefore heavy, it attracts the stress:

ˌ*Okla*'*homa*, ˌ*Argen*'*tina*, *as*ˌ*simi*'*lation*, *op*'*ponent*, *Al*'*toona*
 [hoʊ̯]   [tiː]   [leɪ̯]   [poʊ̯]   [tuː]

Disyllables are ordinarily initially stressed, and monosyllables are stressed:

'*vivid*, '*tennis*, '*ketchup*, '*onion*, '*pickle*, '*bubble*, '*proton*, '*concept*
'*bat*, '*sack*, '*moat*, '*spot*

The rule appears to be somewhat productive, in the sense of chapter 9. For example, a hypothetical word like *palacta* seems to allow only penultimate stress. This is what the rule predicts, since the penult /læk/ is heavy. There are also a few cases where words have been diachronically regularized, receiving new stressings compatible with the rule. For instance, the final stress in the normative pronunciations of *po*'*lice* and *gui*'*tar* date from when these words were borrowed from other languages. Both words are, in certain English dialects, pronounced with a regularized initial stress. *Lemonade* and *cigarette* are likewise often regularized to antepenultimate stress.

Despite this productivity, there are a great number of exceptions. *Savanna*, *Alabama*, and *abscissa* all have light penults ([væ], [bæ], [sɪ]) but have penultimate, not antepenultimate stress. *Galaxy* is unusual for having antepenultimate stress when the penult is heavy [lək]; *impotent* is a similar case if we assume that *potent* justifies an underlying long [oʊ̯]. As noted earlier (§12.4), abstract analyses have been proposed as an appropriate treatment for these exceptional words.

14.5.4   *English stress and the argument for syllables*

Words like the following are of interest for the theory of stress and syllabification. Each row is labeled with the consonant cluster that is found between
the penultimate and final vowel.

/pl/   *discipline* ['dɪsɪplɪn], *panoply* ['pænəpli]

/bɹ/   *algebra* ['ældʒəbɹə], *vertebrate* ['vɚtəbɹət]

/tɹ/   *idolatry* [aɪ'dɑlətɹi], *symmetry* ['sɪmətɹi], *recalcitrant* [ɹi'kælsətɹənt]

/kɹ/   *ludicrous* ['ludəkɹəs]

/gɹ/   *peregrine* ['pɛɹəgɹən], *integral* ['ɪntəgɹəl]

/kw/   *eloquent* ['ɛləkwənt]

/st/   *travesty* ['tɹævəsti], *amnesty*, ['æmnəsti], *pedestal* ['pɛdəstəl],
         minister ['mɪnɪstɚ]

/stɹ/   *industry* ['ɪndəstɹi], *chemistry* ['kɛməstɹi], *orchestra* ['ɔɹkəstɹə],
         tapestry ['tæpəstɹi]

The system set up in this chapter stresses these words correctly, as follows. First,
maximal-onset syllabification creates a final syllable beginning with a cluster (thus,
[dɪ]ₒ[sɪ]ₒ[plɪn]ₒ for *discipline*). The conventions for weight assignment classify these
syllables as shown.

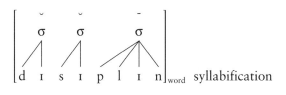

The longest expansion of the English stress rule σ → [+stress] / ___ ((˘) σ)]_word
then correctly assigns antepenultimate stress to such configurations:

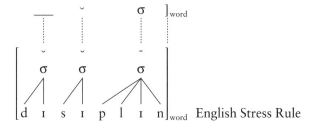

Similar results will be obtained for the other words.

The principles of syllabification clearly play an important role here. If we
attempted to express the English stress rule without syllables, the result would
be quite complex, something like the following:

English Stress Rule (segmental version)

$$V \rightarrow [\text{+stress}] / \underline{\quad} C_0 \left(\left(\begin{bmatrix} \text{+syllabic} \\ \text{-long} \end{bmatrix} \left\{ \begin{array}{l} [\text{-sonorant}] \begin{bmatrix} \text{+sonorant} \\ \text{+continuant} \end{bmatrix} \\ s \begin{bmatrix} \text{-del rel} \\ \text{-voice} \end{bmatrix} (\textrm{ɹ}) \\ (C) \end{array} \right\} \right) V \, C_0 \right)]_{\text{word}}$$

The rule is obviously quite complex. But the main argument is that it misses a crucial generalization: the expression in { } is in fact an outline description of the class of English syllable onsets, which the phonology should characterize in any event. The syllabic rule σ → [+stress] / ___ ((ˇ) σ)]_{word} is simpler because it relies on independently needed syllabification principles.

Exercises

1 Macedonian stress

Examine the Macedonian stress rule and data in §14.3.1 above, and provide derivations in the format of the Polish derivations on p. 275 for the following words: [vo'denitʃar], ['vide], and ['rid].

2 Simple stress rules

Using the parenthesis formalism of this chapter, write a rule to place stress:

a. on the second syllable of a word, with initial stress in monosyllables
b. on the third syllable of a word with at least three syllables, on the final of disyllables and monosyllables
c. on the middle syllable of an odd-syllabled word, and on the syllable just following the midpoint of an even-syllabled word.

   One of the above is a trick question, and has no answer. Explain why not.

3 Alternating stress in Pintupi

Pintupi is an aboriginal language of Australia. Provide rules in the format of this chapter to derive the correct stress patterns for these words. Give derivations similar to those in §14.4 above for examples (d) and (e).

a. ['paɲa]   'earth'
b. ['tʲuʈaja]   'many'
c. ['maʟa,wana]   'through from behind'
d. ['puʟiŋ,kalatʲu]   'we (sat) on the hill'
e. ['tʲamu,limpa,tʲuŋku]   'our relation'
f. ['ʈiʟi,riɲu,lampatʲu]   'the fire for our benefit flared up'
g. ['kura,nʲulu,limpa,tʲuʈa]   'the first one (who is) our relation'
h. ['juma,ʈiŋka,mara,tʲuʈaka]   'because of mother-in-law'

4   Alternating stress in Polish

At least for some speakers and speaking styles, Polish has alternating stress, with considerable free variation.

a. Provide rules in the format of this chapter to derive the correct stress patterns for the words below.
b. Give derivations similar to those in §14.4 above for words of 1, 2, 4, 5, and 8 syllables.
c. What does your analysis predict to be possible for nine-syllable words?

   Hint: for free variation, consult §3.5.

Syls.	Word	Gloss
1	['sen]	'dream'
2	['flaga]	'flag'
3	[sa'moxut]	'car'
4	[ˌtele'vizoɾ]	'television set-nom. sg.'
5	[ˌakompa'natoɾ]	'accompanist-nom. sg.'
6	[ˌtele,vizo'ɾetʃek] OR [ˌtelevizo'ɾetʃek]	'tiny little TV'
7	[ˌakom,paɲato'ɾovʲe] OR [ˌakompa,ɲato'ɾovʲe] OR [ˌakompaɲato'ɾovʲe]	'accompanist-nom. plur.'
8	[ˌakom,paɲa,toɾetʃ'kovʲe] OR [ˌakompaɲatoɾetʃ'kovʲe]	'little accompanist-gen. sg.'
10	[ˌkosmo,poli,taɲtʃi,kovʲa'netʃka] OR [ˌkosmopolitaɲtʃikovʲa'netʃka]	'little, little, little cosmopolitan girl'

5   Syllable weight

a. Divide the following two lines of classical Persian poetry into syllables (disrespecting word boundaries; see p. 281), and classify each syllable by weight.

d͡ʒæhãː	begæʃtæm	o	dærdaː	be	hiːt͡ʃə	ʃæhr	o	diaːr
world	I traveled	and	pain-voc.	in	no	town	and	region

næjaːfətæm	ke	foruːʃændə	bæxtə	dær	baːzaːr
neg.-find-past-1 sg.	that	sell-3 pl. past	luck	in	bazaar

'I traveled the world and, alas! in no town or region did I find that they sold luck in the bazaar.'

b. Even though it looks like there are two slightly different meters, there really is just one. Provide a reasonable guess for why this is so.

6 Classical Arabic stress

Apply the Classical Arabic stress rule (p. 284) to forms (c), (n), (s), and (u) on p. 282. For a possible format to use in your derivations, see p. 275.

7 Stress in Sierra Miwok

Stress in Sierra Miwok, a native language of California, is predictable, as the following data show:

1. ['ʔimmuʔoːk] 'from there'
2. [wa'kalmɨʔ] 'at the creek'
3. ['t͡ʃamʃiʃaːkɨːj] 'him, dying'
4. [ʔɨ'wiːʃaːk] 'he was eating'
5. ['weːlɨjjiʔ] 'he goes to get'
6. ['loːt̪uːt̪aːnɨt̪iː] 'we two try to catch'
7. ['paːpaʔ] 'grandfather'
8. ['t͡ʃamʃiʃaːkɨːj] 'him, dying'
9. [wa'kaːliʔ] 'creek'
10. [pu'lissaʔ] 'drinking basket'
11. ['leppanaː] 'he finished'

a. Figure out the generalization concerning where stress falls in Sierra Miwok, and write a rule to derive stress. Your rule should use parenthesis notation and make use of heavy and light syllables.

b. Give derivations (including syllabification, weights, and rule application) for three words, choosing them to illustrate a maximal variety of types.

c. What kind of syllable (defined in terms of stress and weight) is missing from the data?

8 English syllabification and stress

a. Syllabify the following underlying representation of English using the rules on p. 253: /kɛɹæktəɹ/ (*character*).

b. Apply the English stress rule σ → [+stress] / ___ ((˘) σ)]$_{word}$. For a possible format to use in your derivation, see p. 275.

c. Use the result as the basis for an explanation of why second-language English speakers are occasionally heard to say [kə'ræktɚ].

Further reading

English stress: Chomsky and Halle's *The Sound Pattern of English* (1968, Harper and Row) contains the analysis from which most subsequent work has proceeded. One of the theoretical proposals made there is the set of conventions on parenthesis notation described in this chapter. The analysis is also cited for illustrating the difficulties attendant on analyzing stress without the use of syllable structure.

Mark Liberman and Alan Prince (1977) "On stress and linguistic rhythm," *Linguistic Inquiry* 8: 249–336 pioneered the so-called "metrical" approach to stress, which has been very influential. *Metrical Stress Theory* by Bruce Hayes (1995, University of Chicago Press) analyzes a large number of languages in the metrical approach; it also covers the typology of syllable weight. It should be noted that the approach taken in this chapter, which uses syllables but not metrical theory, is a pedagogically intended mixture. Most work on stress that has used syllables has also used metrical theory.

Iterative rule application is covered in chapter 5 of Michael Kenstowicz and Charles Kisseberth, *Topics in Phonological Theory* (1977, Academic Press). They include self-bleeding as well as self-feeding rules.

Berber quantitative verse: see the reference by Dell and Elmedlaoui cited in Chapter 4. Classical Arabic stress: Michael Brame (1971) "Stress in Arabic and generative phonology," *Foundations of Language* 7: 556–91. Macedonian stress: Steven Franks (1989) "The monosyllabic head effect," *Natural Language and Linguistic Theory* 7: 551–63. Hausa quantitative verse: Russell G. Schuh, "Text and performance in Hausa metrics," downloadable from www.linguistics.ucla.edu/people/schuh/Metrics/Papers/anti_mutadarik.pdf. Latin syllable weight and meter: W. S. Allen, *Accent and Rhythm* (1974, Cambridge University Press). Persian meter: Lawrence Paul Elwell-Sutton, *The Persian Meters* (1976, Routledge). Warao stress: Henry Osborn (1966) "Warao I: Phonology and morphophonemics," *International Journal. of American Linguistics* 32: 108–23.

15 Tone and Intonation

This chapter completes our survey of suprasegmental phenomena with tone and intonation. The chapter also covers the system of phrasal stress on which English intonation depends.

15.1 The Use of Pitch in Phonology

Pitch can be considered as a purely physical phenomenon: the vocal cords can vibrate faster or slower, resulting acoustically in higher or lower fundamental frequency. Frequency is measured in hertz (Hz, cycles per second), and is easily measured and visualized with pitch-tracking equipment.[1]

All (spoken) languages have pitch and vary it systematically. What varies greatly is how pitch is used in the phonological system. There are basically three types of languages.

15.1.1 Tone languages

In a **tone** language, pitch is used to distinguish words, and must appear in the lexical entries of morphemes, just like phonemic segmental information. As with segmental phonemes, one can often find minimal pairs and other sets for tone.

Figure 15.1 shows a minimal quadruplet from Igbo (Benue-Congo, Nigeria). The four words represent the four possibilities that can occur on disyllabic words in a system that has phonemic Low and High tones. In the figure, the accents (´, `) are the IPA diacritics for high and low tone. Tones are also shown in the way they will be analyzed below, with H(igh) and L(ow) elements linked to them with lines. Above each form is a pitch track, which shows the changes in pitch over time.

---

[1] The pitch tracks in this chapter were made with Wavesurfer, a free phonetics package available from www.speech.kth.se/wavesurfer/. To hear the examples, visit www.linguistics.ucla.edu/people/hayes/IP/.

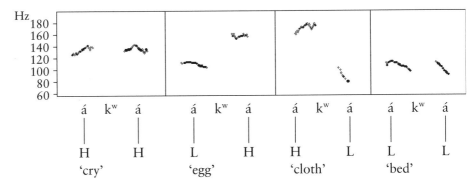

Figure 15.1 Phonemic tone in Igbo

The pitch tracks show that the phonemic representation of tone is, as always in phonology, an abstraction: the tones are not "sung" in level pitch like musical notes, but have gliding allotones sensitive to the segmental and phrasal environment.

Very often, tone languages lack stress; this is apparently true for Igbo. It is also possible for tone and stress to coexist: Bantu languages often have a complex tone system coexisting with a simple penultimate stress pattern.

15.1.2   Intonation languages

In an **intonation** language, pitch does not distinguish words. Instead, there are phrasal-level pitch patterns which convey abstract meanings of their own, usually related to the information structure of the utterance. English and most other European languages are intonation languages. It is typical for an intonation language to have stress.

The pitch tracks in figure 15.2 show the English word *animal* ['ænəməl] as pronounced by the author using statement, then question intonation. The first and last syllables are shown linked to phonological tones, which will be explained in the discussion to follow.

15.1.3   Pitch accent languages

Pitch accent languages are something of an intermediate case. Pitch is phonemic (distinguishes words), and so there are minimal or near-minimal pairs for pitch. Pitch accent languages differ from pure tone languages in that words can only have one prominent syllable. This syllable serves as the anchor point for a pitch change, and pitch in the remainder of the word is predictable, or determined intonationally. The limitation to one prominent syllable is reminiscent of the principle of culminativity in stress (§14.2.1.1).

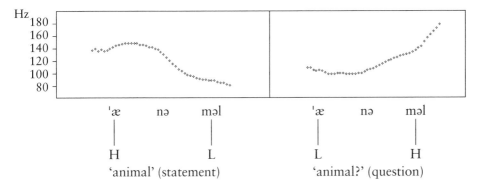

Figure 15.2   English intonation

Tokyo Japanese is a well-studied pitch accent language. Here, one particular syllable in a word can bear a high tone. The choice of which syllable (if any) bears high tone is unpredictable, and high tones must therefore appear in lexical entries. The pitch on all remaining syllables is predictable and can be derived by tonal insertion rules (see Further reading). In addition, many words of the Tokyo dialect have no underlying high tone; for these, all of the tones that appear on the surface are phonologically inserted.

Figure 15.3 shows a minimal triplet for Tokyo pitch accent: 'chopsticks' (initial accent) – 'bridge' (final accent) – 'end' (unaccented), all segmentally [haʃi]. The pitch accent that distinguishes them is designated by the H tone shown in boldface; all other tones are predictable. To avoid the application of a tonal neutralization rule that applies to the isolation form (§8.2), the forms are given in a phrasal context.

The syllable marked for H pitch is called the pitch-accented syllable. The pitch-accented syllable is often phonetically stressed, as in Swedish or Serbo-Croatian, but need not be so; for instance, there is no stress in Japanese.

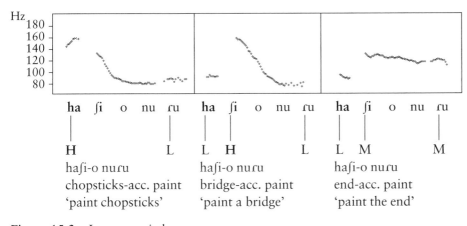

Figure 15.3   Japanese pitch accent

All three kinds of phonological pitch systems are amenable to the same kind of formal analysis, to which we now turn. We will begin with the intonational system of English.

15.2   English Intonation

15.2.1   *Tune and text*

A central idea in intonational analysis is that whenever we produce an utterance in an intonational language, we are simultaneously delivering two related messages: a **text** and a **tune**. The text is simply the words we are saying, conveyed through vowels, consonants, stress, and phrasing. The tune is the pitch pattern with which the words are said. Different tunes can be matched up with different texts.

The terminology is taken from singing, where people often sing an existing tune to a novel text, or vice versa. The analogy is incomplete, for two reasons. First, intonational tunes do not ordinarily involve level pitches, as in music; rather, as already seen, they typically glide smoothly up and down. This is why speech doesn't sound sung, even though pitch is present during any voiced segment. Second, the rhythmic structure of speech is much looser and more flexible than in music, so the freedom of combination of tune and text is greater.

15.2.2   *Tonal autosegments and features for pitch*

The analysis of text (that is, of the phonology of text) has been covered in detail in the previous chapters. For the analysis of tune, we introduce here the concept of a **tone**, or more precisely, a **tonal autosegment**. A tone is like a phonological segment, except that its content specifies only pitch features. For present purposes, let us adopt a simple feature system for pitch, with the following two features:

[Hipitch]: [+Hipitch] uses a relatively higher portion of the speaker's pitch range.
[Lopitch]: [+Lopitch] uses a relatively lower portion of the speaker's pitch range.

These features can be used to define three tones, as follows:

$$\text{High} = \begin{bmatrix} +\text{Hipitch} \\ -\text{Lopitch} \end{bmatrix} \qquad \text{Mid} = \begin{bmatrix} -\text{Hipitch} \\ -\text{Lopitch} \end{bmatrix} \qquad \text{Low} = \begin{bmatrix} -\text{Hipitch} \\ +\text{Lopitch} \end{bmatrix}$$

These will be abbreviated H, M, and L.[2]

---

[2]   For the theory of tonal features in general, see the text by Yip cited in Further reading.

15.2.3 The Declarative tune

The tonal autosegments H, M, and L will be arranged on their own **tier**, which is a distinct level of representation (hence the prefix "auto-" in "autosegment"). The idea of a tier can be made clear if we examine a particular intonational tune of English.

The **Declarative tune** can be heard as the answer to questions (its meaning is discussed further in §15.2.6). The following example is an imagined dialogue in which the second speaker uses the declarative intonation in informing his interlocutor that he lives in Kentucky.

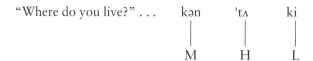

It can be seen that the Declarative tune uses all three of the tones M, H, and L in that order; and that each tone is linked to a syllable. The Declarative tune is defined by the appearance of the sequence MHL on the tonal tier. It can be seen that vertical lines denote simultaneity: for instance, the linking of the syllable ['tʌ] to H indicates that the H tone is phonetically rendered simultaneously with ['tʌ].

15.2.4 Aligning tunes to multiple texts: phonetic interpolation

The example *Kentucky* was chosen to provide the simplest possible alignment of the Declarative tune to a text. It can also be aligned with longer texts, as shown.

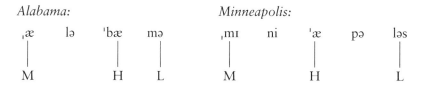

The only novel aspect of the forms above is: what happens on syllables that don't have a tone?

The proposed answer to this question is that the representation should describe only the **critical points** in a contour; that is, the beginning, the end, and the places where the contour changes direction. Between these critical points, what we get is a smooth trajectory, often somewhat droopy, going between one pitch target and the next. These are "don't care" regions (see §4.8), where the phonological system does not specify a value; the phonetic form is instead determined by interpolation.

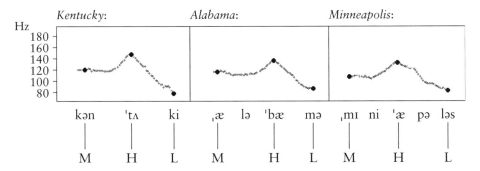

Figure 15.4 Pitch tracks: Kentucky, Alabama, Minneapolis with the "Declarative" tune

These interpolations can be seen in phonetic measurements of the pitch contours involved. The pitch tracks given in figure 15.4 were made by the author, and are pedagogically simplified in the sense that I replaced voiceless segments with nasals ([ælə'mæmə], [ˌmɪni'æmələm]) to avoid gaps in the contour (in real life the ear is able to interpolate through such gaps, but ungapped contours are easier to read). The pitch tracks are also annotated with points indicating the termini or changing points that are determined by the presence of phonological tones.

It can be seen that the relative heights of the points corresponding to tones match fairly well with their tonal category, that is, H, M, or L. Moreover, the shape of the interpolations between tones is not phonologically contrastive, and varies more or less at random. Thus it seems legitimate not to assign phonological representation to such sequences.

The issue of phonetic versus phonological representation also arises when we consider the question of **pitch range**. One can say "Kentucky" in answering a question in quite a few different ways. Figure 15.5 shows a set of four utterances, whose pitch tracks have been superimposed. The lowest curve is likely to sound bored, the highest very emphatic, following the general use of pitch range to convey the speaker's degree of emotional involvement. The question is what these pitch contours are phonologically. One might be tempted to give the various peaks different tones (e.g., Medium High, High, Superhigh, etc.). There are two objections to this idea. First, quite a few tone levels would be needed, in fact probably an infinite number, since it seems possible to vary the pitch on a continuous scale. In addition, such a phonological description would miss the basic point that all the various possibilities above are ways of making a declarative statement.

Thus the sensible approach seems to be to say that, phonologically, all the contours are MHL, and bear the declarative meaning. However, speakers are free to vary the pitch range of their voices to reflect different degrees of emphasis. Thus L, M, H are relative terms. This also applies to comparisons of the speech of different individuals, since individual pitch range varies greatly.

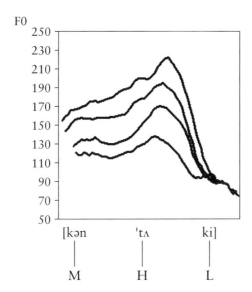

Figure 15.5   Pitch range: "Kentucky" pronounced with four different pitch ranges

15.2.5   The "Emphatic Question" tune

Just as a single tune can go on different texts, the same text can bear many different tunes. Figure 15.6 represents an intonational tune of English that is often used to ask questions, implying that the speaker has a fairly lively interest in what the answer is.

The six cases seen so far illustrate the principle of free combination of tune and text: three texts with two tunes.

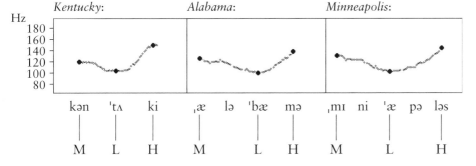

Figure 15.6   The "Emphatic Question" tune: Kentucky, Alabama, Minneapolis

15.2.6   Intonational meaning

Intonational meanings can be rather elusive, and establishing them remains a frontier area of research (see Further reading). Scholars in this area have suggested that intonational meanings are best understood by partitioning the tunes into morphemes, which in English often are single tones.

The H tone of the MHL declarative contour is interpreted as indicating that the speaker intends to add the content of what she is saying to the set of shared knowledge and beliefs resulting from the current dialogue. The analogous L of MLH is the negation of H, indicating that the material is *not* being added to the set of shared knowledge and beliefs; it thus would plausibly be used in a question.

The final tones of MHL and MLH are likewise a pair. Final L indicates a completed contribution of information; that is, that there is nothing remaining to be added to the current contribution to the dialogue, whereas a final H indicates that the information of the utterance is not complete (for example, that the speaker intends to say more, or there is more that could be said, or that the question just asked needs an answer).

15.2.7   Tune–text association

At this point, we can try to formulate the phonological rule system that underlies intonation. Given a text like *Minneapolis* /ˌmɪniˈæpələs/ and a tune like /M H L/, how do we determine what is pronounced simultaneously with what? Not every alignment is well-formed, as one can tell by trying to pronounce *Minneapolis* as shown in figure 15.7.

Thus there is evidence that tune–text alignment is controlled by rules. The rules apply in an intonational derivation, like this:

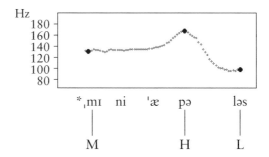

Figure 15.7   Minneapolis misaligned

Underlying form   *Surface form*

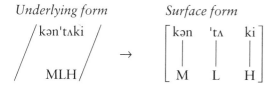

The task at hand is to characterize these rules.

Looking over the data seen so far, the generalizations seem to be fairly simple: the H tone in the Declarative tune and the L tone in the Emphatic Question tune are aligned to the main-stressed syllable of the text; these tones are "stress-anchored." We wish to be able to express this generalization without having to write separate rules for each tune. A way of doing this that is commonly adopted is to mark the stress-anchored tone under discussion with an asterisk or star:

Underlying form for the Declarative tune	/M H* L/
Underlying form for the Emphatic Question tune:	/M L* H/

Stress-anchored tones in intonational systems are often called **starred tones** or **pitch accents**. To avoid confusion with the category of pitch accent languages (§15.1.3), this text will use "starred tone" to denote a tone that is stress-anchored.

A preliminary version of the rules for tune–text association is as follows:

Tune–Text Association Rules for English (preliminary)

Starred Tone Rule
Associate T* with the strongest stress of an utterance.

Edge Rule
Associate other tones with initial and final syllables.

Here is a derivation for *Minneapolis* with the Emphatic Question tune. It is assumed that the underlying representation is the result of the speaker's choice of both a text, shown on the segmental tier, and a tune, shown on the tonal tier.

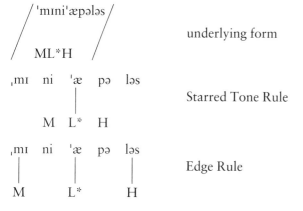

Note that the horizontal alignment of the tones on the page is purely typographical;
only their ordering and their linking to the segmental tier are phonologically
relevant.

These tune–text association rules make some basic claims about English intonation: that the crucial anchor points are the initial and final syllables of the
utterance,[3] along with the stressed syllables; and that the tones of intonational
tunes are classified in the underlying representation into stress-attracted and
edge-attracted tones.

15.2.8   Contour tones and multiple linking

In certain texts, the issue of tonal crowding arises. Suppose, for instance, that the
main stress is on the final syllable. In such a case, the Starred Tone Rule would
link T* to the final syllable. Nothing we have said would prevent the Edge Rule
from linking the last tone to the final syllable as well. This possibility is shown
below with derivations linking the Declarative tune to finally-stressed *Tennessee*
and the Emphatic Question tune to finally stressed *Kalamazoo*:

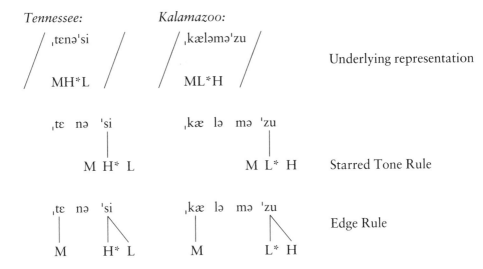

What we get is as shown in figure 15.8, with a falling pitch on the last
syllable of *Tennessee* and a rising pitch on the last syllable of *Kalamazoo*. In
the terminology used in tonal phonology, we can say that the syllable ['si] of
Tennessee and the syllable ['zu] of *Kalamazoo* bear **contour tones**.

This result is a characteristic one in the study of tone in phonology: a fall
or rise on a single syllable is phonologically related to the underlying sequence

---

[3]   In a more detailed treatment we would find that the crucial edges are not always utterance edges
but rather the edges of phrases, as discussed in §10.8.

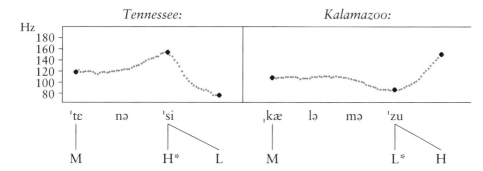

Figure 15.8 Contour tones: Tennessee, Kalamazoo

H + L or L + H respectively. For this reason, many theories of tonal features do not include features like [+rising] or [+falling]. We can do without them, and will have a more general theory, if we stick to simple elements like H, M, and L, letting the contour tones be represented as the association of multiple single tones to one syllable.

When we look at more complex tonal patterns, the virtue of this approach becomes clearer. Some of the more unusual intonations of English can actually put four tones on a single syllable (figure 15.9). This contour can be directed to Anne to express a combination of frustration and surprise. Using multiple simple tones attached to a single syllable is a simpler and more economical way of describing such complex contours, eliminating the need for such features as "[+rising then falling then rising]."

The underlying principle of this approach to contours can be stated as follows:

Static Feature Hypothesis
Phonological features describe static positions.

That is, the basic elements of phonology describe position, not motion: all motion is described in terms of its endpoints, construed as abstract static positions. In extensions of autosegmental theory, this approach has been applied to dynamic segmental entities such as affricates, diphthongs, and prenasalized stops.

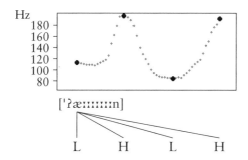

Figure 15.9 A four-tone contour on "Anne!!"

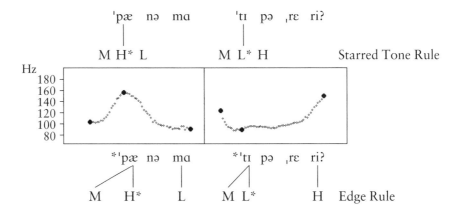

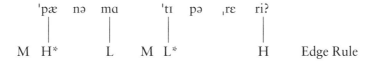

Figure 15.10   Blocking the formation of contours

15.2.9   Blocking the formation of contours

The last section showed how applying the rules of tune–text association can create contour tones when the main stress is on the last syllable. Consider next what happens when the main stress is on the initial syllable, as in words like *Panama* or *Tipperary*. Here, the rules derive the wrong result, as in figure 15.10. The contours generated are impossible, and sound deviant to the native speaker; the pitch tracks above are real, but were generated by the author as a kind of phonetic exercise. Analytically, the point is that the rules can and do generate contours in one context (final stress), but must be prevented from doing so in another (initial stress).

This can be accomplished by placing an extra condition on the application of the Edge Rule, as follows:

Condition on the Edge Rule
Do not associate a tone if it would precede T* in its syllable.

In order to respect this condition, the Edge Rule is blocked at the following stage of the derivation:

   'pæ nə mɑ   'tɪ pə ˌrɛ ri?
    | | | |
M H*   L   M L*   H   Edge Rule

Assuming that tones that aren't linked to a syllable don't get pronounced, these representations suffice as output forms. An alternative would be to suppose that by convention, unlinked tones are automatically deleted at the end of the derivation. Either way, the correct outcome will result: the *Panama* utterance will begin with a fall, and the *Tipperary* utterance with a gradual rise.

15.2.10 The "Regular Question" tune

Questions in which the asker is not so intensely interested in the answer can be asked with the tune L L* H. It can be aligned with the texts so far as follows:

Simple cases: Kentucky, Alabama, Minneapolis

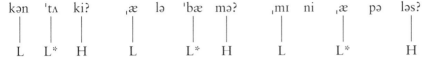

Final contours: Tennessee, Kalamazoo

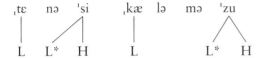

Phonetically, LL*H is like the emphatic question, but with a low level start, as in the pitch track for "*Kalamazoo?*" shown in figure 15.11.

In texts with initial stress like '*Panama* and '*Tipperary*, it is impossible to realize a difference between M L* H and L L* H, since the initial tone gets stranded.

15.2.11 Tune–text association and phrasal stress

We can intonate longer utterances if we consider first how stress is assigned to phrases.

Phrasal stress is a complex topic; but as a rough approximation we can say the following. First, the **grammatical words** (closed-class items like articles,

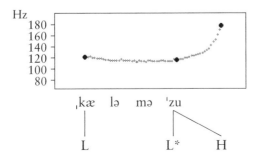

Figure 15.11   The "Regular Question" tune: Kalamazoo?

prepositions, complementizers, conjunctions, and pronouns) are stressless. Second, if there is more than one stressed word (noun, verb, adjective) in the sentence, then the stronger stress falls on the last stressed word.

English Phrasal Stress Rules

1 Grammatical words are stressless.
2 If there is more than one stressed word in a sentence, make the last stress primary, and the others secondary.

Naturally, the rules of tune–text association must apply after these stress rules, since the Starred Tone Rule depends on stress assignment in assigning T*. The following is a full derivation for *He forgot the erasers*. First, the rules of syntax concatenate the words *he*, *forgot*, *the*, and *erasers*, forming a tree:

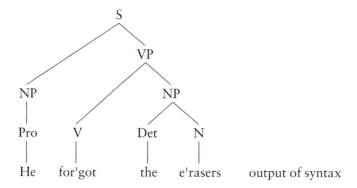

                                                        output of syntax

Within the phonology, the rules of word stress assign the word stress patterns. We note in passing that the final stress on *forgot* is predictable under a full set of English stress rules; final stress is the general pattern for prefix+stem verbs in English, as in *com*['pel], *en*['flame], *be*['friend].

The grammatical words *he* and *the* are stressless. Further, because *erasers* bears the rightmost stress, it is allowed to survive as the main stress of the sentence, while its partner *forgot* is demoted to secondary status.

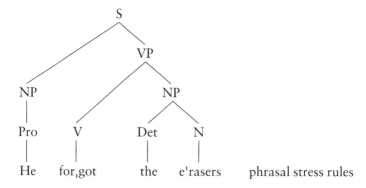

                                                        phrasal stress rules

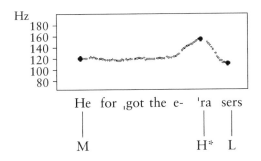

He for ˌgot the e- 'ra sers

M   H*   L

Figure 15.12 The "Declarative" tune: He forgot the erasers

Now, assuming we wish to make a statement, we can associate the Declarative tune M H* L to this text as follows:

He   forˌgot   the   e'rasers   Starred Tone Rule (tree not shown)

                 M   H*   L

He   forˌgot   the   e'rasers   Edge Rule

M   H*   L

This derives the correct outcome, as shown in figure 15.12.

15.2.12   *Contrastive stress: stress differences vs. intonational differences*

It is possible to override the Phrasal Stress Rule in instances of **contrast**. For example, if we wish to emphasize that he *forgot* the erasers (instead of, say, bringing them), we would say:

He for'got the e ˌras ers

M   H*   L

with contrastive stress on *for'got* overriding the phonologically normal stress on *erasers*.

An explicit rule to cover such cases would require a theory of contrastive stress and of the discourse structure on which it depends. For present purposes we can use the following rule:

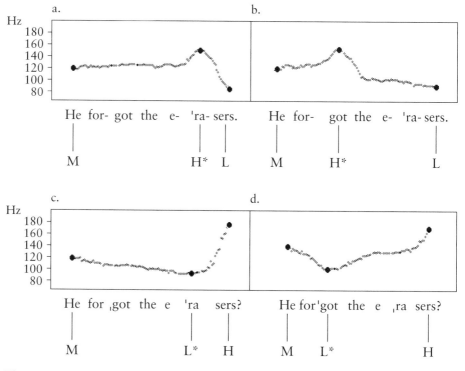

Figure 15.13 Contrastive stress

Contrastive Stress
A word bearing contrastive stress must receive the strongest stress of its phrase.
All other stressed words must bear secondary stress.

Consider now the paradigm shown in figure 15.13. The purpose of the
paradigm is to demonstrate that stress differences and intonation differences are
independent. In terms of our theory, cases (a) and (b) have the same intonation,
namely M H* L; they differ only in how the tune is lined up with the text. Likewise,
(c) and (d) have the same intonation, M L* H. Cases (a) and (c) have the same
stress pattern, but different intonations, and likewise with (b) and (d). Thus phrasal
stress and intonation are separate entities, but they are crucially related by the
Starred Tone Rule, since the phrasal stress pattern determines which syllable will
be linked to the starred tone.

15.2.13 More than one T*: the Surprise tune

The following example illustrates a contour often used to express astonishment.
Suppose one were to walk into a classroom and find that the blackboard had been

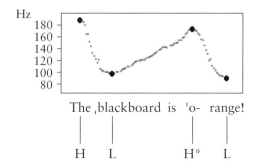

Figure 15.14 The "Surprise" tune: The blackboard is orange!

painted orange. One might, with dropped jaw, say "The blackboard is orange!" (figure 15.14). We will call this intonation the **Surprise tune**, and consider its proper phonological analysis. The nature of the pitch sequence, H L H L, seems fairly clear. Also, the second H is clearly H*, since it links to the strongest stress. The initial and final tones are unstarred, since they link to the edges. But what of the L in second position?

Here, it is useful to compare the sentence in figure 15.14 with the one in figure 15.15. "The canoe is orange!". In this sentence, the position of the L has shifted over onto the third syllable. Evidently this is because *ca'noe* has final stress whereas *'blackboard* has initial stress. The L is stress-attracted, and thus deserves to be classified as L*; and the tune must actually be H L* H* L.

The question now arises of how we are to revise the tune–text association rules so that they can apply to tunes that have more than one T*. In general it appears that it is always the *last* T* in the contour that is selected to link to the main stress. Second, the T* to the left of the main stress seeks out the strongest available stresses. In the examples above, this is the stress on [ˌblæk] in *blackboard* or on [ˌnu] in *canoe*.

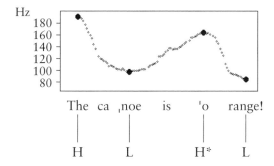

Figure 15.15 The "Surprise" tune: The canoe is orange!

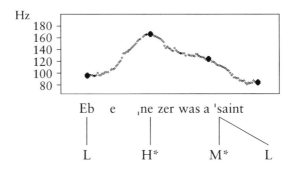

Figure 15.16   The "Predictable" tune: Ebenezer was a saint

This leads us to a revised version of the Starred Tone Rule:

Starred Tone Rule (revised)

1   Associate rightmost T* with the main stress.
2   Associate other T* with the strongest stress preceding the main stress.

The application of this rule in derivations is left as an exercise below.

15.2.14   The "Predictable" tune

The need to associate texts with multiple starred tones is illustrated by another tune of English, L H* M* L, which will be called the "Predictable" tune. Its meaning, roughly, is "the content of what I'm saying is (partially) predictable from the context." Some examples of the usage of the tune are given below.

Suppose that a conversation is about a deceased person named Ebenezer, and that repeated anecdotes are told to show what a nice person he was. After several such stories, a speaker might sum up the discussion by saying "Ebenezer was a saint." (figure 15.16)

The use of L H* M* L signals to the listener that the content of this utterance is largely predictable from what came before. Notice that it would not be appropriate to use the Surprise tune here; the latter would be better as an indignant reply to someone who had suggested that Ebenezer was not virtuous.

The tonal alignment of the Predictable tune works exactly like the alignment of the Surprise tune.

Another, shorter example of the tune could arise when someone reads a book to a small child (which has been read before dozens of times), finishes, and closing the cover says "The end."

Notice that here the first L tone cannot link, since this would prevent H* from being the leftmost tone of its syllable (see Condition on the Edge Rule, §15.2.9).

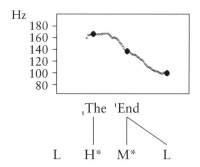

Figure 15.17 The "predictable" tune: The end

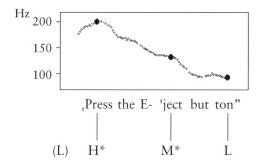

Figure 15.18 The "predictable" tune: Press the Eject button

The function word *the* is exceptionally stressed here and is pronounced as [ˌðiː] or [ˌðʌː].

A third example can be imagined by supposing one has purchased a disk drive, which comes with an instructional video that gives hands-on training in using the machine. It might include the following text (figure 15.18):

"We will now learn about the Eject button. The Eject button ejects the disk from the drive. Press the Eject button."

It makes sense here to use the Predictable tune, since the video is a tutorial, and all along it's been telling you to try out everything it describes.

The same text easily can be rendered with the other four tunes discussed in this chapter. Thus, as an answer to the direct question "How do I get the disk out of the drive?", the Declarative tune is appropriate; if one is told to press the Eject button but there is none, the Emphatic Question tune is appropriate; if one is guessing that the right thing to do is to press the eject button, the Regular Question tune is appropriate; and if one has to tell another person ten times to press the Eject button, the Surprise tune is appropriate for the tenth iteration.

15.2.15   Intonation summary

An intonational system like that of English can be described with a battery of formal devices. First, since the anchoring points for the starred tones are stressed syllables, we need stress rules (both word stress and phrasal stress) to assign the stress contours. There is also a lexicon of intonational tunes, each bearing a meaning and available for assigning to texts. This assignment is carried out in the phonology by tune–text association rules. These occasionally strand a tone that cannot be properly linked, and also can create contour tones by linking two tones to the same syllable.

15.3   Tunes in Tone Languages: The Phenomenon of Tonal Stability

The need for a separate tune and text is easy to see in the case of intonation, where tune and text transmit distinct messages. Yet the same conclusion has been drawn for tone languages as well. The evidence is usually more subtle, but a number of arguments suggest that tones have a similar independence from segments in tone languages.

Etsakǫ (Benue-Congo, Nigeria), has an ordinary rule of vowel deletion, which resolves hiatus (p. 168) by deleting a vowel before another vowel.

Hiatus Resolution
V → ∅ / ___ V   Domain: Utterance

This is the general rule for hiatus resolution in Etsakǫ. It is preceded, and bled, by other more specific rules applying to particular vowel sequences or in particular grammatical contexts.

Since Hiatus Resolution has an Utterance domain (see §10.7), it applies across word boundaries, creating a great many phrasal alternations.

[dɛ́]	'buy'	[útékwì]	'chair'	/dɛ́ útékwì/ → [d útékwì]	'buy a chair'
[kélé]	'look for'	[úkpò]	'cloth'	/kélé úkpò/ → [kél úkpò]	'look for cloth'
[í-dzé]	'plur.-ax'	[élà]	'three'	/í-dzé élà/ → [ídz élà]	'three axes'

What is of interest here is what happens when the vowel being deleted has a different tone from the vowel that immediately follows. The result is a contour tone, with underlying H + L becoming a fall (IPA [ˆ]), and underlying L + H becoming a rise (IPA [ˇ]).

Creation of falls:

[dɛ́]	'buy'	[àkpà] 'cup'	/dɛ́ àkpà/	→ [d âkpà]	'buy a cup'
[ú-dzé]	'sg.-ax'	[òkpá] 'one'	/ú-dzé òkpá/	→ [údz ôkpá]	'one ax'
[ɔ̀ɣèdɛ́]	'banana'		/ɔ̀ɣèdɛ́ ɔ̀ɣèdɛ́/	→ [ɔ̀ɣèd ɔ̂ɣèdɛ́]	'every banana'
[ɔ̀tɛ́]	'cricket'	[èθà] 'father'	/ɔ̀tɛ́ èθà/	→ [ɔ̀t êθà]	'father's cricket'

Creation of rises:

[ówà]	'house'	/ówà ówà/	→ [ów ǒwà]	'every house'
[ájòxò]	'coco-yam'	/ájòxò ájòxò/	→ [ájòx ǎjòxò]	'every coco-yam'

The intuition here is that this is a form of **tonal stability**: when a vowel deletes, the tone it bore remains present, preserved as part of a contour on the vowel that triggered the deletion. The IPA diacritics provide a visual depiction of the stability effect: from underlying /ˊ ˋ/ we derive [ˆ], and from underlying /ˋ ˊ/ we derive [ˇ].

Let us consider what sort of derivation is needed to make this intuitive idea work. For the case of /ówà ówà/ → [ów ǒwa], we would assume that in the morphological component of Etsakọ, the process of total reduplication (p. 105) that forms constructions of the type "every Noun" has the property of copying both the segmental material and the tonal tier. This yields the following representation:

underlying form

The rule of Hiatus Resolution applies on the segmental tier. For this reason, when it deletes the final vowel of the first /owa/, the tone remains, as follows:

Hiatus Resolution

(The association line may be assumed to delete by convention: there can be no simultaneity relation with a vowel that no longer exists.)

To obtain the correct final result, it suffices to provide a rule that reassigns an association to the stranded tone. Adopting the notation T′ for such tones, and the notation of dotting to indicate "add a line," the rule would be as follows:

Contour Formation

Link a stranded tone to the vowel that bears the immediately following tone.

Contour Formation completes the derivation as follows:

The tones linked to the second [o], L H, define a rising contour on this vowel, just as was seen earlier for intonation (§15.2.8), when the final LH of the Emphatic Question tune formed a rising contour when both tones were linked to the final syllable of *Tennessee*.

Quite a bit more could be said about the phenomenon of tonal stability and contour formation. One wonders, for instance, why the stranded L docks rightward to form [ówôwà], and not leftward, which would create *[ôwówà]. It has been suggested that the direction of docking is predictable; the stranded tone always docks on the vowel that triggered vowel deletion. This idea is actually supported by Etsakọ evidence, since in the special syntactic contexts where hiatus is resolved by deleting the second vowel rather than the first, docking of the stranded tone is indeed to the left: /ɔ̀ɣɛ̀dɛ́ ɔ̀nà / → [ɔ̀ɣɛ̀dɛ̂ nà] 'banana-this', not *[ɔ̀ɣɛ̀dɛ́ nà].

Another issue is what happens when the stranded tone is identical to its partner, as in /dɛ́ útékwì/ → [d útékwì] 'buy a chair'. Some theories resolve the identical tones linked to single vowels to a single tone, like this:

Another possibility is to leave them intact, under the assumption that they would be pronounced no differently from a single tone.

Leaving these questions aside, the crucial point of the example is that tonal stability exists, and is interpretable under the basic approach taken here. Specifically, the assignment of tones to a separate tier leads to the prediction that vowel deletion could leave a stray tone behind, which (in languages like Etsakọ) is rescued by Contour Formation. The widespread occurrence of tonal stability has led phonologists to posit autosegmental description as the standard form of analysis for tone. In this conception, even where tones are listed with segmental morphemes in the lexicon, they nevertheless have the status of tune, separate from the text.

Exercises

1 Applying the Starred Tone Rule

Assuming that the Surprise tune is H L* H* L, give derivations to show that the Starred Tone Rule as stated on p. 308 will derive the examples in §15.2.13 correctly.

2 Intonational derivations

For each sentence, assign the intonation contours indicated and show how the rules from the readings apply. You can assume the stress contours given, and just do the intonational part of the derivation. Draw a curve showing roughly what the intonation would look like.

a. I ˌreally don't 'approve of it.   (Declarative, Predictable)
b. Do you ˌthink you'll be 'leaving?   (Emphatic question, Regular question,
                                                            and Declarative)
c. ˌJane suc'ceeded.   (Predictable and Surprise)

3 Etsakọ tone review

Show the steps involved in the derivation /ɔ́ɣɛ̀dɛ́ ɔ̀nà/ → [ɔ́ɣɛ̀dɛ̂ nà], from §15.3.

4 More on Etsakọ

Etsakọ (§15.3) has further tonal alternations that occur in a particular syntactic construction, namely possessive noun phrases of the form "X of Y." Table 15.1 shows representative data.

Formulate an analysis of the alternations seen in these forms, integrating it with the analysis already given in the text. Justify any rule orderings needed. You may find it useful to assume an underlying *floating tone*: specifically, assume that Etsakọ has a word meaning 'of' that has no segments, only a tonal-tier representation.

Table 15.1 Etsakọ data for exercise 4

	[èθà] 'father'	[òké] 'ram'	[ɔ́mɔ̀] 'child'	[ódzí] 'crab'
[àmè] 'water'	[ámêθà] 'water of father'	[ámôké] 'water of ram'	[ámɔ́mɔ̀] 'water of child'	[ámódzí] 'water of crab'
[únò] 'mouth'	[únêθà] 'mouth of father'	[únôké] 'mouth of ram'	[únɔ́mɔ̀] 'mouth of child'	[únódzí] 'mouth of crab'
[ódzí] 'crab'	[ódzêθà] 'crab of father'	[ódzôké] 'crab of ram'	[ódzɔ́mɔ̀] 'crab of child'	[ódzódzí] 'crab of crab'
[ɔ́té] 'cricket'	[ɔ́têθà] 'cricket of father'	[ɔ́tôké] 'cricket of ram'	[ɔ́tɔ́mɔ̀] 'cricket of child'	[ɔ́tódzí] 'cricket of crab'

Further reading

The theory of tone that gives it a separate representation on its own tier was proposed in John Goldsmith's *Autosegmental Phonology* (1976, MIT dissertation; https://dspace.mit.edu/).

Textbooks on tone and intonation: *Intonational Phonology* by D. Robert Ladd (1997, Cambridge University Press); *Tone* by Moira Yip (2002, Cambridge University Press); *The Phonology of Tone and Intonation* by Carlos Gussenhoven (2004, Cambridge University Press). Ladd's earlier book *The Structure of Intonational Meaning: Evidence from English* (1980, Indiana University Press) helps clear away mysteries and confusions that often hinder the study of intonation. Two other works that form much of the basis of current theory are *The Intonational System of English* by Mark Liberman (1975) and *The Phonology and Phonetics of English Intonation* by Janet Pierrehumbert (1980). Both were MIT dissertations and are downloadable, from https://dspace.mit.edu/.

An influential work on the meaning of English intonation contours is Janet Pierrehumbert and Julia Hirschberg "The meaning of intonation in the interpretation of discourse," in P. Cohen, J. Morgan, and M. Pollack, eds., *Intentions in Communication* (1990, MIT Press), pp. 271–311. The discussion of contour meanings above is taken (loosely) from this work, along with the "Eject button" example.

Janet Pierrehumbert and Mary Beckman's *Japanese Tone Structure* (1988, MIT Press) provides a thorough analysis of the Japanese pitch accent system using autosegments and phonetic underspecification.

Igbo tone: examples from the UCLA Phonetics Lab Archive, http://archive. phonetics.ucla.edu/. Japanese pitch accent: examples from the *IPA Handbook* website, cited above on p. 18. English phrasal stress rules: Chomsky and Halle, *The Sound Pattern of English* (1968, Harper and Row); Etsakọ tone: Baruch Elimelech, *A Tonal Grammar of Etsakọ* (1978, University of California Press).

Appendix: On Phonology Problems

1 A Note on Data and Citation

I have not given the data sources for any of the problems given in this book (a few are from my own data). As I recognize, non-citation flies in the face of legitimate scholarship. However, I am aware that phonology teachers usually want their students to solve the problems on their own! I hope that the linguists who did the research on which the problems are based will understand.

2 Writing up Phonology Problems

Phonology teachers often like to customize problem directions, particularly when the problem is being used to teach a particular phonological theory, so be prepared for the possibility of "override" directions from your teacher.

Some teachers like phonology problem answers to be very explicit, while others favor terseness. You should check with your teacher what approach she thinks is best.

A few hints can probably safely be given for any phonology course. It always pays to give your rules descriptive names like "Spirantization" or "Final Devoicing" and use these names consistently in referring to the rules in prose. Rule names like "Rule 1" are not user-friendly. They burden the memory, and may aggravate the disposition, of whoever is doing the grading.

Generally, phonology teachers expect their students to include illustrative derivations. It is good to pick for each rule one form that cleanly illustrates it. By "cleanly," I mean that as few other phenomena as possible are present in that form. It is also good to include comparison forms where the rule does not apply. Finally, it is good to include forms that show how the rules interact, to justify the orderings.

In published research in phonology, authors virtually always *intersperse* the derivations among the forms, so that each example occurs right after the analytical point it is meant to illustrate. The alternative is to put all the derivations at the end, a strategy occasionally preferred by phonology teachers. You should find out what your teacher prefers.

For the more complicated problems, when you write up your answer, it's good to first try to sort the phenomena in order of complexity, and give the simplest first. For example, the presentation of Lardil phonology in chapter 8 begins with what I take to be the simplest phenomenon, vowel height alternation, moves on to the various final deletions, and ends with the interaction of the two. Sometimes one hits an expository conundrum: you can't explain A without explaining B, and vice versa. The solution here is to decide which of A or B is simpler, explain it first with a forward cross-reference ("as we will see below . . ."), then later explain the other phenomenon with a backward cross-reference.

Index